Lives in the Shadow with J. Krishnamurti

RADHA RAJAGOPAL SLOSS

Addison-Wesley Publishing Company

Reading, Massachusetts   Menlo Park, California   New York
Don Mills, Ontario   Wokingham, England   Amsterdam   Bonn
Sydney   Singapore   Tokyo   Madrid   San Juan
Paris   Seoul   Milan   Mexico City   Taipei

Grateful acknowledgment is given to Faber and Faber Ltd. for permission to quote from "The Hollow Men" by T.S. Eliot.

Library of Congress Cataloging-in-Publication Data

Sloss, Radha Rajagopal 1931–
    Lives in the shadow with J. Krishnamurti/Radha Rajagopal Sloss.
      p. cm.
    "First published in England by Bloomsbury Publishing Ltd." — T.p.
verso.
    Includes bibliographical references and index.
    ISBN 0-201-63211-X
    ISBN 0-201-62701-9 (pbk.)
    1. Krishnamurti, J. (Jiddu), 1895-1986. 2. Philosophers — India
— Biography. I. Title.
B5134.K754S64 1993
181'.4—dc20
   [B]   92-35164
                                       CIP

First published in England by Bloomsbury Publishing Ltd.

Cover design by Diana Coe

Typeset by Hewer Text Composition Services, Edinburgh

1 2 3 4 5 6 7 8 9–MA–97969594
First printing, January 1993
First paperback printing, March 1994

To those who gave me my memories and
to those who shared with me their own,
this book is lovingly dedicated

Contents

PART THREE   DENOUEMENT
Lost in a Pathless Land (1947–86)

Preface to the American Edition

Since this book was published in England in May 1991, and subsequently found its way to other parts of the world, I have received numerous letters and telephone calls. Almost without exception all expressed gratitude that the areas of obscurity to which I referred in my first preface have now become clearer. Knowing more of the human side of Krishnamurti, and the inconsistencies between his teachings and his private life, has made his teachings more meaningful rather than detracting from them. On my part, I am grateful for all of these communications. They have reaffirmed my hope that most of us do not fear discoveries that might alter our perception of reality and that we are each free to imbue these discoveries with whatever relevance is essential to us as individuals.

My regret is that Krishnamurti did not live to see this book, for I tried hard to have it published in his lifetime. He might not have read it, but he would have known it was there and at least a part of him would have understood why I had to write it.

Preface

This is not only the story of one person. It is the story of the relationships of J. Krishnamurti and people closely involved with him, especially Rosalind Williams Rajagopal and D. Rajagopal, my mother and father, and of the consequences of this involvement on their lives. Recently there have been biographies and a biographical film on Krishnamurti that have left areas, and a large span of years, in mysterious darkness. It is not in the interest of historical integrity, especially where such a personality is concerned, that there be these areas of obscurity.

Illustrations

xi

Acknowledgments

Recent copyright laws require permission for the publication of a person's letters, either from the writer or his literary estate. Therefore, for obvious reasons, Krishna's letters to my mother have been omitted from this book. They are in my possession and support the facts of the story as I have presented it.

Certain other documents pertaining to the events herein will be sealed for some years. Others to which I have had access are in my father's historical collection.

I would like to thank Matthew Huxley for permission to quote from Maria Huxley's letters; Christian von Ledebur and Ivan Moffat for permission to quote from Iris Tree's letters and poetry; Joan Watts Tabernick for permission to quote from Alan Watts' letter to Blanche Matthias; Beatrice Wood for permission to use any of her letters and writings; and Sybille Bedford for permission to quote from *Aldous Huxley* (Alfred Knopf/Harper & Row, New York, 1974). I deeply appreciate Liz Cowen's sensitive and perceptive editing and the helpful support and advice of Liz Calder and the others at Bloomsbury who helped to produce this book. I would like to add a special thanks to my agent Rivers Scott for his belief in the book and his expert handling of it. I also want to express my gratitude to those many friends who have given me advice and shared with me their recollections. They will know who they are.

Finally, and most importantly, I want to thank my husband, who sustained me with his love, patience and illuminating insights through the often difficult times involved in writing this story; my father for his deep concern and silent support as I wrote; and my mother for her extraordinary generosity in sharing with me all her correspondence as well as the most intimate parts of her life which, but for her regard for the truth, would have remained undisturbed.

Between the idea
And the reality
Between the motion
And the act
Falls the Shadow

Between the conception
And the creation
Between the emotion
And the response
Falls the Shadow

. . . Between the potency
And the existence
Between the essence
And the descent
Falls the Shadow.

T. S. Eliot, *The Hollow Men* (1925)

Introduction

The Sage Garden

I see it still in dreams spun from earliest memories. The large pergola covered with honeysuckle and trumpet vines sheltered a brick terrace. At one end was the rectangular lily pond where my baby ducks swam. Beyond were terraced lawns, shaded by towering pine trees; a patio, arboured by pink roses sprouting from ancient trunks; and finally, the redwood house, painted pale yellow.

Behind all this were the arid foothills of Ojai covered with the often inhospitable, but beautiful chaparral – black and white sage, manzanita, sumac and poison oak. Our garden with its water-thirsty lawns and arbours defied these natural surroundings. In time its nature, like the rarefied innocence of our lives, changed.

The garden was eventually transformed, not only by the sere realities of environment, but also by the practical needs of a productive orange ranch. The orchard's requirement for space and especially for water came first.

The orange ranch was the province of my uncle, Willie Weidemann. With his practical German expertise, he managed the resources of our land. Water came from Big Horn canyon just behind us. Droughts were not infrequent. We adapted to what we were granted in rainfall and weather. In summer the croquet lawn on the top tier was left to wither to a brown carpet of burrs. To further conserve water, the orchard was irrigated at night. I can still conjure up the tsk-tsk-tsk of the sprinklers and the odour the parched earth gave off as it was moistened. The orange trees, glistening pale silver in the moonlight, turned their leaves like hands receiving an answered prayer. In harsh, frosty winters Willie would work all night, turning on sprinklers to raise the temperature, for we had no oil heaters (which we called smudge pots) as they did down in the valley, set in rows along the trees. Yet we were spared the black veil of smoke which shrouded the valley on cold mornings.

As the orchard took our water, it also consumed our space. The pergola, brick terrace and pool – as well as all the exotics in the

1

garden – disappeared. The scent of black sage rubbed between our fingers during walks in the foothills would be better remembered than the scent of honeysuckle arbours. Added to my collection of pet ducks, geese and turkeys were the wild pets of the chaparral – a skunk, a chipmunk, possums, a baby king snake and the tanager with a broken wing. Sometimes too, on moonlit nights, coyotes came as close as the upper lawn to dance and bark before dawn sent them prowling back to the hills. Often the odour of skunk drifted about the house at night. Once we saw a condor soaring high above our garden towards its nest on nearby Topa Topa Mountain.

Our world was a child's paradise and looking back, I think it must have been an adult's paradise too.

The house was already old when I was born. It had grown around a single classroom built long ago for the teachers' daughters from Thacher's Boys' School up the road. It was called Arya Vihara, Sanskrit for House of the Aryan, a name that has always embarrassed me, especially in my school years during the Second World War. It was not easy to explain the meaning to my friends, but there were many things in our household that were not easy to explain; fortunately I was brought up not to feel the need to do so.

It was sufficient that the adults in my life appeared to have found a harmonious balance between the spiritual and intellectual hermitage and the working ranch that existed in that unusual garden of sages.

The frequent visitors to Arya Vihara were cared for by my mother, Rosalind. There were three meals a day: breakfast in bed for those guests who preferred it, luncheon on the lawn or patio in good weather, and dinner in the dining-room. We bathed and changed before gathering in the evening. It was understood by all visitors that there would be no smoking, alcohol or meat.

My father, Rajagopal, worked all day and late into the night, arranging and editing Krishnamurti's talks and notebooks, appearing only for dinner and occasionally for the four o'clock badminton game.

Eventually the row of acacias that lined the path between Krishnamurti's cottage and the main house was also sacrificed to the orchard. But before that happened, I often lurked on a high branch amid the fragrant yellow puffs of acacia blossom. There I would wait for my favourite victim to pass underneath and mischievously pour water on his head. I was blissfully unaware that this person had once been proclaimed the world teacher by leading members of the Theosophical Society. No one used that term in my childhood. As I could not pronounce his name, Krishnamurti, he was known to me always, as Krinsh.

Life changed considerably with the Second World War. There was much more work for my mother. A vegetable garden, cows and chickens, cheeses to be made with surplus milk and hand-churned butter were added chores. There were beehives too. My mother and Krinsh were the ones who put on nets and gloves and tackled the hives while I extracted the honey. We were, in effect, self-sufficient during the war; which was the idea, for as pacifists we did not want to be a burden. Our war effort was sending as much food produce as we could overseas.

It is those war years that stand out most clearly in my memory. Where most people's lives were pulled apart, ours were bound together as they never had been before and never would be again. My father's and Krinsh's travelling was brought to a stop. We were all caught together in Ojai for the duration. During the war my father moved his office from Hollywood to Ojai. Due to petrol rationing, driving was curtailed. We saved all year for enough petrol coupons to take us to Sequoia National Park for six weeks in the summer. There, amidst those gigantic three-thousand-year-old trees, we were joined by a whole entourage from Ojai; family, friends, and the usual single lady devotees who discreetly followed Krinsh everywhere they could.

Those who were closest to us then, those still living, must wonder what went so wrong that such apparent harmony and vitality of spirit and mind and physical enterprise should disintegrate disastrously into a war of litigation. How three people, who for nearly half a century seemed so inevitably bound together in totally unselfish lives, could be involved in bitter and ugly charges brought by one of them against another. How the high ideals of the brotherhood of man, the eschewing of killing or injury to any creature, the search for freedom from ambition, guilt, fear, could have dissolved into such discord. The seeds of conflict must have been sown somewhere along the way, beyond my memories.

In Part One I retrace a path back to the origins of Theosophy, how it related to my immediate family and how it was the catalyst that brought them together. Part Two is interwoven with my personal recollections of incidents and people that had a bearing on our lives and Part Three describes the sad harvest of seeds planted long ago.

PART ONE
EARLY HISTORY

The Path of Discipleship
(Late Nineteenth Century to 1931)

1

The Elders

Growing up with the world teacher, even if he had disclaimed that title four years before my birth, had many side benefits. There was a steady flow through our home of interesting and unusual people, most of them mentally sound. Ours was hardly a life of mystical seclusion or quiet contemplation, although Krinsh certainly fitted 'being alone' into his routine. Because of him I was spared one of the worst effects that befall an only child: that of being the centre of attention. There was clear awareness of who our centre was, and of the circle that radiated from him in undiminishing magnetism to the farthest reaches of the earth. That a man is not always a prophet in his own valley and that even such a luminary as Krinsh had his dark side I would come only gradually to realize.

Long before I was born, both of my parents had committed themselves to Krinsh and to coping with the inevitable complexities attached to life around him. Yet for all her hard work, my mother Rosalind never lost the aura of unselfconscious glamour that had been hers since she arrived in Hollywood in 1919. Nor did the increasing tensions in her life dissipate her talent for spinning fun and excitement out of whatever circumstances were offered. She loved games of all kinds and could play chess with my father as well as badminton with Krinsh.

As a child I saw very little of my father, nor did I see much of him after that, but his personality was so strong that a little of him went a long way and I know now that his influence on me was profound. Those rare moments I had with him I treasured, for there was no trivia in him at all and everything he said, even his humour (in which he abounded), was significant.

There was often an unspoken tension when my parents and Krinsh were all together and sometimes the unspoken broke out into quite vociferous arguments, the basis of which I would not understand for many years. When other people were there these tensions evaporated and the three of them seemed to form a comforting magic circle into which the troubled or spiritually weary or confused could enter and rest. Then there was much laughter; jokes and games broke the routine of 'serious' discussions. The transparent bond between them became almost tangible.

The two images of Krinsh – the public and the private – were engraved in my earliest memory. It did not puzzle or concern me as a child that our private Krinsh was so different from the one who appeared when strangers came to the house. Our Krinsh, whose hair I pulled as a baby, whose lap I sat on, who kissed my bruised knees and braided my hair, who picked me up when I was afraid, who kissed my mother's hand when he greeted her in the morning, who scolded her when she was careless, or allowed her to scold him when he was difficult – this Krinsh never appeared before strangers. The moment Krinsh walked into a room of new visitors or not very intimate friends, both he and they changed perceptibly, especially if they were devotees. The very way he tried to melt into the room, as though he wished no one would notice him, drew immediate attention. Conversation stopped. 'Please do go on, don't let me interrupt,' he would say. But who would dare continue when *He* was there? There was a reverent silence as all the attention and energy in the room flowed toward him and poor Krinsh then had the task of restoring the conversation.

Those occasional people who witnessed our 'normal' behaviour were probably shocked to the core. Fortunately no one was around when my mother, in a cross between exasperation and playfulness, dumped a plate of scrambled eggs on his head. We all ended up thinking that was very funny. It was not the sort of incident that led to arguments between them. Arguments stemmed from causes that were kept secret even from me.

There were other adults in my childhood who did much to shape my outlook. My grandmother, Sophia Williams, with whom I spent many of my first nine years, gave me her love for music and her eldest daughter, my Aunt Erma, gave me her love for books and history and nature. Another of Sophia's daughters, Grace, had married Willie and their son David was one of my two playmates, the other being Krinsh. As the Weidemanns lived next door, on the same ranch, David and I were inseparable from breakfast until dinner.

It was largely from Erma that I learned about the roots of our lives. It was from Erma that I knew how my mother, an American girl from Buffalo, New York, had met three young men from India in a distant California valley; Krishnamurti, his brother, Nitya, and Rajagopal, my father. This all happened because of Theosophy. During my early childhood only Erma discussed Theosophy seriously with me. The great rift between Krinsh and the Theosophical Society had taken place a few years before my birth. It was Erma who told me many accounts of the founders and their principles. She told me also that the meeting and marriage of my parents illustrated the basis of Theosophy: the bringing together of East and West, the universal brotherhood of man, the breaking down of cultural barriers and prejudices. No matter what their attitudes in later life, there was no doubt in Erma's mind that all my adults owed a great deal of their present condition, philosophical, psychological and material to their Theosophical elders.

Erma explained that the Theosophical Society, founded by a Russian and an American, was based largely on their interpretation of Buddhism, Hinduism and a blend of various occult theories unique to the founders. Its aim was to explore the mysteries of nature and the latent powers in man on which the study of Oriental philosophy could throw some light. It was open to believers and non-believers, the orthodox and the unorthodox. In the early days Theosophy had a strong appeal to those who found little solace or satisfaction in orthodoxy and yet were not content to count themselves as atheists. It also attracted that small but articulate group of freethinkers and avowed atheists searching for some order of spiritual sustenance amidst the seeds of nineteenth-century science. In the late nineteenth century it was inevitable that the range of ideas and activities Theosophy proposed would attract an equally wide range of people. There were those who, as scholars, were interested in pursuing the intercultural aspects of this new society. Many budding politicians in India, after decades of suppression and denigration by the British, found hope and support in the idea that Westerners would take such an interest in their cultural and philosophical heritage. Almost every country in the Western world, as well as Asia and Australia, eventually had national and regional chapters in the society. The colourful and sometimes sensational claims and activities of certain of its members intrigued the world's press which, for many decades, hovered close by.

As a young person I found Erma's accounts of these early Theosophists far more colourful than the philosophy Krinsh had formulated as he detached himself from the society. In spite of the often expressed scepticism about Theosophical ideas and incidents that would float around the dining table (especially in the company of such guests as Aldous Huxley), Erma would later provide me with the background of that early history. Her beautiful hazel-green eyes wide with amazement, she offered these accounts, not out of defiance or contradiction, but as a vital component of her own psychological memory.

Thus I learned that in 1873, Helena Petrovna Blavatsky, a Russian emigrant, and the granddaughter of a Princess had arrived in New York. With her quizzical interest in spiritualism, she soon found her way to a meeting with Colonel Henry Olcott, a lawyer who had served in the Civil War as a fraud investigator. Olcott was, at the time, observing the activities of a group of spiritualists for a series of newspaper articles. Together, in a few years, these two explorers in occult phenomena would form the Theosophical Society.

Erma seemed to accept comfortably Blavatsky's claim that since early childhood she had been visited by a tall, dark, mysterious person whom she took to be her protector. Blavatsky felt he had saved her from several brushes with death or serious injury. Later she would identify him as the Master Morya who, along with another adept, the Master Kuthumi, had chosen her as their earthly messenger.

Blavatsky believed these adepts to be mortal, born as we are born and eventually subject to death. Their purpose was to help mankind through its most difficult periods. Throughout her life, Blavatksy claimed to feel their protection and her writing was closely associated with them. She made them the cornerstone of the Theosophical movement. In time, other members would claim direct communication with them, alleging to also receive the Masters' instructions and guidance. As even Erma had to admit, these independent communions would sometimes lead to conflicts and splits within the society. When I would venture to check out the idea of Masters with Krinsh he would snort, 'That is all irrelevant.'

I found Blavatsky and her Masters far too interesting to be dismissed with a snort and I would soon beg Erma for more tales. I learned that Blavatksy was a wilful and unconventional young woman. To spite a governess, who tauntingly told her no one would ever marry her, she became engaged to a man three times her age. Horrified at what she had done, she tried unsuccessfully to break the engagement. Displaying considerable ingenuity and courage, she then eluded the close surveillance of that disappointed husband and at seventeen embarked on extensive travels. Strangely, Krinsh seemed to countenance Blavatsky's exploits on the worldly plane with better grace than those on the occult. It was acceptable to believe that she had joined the forces of the Italian patriot Garibaldi in his campaign to unify Italy. Colonel Olcott claimed to have been shown her left arm, broken in two places by a sabre when she served as a volunteer at the battle of Mentana. She also revealed to him the trace of a musket bullet still embedded in her shoulder and another in her right leg. A scar just below her heart recorded the spot where she had been stabbed by a stiletto – a wound so profound that she had been left in a ditch as dead. Blavatsky apparently did not intend these details for the public for when she read an account in the *American Mercury*, she declared it was a lie and nobody's business, that she had never been on Garibaldi's staff and had just gone with friends to Mentana to help shoot the papists. (Krinsh loved the part about shooting the papists.)

As the episode at Mentana circulated among Theosophists, however, it gained even more colour. One version was that Blavatsky had died at the battle of Mentana. She was dead in the ditch when the Master Morya interceded, deciding that her body would make a good vehicle for another *Chela* (student disciple) to assume and carry on the work of the adepts. Strange as this account might be, it was given some support by Colonel Olcott. This long-suffering, rational, but sometimes gullible man had many difficult moments with Blavatsky's temperamental and powerful spirit, which he had trouble reconciling with the physical exterior of a Victorian lady. Olcott sometimes came upon Blavatsky late at night, working on her memoirs. Unaware of his presence, she would be going through the motions of parting and drawing over each ear an invisible beard. She gave so graphic a pantomime that Olcott could almost see the long wispy beard, worn in this Rajput style by one of the Masters.

Certainly many stories about Blavatsky's life, apocryphal or not, are extraordinary, even when applied to a lady of an age abounding in extraordinary women. She once amazed a sea captain, who later recounted he had seen her light her cigar, without matches or other observable assistance, while standing at the rail in the midst of a furious storm. Every other living creature had been driven below deck. Of greatest significance to Blavatsky, in her spiritual evolution, were the years she claimed to have spent living and studying with the Masters in their occult dwelling place, Tibet. She learned to materialize objects and to receive written messages from the Masters. When Aldous Huxley came into our life, he maintained that Blavatsky was a complete charlatan, referring to her materializations as hoaxes. Seeing the allegedly materialized objects in the Theosophical Museum in Adyar some thirty years later gave me no additional illumination.

It was Blavatsky's special mission to form the Esoteric Society within the Theosophical ranks. The Theosophical Society welcomed any sincere person to membership. The Esoteric Society, or ES as it came to be called, was strictly for those who had proved their dedication to Theosophy, mostly through work. These select members were deemed ready for exposure to the ancient wisdoms which would help them along 'the Path' of the Masters. Membership of the ES was supposed to be absolutely secret. But I soon gathered that at one time Krinsh and my father, as well as Erma, had belonged to it.

To the end Blavatsky retained a strong antipathy toward religion, especially Christianity (an attitude that won her many enemies). She saw modern religions as decayed forms of the original 'wisdom religion'. She also disliked ceremony and ritual, never committing herself to personal restrictions in behaviour or diet, such as vegetarianism, usually embraced by her fellow Theosophists.

Erma used to say that an inevitable chain of circumstances leading to my parents' marriage was set in motion the day her grandfather, Carl Waldo, met Madame Blavatsky. Carl Waldo had left his aristocratic background in Germany as a young man to emigrate to America, where he eventually made a fortune in hansom cabs. He was also excommunicated for becoming a Freemason. This grandfather was the original source of Erma's involvement in Theosophy, an involvement that would affect not only her life but the lives of her mother and her three sisters.

'It all started with a body,' Erma told me one day, 'no, not an astral body – a corpse.'

One day in May 1876 Carl Waldo went down from Buffalo to New York City to attend a funeral in the Masonic temple. The deceased Bavarian nobleman, Joseph Henry Louis, Baron de Palm, Knight of St John of Malta, Prince of the Roman Empire and Fellow of the Theosophical Society, would attain more fame as a corpse than he ever had alive. He had left his worldly goods (which were nil) and his body, which would prove to be more significant, to the executorship of Colonel Olcott. The Baron specified that he wished to be cremated. This was not a simple request. Olcott had to wait six months after the funeral before the first crematorium in America was completed. The Baron's was the first body in the United States to be publicly cremated with official sanction; an event covered extensively by the national press.

At the funeral in New York City, Carl Waldo found the Masonic Temple full of spiritualists, journalists and hecklers. In that audience, giving her moral support to her friend Olcott, was Helena P. Blavatsky. Although this occasion awakened Carl's interest in Blavatsky and her fledgling society, he went home to Buffalo as uncommitted to Theosophy as he was to all the many philosophies he had explored throughout his life. But his account sparked an enduring interest in his granddaughter Erma.

The Elders

Erma's forebears were a mixture of idealists and atheists, pacifists and eccentrics. She would always remain proud of them. Her father John Williams was, if not an avowed atheist, totally against any churchgoing. Yet he could quote scripture to his advantage when he chose to do so.

By the time Rosalind was born in 1903, the last of four daughters, her parents' marriage had become increasingly unhappy. Sophia Williams had married John on the rebound and had never come to love him. She had wept through her first pregnancy and wept through all the three following. John's once equable disposition became erratic. Erma said he would go out of the house like a lamb in the morning and come home raging like a lion, or vice versa. In spite of his dedication to politics (he was elected to the New York State Assembly twice), John never forgot he was an artist and he spent long hours painting in the attic at night, making Rosalind hold up a lantern for him until she thought her arm would wither at the shoulder. In 1919 when Rosalind was sixteen, Erma Williams led her family to California, her mother away from an estranged husband and her sisters from a tyrannical father.

Both Erma and Rosalind were endowed with adventurous natures. As the train carried them across the prairies and deserts their minds cleared and stretched with the skies. The terrain of the far west spread in ever-increasing immensity before them. They did not then imagine how open they would have to be to embrace the future that awaited them.

Nestled in the hills a few blocks from the glamour of Hollywood Boulevard was the Theosophical enclave. Here, in architectural fantasies ranging from English cottage to Hindu templesque, dwelt an international assortment of Theosophists. They were, of course, not drawn to Hollywood for its movie world, but for the pure air and sunshine, the oranges, and the ambience of spiritual freedom that the Los Angeles basin offered.

Rosalind, with her classical face, golden hair, and naturally high colouring, was stared at and often taken for a young actress, much to her mother Sophia's dismay. In those days, Hollywood Boulevard, with its streetcar in the centre, was the scene of much exotica. Pola Negri walked her pet leopard there, the Sennet bathing beauty, Gloria Swanson, strolled by, and Harold Lloyd perfomed his stunts on the Taft Building. A mile or two away, along the still rural Sunset Boulevard, flamboyant mansions were being erected for the movie stars and moguls.

Mary Gray, an eminent Bostonian and Theosophist, offered Erma a position running her small School of the Open Gate in the Ojai Valley, eighty miles north of Hollywood. Mrs Gray had transplanted herself and her children to this valley, already a Theosophical centre. Erma soon arranged for her family to come up to Ojai. Rosalind stayed in Mary Gray's house with Erma, while Sophia and Grace lived in a small bungalow on the property adjacent to Mary Gray's estate.

Sophia, a talented pianist, then in her fifties, never learned to like the country. She had moved from her birthplace, where she had lived her whole life amid a closely knit family of brothers and sisters, with strong musical ties, to a rustic little cottage in a dry rocky valley, amidst a group of Theosophists towards whom she felt neither interest nor disapproval. Her move to California had taken a lot of fortitude. Innately a city person, she returned to Hollywood, to settle there for the remaining twenty years of her life.

None of my elders had ever actually met Blavatsky so the differences in their opinions about her were not so puzzling, but there was another colourful person of those early days whom both of my parents and Krinsh had known well. I would remain disturbed for many years by the marked divergence of opinion between Krinsh and my parents when it came to Charles Webster Leadbeater. It was clear that Leadbeater had played a key role in both my father's and Krinsh's lives. It was he who 'discovered' them as young boys, and lifted them from their backgrounds and families to be launched on what he proposed to be extraordinary futures.

They all agreed that Leadbeater was an awesome figure with his strong, intent face, white beard and piercing eyes. I was once told a story about his arrival in Hollywood, where, during a lecture tour, he was to stay with fellow Theosophists. After watching two burly men struggle to lift his very large trunk up the steps, he remarked with withering scorn, 'Humph! Meat-eaters!' and hefted it on to his own shoulders with no difficulty.

My mother remembers Leadbeater as a kindly, though firm, old man who aroused no fear in her. My father, who knew Leadbeater primarily through a steady correspondence that lasted for over a decade, always spoke of him with affection and gratitude for his practical and spiritual guidance. Erma had Theosophical faith in Leadbeater's occult knowledge. Krinsh portrayed him as harsh and overbearing. Although he owed to Leadbeater his early education, restored health and incredible future, I sensed neither gratitude nor fondness in his references to his old protector. Neither of my parents ever questioned Leadbeater's integrity. Not even Krinsh doubted his veracity on the earthly plane, although by the time I was born he sounded as though he had rejected the occult findings of this man, who claimed to have found him through occult knowledge.

The adventures in Leadbeater's life are as fantastic as Blavatsky's. He had a vivid imagination. His style of writing drew no line between fact and fantasy. One could easily believe that every word was rooted in fact, for his descriptions were impressive and convincing. For example, he could put into simple words complex observations in the developing field of molecular science.

When one is confronted with the total body of Leadbeater's writings, which explores everything from the metaphysical evolution of man, to the solar system, the astral plane, thought forms, molecular structure, the consciousness of rocks, transubstantiation and elementals, it is understandable that some believe it could only have been achieved through clairvoyant means. His writings are a phenomenal effort closely matching the achievement of Blavatsky herself.[1]

One of my favourite Leadbeater stories is an account of his exploits in South America, where his father was directing the construction of a railway. On a trip into the jungle, Charles, his brother Gerald and their father were captured by rebels, whose leader demanded that they join his army or be executed. The rebels prepared to administer an oath of allegiance which involved trampling on a crucifix. Leadbeater's horrified father made a sudden dash into the jungle and disappeared. Gerald was then ordered to trample on the crucifix. Refusing to do so, he was killed. Charles was tied between two trees, and a fire set under his feet. Fainting from pain, Charles suddenly saw his dead brother Gerald standing in front of him, looking peaceful and happy. Leadbeater was reassured by this vision and held on until the middle of the night when his father returned and rescued him. When a band of volunteers left to fight the rebels, Charles begged permission to ride with the men, hoping this would give him the opportunity to avenge the death of his brother. Eventually Charles found himself attacking the leader with a sword. Although he was pitted against the 'best swordsman' in South America, the young Charles leapt on top of his foe, holding the point of his sword to his throat. Just then the silver and ebony crucifix around Leadbeater's neck fell out. Seeing it, the rebel leader cried out for mercy. Unmoved, Leadbeater was about to plunge the sword into his victim's neck. However, he felt his arm being held back. Turning, he saw his dead brother Gerald. The rebel saw him too and was terrified. Unable now to carry out his vengeance, Leadbeater left his fallen enemy lying on the ground and walked away, 'saved by a ghost' as he later entitled this story.[2] (That was not the end of Gerald, who, according to Leadbeater, later reincarnated into a young Singhalese, Jinarajadasa, whom Leadbeater discovered, educated and took into the fold of the Theosophical Society, to one day become its President.)

Leadbeater's early biographies recount his attendance at Oxford and his ordination into the Church of England. He soon found he was unsuited for such orthodoxy. The Church fully concurred.

Once, on a sea voyage, Leadbeater had spoken with the same captain who had observed Blavatsky lighting her cigar in the storm. Leadbeater was so intrigued that he investigated this extraordinary woman. His findings led him to the Theosophical Society, which he joined in 1883.

The following year he met Blavatsky and travelled with her to India, where he hoped to meet the Masters. His faith in the society and in Blavatsky was already so great that he gave up everything to do this. In 1885, Colonel Olcott invited him to Ceylon to help revive an interest in Buddhism there. In this they were both eminently successful. In Ceylon Leadbeater eventually founded an English school for boys which would grow into a major college.

Gregory Tillett's biography of Leadbeater, published in 1982, has cast doubt, at least among non-Theosophists, on some of Leadbeater's accepted history. Tillett unearthed a birth date that would make Leadbeater too young for his South American exploits at the time alleged. Tillett found no record whatever of the younger brother Gerald. It is possible, as it is possible with Blavatsky, that Leadbeater was subject to an urge to embellish or rewrite his early history to accord more closely with the role he felt was his destiny.

I was aware from overheard conversations that Leadbeater was the cause and centre of many storms within the Theosophical Society, but my adults were united in repudiating the allegations that had been made from time to time about Leadbeater's morals.

Whatever one's view of Leadbeater's occult histories, experiences and morals, he had, as my father always emphasized, many admirable qualities. He devoted the last half of his life to various aspects of Theosophy. He was dedicated to education and worked diligently to expand the consciousness of the young people around him. This was his principal life work. Many of his ideas, particularly those concerned with what today would be called sex education, were far enough ahead of his time to cause outrage in the Victorian age.

There was one person about whom all my elders were in complete accord – Annie Besant. She, more than anyone, inspired them to embark on those separate and confluent paths that led to their life work.

Those in our circle, everyone I ever met who had known her, spoke of her with the highest – almost reverential – esteem. My father feels to this day that he owes everything good in his life to her. My mother was guided by her on levels some of which only surfaced in later years. Even Krishna, who nearly broke her heart, expressed his love for her long after her death. They knew her for the last two decades of her long and many faceted life – after she had become a Theosophist.

My mother described her extraordinary penetrating blue eyes and her beautifully shaped head with its full crop of white hair that she loved to have my mother brush. She took a firm but always kind hand with the young people around her, teaching through her own example, her personal fastidiousness, sitting quietly without fidgeting to conserve valuable energy, her punctuality, reliability and dedication to whatever one chose as one's vocation. She was steadfast and loyal in her friendships.

Annie was proud of being three-quarters Irish. When she was only five, her father died of tuberculosis. Her mother had foreseen her husband's funeral, but then was too ill with grief to attend. At first Annie had attributed this not uncommon clairvoyance of her mother's to a psychological aberration. Later, as a Theosophist, she found it easier to explain.

In 1867, Annie married a young clergyman, Frank Besant. Their mutual interest in the Anglican church had drawn them together, but the marriage was doomed from the first to be unhappy. Frank Besant displayed a cold and unrelenting insistence on his wife's obedience, which he often reinforced with physical violence.

The birth of their first child, Arthur Digby, followed a difficult pregnancy. Annie almost lost her second child, Mabel, to a severe case of whooping cough. She sat for days with the suffering baby on her lap, powerless to give relief. The doctor, believing death inevitable, finally left a small bottle of chloroform to alleviate the agony. Annie's careful administration relaxed the paroxysm enough to allow breathing, which turned out to be the cure. This brush with death and witnessing the suffering of an innocent creature pushed Annie on her first step toward atheism. After deep inner scrutiny and searching interviews with some of the Church of England's most influential spokesmen, she finally concluded that God did not exist. She left her husband, then turned philosophically to scepticism and materialism, a course which provoked Frank Besant to gain custody of both children. (Initially

Annie had been granted custody over the little girl, Mabel.) Rather than involve Digby and Mabel in bitter conflict, Annie accepted this harsh judgment. However, she never lost faith that in maturity her children would return to her of their own will. In this, as in much else, she was correct. Although she refrained from engaging in a protracted legal battle with her husband over her rights as a mother, she resolved that other women should not so easily suffer the same fate. She worked to change the law regarding women's rights in divorce. She also resolved that no homeless or abused child would cross her path unnoticed. She put her energies into active reform movements.

By the time Annie was forty she was known throughout the English-speaking world as one of the great orators of her time and as a courageous woman who plunged into those areas of reform that most horrified the conservative society of the 1880s: birth control and union organization. She bore with courage and dignity the ridicule as well as the renown which her activities drew upon her. She moved in the radical circles of Charles Bradlaugh, a noted materialist, of Fabian socialists and of suffragettes.

When, in 1888, she met Blavatsky, having already read and reviewed Blavatsky's latest book on the mysteries, *The Secret Doctrine*, Annie Besant was ready for a sweeping change. She had come to feel that a materialistic philosophy no longer sustained her. She believed her work for the brotherhood of mankind could better flourish under the banner of Theosophy. But if Theosophy wrought deep changes in her, she too would bring changes to it, through her altruistic nature and humanitarian interests. Blavatsky claimed that materialism and atheism were no impediments to being a Theosophist. Nevertheless, Annie Besant quickly moved away from her own scepticism. She came to believe, without reservation, in the existence of the Masters and in the occult plane on which they sought to guide the world out of its conflict, a conflict being fought between the dark brotherhood and the white brotherhood, black and white magic. She and Blavatsky became close personal friends, after which Annie underwent a series of mystical experiences which had a profound affect on her, sustaining her in later difficulties.

One of Annie's closest friends was George Bernard Shaw, who had long admired her for her intellect as well as for her charm and magnetism. Shaw had introduced her to vegetarianism as an ethical practice some years before she became a Theosophist. But he was astonished and perplexed, even vexed, by this amazing change in a woman he so deeply respected for her rational and effective activities on the worldly level. He had once even suggested marriage with her, but she declined, instead drawing up a contract under which they would live together. Shaw, when he read this document threw up his hands and exclaimed, 'Good God, woman! That's worse than any marriage.' However close they remained, he never followed her into her new philosophy.

Unlike Blavatsky who, to the later embarrassment of Theosophists, smoked cigars incessantly, ate meat, uttered profanities, and often had a biting tongue, Annie Besant adopted a strict Hindu code in her daily life, including Indian dress and *puja* (purifying rituals of cleanliness). Yet she never sought to impose her own convictions on anyone else.

Even when she became President of the Theosophical Society in 1907, Theosophy did not become Annie's whole world, absorbed by it though she was. Her great interest lay in the cause of Indian independence. The time came when she deliberately set aside her occult life to again make a place for her political one. She never lost those powers of oratory and endurance that had come with years of frontline fighting for human rights and a better social order. It would be difficult to find a person in any era who so successfully tackled so many causes to improve the human condition.

While Annie Besant would always have certain revelations of her own, as she became more occupied in her fight for Indian Home Rule she allowed herself to be guided more strongly by Leadbeater's occult knowledge and experiences with the Masters. In Leadbeater she found a spiritual friend on whom she relied for many of her most crucial decisions – those made on that supersensible region believed to exist beyond the tangible world – the astral plane.

Leadbeater, whether through occult means or through a keen intuitive insight, had a talent for choosing young people of promise. Jinarajadasa, who he believed to be the incarnation of his brother Gerald, was but the first of these discoveries. Six years later, in 1907, Leadbeater made his second find, one that would have grave consequences for the society and many of its members, and above all for Annie Besant. This new discovery would lift her to the heights of spiritual hope and expectation and then usher her into old age, broken both in health and spirit.

2

The Vehicle

All our lives are rooted in a past; sometimes mysterious and half-forgotten, sometimes well chronicled with family pride. Among immigrants there is usually, in the resettlement, a grafting on of the old culture to the new. 'Setting down roots' has been, until recently, a widespread and respectable goal. My family were unusual in their time for considering both respectability and roots inconsequential. Yet they would have had to admit that for fifty years they allowed a fourteen-acre piece of land with a house called Arya Vihara to draw them into a fold and to be their fixed compass point. From here their lives rotated around the world singly and together. I learned of their childhoods from a series of anecdotes told to me by them and others, but I never sensed that the past and from where they had come held much importance for them. When I asked my mother where she felt her real homeland was, she replied it had been many places – wherever she was at the time, that she didn't feel bound to a place. Neither did my father. When I asked Krinsh this question, he replied, 'homeless'. To a degree I inherited from my adults this rootless philosophy, but for the first twenty years of my life I looked on Arya Vihara as my home. Now it is painful to return there, just as it may have been painful for them to return to their first homes. Yet I still harboured a certain curiosity about those places and the pasts that went with them.

Five days before he died I saw the house where Krinsh was born. We were driving across South India, my husband, son and I, on the main trunk road between Bangalore and Madras. It was a spontaneous and unscheduled detour, for I had seen a small dot – Madanapalle – on the map. The pavement of this secondary road soon gave way to dust and gravel. Still we went on, drawn by an unlikely quest for the house in which Krinsh had lived ninety years before, and then drawn by the increasing beauty of the countryside, the jade green of newly planted rice, water buffaloes slowly tilling rocky fields, an isolated thatched-roof mud cottage. In the distance, as though scattered by a gigantic hand, lay the most ancient rocks in the world, or so I had always heard.

Near these he had been born in 1895: Jiddu Krishnamurti, the eighth-born son of a high-caste Shaivite Brahmin, Telegu-speaking family, in the town of Madanapalle, Andhra Pradesh, South India. Lord Krishna, according to legend, had been the eighth-born son. Traditionally in India the eighth-born son is called Krishna.

From his earliest years, according to his own accounts, Krishna was vague to the point of appearing moronic. I grew up on his stories of being beaten at school for inattentiveness and for failing to learn his lessons. At home, too, he had difficulty in performing the simplest task correctly. But while his mother was alive, his life was relatively happy. She had a deep love for him. According to Rukmini Arundale, whose family and Krishna's were close friends and neighbours, his mother also believed that this son was destined to be a great person and to have an extraordinary life. She was so certain of this, even before he was born, that breaking orthodox rules, she insisted on giving birth to Krishna in the *puja* room, a place traditionally reserved for prayer and meditation.

I find Krishna's later assertions that he had no memory of his early years hard to believe in the face of so many vividly recounted childhood tales. He would say that they were not from his own memory but were based on what others had told him later. There is no doubt in my mind, however, that Krinsh remembered his mother and his love for her. He used to tell me how, in conventional Brahmin fashion, he kissed the hem of her sari when he greeted her every morning. The very mention of his mother evoked a noticeable depth of emotion in him that moved me as a child. Whatever scant youthful happiness he experienced was related to her. She seems to have had the gentle and loving nature of the model Indian mother, who would replace discipline with love and attention.

When speaking of his father Narayaniah, Krinsh did not display the same emotional warmth. I heard how Narayaniah worked under the British administration as a revenue collector. Krinsh did not seem particularly proud of his father's profession. And in spite of this stable employment, the family was not well off, though not impoverished. Narayaniah was transferred frequently and had to move his family with him. Only six of the eleven children survived to early adolescence. While staying in one town, Cudappah, a bad malarial area, young Krishna, at the age of two, contracted this disease. He would suffer recurring symptoms for many years.

Although Narayaniah had become a Theosophist before Krishna's birth, the usual orthodox Hindu rituals were adhered to. Krinsh recounted with a certain pride how he underwent the sacred thread ceremony when he was six. Bathed and in all new clothing, he sat on his father's knee while his mother guided his finger to trace the word AUM in grains of rice on a silver tray. The priest chanted mantrams. The family drove on a cart drawn by white bullocks with brightly painted horns to the temple. Here they prayed for his good future. Then they proceeded to the school where his intellectual training was officially entrusted to the schoolmaster. In Hindu tradition, this day marked the beginning of Krishna's real birth into the world. It was also the beginning of his difficulties. Discipline begins in school. There the child, having experienced his sacred thread ceremony, is prepared for the harsh realities of life. Krinsh suffered more than most children in school, for he could not learn or concentrate. When he failed to answer the questions, he was sent out on the porch, where he would often stand forgotten for the rest of the day. He might have stayed there all night too, in a vacant trance, if his little brother Nitya had not remembered to take him home. Krinsh was frequently caned. He would forget his books and slate and, when he had not forgotten them, would sometimes offer them to a poorer child who had none. This generosity only earned him another caning.

Krinsh was always conscious of being a high-caste Brahmin. Often he told me of the meditation sessions every morning in his house, when he had to sit without moving a muscle or his ear would be pinched by his father. He believed that such training, plus centuries of Brahmin genes, had developed a superior intelligence in Brahmins, an opinion that my American side of the family found undemocratic. It was obvious that he esteemed his birthright of Brahmin fastidiousness. He recalled his father's overseer, an Englishman, who occasionally dropped by for tea, thinking that he was honouring the family with his visits. The overseer could not have suspected that on his departure every utensil he had used had to be broken and discarded and the whole house scoured from floor to ceiling, so badly was it polluted by the presence of this foreigner.

Krinsh often told me these stories, but he never made much of having seen ghosts. Perhaps he did not want to fill my mind with such immaterial concepts.

Krishna was close to his older sister. The first tragedy of his life was her early death. One day he became alarmed when he saw his mother conversing in the garden with someone he could not see. His mother explained that it was his dead sister and if he so wished he could see her. At first he laughed and then, perhaps to please his mother, he said he could see his sister too. No one else in the family had this ability. His mother also claimed to see auras. Before long the little boy followed her example in this as well. It was natural that he should exhibit a childish effort to please his mother by sharing her psychic disposition. Krishna was born into and grew up in an environment not generally sceptical of the occult or mystical. His Hindu family and his later Theosophical 'family' were alike in this.

Later he claimed that none of these things, including the canings, had conditioned him at all or left any marks on his mind. His memory or lack of it is one of the most complex and elusive aspects of his personality. It is also basic to the understanding, not only of his observations on conditioning, consciousness and freedom, but of his own actions.

In 1905, when Krishna was ten, his mother died and what had been a difficult existence now became a grim one. The little boys were left in the care of an already overworked father. Krishna would see his mother after her death, hear the sound of her bangles following him to school, and try to grasp her sari as she climbed the stairs, only to have the apparition vanish when she reached the top. Her loss would haunt him for many years if not for all of his life.

Eighty years later I looked up at those stairs. We had found the house through a series of inquiries starting at a local Rotary Club. From there we had been directed to a textile merchant who was an old friend of Krinsh's family. 'My father sat on the same school bench with Krishnamurti,' he told us.

The house stood in a quiet narrow street in the centre of the bustling town. It had recently been sold and was now vacant and padlocked. The stairs to the upper rooms opened directly on to the street. The original thatched roof was replaced and the house had been improved, but a small cistern in front still stood filled with water. I saw no ghosts, but had a strange and unhappy premonition that this inadvertent pilgrimage to his birthplace signified my final farewell to Krinsh.

The Theosophical headquarters at Adyar, which stand in 300 acres, are still an oasis. Beyond the guarded gates lies the tranquil beauty of another age. Except for a few additional buildings, little has changed since the first decade of this century. The now polluted Adyar river still flows along one boundary, the beach still stretches along another. A tree-lined road winds gracefully through groves of palms and exotic gardens, past the second largest banyan tree in India, to Leadbeater Chambers, three storey living quarters built during my father's boyhood. Individual members have added private dwellings here and there and passed on, leaving these houses to the society. It is necessary when walking at night to carry a flashlight and beat on wood as a precaution against cobras. The winter climate is never chilly and in summer the intemperate heat is modified by the cool green landscape and the breezes from the sea.

When Narayaniah retired in 1907, his pension could barely support the four boys still under his roof. He attempted to get a post in any capacity at Adyar in exchange for food and lodging. Mrs Besant was averse to having the distraction of children on the compound and turned down the request. But this did not discourage Narayaniah, who persisted with his appeals and was finally given work, but not living quarters, in the compound. He had to settle his family in a shabby little cottage outside the gates. The three-mile walk across the river to school in the Madras suburb of Mylapore and the insanitary conditions of their house were not much of an improvement for the little boys. Nevertheless, the proximity to the Theosophical oasis was to bring about a major change.

In the four years before Krishna's arrival at Adyar, Leadbeater had won high acclaim for his American lecture tour, only to fall from grace due to a charge of moral misconduct. This put a strain on Leadbeater's friendship with Mrs Besant and forced his resignation, under pressure, from the society. Today it seems likely he was a victim of his times, for he believed the pressure of sexuality on young boys and girls was increased by ignoring the subject and refusing to talk about it. He objected to the orthodox view that thoughts do not matter as long as they do not become overt, and he wrote explicitly about the ameliorating effects of masturbation in ridding the mind of such thoughts. He felt that not to do so could lead to more serious consequences, quoting St Paul that it is best to remain celibate but it is better to marry than to burn. Leadbeater concluded in his best style that the 'average doctor cannot see the horrible astral effects of perpetual desire'.

'It is better to marry than to burn.' How often I had heard Krinsh mutter that in some vague moment to no one in particular. It would be many years before I realized the significance it had for him.

Mrs Besant, liberal as she was on other fronts, was torn between Victorian shock at Leadbeater's views and her feelings of loyalty to an old friend. The same wave of confusion was felt throughout the society. Some members did remain loyal to him, like Jinarajadasa, who asserted

The Vehicle

that he had never in all his years of closeness to Leadbeater encountered the slightest impropriety. The pressure against Leadbeater was so strong, however, that even Jinarajadasa had to resign temporarily.

When Mrs Besant became President of the Theosophical Society in 1907, she gradually warmed to Leadbeater again. She even took up cudgels in his defence, stating that he had been wronged by her and the society. Leadbeater returned to Adyar, where he confined himself for the time being to occult investigations into the earth's past and the past lives of those upon it.

If Mrs Besant had expressed doubts about his sexual theories, she had none whatever about his occult reliability. She continued to accept without question the messages and instructions that he transmitted to her from the Masters.

Blavatsky had quite emphatically denied the coming of a new world teacher in the near future, writing that:

> No master of Wisdom from the East will himself appear or send anyone to Europe or America . . . [at least] until the year 1975 . . .
> He will appear as Maitreya Buddha the last of the Avatars and Buddhas, in the seventh Race. Only it is not in the Kali Yug, our present terrifically materialistic age of Darkness, the 'Black Age', that a new Savior of Humanity can ever appear.[1]

She also stated emphatically: 'With the advent of Theosophy the Messiah craze has surely had its day and seen its doom.'[2]

In this she was mistaken. The idea of an imminent incarnation of the Lord Maitreya as world teacher was definitely in the air, at least for Mrs Besant and Leadbeater who, despite Blavatsky's clear pronouncement, set out to find the proper vehicle for the new incarnation.

It had become a habit for Krishna and his younger brother Nitya, from whom he was inseparable, to stop at the beach on their way home from school in the hot summer evenings. Here they would shyly watch a group of young Theosophists cavorting in the waves. One day Leadbeater happened to notice Krishna. He later said that he had been struck by the unusually pure and generous nature of the boy, as revealed in his aura. Leadbeater concluded from this initial impression, that Krishna might prove to be the vehicle that he believed the Masters were directing him to find. Before long he stated he had been instructed by the Master Kuthumi to train this boy. There were those around Adyar who found this choice very surprising. One young

Theosophical scholar, Ernest Wood, who had been helping Krishna with his homework, found him particularly dimwitted. Early descriptions of Krishna and even his own later descriptions of himself evoke a scrawny, dirty, cough-racked, lice-ridden, crooked-toothed boy with rickety legs.

The younger brother, Nitya, who was alert, charming, and easy to teach, might have seemed a better candidate. But for all Krishna's unpromising appearance, Leadbeater became more and more certain that this was the vehicle for whom he had been waiting. Meanwhile Mrs Besant, unaware of Leadbeater's find, had dispatched to Adyar from the United States Hubert Van Hook, a young American whom she believed to be a promising candidate for the vehicle of the world teacher. Hubert arrived in Adyar with his mother in November, a few weeks before Mrs Besant's return. It must have been a considerable shock for Hubert to find that he had already been upstaged by a rather scrawny young Indian. Nevertheless, the two Indian brothers and Hubert joined together in their lessons. For some time Hubert and Nitya were to be Krishna's only youthful companions. The supplanting of Hubert, however, would not be forgotten by the Van Hooks. In the future their cry of immoral conduct would be added to yet more charges against Leadbeater.

Besides nurturing Krishna's astral body Leadbeater had the even more difficult task of nurturing his physical body and mind, both of which appeared to be below normal development for his age. This in no way deterred Leadbeater, who would continue for a few more years to be convinced that he had chosen correctly. He had soon convinced Mrs Besant too. Both Krishna and Nitya were removed from their father's house, and from the school where Krishna had continued to receive cruel treatment. In fact, they were removed altogether from their family circle, never to return.

Leadbeater had been spending years working out and tabulating the past lives of people, important and unimportant, based on an occult source of knowledge which was evidently only available to him. He now began research on the past lives of Krishna (who was identified for this purpose as Alcyone). The thirty lives of Alcyone took up two volumes. Leadbeater's charts involved hundreds of people all related to each other through thirty incarnations. What would become of utmost importance in the present incarnation of these people was their previous relationship to Alcyone. One can imagine a near epidemic of spiritual pride and jostling when Leadbeater published his charts. Shiva Rao, then a young teacher at Central Hindu College in Benares who would have a long future with Krishna, assisted Leadbeater in these tabulations. He later commented that, while it would be impossible to prove that they had a genuinely clairvoyant origin, the complex interweaving of so many thousands of detailed family connections through so many lives, without error, was a mental feat even more difficult to explain.

Leadbeater had his own spiritual evolutionary plan in which there are ten different levels or initiations to pass. To reach even the fourth initiation or Arhat level is more than most individuals can expect in one lifetime. To hasten the naturally slow process of evolution, one may become a pupil of a Master and be placed on probation. Masters have passed the fifth initiation. After the sixth initiation individuals may pass out of the earthly orbit altogether, or they may remain as members of the occult hierarchy, still concerned with governing the inner plane. Above the sixth level are the three offices that administer the occult world: the *Mahachohan,* the *Bodhisattva* and the *Manu.* Alone, on the eighth level is the Buddha. Above the Buddha is the Lord of the World. At the very top, on the tenth level, resides the Trinity of the Logos.

Gautama Buddha had once held the office of the *Bodhisattva,* but no longer. It was now occupied by the Lord Maitreya, who had incarnated into Jesus, known during that period as the Christ. The population of the earth has passed through a series of root and sub-root races, some overlapping through successive periods. The present stage is the Aryan or Teutonic, whose characteristics are largely commercial, scientific and individualistic. This stage will soon evolve into the Austral/American or sixth sub-root race, which will be intuitive and co-operative in nature. To help in the emergence of this new race, the Lord Maitreya, whom Leadbeater envisioned with long red-gold hair and beard and violet eyes, would soon reincarnate into the body of one of his pupils – hopefully into Krishnamurti.

It was no wonder that the preparations for this imminent incarnation would cause such a stir in the Theosophical world. Word spread rapidly and many eyes and ears were focused on Leadbeater and the two little Indian boys he had found on the Adyar beach. Leadbeater was fully conscious, however, that first there must be many trials along 'the Path' that could result in failure; Krishna was not to be taken as a final choice. The course of preparation was all important and there would be signs to watch along the way that would verify or discredit the candidate.

To begin with, Leadbeater spent many hours reading to Krishna about his former lives. But as the boy knew very little English at that time, it probably passed through his mind as cleanly as had his boring school lessons. He would later describe himself as a sieve, absolutely untouched and unconditioned by these ideas.

For five months, while his body was left comfortably in bed, Krishna was supposed to be making nightly astral journeys to the Master Kuthumi's house in the Himalayas for instruction. He would spend the following mornings, back at Adyar, painstakingly recording these meetings in notes that would become his first book, *At the Feet of the Master*. Several Theosophists later vouched that Krishna had written these notes in his own words and that only the spelling and punctuation had been corrected. Given the probable level of the boy's progress in English, it seems likely that this was a slight exaggeration. Ernest Wood, who had already expressed surprise at Leadbeater's choice of candidate, noticed that the book was in Leadbeater's style and even had some sentences remarkably similar to those in one of Leadbeater's own books about to go to press.

It is sometimes difficult to distinguish with certainty the boundaries of the possible or to drive a straight course through the occult areas of Theosophy. On one side are cries of hypnotism, and self-delusion and on the other the claims made by those who believe implicitly in these phenomena and whose lives proclaim them to be honest and reliable individuals. For those who find it impossible to believe in the occult happenings of the Theosophists, an explanation less complex than hypnotism is that personalities as magnetic and powerful as Blavatsky's and Leadbeater's (and as Krishna's would become) are able to create an atmosphere in which the 'willing suspension of disbelief' is over-whelming.

Eventually Krishna would disavow all these claims made on his behalf. They would be an embarrassment in his search for an independent path to the truth. Then he would find for himself a neat way out of that dilemma. In 1929 he would claim to remember nothing of his earlier years. As a result he never needed to offend his benefactors by denying the authenticity of that first little book, nor did he need to claim responsibility for it. Where Blavatsky and Leadbeater may have re-arranged their past to fit, more appropriately, their present, Krishna chose to blank out his youth altogether. However, while Krishna would later claim that he had been untouched by Theosophical ideas, he retained certain concepts and imagery given him during this period and would later incorporate them into his own teachings.

Certainly, a key influence in Krishna's early training was Mrs Besant. Her published talks on *The Way of the Path* must have been easily accessible to him. In these she had described her version of the route of spiritual evolution. Mrs Beasant enumerated the first steps towards probation, involving various requisites and tests that must be fulfilled. After these preliminary steps were fulfilled, one might proceed toward preparation for discipleship by attracting the notice of a Master for guidance along the probationary path. One is not expected to perform perfectly but to practise and attempt. Gradually learning to discriminate between the real and the unreal, one becomes indifferent to worldly objects. One learns control of the mind, senses and body, also tolerance and endurance. One may now choose a short cut, leave the beaten track and climb straight up the mountain. This entails paying in difficulties what one has gained in time and drawing on oneself immediately the whole karmic debt which might have been played out through many lives.

Before the second initiation one must be rid of three things: the *illusion of personal self, doubt* and *superstition*, or that 'reliance on external sectarian rites and ceremonies for spiritual help' which are necessary only in the lower stages to climb the ladder toward reality.[3]

As Krishna soon discovered, 'the Path of Discipleship' was not always easy. In the future he would chafe at the bit quite often until he found his own short cut to the top. For the present, the nightly visits on the astral plane to the Master Kuthumi, on which Leadbeater told Mrs Besant he accompanied the boys, were not arduous. Leadbeater was soon able to announce that Krishna had been placed on probation and was well on the way to the next step on 'the Path', acceptance by and close unity with the Master.

For a child who, initially, had been considered by some retarded, Krishna began to make remarkable progress in those first months at Adyar. He would retain his difficulty in learning, at least in certain subjects, but he exhibited no difficulty then or in later life in learning what he *wanted* to learn.

Both brothers found their new surroundings a true paradise even without comparing them to their impoverished home and harsh schooldays. They soon outgrew the intrinsic fear, from which young Indians often suffered, of Europeans with their overbearing sense of superiority.

At the age of fourteen, only eight months after being discovered by Leadbeater (when he had known no English at all), with Leadbeater's probable assistance, Krishna wrote affectionate and grammatical letters to Mrs Besant. He saw her as a new mother and begged her to let him address her as such. That warm and generous-hearted lady who had fought so hard for the underprivileged must have been touched by the motherless boy who thanked her for her kindness, for his bicycle, for the use of her room, in which the brothers slept when she was away. To be removed from the mud-floor cottage outside the Adyar gates to the quite magnificent two-storey stucco headquarters with its spacious rooms and breezy verandas; to be nourished physically on the excellent vegetarian food and nourished mentally by half a dozen devoted young tutors was indeed much to be thankful for. There was also the glorious future for which Krishna was being prepared.

A photograph, taken in 1910 on the roof of the ES building in Adyar, prophetically records the emerging new Krishna. He faces his little brother Nitya and Leadbeater, who has protectively placed a large white hand on the younger boy's thin shoulder. The graceful curve of Krishna's posture states his mother's expectations, instilled in him long before being re-affirmed by Leadbeater. It asserts his self-confidence, even arrogance, standing in opposition to his benefactor.

Krishna's later memories of Leadbeater, those that edged through his wall of oblivion, were not at all warm. He used to tell me, as he had often told others, how Leadbeater, having urged him repeatedly to keep his mouth from hanging open, had one day jolted him with a sharp sock on the chin. Krishna never held his mouth open again. Nor did he ever forgive Leadbeater. Another time he and Nitya had asked to have oatmeal for breakfast. As a result they were served nothing else for the next few weeks. Krishna offered an even more graphic example of Leadbeater's stern discipline. One day the two brothers had been swimming in the as yet unpolluted river with Leadbeater. It was getting late. Noticing an ominous dark spot, they avoided it and swam to shore. They felt they had got away with this harmless evasion. No sooner were they safely on the river bank, than Leadbeater said, 'Now we shall go back and swim through that spot.' This view of Leadbeater's severity seems unique to Krishna. According to my father and mother and according to their recollection of Nitya's view, it was quite out of character. This was corroborated by Rukmini, who told me she could not imagine Leadbeater ever striking anyone. Yet as it was of utmost importance to him to eradicate fear, it is possible that he felt strong measures were necessary in the preparation of the vehicle. That he did not succeed in this particular attempt will be seen. Fear would remain an intrinsic part of Krishna's personality and would become a basic factor in his later philosophy. His approach to the problem would be diametrically opposed to Leadbeater's. Krinsh told me these stories about Leadbeater many times. While he may have preferred to claim that they were not his own memories but transmitted to him by others, they seemed to me to be told with first-hand poignancy.

30

The Vehicle

There was too much emotion, sometimes even a perceptible shudder, when he spoke of Leadbeater, making it hard to believe that his own recollections were no longer available to him.

Although the now demoted Hubert was allowed to play with Krishna and Nitya, he was not allowed to touch any of Krishna's belongings. Leadbeater believed that even inanimate objects could receive bad vibrations and pass these on to another. While this restriction may have been hard on Hubert, who had been led to think he would be the candidate for the vehicle, it did not seem to affect Krishna's generous nature. He persisted throughout life in wanting to share his possessions, at least with his favourites of the moment.

It is certain that from the time Krishna was taken into the inner fold at Adyar both he and his brother Nitya were showered with every intellectual, material and non-material benefit. Along with this went a strict routine of exercise, cleanliness and personal grooming. As part of the physical fitness programme, Krishna was encouraged to cycle. According to Richard Balfour-Clark, one of the boys' tutors at Adyar, whom I was fortunate to meet in 1973, Krishna showed considerable prowess in cycling long distances. Leadbeater was determined to replace Indian with European ideas of personal cleanliness. While Brahmins found the English habit of soaking in one's own dirty bath water quite revolting, Leadbeater disapproved of the Indian way of sloshing water over the body while clad in a loin cloth, a procedure he considered inadequate. Within two years the brothers had been sufficiently prepared, in Mrs Besant's opinion, to make their European debut.

In the spring of 1911 Krishna and Nitya accompanied Mrs Besant to England, where they were greeted with a considerable fanfare by Theosophists. Krishna's recently published *Lives of Alcyone* had preceded them. Doors of the highest circles were thrown open to them, for there were many wealthy and aristocratic Theosophists in that era. Among these was a person who would be as close to Krishna as anyone during his youth, a Lady Emily Lutyens. She was the daughter of the Earl of Lytton, Viceroy of India, and the wife of Sir Edwin Lutyens, the renowned architect who designed the government buildings of British New Delhi. At the time Lady Emily met Krishna she was a recent adherent of Theosophy. Like Mrs Besant, Lady Emily was drawn to the increasingly handsome but still frail and motherless boy. Until her death, nearly half a century later, he addressed her as 'Mum'. The chord he struck in her was one he would strike in many women throughout his life.

Along with all the luxuries of life amid England's upper crust,

31

Krishna, now only sixteen and Nitya three years younger, were subjected to a well-planned and rigorous anglicization. They had to endure uncomfortable European shoes, expensively tailored suits, neckties and, worst of all, food which for several years caused them severe indigestion. As this diet had been prescribed by the Master Kuthumi (via Leadbeater), no one would have dared to interfere with it. Years later Krinsh described to me the discomforts of two young Brahmins transplanted to England. He made clear his dislike of English cooking, his revulsion at the lack of basic cleanliness – the butler who spat on the water glass to make it shine – the young aristocrat who changed his collar but not his shirt. Krinsh told stories too of life in public school, of the ice-covered water with which they had to wash their faces in the mornings, of the appalling food and finally of the bullying which he and Nitya terminated by a claim, though sheer bluff, of knowing jujitsu. However, these schooldays did not last long.

In 1912, the boys' father, Narayaniah, took action to have his sons returned to his custody. Whether he was genuinely disturbed by the rumours about Leadbeater and wanted them removed from his influence, or whether he felt the original promise of furthering the boys' education and opportunities had taken an undesirable turn, was never quite clear. However, while the case was being fought in Madras, Krishna and Nitya were safely sequestered in the idyllic town of Taormina on the island of Sicily, well out of their father's grasp should the verdict fall in his favour.

In spite of her brilliant defence arguments Mrs Besant lost the first rounds in the Indian courts. But she won her appeal to the Privy Council in London. This gave her the control she needed over her wards to ensure Krishna the future she believed to be his destiny. She was even awarded the court costs, but charitably declined to collect from the defeated Narayaniah. Krishna was exultant and congratulated her on this victory that would ensure his 'marvellous future'.

3

The Vehicle Takes the Wheel

Among the group of important Theosophists in London was an American who would play a vital financial role in both Krishna's and my parents' future. She was Mary Dodge, the heiress of the Phelps Dodge copper fortune. Miss Dodge supported not only causes but many people and their perpetual travels on behalf of Theosophy. She herself was too crippled by arthritis to travel and once told my mother that the one ocean voyage she had embarked on from America to England had caused her such seasickness that she had decided to remain in England for the rest of her life. She shared her home, Westside House on Wimbledon Common, with a fellow Theosophist, Lady De La Warr. Mrs Besant was always welcome there along with her wards. Miss Dodge even offered Krishna a house on Hampstead Heath. She also settled on him £500 a year for life. This generosity toward a young Indian boy she scarcely knew is a mark of not uncommon Theosophical faith in their leaders. Krishna had not yet attained the magnetic force that he soon would display. But those who knew Mrs Besant trusted her absolutely. If she said she believed Krishna was to be the vehicle for the world teacher, they did not question her judgment and did all in their power to assist her.

In spring 1913, not long after this financial boon, Krishna began to reveal a new side to his character, different from the affectionate, dreamy, sometimes vacant boy of only four years before. With the approach of his eighteenth birthday Krishna began to show his dislike of criticism and to flex his independence.

Mrs Besant had asked George Arundale, the head of Central Hindu College, which she had founded, to come to England expressly to tutor Krishna and Nitya. She had also asked Jinarajadasa, now an important member of the Theosophical Society to join them. Being loyal Theosophists, these two men did not hesitate to give up work that greatly interested them for this new task – a task not made easier by Leadbeater's assertion that while they were both Krishna's teachers, the Master Kuthumi had revealed that they were also his disciples. One can imagine that being tutor to a teenage boy who knew you were his disciple was not an easy undertaking.

Theosophy had a way of generating a great deal of excitement, particularly among its higher echelons. Mrs Besant was still an indefatigable lecturer. She travelled widely, lecturing on the precepts of Theosophy and on the preparations for the coming world teacher. There were already 15,000 worldwide members of the Order of the Star, a society formed within Theosophy to prepare themselves and the world for 'the Coming'. A publication called the *Herald of the Star* kept these hopeful people abreast of the latest developments. Krishna was prominently featured as the editor, although George Arundale did the work.

In spite of the responsible efforts of Jinarajadasa to instil some culture into the prospective world teacher, the fun of the details of publishing, such as choosing fancy ink and paper, easily occluded any thoughts of Shakespeare and Sanskrit from Krishna's mind. Jinarajadasa soon discovered for himself the change in this once docile young man. Krishna had no intention of giving up his exciting new life for studies that bored him. As well as disliking criticism, Krishna also disliked discipline. He had probably suffered from it as a child. Those who took too firm a hand with him quickly lost his favour. Among these was his once beloved tutor Jinarajadasa. As part of Krishna's proclamation of independence, he wrote to Leadbeater objecting to the Master's instructions being transmitted to him through others. He felt he could carry out the Master's instructions better if they were not forced upon him and made unpleasant. Miss Dodge's generosity would now, theoretically, make it possible for him to plan his own living arrangements. In this plan he eliminated Jinarajadasa from whom, he said, he could not possibly learn Sanskrit. The younger George Arundale was much more to his liking and was someone – at that time – Krishna felt he could control.

Yet he was having some problems with George too, stemming from his relationship with Lady Emily. George and some of the elders on the scene were critical of the evident affection between Lady Emily and Krishna. The fact that she was old enough to be his mother did not mitigate their opinion. But Krishna had found in Lady Emily the gentle motherly qualities for which he had yearned since the loss of his own mother. Mrs Besant loved him deeply and gave him warmth and affection, but he was seldom with her. She was always involved in momentous activities and he was not her only focal point. To be the single object of a woman's focus and love would be his lifelong need. Lady Emily was but the first to fill this role.

By this time Krishna had finally acquired a facile command of the

English language. His natural aptitude for languages, the one subject in which he could excel (though he could not pass the examinations) coupled with an ear for poetry and a gift for elocution would serve him well – to say nothing of his now striking good looks. With his hair elegantly cut, his teeth straightened, and his poise awakened, he had moved far away from the rickety, unkempt little boy with lice in his eyebrows and a vacant look in his eye.

Theosophists like good Hindus were imbued with qualities of faith and *dharma*, or duty. Many of them also sustained trust in the existence of the Masters and the reality of messages sent through messengers like Leadbeater. While Blavatsky had been highly sceptical of phenomena occurring outside her own experience, Mrs Besant had become a trusting, if not gullible, person. Her faith was based initially on her own experiences but for some years she had placed a large part of her occult trust with Leadbeater.

Krishna's first signs of independence were taken by his elders as a natural display of adolescent rebelliousness. His protectors (or protectors of the order, as Mrs Besant and Leadbeater referred to themselves), tended to explain away his difficult behaviour as symptoms of insufficient readiness in the vehicle. They apparently failed to perceive the true nature of that incipiently independent mind; a mind that would ultimately seek its own short cut up the mountain.

Krishna's new display of independence was, on another level, also part of a lifelong pattern of behaviour, that of suddenly showing an interest in and demanding control over affairs that had previously not interested him at all. His insistence on autonomy was understandable, but his methods for gaining it would sometimes create confusing and difficult situations. In the future many people close to Krishna would believe they were in the presence of an egoless and perfect being, yet find his ways obfuscated and bewildering.

As a result of Krishna's protest to Leadbeater, Jinarajadasa was recalled to India. But evidently the Masters would not co-operate with Krishna's wish for direct communion with them. So, if for nothing else, Krishna was still dependent on Leadbeater to relay his advancements along 'the Path', just as were others in Krishna's small circle, including Lady Emily. Perhaps not coincidentally, no new advancements came through for any of his favourites for some time.

Realizing his rebelliousness had incurred Leadbeater's displeasure, Krishna wrote a very long apologetic letter, begging forgiveness for his bad behaviour and acknowledging that he owed everything to Leadbeater. What Krishna did not know at that moment was that Leadbeater was no longer placing all his expectations in Krishna. He had just announced a new discovery in the person of D. Rajagopalacharya, a thirteen-year-old Ayyangar Brahmin who was said to have 'a marvellous past and a great future'. Privately Leadbeater expected that this boy might even fulfil the role assigned to Krishna should Krishna in some way fall short. While Mrs Besant appeared to have unequivocally committed her faith and her love to Krishna, Leadbeater, fond as he was of the young man, would not find it impossible to admit that he had made a mistake in his initial choice.

Meanwhile Krishna's wish for more independent living arrangements had been overruled, if not by the Masters, at least by Mrs Besant, who, in the summer of 1914, moved the brothers to Bude, Cornwall. They remained there for a year, continuing their studies under George Arundale in preparation for Oxford.

Krishna never found formal academic endeavour either interesting or easy and this year could not have been very comfortable for him. Nitya, on the other hand, loved his studies and applied himself with an enthusiasm that might have been the cause of his severe eye strain and his generally run-down condition. Krishna felt both sympathy and impatience with Nitya's poor health. He sometimes complained of his brother's bad humour, a view that is very much at odds with any offered by those closest to Nitya, either then or later. All who knew Nitya well, remarked on his warm, loving nature and his beautiful and spontaneous laugh and smile. He did not have Krishna's physical beauty, but his charming personality made up for that. From the beginning, however, neither Nitya's wishes, his abilities, nor his health would ever be placed ahead or even on a par with Krishna's. He would always be considered an inseparable part of the older brother's future, a part that was decreed by the Masters.

Predictably, Krishna failed the entrance examinations for Oxford. The university made it clear in any case that it preferred not to include a messiah in the student body. This was the first of Krishna's academic disappointments and it would have an influence on his attitude toward intellectual endeavour. For the rest of his life, he emphasized, with more pride than regret, his inability to pass examinations.

The First World War had a minimal effect on Krishna's life. In spring 1915 Nitya went off to France to join the Red Cross as a dispatch rider. Krishna was disappointed not to be allowed to accompany him. As compensation for having to remain in Cornwall, he was given his own motorcycle. In June the brothers were reunited in London and it was decided they should both study for admission to London University.

The Vehicle Takes the Wheel

At this time they met an eminent and kindly barrister named Harold Baillie-Weaver, who took the two boys under his wing. From him they acquired a taste for fashionable clothes (Baillie-Weaver had the same tailor as the Prince of Wales) and for perfect grooming, which included the art of polishing shoes, an art which Krishna never lost. The serious Theosophists around him noticed the emergence of a new, distinct aspect of Krishna's personality. He acquired not only a passion for expensive clothes, but also for fine motorcars, the cinema and for sports. Despite these fashionable tastes Krishna and Nitya also volunteered for clean-up chores in a war hospital, duties that for Brahmin boys must have been highly distasteful.

Much as they would have liked to move in with the Baillie-Weavers, the boys were not yet to be permitted even this much independence. For the next few years they had to live under close supervision in a gloomy rented house in which they never felt at home. All their capers, innocent as they might be, were relayed to Mrs Besant.

In 1920 Nitya passed his Matriculation with honours. It was decided that Krishna, who had repeatedly failed, should go to Paris and study French. Nitya remained in London, reading for the bar, and to a certain extent, living his own life, which included placing a bet on a winning horse. At the time Krishna displayed a sanctimonious attitude when he heard of his brother's triumph, reminding Nitya how much others must have lost for him to have won. Yet, by the time I heard the story from Krinsh, he showed pride in Nitya's accomplishment and wry humour in his own failure in a similar escapade.

Only two months after his harsh judgment of Nitya, Krishna demonstrated that he was not above gambling himself. Accompanied by a Theosophical comrade, he went to the Casino in Nice with the ambitious intention of ruining the bank by using his will power to control the ball. At first he turned ten francs into a hundred, but in the end he came out twenty short.

Nitya's winnings, on the other hand, bought for him an Isotta Frascini car. When Mrs Besant heard about it, she seems to have shared Krishna's initial disapproval. She made Nitya return it. This incident, however, strengthened Nitya's determination to become financially independent. With the help of a well-to-do Indian in Bombay, he worked out a plan to import motorcars and tractors into India. He was also stopped cold in this enterprise by Mrs Besant, to whom he had written announcing that he was postponing his examination in criminal law. She reminded him that his duty was to look after Krishna, still in Paris, and to remain within reach should Krishna get into difficulties. She recognized that it was the younger brother who must look after the older, a sacrifice expected and demanded of Nitya.

On a brief trip to Paris in February 1920, Nitya had met a charming French family, Mme de Manziarly and her four children, who would be closely associated with both brothers. Actually Mme de Manziarly and her eldest daughter Mima would be among those few people who gave Nitya first place, over Krishna, in their hearts. He confided to them during his short life some of his deepest feelings. 'I've never yet enjoyed anything for which I've not paid dearly, I think it must be because my enjoyments are among the forbidden ones, and those that are permissible are not enjoyable.'[1]

Krishna, meanwhile, had been attempting to live on his own in a flat in Paris, but he spent his whole allowance in the first few weeks and was soon practically starving. He admitted then and later that he could never manage money. It was quite clear, particularly to Mrs Besant, that he would always need someone at his side with firm guidance over his worldly affairs.

At twenty-five, Krishna was fluctuating between a wide range of moods. Sometimes cloaked in a romantic depression, he seriously doubted the things he had been told about the Masters and his own future. Sometimes showing a new maturity, he would resolve to search for his own philosophy of life, to meditate, and to work hard to prepare himself to help others. He was already aware that to do this he must first find himself, that he must develop sympathy, understanding and love. The next moment he would rudely (and privately) blast off at the Theosophical leaders, always exempting Mrs Besant from his outbursts.

Serious philosophical pursuits were not the only ones that occupied Krishna that summer in Paris. The two younger de Manziarly daughters brought a new sense of fun and gaiety into his life. Krishna found his first romance with Marcelle de Manziarly, and admitted that he could fall in love with her, but maintained that marriage was out of the question. He expressed his sense of higher purpose.

His love life was naturally something Krinsh never discussed with me. I doubt if he ever seriously discussed it with anyone except, in the very early years, in his almost daily letters to Lady Emily. Most people have the impression that nothing of the sort could ever have existed for him. We shall see, however, this is very far from the truth.

Serious reading was added to his repertoire of new activities. The intellectual circle around Mme de Manziarly fed him such books as *The Idiot, War and Peace* and *Buddha's Way of Virtue*. In the last he found a passage that might have echoed his own inner development at that moment. 'All conquering and all knowing am I, detached, untainted, untrammelled, wholly freed by destruction of desire. Whom shall I call Teacher? Myself found the way.' This could well be taken for the kernel from which his philosophy would gradually emerge. He would eventually claim that all his past conditioning had fallen away along with his past memory.

He persisted in his rebelliousness – wisely unrevealed to Mrs Besant – but abetted by the young de Manziarlys, with whose help 'he hoped to change the world'. To these sisters he hinted at the contempt he would one day express for certain Theosophists, saying he was fed up with the whole crowd of fools. Yet, in 1920 he still felt integrally bound to the society and hoped to make it eventually conform to his view of the right path. This view was still unformulated and it would be nine years before it became publicly known.

At this point a new personality would enter his life who would become for the next fifty years his closest associate. But first Krishna's initial jealous reaction to this new 'rival' would be another revelation of his character.

4

The New Discovery

My father has always avoided the limelight. He would never have looked upon himself as Krishna's rival. Leadbeater and Krishna himself did that. Ever since I can remember he was a private person, living a life apart from us, joining us only for meals and special occasions.

From the stories he told me of his childhood I visualized a happy home, clean and fastidious by the highest Brahmin standards. He had loving parents. Among his six siblings was an especially beloved younger sister and a rather overbearing older brother.

He was born in the state of Madras, now called Tamil Nadu, on 7 September 1900, the fourth of seven children and named Desikacharya Rajagopalacharya, Desikacharya being his father's given name. (In South India a child's given name is prefaced by the father's given name.) My father's family was Ayyangar Brahmin, Vaishnavite, one of the highest and strictest of Hindu castes. His father, V. K. Desikacharya was a judge and also a Theosophist, a member of the ES, and the President of the local lodge of the society.

My Indian grandmother, Doraichi, was deeply religious. Even at the age of ninety she still made a daily pilgrimage to the temple, a mile each way from her home. Of her seven children, only my father, like his father, became a Theosophist.

In spite of the liberalizing influence of Theosophy, the family adhered strictly to certain orthodox Hindu customs. Eating onions or root vegetables, for which my father had an unfortunate liking, was forbidden. Liking foods that were either forbidden or bad for him would be a lifelong habit with Raja. One day, hiding behind an old shed munching a raw onion, Raja was caught by his older brother in this defiance of the family's caste restrictions. As is so often the case, the discipline of an older sibling can be much more severe than that of the parents. On another day in December 1913 Raja was again in tears after some such incident with his brother. His mother suddenly suggested that Desikacharya take his young son along to the Christmas convention of the Theosophical Society to be held at Calicut, a day's train journey away.

As an Ayyangar Brahmin Desikacharya would not eat food prepared by anyone other than a member of the same caste. Therefore the cook had to accompany them. Unfortunately, at one of the junction stations the cook wandered a bit far and missed the train, causing Desikacharya and Raja, to arrive at the conference a day late. This incident would not have been memorable except that Leadbeater, who was to preside over the conference, stated later that the night before leaving for it he had been told by the Master Kuthumi that he would find there someone new and very special. He looked around carefully on his arrival and saw no one, or rather no aura, out of the ordinary. Although puzzled, he did not doubt the Master's word. When Desikacharya and his son turned up the next day and Leadbeater saw the boy's aura, he recognized that this was the person he had been looking for. He entered in his diary for 26 December 1913, 'Met D. Rajagopalacharya and instantly recognized him as one of us.'[1]

The fact that for the past six months Leadbeater had been coping with Krishna's continuing rebelliousness might have prompted him (or the Master Kuthumi) to continue the search for the vehicle. News of this 'discovery' would eventually reverberate all the way to Europe.

For Raja, this moment was the beginning of a new and long path. Desikacharya was naturally pleased that his young son had drawn the notice of a leader in the society. Although personal encounters with Leadbeater would be few and far between for Raja, the older man was to take a profound and enduring interest in the boy that started with daily letters. His English was still limited, but Raja responded with letters of his own 'full of affection, and always asking for guidance how to live the life of dedication to the Master, which he had accepted with joy'.[2] This time Leadbeater had chosen a candidate who was well nourished, eager to learn and willing to obey. (Except when it came to food.) At some point Desikacharya must have mentioned his eldest son's discipline of Raja over his eating habits. This evoked a strong plea from Leadbeater.

'A thousand chilli cakes are not worth upsetting the feelings of this great soul,' said Leadbeater, who then firmly recommended that Desikacharya prohibit that elder brother from interfering with young Raja in any way, as he evidently was not capable of understanding his young brother's true nature. Leadbeater himself would often caution Raja to take better care of his health. But Raja did not perceive this advice as anything other than affectionate concern and would never resent Leadbeater.

Two months later Leadbeater was to set off for Australia on what he then intended to be a short stay of six months or so; but he would be absent from India for twenty years. Concerned about the future of his new discovery, before leaving he sent for Raja to visit Adyar for a few days so that he could inspire him to pursue his education. Jinarajadasa, who at Krishna's instigation, had just been recalled to India, was asked to look out for Raja in Leadbeater's absence. With his family's blessings, Raja was sent to the Theosophical school in Benares. He made lifelong friends there, among whom was Yagna Shastri, Rukmini's brother.

Yagna was the same age as my father. I first met him when he was seventy-four while we were staying at Leadbeater Chambers in Adyar. One morning Yagna appeared on the veranda in his immaculate white kurta and pants with a small boy's smile on his face.

'Isn't it just like your father's?' were his first words to me. He pointed at the short wide nose that can be found on ninth-century Chola sculpture as well as among the present population of Tamil Nadu. My father had never told me about Yagna. In a few minutes Yagna told me a great deal about my father.

'The first day Raja arrived at school I threw mud on his eggs, partly to tease and partly because I thought it wrong for the Theosophists to make us eat eggs, strictly forbidden to Brahmins.

'He was homesick and that made him cry. I remember that moment so well – how he felt and how I felt.

'Our true friendship only started forty years after those schooldays in Benares. I was jealous of Raja then. I saw him as a spiritual rival – such rivalry had already descended to the young. I even hit him once for no reason at all and he never hit me back. He was everyone's favourite. They all loved him.

'Raja and I belonged to a small group of boys, singled out by Leadbeater because of our significant past lives and future potential. We certainly felt our special status, and created a good deal of mischief. Not Raja, he was never a troublemaker, but some of us refused to address the teachers formally as Sir, and we threw the brass washing pots at other boys during their bath.

'Poor Shiva Rao, our tutor [formerly Krishna's tutor at Adyar] finally felt compelled to write to Leadbeater and complain about his boys. He got small satisfaction from that! Leadbeater replied that if Shiva Rao couldn't control his boys he was not fit to be their teacher.

'We would both come down to Adyar for holidays and scramble together over the open beams of this very building, which was being constructed then. The only naughty thing I ever saw your father do was frighten Mrs Jinarajadasa with a coiled-up rope. She thought it was a snake and nearly had a heart attack. We thought she was a very prim and proper Englishwoman and laughed at her accent. Later of course we were all good friends, but the idea of an Indian marrying an English-woman was very odd in those days. It was even upsetting when my sister, Rukmini, married George Arundale. Then I married an American and so did your father. That's what Theosophy did for us all.'

From 1914, when Raja left home for Benares, he never returned to his family, except to visit. His closest relationships would be based on a brotherhood of ideals rather than a kinship of blood. If his family resented this, and, according to Rukmini, they sometimes did, they also felt deeply grateful for the help he would unfailingly give them for several generations. Raja's older brother, however, who remained an orthodox Hindu, continued to feel that Raja was being 'led astray' by the Theosophists, who did not adhere to traditions. (He may have been right, from his point of view, for when their father died, Raja, then eighteen, defied his brother and upheld Desikacharya's wishes that his widow be spared the orthodox Hindu forms of mourning, such as shaving her head. This eccentric behaviour caused so much gossip in Tanjor, where they were then living, that Raja took it on himself to move the whole family to Madras.)

After one year at Benares, Raja decided he would prefer to go to the Theosophical school and college at Madanapalle, Krishna's birthplace. By this time Leadbeater had decided, through his unique investigations, that Raja, in his last incarnation, had been St Bernard of Clairvaux. The political and the stirring oratorical abilities of this saint, demonstrated by his healing of a schism within the church, preaching for the crusade in AD 1145, his organizational talents in planning and building monasteries and his love for and preservation of books and manuscripts had been described in biographies of St Bernard, published in English in the 1890s. Those books were available to Leadbeater. Some of these qualities are also thought to be inherent in the true Vaishnavite, adherents of Vishnu, the Preserver. When Raja stayed at Adyar, his small bedroom in the headquarters building was adjacent to the room and library of the absent Leadbeater. He was free to avail himself of the library and was to develop a lifelong cherishing of books. Who can say with certainty whether Raja's later manifested traits and talents were due to the awareness of his alleged former incarnation, the influence of Leadbeater, or were simply natural to him? It would not be easy to separate the influences he had as a young boy among the Theosophists from the rigorous brahmanic training in his own home. There is no doubt that he eventually developed a strong will directed unwaveringly toward what he perceived to be his own life purpose or *sva-dharma*, a concept perfectly exemplified by Arjuna in the Bhagavadgita, when he casts aside his horror of entering the battle in order to fulfil his intrinsic nature and duty as a warrior.

On one subject Raja would remain intractable for his whole life. Exercise. He simply would not do it, except on sporadic and rare occasions when impelled by some peculiar motivation. During Raja's holidays, he stayed at Adyar with Jinarajadasa, who urged him to go for a good bicycle ride every afternoon. He was probably convinced that his advice was being taken. Raja appeared to ride off down the road and be gone for a good two hours. But just around the corner, practically next door, lived Rukmini's family. Here he was warmly welcomed to tea and whiled away the afternoon in the company of two very beautiful young girls. According to Rukmini, her sister Shivakamu was the main attraction. Raja would urge Rukmini to go and try on an endless array of saris which, one by one, she would come in to model for him while he conversed with the other sister. Whatever benefit Raja lost from lack of exercise, he gained in the warmth and fun of these afternoon visits. Even heavily chaperoned, this socializing between boys and girls was highly unorthodox and an example of the liberalizing effect which Theosophy could have on Hindu culture. The unselfconscious and lasting friendships that developed helped to shape their later lives, lives of complexity and idealism, that would bridge diverse cultures. These times at Adyar also exposed Raja to occasional currents of dissension between his elders. Once sitting unobtrusively and unnoticed he heard Jinarajadasa reprimand George Arundale, who had just left Krishna in England.

'You were supposed to stay there and look after him.'

'I could take no more,' replied George.

This exchange had no meaning for my father at the time, but it remained in his memory. Years later he would see letters between these two men who had been so devoted to Krishna, expressing their disillusionment over Krishna's early powers of manipulating and exploiting those trying to help him.

By the time he was sixteen, Raja began to fulfil, in a very concrete way, Leadbeater's initial hopes for him.

He had found several villages around Madanapalle without any school. To him it was a tragedy to see children as well as their elders unable to read or write. He got the villagers to clean out a shed and persuaded his fellow students to teach night school. He raised money for books and lights and organized the programme. Succeeding with the first school, he went on to set up others. This idealism did not go unheeded by Annie Besant.

In 1919, Raja was invited to accompany the Jinarajadasas to Australia, where they would visit Leadbeater in Sydney. It would be the first time in five years that he would see the man who had recognized his potential for a 'marvellous future'. On the way to Australia they stopped in Java. Here Raja exhibited one of his rare but dramatic instances of physical endurance. He walked barefoot up a volcano. My father's ability to withstand these unprepared-for exertions with no ill after-effects, was exhibited throughout his life and was often the envy of those, like Krinsh, who arduously, for many days, prepared themselves for such an undertaking.

When Raja and the Jinarajadasas arrived in Australia, they were immediately confronted by Leadbeater's continuing difficulties with unsubstantiated charges of sexual misconduct. In fact, he was being attacked not only on grounds of immorality but of lunacy as well. The latter charges stemmed from his predictions about the coming of the world teacher. Leadbeater had also become a Bishop in the Liberal Catholic Church, once called the Old Catholic Church, which had been formed as a protest against papal infallibility. It followed the ritual of the Roman Catholic Church in the Mass, but there was no confessional in the Liberal Catholic Church and celibacy was not required of the priesthood. The English liturgy had been composed by a joint effort of Mrs Besant and Leadbeater.

The evidence against Leadbeater was largely based on Hubert Van Hook's claim that Leadbeater had made improper advances to him in Adyar and had faked the *Lives*. However, since Hubert's future as the vehicle, before being given a fair chance, had been abruptly terminated by Leadbeater's discovery of Krishnamurti, Hubert was not an unbiased witness. And one might wonder what proof of fraud anyone could offer as to whether the *Lives of Alcyone* were dictated by Leadbeater's occult knowledge or by his fertile imagination.

Jinarajadasa was horrified at the implied collapse, inherent in this scandal, of the whole occult hierarchy from Leadbeater on down – to say nothing of the Liberal Catholic Church and the reliance on Leadbeater's reports of initiations for countless hopeful people. But as it had in the past, the furore soon died down. One of the central tenets of Theosophy was to shun gossip, and most of the charges flying on all sides turned out to be no more than that.

In the summer of 1920 Raja sailed with Jinarajadasa to England, where he stayed with Miss Dodge while preparing to take his entrance examinations for Cambridge.

When Krishna and Nitya heard of the imminent arrival on their stage of Leadbeater's 'new discovery', their reaction was, to say the least, surprising in those being prepared for such high purpose. Nitya who had been enjoying living on his own at long last, was furious to find that he would soon have to share his flat. Yolande and Marcelle de Manziarly teased Krishna about being jealous of his new rival, to which Krishna retorted that he would gladly hand over to that 'blinker', Rajagopal, his place. He made fun of the name, however, and scoffed when he heard Raja wore white gloves. (Raja would not know of Krishna's taunts until thirty years later when he read of them in Lady Emily's biography.) On a more serious level, Krishna had been venting his increasing impatience with the Theosophists and with the notions that had surrounded him since his own discovery. Soon he would be pleasantly surprised to find in Raja a friend with strong rational and intellectual capacities to whom he could look for support in his struggle for total independence. But it was Nitya who became Raja's closest friend. They had more in common intellectually and temperamentally than either of them had with Krishna.

Raja was, in at least one respect, more fortunate than the brothers. Being less the centre of attention, he was able to pursue what he most wanted to do: to avail himself of the opportunity to study at Cambridge. Nitya, who had a brilliant mind, had passed all his examinations and was reading for the bar in London, still hoping to gain financial independence. Because of Krishna's needs, and his own ill health, he would not be able to continue this pursuit much longer.

Thanks to Miss Dodge, Raja's life at St John's College, Cambridge was not only intellectually interesting but also comfortable. He had a set of rooms with his own furnishings, in short, the facilities that any upper-class young Englishman would expect. Because he was in a university and working hard from the beginning to make the most of this opportunity, ultimately getting his degrees with honours, he was spared the upper-crust English snobbery which had so badly infected Krishna and Nitya in their early years in that society. Raja took very strongly to Western culture, studying Greek and Latin. He specialized in European and English history and law. He developed a keen ear for Western classical music but would always retain his love for Indian music and culture.

Having been drawn quickly into the inner circle around Krishna and Nitya, Raja was held in great affection by those closest to the brothers and by the brothers themselves. He was also taken quickly into the confidence of this circle. Leadbeater's expectations of Raja had preceded him. He had a shy and deferential manner toward his elders. Miss Dodge was sufficiently taken with him to confide her growing concern over Krishna's behaviour. She would not go back on her promised financial support to Krishna out of regard for Mrs Besant, but she settled an even larger amount on Raja. A few years later Krishna would suspect this and question Raja closely, but his curiosity was given no satisfaction.

They all spent holidays either with Lady Emily and her daughters, or the de Manziarly family, or both. According to Marcelle and Yolande, Raja was very shy but loved to laugh with them. They teased him a great deal, trying to frighten him with strange noises outside his room at night. At that time Raja and young Mary Lutyens also became good friends. They would sit under a tree reading Shelley. He and Lady Emily developed a lifelong affection as well, although she never showed for him, or even for Nitya, the adoration she had for Krishna.

In February 1921, Nitya, still living in London, had such a severe bout of chicken-pox that his health was permanently weakened. Krishna had also been ill with a sinus infection and bronchitis and was so impressed by the de Manziarlys' naturopath doctor that when in May Nitya had his first haemorrhage, Krishna insisted he come to France to be treated. By September Nitya was not better, in spite of his invalid's existence. So the two brothers and Raja went to Villars in the Swiss Alps.

A beautiful five-thousand-acre estate with a moated castle had been offered to Krishna by the Dutch Baron, Phillip van Pallandt. Leaving Nitya in Raja's care in Villars, Krishna went to Holland to accept Eerde Castle in the name of the Order of the Star. It was on this trip to Holland that Krishna met his first 'serious' love, a seventeen-year-old American girl, Helen Knothe. It was a most inopportune time to make such an attachment, for he and Nitya were destined to soon return to India for the first time since they had left in 1911.

After his quiet summer, Nitya was deemed well enough to undertake this journey. The lives of both brothers were still in the hands of their protectors. Over major decisions neither had any control. Krishna was miserable at leaving his new-found love and felt it a great sacrifice on his part to do so. But if it was inopportune for Krishna, the trip would herald disaster for Nitya, whose recovery had not been as complete as everyone had assumed. While the brothers boarded ship for Bombay, Raja returned peacefully to Cambridge.

5

Back on the Path

In India, everywhere they went, from Bombay to Benares, Theosophists greeted Krishna and Nitya with warmth and excitement. The brothers had left their homeland ten years before as shy, unsophisticated little boys. They returned now in their Savile Row suits with elegant haircuts, but had sufficient taste to assume Indian attire very quickly, which was also considerably more comfortable. Krishna was flung immediately into a display of adoration that may have existed on a smaller scale in Europe but which would always be highly magnified in India. The sheer numbers of people greeting him at train stations, stretching to touch his garments or his feet, thousands of smiling brown faces rising from white kurtas and radiant saris – all this directed at a young man of twenty-six, who had not yet publicly (or privately) proven his proclaimed destiny – was overwhelming.

George Arundale had meanwhile married the beautiful young Indian girl, Rukmini, the childhood friend of Raja who had also been, many years before, Krishna's neighbour. Rukmini, along with everyone else, was full of anticipation at their arrival. She remembered that Krishna came up to George, who tried to introduce her as his bride. But Krishna merely interjected, 'George what is wrong with you and Jinarajadasa?' George replied, trying to sound good natured, 'Oh dear what have I done now?' It was clear to Rukmini that Krishna disapproved of both men's marriages. This first meeting, at which she felt very much put down, would affect Krishna's and her relationship until the end of their lives.[1]

Nitya had persuaded Krishna that they should attempt a reconciliation with the father they had not seen for ten years. Krishna, characteristically, would say later that he remembered nothing of the meeting, which we can imagine was not too happy. Nitya wrote to Marcelle de Manziarly that they had found a gaga father and a mad younger brother.

From India the brothers went with Jinarajadasa to Australia, via Colombo. Travelling on European ships in those days was often an ordeal for Indians, especially those like Krishna and Nitya, who, for

48

the most part, had been protected, but were sometimes unavoidably exposed to hostile European bigotry. Krishna was by nature shy, as many Indians are, shy and non-aggressive. He appeared to meet the challenge of his new role with poise but was sometimes inwardly miserable when required to be on public display. He often spoke of that and similar voyages, his remembered unhappiness thinly masked by the sardonic humour of twenty years' hindsight. It is possible that his inward nature and his public life were already at odds and causing a division in his personality that would be the source of many problems in his later relationships.

With a little imagination one could visualize the slender, graceful young man; the beauty of his face with the slightly aquiline nose, the full mouth that so easily revealed his changing aspects, the large giraffe eyes with straight long lashes that veiled them from the over curious. One could feel him torn between his ineradicable Brahmin pride – his scorn for his fellow passengers' opinions, and his sense of inadequacy in living up to a role he had not chosen for himself – wondering how he could face the multitudes whom he knew would come to meet him on his arrival in Perth, the first stop of this Australian tour.

On shipboard, he witnessed a small humiliation of Jinarajadasa who, when he took a seat on a sofa next to an Englishman, was rudely told to move on. Krishna admitted to an impulse of violence, which he managed to restrain. At times, he felt the public speeches and the devoted crowds went against his nature. There was another side of him, however, which steadied his performance. Like many public figures he learned that energy could flow from the crowds to him as well as the other way.

The Australia of that era, with its strong racial bigotry on the one hand and the pioneering spirit on the other, which drew many adventurous spiritual seekers to Theosophy, was a true testing ground for a young world teacher and this first trip established him in many hearts as that.

After stops in Perth and Melbourne they arrived in Sydney for the Theosophical Convention. Here they were warmly welcomed by Leadbeater, whom they had not seen for ten years and who had apparently mellowed since the Adyar days. Where once he had avoided women, they now found the old man kind to the old ladies and admitting young girls into his circle.

But they were soon to find some very un-Theosophical happenings were going on around the Convention.

Some dissidents had formed a Back to Blavatsky movement: Theosophy without personality cults, the Liberal Catholic Church, initiations, the Order of the Star, *or* the coming. The last would have eliminated Krishna, or rather his role as vehicle for the world teacher. In future Krishna's own position would come to resemble on some counts this divergence. But at this time, his basic loyalty to Leadbeater was still intact. This must have made all the more painful the naked vulgarity of a renewed uproar against his old protector, Leadbeater. All the previous immorality charges were rehashed. All, according to Krishna, were lies. He did not waver in his defence. With Nitya's support, Krishna upheld absolutely Leadbeater's purity, although he would make no such commitment to his clairvoyance. Some years before, Mrs Besant's doubts about Leadbeater had been just the reverse. Much later, when Krishna himself turned against Leadbeater, it was not on grounds of morality.

In Sydney a doctor diagnosed that Nitya, again in a weak condition, had tuberculosis in his right and left lungs. This was a terrible blow. Nitya was sent immediately to the mountains. Krishna accompanied him, but not before he had met and been mildly attracted to an English girl, Ruth Roberts, who was among the young circle around Leadbeater. Ruth was tall, dark and stunning, and Krishna's attraction to her did not go unnoticed, but he was also aware of the rumours and gossip that floated incessantly around him. He was, after all, as confused as any young man who is torn between two attractive girls, Helen, his first real love left behind in Holland, the other beside him in Sydney. On top of this common dilemma was the realization that he was, in fact, expected to renounce any such feelings altogether.

After only ten days in the mountains, where he had begun to feel better, Nitya had to return to Sydney with Krishna to greet Mrs Besant when she arrived.

The harassment of Leadbeater and those close to him continued, both in the press and on the streets. The brothers were referred to as 'dandy-coloured coons', their well-cut suits scoffed at. People nudged each other, pointed out Krishna as the messiah, 'that fellow with thirty lives', and laughed loudly. Krishna said he would have laughed too if he had not been involved, indicating that inwardly he was already beginning to question his position. Leadbeater must have discerned Krishna's misery. A few days later he comforted him with a message from the Master Kuthumi, which stated that the Masters had the highest hopes for Krishna, but that he must work hard to find his true self, to be tolerant, and to help others.

Krishna took to heart this advice. He talked with Mrs Besant and told her that he wanted to drop all Star and Theosophical work for a while and to study seriously philosophy, economics, religion and education, that he wanted to improve his mind and also to develop in himself love, tolerance and compassion.

Nitya's health failed to improve, and it was deemed imperative by those close to him that, as soon as possible, he return to Switzerland.

As the voyage via India and the Red Sea would be too hot, Mr Warrington, the President of the Theosophical Society in America, who was then in Sydney, suggested they go via California and break the trip in the Ojai Valley, where he had a friend who could accommodate them for the summer. This unscheduled detour would have a significant effect on both their lives.

6

California

The two weeks' voyage across the Pacific, while rough enough to have caused Nitya seasickness, appeared to improve the condition of his lungs. Krishna, never subject to travel sickness, had found the voyage dull. Perhaps unpleasant would be a better word. In spite of Mr Warrington's presence, he was plagued by the unwanted attention of curious women on the one hand and offensive men on the other. One Australian asked belligerently why these 'dark men' were allowed to travel first class.

All this unpleasantness dropped behind him as the steamship entered the Bay and there, rising above the summer fog that lapped at the city's foundations, Krishna saw the hills of San Francisco.

They were met by a Theosophist who was also a Professor at Berkeley. She had invited them to stay with her. The next day, which happened to be the Fourth of July, they ferried across the bay to Oakland, where they caught the train to the University of California at Berkeley. The campanile tower reached toward a clear sky and the pale grey granite buildings gleamed in the sunlight. July was mid-winter in Sydney. This perfect California summer day, with mild cooling breezes from the Pacific, wrought immediate changes in Nitya's health and in both their spirits. Krishna's first mingling with Americans was on a campus that would still be a stronghold of racial tolerance and democratic idealism more than half a century later. Berkeley on Independence Day might well have had a heightened atmosphere that Krishna could not fully grasp. He was, however, instantly smitten with what he saw, and would not forget this first impression of America: the open forthright manners of the students, who, boys and girls alike, looked him straight in the eye; the atmosphere of freedom and equality. He liked the attitude between men and women. He could drop the self-consciousness about his own background which stemmed from childhood memories of English superiority. Mixed with his enthusiasm for this American institution was a yearning for India to have such a beautiful university on its soil. At that time he felt that Indians were more suited than any people on earth to a true scholastic atmosphere. (When he came to

52

know more Indians in academic settings, he would display frequent impatience with the rigidity of their conditioning.) He would always reveal a certain confusion in much of his attitude toward education.

The following evening they boarded the night train for Ventura, three hundred and fifty miles south. It was unfortunate that most of this first trip through California would be travelled in darkness. But they could at least see the dawn silhouette the coastal mountain range and the first light of that summer morning shimmering on the Pacific Ocean. They arrived by mid-morning at the small farm centre of Ventura. There they were met by a tall dark-haired woman with an aristocratic bearing and accent, a strong face and impeccable clothes; altogether an improbable and unanticipated figure standing in that small rural station. This was Mary Tudor Gray, who, as a descendent of an old New England family, felt herself as much a 'brahmin' as her two young Indian guests. She would be their hostess for many months.

Ojai lay fifteen miles inland and the dry daytime heat, dispelled at night by the sea air, was just descending upon the valley. Mr Warrington burst into song, 'Ojai – Ojai,' as they rounded the final turn and saw the spread of dark green orange groves surrounded by the protective sage-covered hills.

At the eastern end of the valley beneath a sheer oblong bluff called Topa Topa lay Mary Gray's estate, nestled against low foothills scored by miles of horse and footpaths, maintained by neighbouring Thacher School.

The valley might have been set in any number of places in India with its softly contoured hills and dry underbrush. But closer familiarity would soon distinguish its virginal quality. Few people had ever lived there. Some parts of the Ojai had been sacred to the Chumash Indians. In 1922 there were only a few hundred people scattered over fifty square miles, mostly orange ranchers.

Although her house was large, Mary Gray had turned over one of her small rustic guest cottages to the brothers. While she did not want to risk exposing her young children to Nitya's tuberculosis, she did share with them her excellent vegetarian cook. They took delight in the fresh fruits and vegetables that were in plentiful supply. There were horses available for riding and walks up the stream that would generally run dry by midsummer. But this year there was still a clear trickle to fill the rocky pools. Here they took hip baths in that untrammelled paradise.

In spite of all this healthful living, Nitya suddenly took a turn for the worse, running a temperature night and day. Krishna felt the strain of caring for him and complained that his brother was temperamental, irritable and would not do anything he told him.

Mr Warrington had arranged for his daughter to help out with the two young men. But this task soon proved too much of a burden for her.

It was Erma who came up with a solution.

For the past three winters, Rosalind had been working and living with her mother in Hollywood. During the summers Mary Gray, who had become very fond of Erma's family, offered them her summer house in Montecito and encouraged Rosalind to take summer courses in the state college in Santa Barbara. Mary Gray felt she should further her education, and had even offered to send her to Radcliffe, if she would complete the necessary requirements. In addition to her courses, Rosalind entered the summer tennis tournaments. Tennis had always been her greatest passion. Her summers in Buffalo had been spent on the courts, perfecting a form which was not conventional, but which was effective enough to have won the attention of the Lawn Tennis Association in the Santa Barbara tournaments. They wanted to take her on and train her. Once by another player's default she came up against Helen Wills, then in her prime, who sportingly allowed her one game a set. Neither Erma nor Mary Gray approved of a tennis future for Rosalind. They felt she had too much potential to waste her life on sport.

But Rosalind was thoroughly enjoying her usual summer studies and tennis in Montecito. She did not share Erma's Theosophical interests. She was nineteen, high-spirited and had a fun-loving nature. She was devoted to her mother, Sophia, who was wise enough to give her youngest daughter free rein. Sophia trusted Rosalind's intrinsically generous and truthful character to pull her through whatever difficulties her impulsive spirit might lead her into.

Erma arrived one day with the suggestion that Rosalind replace Mr Warrington's daughter in the care of two young Indians who had recently arrived in Ojai. It was typical of Rosalind, playful though she was, to give up her own interests and a delightful summer to care for two young men she had never met – one of them quite ill.

Rosalind never forgot that first meeting. Nitya took her hand between his, looked into her eyes and said, 'Why, I know you,' and even then she knew exactly what he meant. She did not notice his blindness in one eye, the frailty of his body or the feverish flush from which he most often suffered. She heard the beautiful timbre of his voice and the exuberance of his laugh. She was touched by the warmth of his smile and was instantly drawn to him. She scarcely noticed Krishna, who was almost always the centre of everyone's attention. It would not have occurred to her, or to anyone else, to wonder what his feelings toward her might have been. To the ailing Nitya, this vital and warm American girl, fresh from a summer on the tennis courts, her fair skin slightly tanned and her blue eyes radiant, held a special fascination. Westerners often seem uncouth to Indians, especially to Brahmins who have a rare fastidiousness in their personal cleanliness. (It was ironic that Leadbeater, an Englishman, should have found it necessary to make such a point of training the brothers to bathe properly, but that was probably due to their neglected condition.) Nitya would complain later to Rosalind of the unfastidiousness of the English girls he had known, and how he had been put off a close relationship with one of them for this reason.

Sophia had imparted her meticulous sense of cleanliness to her four daughters. Rosalind's upbringing as a vegetarian, due to a quixotic whim of her father and her passionate love for animals, were further attributes in this new relationship. Above all, she had an innate talent for mothering. A sick or hurt creature, no matter what its species, drew her immediate care and instinct for healing. She poured into Nitya not only love but vitality.

Krishna was relieved by his brother's response to Rosalind's care. Nitya did exactly what she told him to do. Krishna was also immensely impressed with what he thought were her natural American capabilities.

The very first dinner she cooked for them, however, was a disaster. Rosalind had prepared a cheese soufflé, imploring the two young men to appear on time for dinner. The brothers quite forgot about this and took off for an afternoon walk, arriving late. They were confronted by a fallen soufflé and a crestfallen cook.

It is surprising that Rosalind's family did not share Mary Gray's quite reasonable concern for this close association with a tubercular patient. Erma may well have let caution be swept aside by the extraordinary opportunity for her young sister to care for someone so close to the vehicle, but Sophia did not believe in all this. One can only wonder. My grandmother was never a person who insisted on having her own way, and perhaps she had her own kind of faith in the good sense and good health of her youngest daughter.

In any event, Rosalind never suffered any ill effects from the love between her and Nitya. Perhaps because she only knew him for three years before his death, this love, with its innocent and magical quality, haunted not only her and her marriage, but also my childhood. Such love, eternized by death, may not survive the realities of a living relationship.

7

The 'Process'

While Nitya had at last found the love for which he so long yearned, Krishna was left very much on his own. In Ojai he was without his old friends, the de Manziarlys, Helen or Lady Emily. While he rejoiced in the improvement that Rosalind's care brought to Nitya, he too longed for comfort and affection.

Theosophists of that period believed in sublimating sex, even within marriage. It was certainly assumed that Krishna would be chaste. At the age of twenty-seven he had never had a fulfilled love relationship. His love for Helen was on a 'higher' or at least an entirely 'pure' plane. According to Helen's own testimony it was never anything else. During a visit to Ojai in 1984, Helen Knothe (the recently widowed Mrs Scott Nearing) stated that she and Krishna had sometimes lain together in bed but had never had sex. She doubted that he had ever had sex with anyone.[1] What symptoms might emerge from suppressed sexuality in a highly sensitive, imaginative, and warm-natured young man, is a matter for clinical conjecture, but in the light of what soon transpired conjecture cannot be totally ignored. Leadbeater had evidently offered advice along these lines to other boys, which, as we have seen, brought him serious trouble. Krishna, however, always maintained that Leadbeater had never touched on such matters with him or Nitya. It must have been assumed by all his elders that he was on quite another plane from most young men.

While Krishna would often state that neither the pleasant nor the unpleasant experiences of life touched him, it is difficult to believe that the recent events in Sydney had not shaken him. The crudity of language and behaviour to which he had been subjected, the charges hurled against his old protector, Leadbeater, must have distressed him to some degree. He was also faced with the graphic illustration of how even an exalted member of the Theosophical Society could suffer from a tarnished reputation. He and Nitya had both come to Leadbeater's defence, but the whole affair had shaken Krishna's view about much of his Theosophical world.

The 'Process'

Krishna also had health problems, real or imagined. A Theosophist and Swedish chiropractor, Dr John Ingelman, had introduced Nitya to Dr Strong in Los Angeles, a medical disciple of the famous Dr Abrams, to try the Abrams diagnosis and treatment. Dr Albert Abrams had the highest medical qualifications and was not generally considered, in his time, a quack. He claimed he could cure tuberculosis, cancer and syphilis by means of an Oscilloclast machine which sent electrical pulses through the affected areas. He believed that smallpox vaccination was the cause of most diseases including syphilis, which he thought to be far more widespread than people realized. With a few drops of the patient's blood he diagnosed these diseases and prescribed the treatment on his machine. Many celebrities, including the writer Upton Sinclair, swore by his cures. Dr Abrams diagnosed Nitya as having tuberculosis in his left lung and both kidneys and syphilis in his spleen. After two weeks of the treatment the new blood tests showed all these germs had disappeared from his body. Krishna, totally convinced by this, then sent in samples of his blood. He was told he had cancer in his intestines and left lung and syphilis in his spleen and nose. After treatment on the Oscilloclast machine, he felt much better. He was wise enough, however, not to mention the diagnosis of syphilis to anyone but Lady Emily.

In spite of the optimistic reports on Nitya, it would be found in later tests that he still had spots of tuberculosis on his lungs; stress of any kind would set him back considerably. He was still an invalid and Rosalind cared for him tenderly every day. The brothers had moved to the little cottage where Sophia had once stayed. They enjoyed the increased sense of privacy here and thought the cottage had the atmosphere of a small ashram. In fact they preferred not to have any strangers around. So Rosalind helped regularly with the cooking, coming over by day from Mary Gray's house next door where she was staying. Dr Ingelman had, for those times, an advanced knowledge of nutrition, especially as applied to a vegetarian diet, and his guidance was invaluable to Rosalind. Krishna did his best to help. He disliked the appearance of being waited on and would always be the first on his feet to offer assistance.

The vicissitudes in Nitya's health did not prevent Rosalind and the two brothers from having some very good times. She did not see Krishna as a special person, certainly not as a world teacher. But alongside her love for Nitya, she developed a great fondness for his older brother. They read aloud and memorized Milton, Keats, Shelley and Krishna's favourite, the Song of Songs. They walked together in the foothills and on very hot days went with the Gray family to the beach.

Ever since he had received the Master Kuthumi's message in Sydney, Krishna had shown signs of a changed attitude about the Masters, Theosophy and his role in 'the Work'. Now he took an even more serious turn, perhaps due in part to the absence of luxuries and distractions afforded him by upper-class European and English life. He was also, for the first time, cut off from the vigilance of his protectors. He was freer than he had ever been and in an atmosphere conducive to spiritual concentration. He appears to have made the most of this and took up meditating regularly, predictably setting aside his intentions for intellectual improvement.

Rosalind had relieved Krishna from the pressure of caring for Nitya, freeing him from that responsibility which he had felt as a burden. Nitya was far too sensitive to Krishna's needs to ever knowingly pre-empt his older brother's place in any relationship. His love for Rosalind could only have flowered under the belief that Krishna did not share a similar feeling for her. Nevertheless, considerate though they may be, two people in love tend to isolate a third person from their charmed circle. Krishna would always claim he was incapable of loneliness, yet there would be times in his life when enforced isolation produced some strange reactions.

Stemming ostensibly from his meditation sessions, Krishna suddenly developed disturbing physical symptoms that progressed from discomfort to pain. Along with this came a series of peculiar experiences.

Both Krishna and Nitya wrote accounts of these experiences (which Nitya called the 'process'). They lasted this first time for a period of about three days. These accounts were typed by Erma and sent, at Krishna's request, to Leadbeater and Miss Dodge. Additional copies were made later by Rajagopal to be given to Mrs Besant and Lady Emily. Everyone involved was sworn to a lifetime of secrecy by Krishna. (Lady Emily would be embroiled in a tempest when, thirty years later, she wanted to publish these accounts in her biography, *Candles in the Sun*. Twenty years after that Krishna dropped his objections and allowed Lady Emily's daughter Mary Lutyens to do so.)

Rosalind was well aware that Krishna was experiencing some strange symptoms. He complained of an acute pain in his neck and she detected a slight swelling there, but saw nothing alarming. After a few days he described what sounds like a classic psychic or *samadhi* experience. He felt at one with a distant workman, with the very tool in his hand and the stone he was breaking, the grass, the dust, the birds and the trees. He then passed into a semi-conscious state.

This condition gave way the next day to worse physical pain and a mental distress that made him feel everything around him was filthy. The small front room of the cottage was dark and stuffy on hot summer days, the front veranda and the screened porch on the side, where Krishna slept, kept out the sunlight. In a dark corner he cowered in misery and allowed only Rosalind to hold his head in her lap and comfort him.

Nitya, who witnessed both the ecstasy and the suffering of his brother, wrote his own account which he later sent to Leadbeater, describing the daily events over four days. He deferred to Leadbeater for interpretation but his description is full and sincere though somewhat intensified by his feverish condition and poetic imagination.

On the first day Krishna began to feel restless and a painful lump developed in the back of his neck. The next morning all was well until after breakfast when Rosalind found him tossing about on his bed in evident pain. She could not determine the cause of his suffering. Nitya thought it was like an attack of malaria which he knew Krishna had first contracted as a young child. But Krishna was complaining of intense heat rather than chills.

Nitya was continually touched and filled with admiration as he witnessed Rosalind's skill and tenderness while nursing Krishna. The nineteen-year-old girl had no experience of nursing and no interest in Theosophy, yet her care, bestowed with what Nitya perceived to be a remarkable combination of unselfish and yet impersonal love, was to make both young men wonder if she were the incarnation of their long-dead mother.

On the third day, when Rosalind had been almost continuously at Krishna's side, Nitya felt the whole house filled by a great force and Krishna as if possessed complained of filth in the house and in his bed, though everything was spotlessly clean. He allowed no one near him, crying aloud that he wanted to go into the woods in India, and he huddled in a dark corner. Nitya, Rosalind and Mr Warrington waited on the veranda, watching the sky darken after sunset. They could still see the shape of a young pepper tree a few yards away, which all day harboured bees and small birds, drawn by its fragrance. Mr Warrington then persuaded Krishna to leave the cottage – still stuffy with the afternoon's heat – and enjoy the evening coolness under the tree.

Krishna had eaten nearly nothing for three days, yet now seated under the tree he began to chant mantrams. Nitya was reminded of a moment long ago in Taormina when Krishna had gazed upon a painting of Gautama Buddha in beggar's robes and they had both felt they had received a divine thought. Afterwards Nitya told Rosalind that he had again felt this presence and had seen a great star above the tree. He was convinced he saw this glorious moment reflected on her face – and he told her that she had exclaimed repeatedly, 'Do you see him?' Nitya had assumed without question that she was referring to the Divine Bodhisattva. Although neither he nor Mr Warrington were able to share her vision, they heard the music of the divine Gandharvas.

All this lasted nearly thirty minutes and then, as Krishna rose and approached them, Rosalind fainted. When she recovered, much to Nitya's distress, she remembered nothing except hearing music.

Rosalind, who, according to Nitya, was the only *actual* witness of the occult phenomena, does not accept what he assumed she had seen. Night after night Nitya, Rosalind and Mr Warrington gathered on the veranda of the cottage for meditation. Rosalind usually fell asleep and on this occasion awoke to be told she had witnessed the coming of the presence. To this day she often awakens hearing music, as she has done all her life. She had from birth gone to sleep to the sound of chamber music performed by her mother and aunts. Not sharing the preconceptions of the others, she allowed them their interpretations without accepting them as her own. She believes that whatever Nitya read on her face stemmed from her own dreams. She remembered nothing and did not feel anything remarkable had happened.

She was in an exhausted state. All her days were spent taking care of Nitya and then, as his symptoms began to occur, of Krishna. Rosalind never found these symptoms as strange or alarming as did either Nitya or Krishna. Krishna, moaning about a swelling in his neck, back pains and an upset stomach, would put his head in her lap for comfort. He sometimes also fondled her breast. She attributed this behaviour to his strong need to be mothered. But it hardly helped confirm, for her, the spiritual implications of this event, so exciting to the others.

For the past ten years there had been considerable activity throughout much of the Theosophical world in anticipation of the coming of the world teacher, as forecast by Leadbeater. Money had been raised, publications started, land donated, and thousands of individuals were working hard to advance their own spiritual preparedness. Krishna's 'process', as Nitya first called it, took place against a backdrop of intense anticipation and excitement.

Given the mental condition of everyone except Rosalind at that moment, it is no wonder that they concluded the supposed phenomenon was happening. Nitya, due to his feverish condition, on top of being in love, may have greatly exaggerated the look on Rosalind's face. Nor was he of a sceptical nature. He did not live long enough for us to know whether he would have followed his brother in an eventual rejection of Theosophy. As we shall see from what transpired between them before his death, it seems unlikely.

If one is not given to a belief in the occult, Krishna's physical symptoms might be explained by a variety of ailments, such as recurring attacks of malaria, which he had first suffered at the age of two and which were known to have afflicted him in later life.

When I was a young girl, I told Krinsh one day about an epileptic boy in my school. I described the terrifying seizures and how we were all trained to help the boy by putting a handkerchief in his mouth so he wouldn't bite off his tongue. And then I added that Warren had admitted to me that several times he had faked these attacks to avoid a difficult situation, and had fooled even the teachers. Krinsh replied that he knew all about that affliction, for his own mother had suffered from it. I was duly impressed and repeated that comment to my father, who said very seriously that I must never repeat it again or discuss it with anyone. Krinsh never again referred to it. I have found no reference to this possibility in any of the literature about him, but his words remain a clear and definite memory. Epilepsy is a complex disorder and manifests itself in a wide range of symptoms, such as seeing visions and other symptoms at that time not readily diagnosed.

The most plausible explanation could lie in a complex of factors that include the dissociation of personality, the often accompanying hallucinatory symptoms, and the subsequent emergence of one or more partial but distinct personalities.[2] No one thought to call in a doctor of any kind when Krishna's first symptoms emerged. Even before the popularity of psychosomatic medicine, a competent physician might have suggested that Krishna's symptoms were quite simply the result of a conscious or unconscious intense need to receive the mothering and love that Rosalind had been bestowing on Nitya. In the future these symptoms would be witnessed usually by a woman for whom Krishna felt a special involvement or love. What is important is where these manifestations led and why and how the acceptance of the occult interpretation shaped his future.

It is not easy to define a mystical experience, although to the authentic experiencer the veracity of it seems unquestionable. The state of feeling a departure from the body or a drifting away and looking down upon it is not uncommon. It happens to people who have suffered prolonged bouts of dysentery, sunstroke or other physical ailments. Classically, in Buddhism as with some of the Christian mystics, a *samadhi* or mystical experience seems to be, simply put, a dropping away of the ego and a sense of oneness with the universe, or as Blake expressed it with such precise beauty:

> To see a world in a grain of sand
> And a heaven in a wild flower
> Hold infinity in the palm of your hand
> And eternity in an hour.

This usually temporary state of egolessness should have an effect on the personality which is lasting even though the ego condition returns. The very essence is the dropping away of the ego; there can be no advantage made of it or use for future benefit or sense of authority and knowledge on the part of the experiencer. In other words there can be no profit motive. The mystic Meister Eckhart said: 'Some people want to see God with their eyes as they see a cow and to love him as they love their cow – they love the cow for the milk and cheese and profit it makes them.'

Surely if the illumination derived from *samadhi* is used to promote ego-born wishes, or beliefs, or to elevate the position of the individual in any way, grave suspicion may be cast on the integrity of the whole experience.

Krishna's experience on the first day, his feeling at one with his surroundings, rings true in that it puts no undue demands on credibility. It is not occult. It requires no interpretation, nor does it seem to place the subject in a position of hierarchical advancement. It could, in other words, happen to any of us and we might hope that if it did, as the result of this instant of egolessness, we would henceforth see the world in a new dimension. It can bestow no authority to *lead*, only to *share* and by sharing to offer others the hope of the sense of reality imparted. Some day Krishna himself would proclaim that truth is a pathless land. But he had not arrived at that point yet. While he demanded a shroud of secrecy from the public at large, he allowed copies of the account to be sent to his protectors and he did not protest when his experience under the pepper tree was taken by them as a sign of his rapid advancement along 'the Path'.

8

Trouble on the Path

The 'process' continued through the summer and autumn at Ojai but without the ecstatic aspects. Krishna appeared to suffer only the physical discomforts. In certain circumstances these would continue to manifest themselves throughout the years to come. The 'process' *only* occurred in Rosalind's presence – at least up until then. Krishna professed to believe that Rosalind was his long-lost mother. He and Nitya even wrote to ask Leadbeater if it were possible that she could be the reincarnation of their mother. The inconvenient fact that Rosalind was nineteen and their mother had died only seventeen years before was not lost either on them or Leadbeater, but they hoped that the Masters could account for such untimely paradoxes. The whole experience of Krishna's, 'process' had urged both the brothers into a renewed enthusiasm for the work and service to the Masters, which included Krishna's declaration to Leadbeater of his love and respect and some apology for his past obstreperous behaviour.

This would be in accordance with Mrs Besant's description of the way of 'the Path', although, according to that code, Krishna's behaviour had been far too recalcitrant for one who had passed the second initiation. Nevertheless Leadbeater appeared not to have doubted that Krishna's experience under the pepper tree signified that he had passed the third initiation. The physical symptoms, however, puzzled him. He believed that both he and Mrs Besant had travelled the same stages on 'the Path' but without pain. Leadbeater pondered this question for a month while Krishna awaited his response without total patience. He would never receive a fully satisfying answer. Leadbeater appeared to find it difficult to fit Krishna's symptoms into his scheme. In Leadbeater's eyes Krishna was still a pupil and had a long path ahead, filled with pitfalls, to travel. His ultimate destiny was not, by any means, assured. On the other hand, many of the Theosophists surrounding Krishna were willing to see him as an already perfect being. This made them and their lives much more immediately meaningful and important. Leadbeater's insistence on an arduous step-by-step path to divinity might have made

Krishna impatient, to say the least. Yet in Krishna's public talks with young Theosophists, with whom he was very busy during this year in America, he attributed to Leadbeater's training of him his present state of spiritual development. He was, at the same time, fully conscious of the permeating religious culture into which he had been born and of the role his mother had played, during those early pre-discovery years, in training his young mind to focus on religious figures, Lord Krishna, Maitreya Buddha, whose pictures were in the family shrine room. He had been told to meditate three times a day, even briefly, on great things.

But it was Leadbeater who gave him the cohesive and rigorous training both in habits of thought and of physical care – personal cleanliness being of foremost importance. He repeated to the American youths Leadbeater's view that there was no virtue in being a filthy holy man or saint, either Christian or Hindu, though he added rather melo-dramatically that Leadbeater's nagging about cleanliness had made him temporarily miserable. In 1923 he was still willing to grant Leadbeater a vital role in his training on these levels and he advocated for others the programme Leadbeater had laid out for him: to read a great many novels in order to gain varied points of view and ideas; to learn about ways of life different from one's own, even to read trash; above all, read religious books.

The fickleness of Krishna's affections for Leadbeater would continue for some years, resolving, on certain occasions, into a display of abhorrence at the very mention of Leadbeater's name. This attitude on Krishna's part would one day be the cause of a serious quarrel between him and Nitya, for Nitya remained true to his protectors and to Theosophy.

When the autumn rains came to Ojai in early November, after the usual six months' dry period, Krishna was enchanted by the miracle of green sprouting through the parched dry brown of the terrain. He saw it was a green unlike that of the spring in a cold climate which comes with a gentle mellowing of the weather. In California the grass appears almost overnight, laid like a carpet over the contours of the hills. Tender shoots of poison oak emerge on the dry stalks. The dark green leaves of the live oaks, washed clean from the summer dust, shine. The streams run with crystal water over the white granite rocks. Krishna would carry this image of California with him ever after.

The brothers' love for the Ojai Valley increased, as did their longing to have their own home. With donations raised by Mrs Besant, mostly from Miss Dodge, the six-acre property adjacent to Mary Gray's estate was purchased for them. This land included the cottage where they had been staying and the large, L-shaped main house with patio and front veranda. This they named Arya Vihara (house of the Aryan or nobleman) even though it was merely a ramshackle California redwood ranch house, poorly furnished and in need of paint. Later Miss Dodge bought for them another seven acres so that the privacy of their property was safeguarded. Krishna was already astute enough to refuse to own property personally, perhaps realizing that a young man with his spiritual future must appear to be materially unencumbered. A trust called the Brothers Association had been formed to hold the estate. Of course this was in any case a necessity, for under the California land laws of that time Orientals, as Indians were incorrectly categorized, could not own land. Whatever the technicalities involved, Arya Vihara was to be Krishna's beloved home for many years. Yet there would always be an ambivalence in him which made him long for India when he was in California and for California when he was in India.

By June 1923, Nitya's health was vastly improved and the brothers finally returned to Europe. Rosalind did not go with them. For her and for Nitya the parting was sad and difficult. The love between them had become very strong. But they had both realized that in Krishna's circle 'the Work' was all important and the pursuit of personal happiness must take second place.

Meanwhile Raja had been spared the endless distractions and excitement generated around Mrs Besant and the brothers. While they were in India and California, he had been able to concentrate totally on his studies and had just passed the first set of examinations for the Tripos. Life at Cambridge suited him to the centre of his being. He was a natural scholar, his life was comfortable, and he quickly won the respect of his tutor.

In deference to Nitya's health, it was arranged that August would be spent in Ehrwald in the Austrian Tyrol, where a chalet had been lent to Krishna. Raja was invited to join the large party, which included Lady Emily with her daughters, Betty and Mary, Helen Knothe, Ruth Roberts and Marcelle de Manziarly.

During this seven-week holiday Raja was for the first time on hand, (though not actually present) during Krishna's 'process'. When the 'process' started again in Ehrwald there was no pepper tree; no music, or great star, or shining beings and, of course, no Rosalind. In any case Krishna would not have wanted her; for now very definitely he wanted Helen.

To those on the sidelines with their imaginations and expectations ripe for a miraculous happening, the atmosphere seemed charged with powerful presences. Most of them felt encompassed by extraordinary vibrations. But the whole business of Krishna's 'process', in spite of the assumed implications, must have been worrying if not terrifying to Nitya. While similar experiences had been claimed by Blavatsky and other Theosophists, as well as occultists at large, according to Leadbeater they had not recorded having Krishna's physical misery. Yet Nitya and Krishna were not receiving any clear diagnoses either medical (for they would not consult regular doctors) or occult (from their usual source, Leadbeater). In accordance with Krishna's wishes, it was still a matter of extreme privacy and very few people were supposed to know of it. Although not untypically in such situations, the very cloak of secrecy warmed and spread the secret.

In September the party removed to Eerde Castle in Holland. A trust was being set up to hold the castle for, as with Arya Vihara, Krishna maintained that he did not want personally to own property.

When I last saw Eerde Castle it had survived the Second World War and was a private boarding school. The moat was dry and the romantic atmosphere of a magnificent early eighteenth-century castle was diminished. As a child, I remembered the large fish swimming in the moat, fed by a natural stream, and the row of great trees lining the long entrance drive. The property encompassed five thousand acres of pine forest with small ponds and farms. It was an unbelievable gift to anyone – even a world teacher.

The impetuous love that Krishna had proclaimed for Helen the previous year had mellowed considerably, in spite of her help with his 'process', although he still continued for a few years to write love letters to her.

Nitya had now become close friends with Raja. That summer he had asked Raja to take a year's leave of absence from Cambridge and return with them both to Ojai for the following winter, as he felt his presence might be a help if the 'process' were to continue at Ojai. This Raja agreed to do. He had heard at length about Rosalind from Nitya, whose love for her touched Raja. (Much later he would tell Rosalind that he thought he had fallen in love with her listening to Nitya talk about her on the train across America.)

Serious as the framework of their lives might have been, they were still young and certainly capable of enjoying the possibilities of romance and falling in love. There was never any question of a triangle. They were all very close and Raja would keep to himself whatever serious feelings he had for Rosalind. He would never have interposed himself between her and Nitya. Fortunately neither Nitya nor Raja had jealous or possessive natures.

Now Rosalind had three young Indians to care for. She found in Raja, as had Nitya, a steadfast friend. He taught her to play chess and the love for this game would be a long bond between them. While Raja would never be much of an athlete, he became quite good at badminton, a game at which Krishna excelled.

Rosalind stayed with Erma in what was now called Pine Cottage, which her mother had once occupied, while the young men moved into Arya Vihara. This they all set about to paint in the Victorian décor of cream yellow with dark green trim. Supposedly they were all sharing in the cooking and housework too, but it does not take much imagination to picture who really did the work, putting up with token help from three young men who had never attempted such chores.

Work was relieved by walks together in the hills and trips with the ever generous and loving Ingelmans to the Grand Canyon and to Yosemite. It should have been a very happy existence for all four young people in that idyllic valley. Rosalind was preparing for Radcliffe which she intended to enter in the autumn and was being tutored in French by Mary Gray, in algebra by Raja and in poetry by Nitya. These latter sessions were her greatest delight and Nitya's exceptionally beautiful voice as he read poetry would linger in her memory for the rest of her life.

One day, feeling his health strengthening, Nitya expressed his hopes to Krishna that he might marry Rosalind. But as with all his previous personal yearnings, these hopes were abruptly dashed. He came to Rosalind with a sadness she had never seen in him before and said that Krishna had been outraged by the idea and had insisted that his younger brother must dedicate himself solely to 'the Work'. Much as she loved Nitya, marriage was still far from Rosalind's mind. Neither would it ever be a tendency in her to worry about the future.

There was another aspect not so idyllic to that summer, which caused pain not only for himself but for those around him. Krishna again started his 'process', which continued unabated for weeks and weeks. This time he refused to have Rosalind near him and occasionally called instead for the absent Helen, but mostly he wanted no one.

Having read the accounts of the 'process' the year before and of the role Rosalind had played, Raja was struck by the bewilderment he saw in Rosalind at Krishna's sudden rejection of her. Privately his heart went out to her. Who would have guessed that the hurt in Krishna's heart was behind this rejection? His feelings for Rosalind would remain undeclared as long as Nitya lived (as would Raja's), but he might well have foreseen in Raja yet another rival for her love and this in a man he had already seen as a rival on another front. Yet Raja was gentle and affectionate with a fun-loving side to his shy and often serious nature. It was hard to dislike him. Krishna even admired many of his qualities.

Krishna and Nitya were aware that Raja was also a protegé of Miss Dodge. Krishna was curious as to whether Raja was receiving an income comparable to theirs and often questioned Raja about this. Raja, who had been informed of their allotment, refused to discuss his finances with Krishna. He realized that the fact he was receiving a substantially larger income – perhaps because of his expenses at Cambridge, but perhaps also because of Miss Dodge's special confidence in him – would only cause some resentment in Krishna. That he was right in this assumption was soon indicated.

One day he asked Rosalind to go to Hollywood with him to help him buy his own car. He had saved money for this but did not know how to drive. He and Rosalind returned to Arya Vihara in the late afternoon, driving up in a modest enough Buick. Raja, feeling delighted with his new possession and expecting his excitement to be shared by his friends, was taken aback to be greeted by Krishna's scorn and disapproval. Krishna had by then received a series of much more elegant automobiles. In fact that year, through the generosity of John Ingelman, he was the proud possessor of a pale blue Lincoln.

'That car cannot remain here,' Krishna decreed. 'It is not appropriate for us to have two cars on this place. You must take it right back.'

Raja, though somewhat shaken, ignored this command, the first but far from the last such encounter he would have with Krishna. This early though minor mutual clash of character between them could have been taken as a significant forecast for the future.

Krishna would always assume a superior attitude toward Raja when it came to cars and driving. He considered himself a first-rate driver and Raja a very erratic one, although it was he and not Raja who chalked up speeding tickets and had several near fatal accidents. Automobiles would always play a special part in Krishna's life. He had learned well from Miss Dodge's chauffeur how to wash and polish a car. Although he made an effort to appear mechanical and showed a great interest in the engine he never developed true skill as a mechanic.

Trouble on the Path

In spring 1924, before the three young men were to return to England, Krishna prevailed upon Rosalind to give up Radcliffe and go instead to Australia, to stay in the Manor House and be 'brought on' by Leadbeater, who believed that her care of Nitya had entitled her to be placed on probation. Erma, much as she would have cherished a higher education for her younger sister, undoubtedly was too good a Theosophist to challenge Krishna's advice. There was certainly no one else prepared to do so. Rosalind, while not believing in the Masters, did not strongly disbelieve either and was willing to defer to Krishna's judgment. It was arranged that she would go down by boat with a well-to-do Dutch Theosophist, Koos Van der Leeuw, as her guardian. Again Sophia proved herself to be an exceptionally unpossessive and tolerant mother. Rosalind was very dear to her and had been a great support since leaving Buffalo. Although Sophia never came to espouse any of the Theosophists' notions, she didn't interfere with her daughter's future among them.

That summer of 1924, the first Star Camp was held in Ommen on the new land given by Baron van Pallandt. The conditions for most of the few hundred people who attended – those not privileged to stay in the castle – were extremely primitive. Krishna's topic included the qualities needed for the path of discipleship – a concept he would soon reject completely. Raja had accompanied the brothers there before returning in the autumn to Cambridge to finish his degrees in law and history. He could not have guessed that summer how deeply he would soon be involved in these camps.

Nearly the same group as the previous year went on to a holiday at Pergine, in the Italian Dolomites, where a square-towered castle had been converted to a small hotel overlooking a pristine lake. Krishna and his companions would always be blessed with the most scenic holiday spots the world had to offer. But at this time, the ostensible purpose of these close gatherings of friends was to learn from Krishna the way of 'the Path', to have serious meditations, and to hope that his evolved condition would somehow pull them along. This high purpose did not preclude those frequent moments of fun and games and sometimes off-colour jokes, instigated by Krishna himself and often bolstered by the mischievous streak in Raja. Unexpected outbreaks of mild ribaldry bewildered and shocked some among Krishna's circle of devotees and charmed others, who felt he could never be tainted by vulgarity, even his own, and that the very perfection of his being could elevate such behaviour to a higher plane.

Once again the 'process' continued with Krishna, on his own as at Ojai, except for Nitya's presence. The agony he appeared to suffer was again heartrending for the younger brother, now even more frail. In California, Dr Strong had warned that Nitya should never return to India or he might die. But as usual Nitya's well-being did not receive first priority. Krishna disregarded medical opinion in preference to that of the Masters – or his own judgment. Nitya's place beside Krishna in the work had been so strongly emphasized by the Masters that it was difficult for those who believed in them to think they would permit anything to happen to Nitya. Krishna advised, just as he had advised Rosalind, that Lady Emily should take her two youngest daughters, Mary and Betty, to Leadbeater in Sydney to be 'brought on'. He also advocated the same course for Helen Knothe and Ruth Roberts, the young woman he had found so attractive in Sydney in 1922.

Mary Lutyens, at the age of sixteen, had developed a strong attachment for Nitya, whom she had known since she was three. It seems unlikely that he could have felt more than a brotherly affection for her for he had told both Krishna and Raja and others close to him such as Mme de Manziarly and Mary's own mother, Lady Emily, that Rosalind was the love of his life. But he had not yet told Mary. He did tell her that he had haemorrhaged again just before they landed in Bombay. He had also warned her that things would be very different once they reached India, the constant crowds of people around Krishna, the meetings each morning in his room, including all the 'gopis', the group of young women who had followed him from Europe. (Gopis, in Hindu mythology, were the cow girls that flocked around Lord Krishna and with one of whom, Radha, he fell in love.)

Nitya's condition declined from then on and he would never again be strong. In India he tried to keep going and to accompany Krishna on the arduous whirlwind of activities and meetings, but it was soon evident that he was too ill to participate.

There was another problem that no one would know of until Nitya saw Rosalind again in Sydney. He was becoming increasingly disturbed by Krishna's behaviour toward the Theosophists and in particular their old friends and protectors. Privately to Nitya Krishna was making sarcastic and sneering comments and paying no attention to his brother's objections. Nitya's escalating illness may have made him more sensitive than usual, but he felt he could not deter Krishna. Neither could he endure behaviour which ultimately hurt him so deeply that he withdrew from Krishna and preferred not to talk to him at all. Krishna, meanwhile, appeared to be oblivious to his brother's feelings and continued in his behaviour and activities. He was elated to be back in Adyar, even though Nitya had not been able to accompany him. Nitya had gone up to the hill station of Ootacamund with Mme de Manziarly to care for him.

'Ooty' in those days was as close to paradise as one could get in India; a pine-studded retreat that rose above tiers of coffee and tea plantations. There was a maharaja's villa and many more modest and not so modest villas of well-to-do British. There were clear lakes and mountain walks and the friendly Toda tribal people who lived in huts on the hillsides. But for Nitya, lying ill and lonely in an isolated cottage with no one but Mme de Manziarly – devoted though she was – for company, life could not have been very bright.

The significance of Nitya's silent withdrawal must finally have touched Krishna. One night he had a dream in which he had gone to the Master's house to beg that Nitya would get well and live. Finally he was led to the Mahachohan himself, before whom he vowed that he would sacrifice anything if only Nitya could live. In telling of this vision, or visit, Krishna was admitting his direct experience with the Mahachohan, but it did little to help Nitya, who felt himself once more on the edge of death.

Rosalind had arrived in Sydney in the previous June, 1924. On the voyage down, there happened to be on board the American Davis cup team, which made her time aboard ship anything but dreary with dances every night and deck games during the day. What did the serious-minded chaperon, Koos Van der Leeuw think of all this? At the time about forty, he was a rather stern and upright Dutchman who felt it his duty to send her to bed at a reasonable hour and to try to keep her mind on the serious purpose for which she was going to Australia. While Rosalind had even then a serious enough side to her nature, it is doubtful that he was very successful in this endeavour. However, Koos and his brother Kees remained her close lifelong friends.

The Manor House was something of a monstrosity. Situated across the harbour from Sydney with a lovely view, it was inhabited by as many as fifty people at a time. The overall management was soon assigned to the capable Koos, who put Rosalind in charge of the meals and dining-room. Her knowledge of a proper vegetarian diet learned from John Ingelman was a great help to her. Being a vegetarian at that time was not always easy and there were very few people who understood how to make a balanced diet of it.

Affairs at the house were in a bad way. The servants were unreliable and stole constantly, even though they all had impeccable references.

One day Rosalind went down to the employment agency and sat and watched applicants come and go. At length a rosy-cheeked young man walked in who had a rustic and ingenuous appearance. 'I will take him,' she told the agent, who warned her that he had no references or experience. 'I will take him anyway.' The young man turned out to be hard working and devoted and ended up staying with Leadbeater for many years. Although Rosalind worked hard, there was the companionship of other young people, the opportunity occasionally to go riding in the hills, play tennis and to swim in the shark-ridden waters (supposedly protected from sharks by nets across the harbour and a watch that fired a cannon if sharks were spotted).

On Hallowe'en night when there was a serious occult meeting going on, Rosalind and some of her less pious friends dressed in sheets and terrified the occupants of the hall by appearing in the windows. Bishop Leadbeater could not have been too formidable if these young people would dare play such a prank on him. Rosalind did annoy him considerably once when she moved his cat off a chair on which she hoped to sit. As to training of any sort on a higher plane, there was none that she could discern, unless it was taking place without her awareness.

Krishna and Nitya left India for Australia in early March 1925, still in the company of Lady Emily, her two daughters and Jinarajadasa. There were stops on the way in Colombo, Fremantle, Perth, Adelaide and Melbourne, at several of which tracts of land were offered to Krishna and thousands came to hear him speak. All this did Nitya no good and the little ground his health had gained in Ootacamund was quickly lost. During the voyage Krishna decided that they must return as soon as possible to Ojai and take Rosalind from Sydney with them to look after Nitya. By the time they arrived in Sydney Nitya had suffered another haemorrhage.

On 3 April 1925, the brothers with their entourage sailed into Sydney Harbour. One look at Nitya convinced Rosalind of his critical condition; everyone concerned feared he would not get through the night. It was in a quiet house away from the Manor on that first night that Nitya, ill as he was, burst into sobs and told Rosalind how miserable he had been over Krishna's behaviour toward the Theosophists, of his sarcasm and the ridiculing even of Mrs Besant behind her back. Krishna had never publicly, or privately so far as anyone has revealed, spoken a word against Mrs Besant; therefore what Nitya had to say that night is an extremely important glimpse into his brother's inner feelings. He was the one person before whom Krishna would have felt safe to speak his mind. Nitya told Rosalind he was so upset over it that he had not spoken to Krishna for three months. He swore her to secrecy and went on to say how the whole strain of that had added to his already desperate condition.

Rosalind was concerned that night only for Nitya. When morning came she could think of nothing else than that he was still alive. The next day Krishna came to her in a most unhappy mood and begged her to find out what was wrong. He could no longer avoid recognizing that Nitya was upset with him. Rosalind was in a terrible position. She had given her word to Nitya to say nothing. Yet fearing he would die and leave Krishna in this state without a reconciliation, she broke her word, although it caused her a great deal of pain to do so, and told Krishna how Nitya felt about his behaviour, begging him to make up the quarrel immediately and warning that if he gave her away she would never forgive him. Krishna went to his brother at once and whatever he said appeared to have relieved Nitya's distress. Krishna kept his promise to Rosalind.

Krishna was determined that Rosalind should return with them to Ojai and gave her the impression that he had to stand up adamantly to Leadbeater to ensure this. Leadbeater, Krishna said, felt she should remain in Sydney. Leadbeater undoubtedly found her useful but may well have had his more occult reasons too. However, Krishna won and Leadbeater finally gave his blessing to her going back to Ojai.

In spite of his reconciliation with Nitya, Krishna found the schism between himself and Leadbeater widening. He allowed his boredom to show at the lengthy rituals that were all important in the Liberal Catholic Church and he mocked the 'gopis' for their participation, even though he had suggested that they come to Sydney to be with Leadbeater. He did not need to mock Rosalind. She had never developed any interest in that aspect of Theosophy. In fact one might well wonder what benefit on a spiritual or intellectual level her whole year in Sydney had been. She had found a fair share of good times and had worked hard to keep the Manor dining-room running smoothly. It was not in her nature to question whether that year might have been better spent at Radcliffe, where she was headed before Krishna took her destiny in his hands.

By June Nitya was pronounced by the specialist well enough to sail to California. Krishna had sent for John Ingelman to come all the way to Australia from Los Angeles to accompany them back, and help to care for Nitya.

9

A Left Turn

After receiving his MA and LLB Raja found himself at a critical point in his life. He had just been offered a postgraduate place at Cambridge. His tutor, of whom he had become very fond, was encouraging him to accept it. But Mrs Besant asked him to give up the offer and help in the work for the coming world teacher. She still believed, as did Leadbeater, that Krishna was no more than the vehicle for this coming and that there was yet a great deal of preparation to be made. Raja complied with her request and declined the offer from Cambridge, not hesitating to follow the path she advocated.

Krishna had cancelled the Ommen camp for that summer of 1925, realizing that because of Nitya's health they would have to remain in Ojai. It was an indication of the growing rift between him and George Arundale that Arundale decided to run it anyway, saying he and others could carry on the Master's work without Krishna there.

In July, before the camp was to start, George had gathered a group at Huizen in Holland. At his urging Mrs Besant had changed her plans in order to join them there as extraordinary initiations were said to be taking place. George announced the acceleration of his young wife Rukmini's advancement along 'the Path'.

Raja accompanied Mrs Besant, Lady Emily and Shiva Rao on the night train to Huizen. In an atmosphere of intense excitement, he received his second initiation and was made a deacon in the Liberal Catholic Church. He would also be considered as one of twelve apostles. Although there was some confusion as to who exactly the twelve were, they included Mrs Besant, Leadbeater, Jinarajadasa, George, Rukmini, Nitya, Raja and Lady Emily.

One day during this time at Huizen, Rukmini and Raja were alone with Mrs Besant, taking their initiation in the Co-Masonic Lodge, when suddenly Rukmini was overcome by giggles which soon infected Raja. They struggled with their hands over their faces to conceal this from Mrs Besant, never feeling certain whether she noticed or not. According to Rukmini, Raja had always been shy but was trying to get over it, as Leadbeater said shyness was a form of pride. In spite of the giggles Rukmini felt that from this time on Raja's nature changed. He told her then that he wished his character to develop more in the direction of Mrs Besant's, to become more serious and purposeful.[1]

Raja's further initiations were abruptly interrupted when Krishna wrote asking him to come immediately to California to help with Nitya. After consulting with Mrs Besant, who said he should go if he wished, Raja left Huizen on 3 August, arriving in Ojai on 24 August. He found Rosalind and Krishna exhausted. Nitya had recently suffered another serious haemorrhage. Rosalind was still the one to carry the major burden of nursing Nitya, and the presence of Raja under these grave and sad circumstances would be the cornerstone for a long-lasting relationship between Krishna, Rosalind and him.

Meanwhile in Holland the scene of spiritual advancements had moved from Huizen to the Ommen Camp, where it was disclosed that Krishna and Rukmini had arrived at the fourth or arhat level of initiations and were therefore allowed to ask special boons. According to George Arundale, who seemed to have a unique vantage point from the astral plane, Krishna had asked for Nitya's life and Rukmini for a closer union between England and India. The first of these wishes would be denied, the second delayed for many years. Nevertheless, the wheels were still grinding and on the last day of camp it was announced that Mrs Besant, Leadbeater, Krishna, Jinarajadasa and Arundale had all taken their fifth and final initiation – but they still expected to be treated as before by those struggling along on the lower levels.

In Ojai, Raja found that Krishna was very disturbed by what he had heard of the happenings at Huizen and had already written to question Lady Emily as to whether or not Leadbeater had confirmed them. Leadbeater had, in fact, cast serious doubt and disapproval on the whole business and would continue to do so. Krishna had not revealed in his letters to Mrs Besant how strongly he felt, although he had written of his distress to Lady Emily, asking her to destroy these letters for fear of revealing to others his criticism of Mrs Besant, who was now taking full authority for the proclamations.

Apparently Krishna did not believe in or approve of the idea of the apostles or the rapid initiations which had taken place. However, he said he still believed in the Masters, and believed that they would not let anything happen to Nitya as they had stated that he was essential to 'the Work'.

The strain of seeing his brother so ill sometimes caused Krishna to needle him into a will to live. Once he even told him that in a vision the Mahachohan himself had said that Nitya must pull himself together and get well or he might die. Raja found such tactics as surprising as the frequent tension between the brothers, which he could not avoid noticing. One afternoon, when Krishna was in the living-room discussing some arrangements with a young Theosophist, Nitya became quite agitated and asked Raja to 'go and keep an eye on Krishna and see what he is up to'. It is probable that Nitya alone realized the seriousness of the inner revolution that was simmering in Krishna and which sometimes boiled over in the form of increasing disrespect toward the Theosophical leaders. With Mrs Besant unquestioningly accepting George's announcements about the initiations, with Leadbeater isolated in Australia, and with Nitya evidently untouched by the doubts which were more and more besetting him, Krishna was certainly in a delicate position. Having been proclaimed an arhat, even though he had to share that distinction with Rukmini, was he then to question the whole performance at Huizen and Ommen? It must have become clear to him at about this time that he would have to find a way out for himself from what he saw as a rapid descent towards the ridiculous.

Mrs Besant had expressed the hope that Krishna would attend the Theosophical Jubilee in Adyar that autumn. It was still of utmost importance to him not to offend her and he had yet to work out the careful course he must tread through the polarizing factions within the society. By October he felt there was enough improvement in Nitya's health to allow him to comply with Mrs Besant's wishes. Raja, who was expected to go too, was surprised by Krishna's insistence that Rosalind should leave Nitya and accompany them. Rosalind was most reluctant to do so. Without her knowledge, Krishna had arranged for Mme de Manziarly to come from India and arrive in time to take over the care of Nitya while they were all away. Considering, in that age of travel, the time involved that it would take to implement such plans, it certainly was not a last-minute decision. According to her daughter Mima, Mme de Manziarly knew the moment she saw Nitya that he was dying. Probably Nitya knew too. But Krishna, whether by fact or illusion said he had received in person, *direct* confirmation, not only from the Masters, but from the Mahachohan himself, that Nitya's life was essential to 'the Work', therefore he could not die. Also, he and Rosalind had both been assured by Dr Strong that 'the thread of life was turning upward and that Nitya would live'.

Rosalind, suffering from an acute case of urticaria, a severe skin rash brought on by exhaustion, had allowed herself to be reassured by this too. She had been caring for Nitya night and day for many months without a break. It was a tragic error – certainly for those who loved Nitya and would have wanted to be with him to the end.

One day Nitya talked very seriously to both Raja and Rosalind, asking them to promise that no matter what the difficulties, they would always stay with Krishna. Later they would look on this as a solemn deathbed promise. In the far distant future this vow would prove to be a terrible millstone around Raja's neck.

On the day of departure, Rosalind, distraught and exhausted and still reluctant to leave, threw her things in a suitcase and ran out of the house, not even noticing that she had no proper shoes until she was on the way to the railway station. Mary Gray kindly took her own shoes off her feet and gave them to her.

The voyage to England calmed and rested them. Although Raja did not completely share Krishna's evolving doubts, by standing with Krishna at this moment he and Rosalind were together taking a new direction which would drastically alter their lives. Yet they had and would continue to have quite separate views of Krishna, just as they had of Theosophy.

Rosalind had never espoused the occult aspects of Theosophy and had not herself even joined the society. Erma had in fact joined her up as a life member. But if Rosalind was aware of this at all at the time, she would later forget it. She had a tremendous love and respect for many Theosophists, Mrs Besant, Miss Dodge and several others, to say nothing of her own sister Erma, and would not have let any difference of belief impose on those relationships.

She had reservations about Krishna where his role as the vehicle was concerned. One would have to believe that there are Masters in order to believe that they had chosen him to be the vehicle for the incarnation of the Lord Maitreya. Rosalind had neither denied nor accepted this belief but had simply watched, without feeling either intellectually or spiritually involved. Her background may have played a role in this attitude. Even if she had not been sceptical by nature, her father had been during most of her childhood an agnostic, if not an atheist, and had expressed strong feelings against spiritualism. He had insisted on selling a lovely summer retreat that Sophia's family had owned, simply because of its proximity to a spiritualist centre called Lily Dell. It is true that Erma had managed to espouse Theosophy in spite of her father, but she had been driven away from home by his disapproval.

Raja on the other hand, had been surrounded since birth by the devout Hinduism of his mother and the Theosophical ideals of his father. Until this point he had no reason to question the utterances of the Theosophical leaders. Now there were serious differences among these leaders, but none of this would shake his deep inner faith in a destiny somehow purposefully guided by the Masters. Nor would he ever lose sight of what he personally owed to Leadbeater and Mrs Besant. This was an important distinction between Raja and Krishna.

While Krishna was deeply distressed and unhappy about the events at Huizen and the pronouncements at the Ommen Camp, he was afraid that if he were to openly speak against all these things in which he disbelieved totally, they would say he had failed and was taken over by the dark forces. He claimed to have tried several times to speak to Mrs Besant, but she did not take it all in. There is a different version, however, of the way in which Krishna dealt with this problem.

> Krishna rejected all the revelations about Initiations and Apostles, the World Religion and World University and such things, but was unwilling to tell Mrs Besant himself. But he was determined that she must be told. He sent Professor Marcault, an official of the World University, to break the news whilst he, Krishna, remained in the car outside Mrs Beasant's London residence. Marcault told Mrs Besant as simply as he could and departed, leaving her deathly pale and severely shocked. For some time afterwards she was physically ill, and thereafter showed signs of rapid aging, loss of memory and a tendency to focus on the past. She was torn between a series of opposed loyalties and demands and remained in a state of uncertainty and conflict for the rest of her life.[2]

On 3 November 1925 Mrs Besant, with her entourage, boarded ship for India. Rosalind was sharing a cabin with Lady Emily and Krishna with Shiva Rao. They stopped briefly in Rome, where they were joined by George Arundale and Rukmini. Now it was Krishna's turn to be reprimanded by the Mahachohan – through George as intermediary. Krishna was reproved for his scepticism, and warned that he could ruin his chances.

This voyage was certainly not destined to be easy. Rosalind, Krishna and the Arundales spent a good deal of time on deck playing bridge. One can imagine that the atmosphere around the bridge table must have been tense, with Rosalind pining for Nitya, the increasing hostility between Krishna and George, and George's irritation with Rukmini, whose eyes sometimes followed her old childhood friend, Raja, as he paced around the deck.

Just one day after sailing from Naples they received a telegram saying that Nitya had the flu. Five days later at Port Said they received a telegram from Nitya saying his flu was more serious and asking for their prayers.

In spite of the scepticism that Krishna had recently exhibited, he still believed that the Masters would not have let him leave Ojai if Nitya were going to die. That night George suggested they all go to bed and try to get in touch with the Masters about Nitya. The next morning he reported that Nitya was destined to go on to great things, both in Krishna's future and in India's. All felt he would be well, except Rosalind, who told only Lady Emily about her experience. It was quite different from everyone else's. She saw Nitya with a white silk scarf around his neck and she knew he was dying. He seemed in good spirits and happy to talk to her. He told her many things and said she must remember this conversation. She said she was a 'doubting Thomas' and how could she be sure when she woke up that it was not just a dream? She remembers his eyes looking around the room and then fixing on the scarf around his throat.

'Remember this scarf,' he told her.

She asked him why he had the scarf around his neck and he said his throat was very sore. She was puzzled by it because she did not recognize it as an article of his clothing, each piece of which she knew well as she had so often done his packing.

Lady Emily asked her not to tell Krishna what she had seen as it would upset him. That same morning a telegram came informing them of Nitya's death. It had been sent during the night but had been held up by a violent thunderstorm as they were entering the Suez Canal. Later, when Mme de Manziarly arrived in Adyar with Nitya's ashes, Rosalind asked her about the scarf and she said it was her scarf which she had put around Nitya's throat because it was sore. While so many around her were claiming to have the most incredible occult experiences, Rosalind never made much of that one very real and poignant final moment with Nitya. With a resilience that she would display throughout her life, she kept her grief deep within her. By the time they reached Adyar, Krishna too seemed outwardly recovered from signs of grief, at least in public. Yet Nitya's death meant more to him than the loss of his brother. It meant also that he had allowed himself to be swayed by false illusions. He had evidently believed until that moment that the Masters would protect and guide him. Now he felt not only betrayed but doubtful of the Masters' very existence. It was the beginning of his overt break with Theosophy.

At Adyar Rosalind stayed with Lady Emily and a large group of young girls, while Raja and Krishna moved into their old rooms at the headquarters building.

As Rosalind was still suffering from the urticaria that had plagued her in Ojai, and was reluctant to be seen, she felt touched by the great care and kindness Krishna showed in keeping her near him during the day and letting her rest in his spacious apartment, tenderly treating her affliction. Rosalind assumed, quite naturally, that this was for her sake, but one day Helen Knothe came and hugged her and said how important it was for Krishna to be with her because of her closeness to Nitya. Helen, because of Krishna's previous attachment to her, might well have anticipated that he would now turn solely to her for comfort; her words to Rosalind show her lack of pettiness. Yet, as we shall see, he did not exclude Helen either. Krishna said that he and Nitya were now one in body and spirit, which might explain his need to be close to the person Nitya had so deeply loved. But just as valid an explanation could be that Nitya was no longer between him and Rosalind. Krishna had not, after all, hesitated in his insistence on taking Rosalind to India and denying his critically ill brother the solace of her care.

But while Krishna had drawn closer to Rosalind, Rosalind had drawn closer to Raja. One evening to get the cool air, she and Raja had gone up the outside staircase of the headquarters and were sitting on the flat roof, momentarily setting aside the strain and unhappiness of the past months, talking and laughing and enjoying the lovely view which swept over the compound and across the river. Suddenly Krishna appeared and, directing his annoyance entirely at Raja, asked just what they were doing up there. They had not remembered that they were right over his room, but Raja had the distinct feeling he was being reprimanded for enjoying these few moments alone with Rosalind. Many years later Helen would recall that she and Krishna were together in his room when they heard Rosalind and Raja on the roof and that Krishna was shocked that they could laugh and joke so soon after Nitya's death.[3]

Meanwhile Leadbeater expressed his frank disapproval of the happenings in Holland. He did not believe anyone had so rapidly passed initiations which he and Mrs Besant only hoped to do in their next life. That any of them should have passed the fifth initiation and be on the same plane as the Masters was totally unacceptable. Even as the vehicle, Krishna was not expected to attain that height and his vehicleship was still in question as far as Leadbeater was concerned. This did not deter Leadbeater from relaying his own version of initiations and the faction led by George began to hint that Leadbeater's powers were failing him or, worse, that the 'blacks' had got him. The unpleasant implication would soon be applied to Krishna as well.

These conflicts within the inner circle did not dim an undercurrent of great excitement and expectation in the less advanced, among whom word had spread that the Lord would manifest himself in Krishna during the Jubilee. When scores of people all expect the same happening, which they had all read about, heard about, and dreamed of for more than a decade, it is not entirely surprising that they should indeed all see it come to pass – at least most of them.

On 29 December 1925 in his talk to members under the great banyan tree, Krishna suddenly changed his use of personal pronoun from the third to the first. Those like the Arundales, who had reservations about the vehicle's readiness, claim to have noticed nothing out of the ordinary and merely thought he was quoting scripture when he said: '*He* comes to lead us,' and then switched to: '*I* come not to destroy but to build.'

Rosalind, who had been with Krishna while he dressed and prepared with unusual care for this talk, had been somewhat surprised when he suddenly said, 'You watch! I'm going to show them something.' And she did notice the extraordinary magnetic power he seemed to cast over his audience.

This was a critical moment in Krishna's life, for Mrs Besant took the change of person and, as some noticed, the change of voice as evidence that the coming had begun.

Leadbeater, at this time, was giving Krishna his full support, saying there was no doubt that He had used the vehicle and would continue to use it, *but only intermittently*, in other words on appropriate occasions, not when the vehicle was eating or taking trains.

For the moment, Krishna accepted this position and did not push for more, although the time would come very soon when being a mere vehicle was not nearly enough.

Meanwhile Rosalind was travelling through India with Lady Emily and her daughters and staying in luxurious homes like that of Lady Emily's brother, Lord Lytton, Governor of Bengal. A few months later she travelled with Mrs Besant in a very different style, staying with Indians and really getting to know the people and the country. With Raja, she visited the small village near Madanapalle, Krishna's birthplace, where as a boy of sixteen Raja had started the school of adult education in conjunction with the college near by. All the villagers came out with garlands to greet them. She met many Indians with whom she would be lifelong friends and she also met Raja's mother, although neither of them guessed at that time what their relationship was to be.

Raja was now asked by Mrs Besant to take over all the work of the Star which Nitya had been expected to do had he lived. In reality Nitya would probably not have had the strength to shoulder the burden of what the Star was to become. No one then foresaw that Krishna would sever his relationship with the Theosophical Society and need his own independent organization to fund and make possible his continual travels for worldwide talks and meetings. Raja had displayed an early talent for this work, which Leadbeater had seen when he first chose the young Raja to be one of his special pupils, and of which Mrs Besant had been well aware for many years. She clearly reaffirmed her faith in Raja's abilities the following year when she addressed a meeting of the Star Council, at Eerde Castle in Ommen.

> It is I think, a very fortunate thing for this Organisation, that you have not only my son Krishnaji, but one whom I have known from quite his youth, Rajagopal, who adds to a very brilliant literary ability, I am glad to find, very considerable business faculty, a quality essential in work of this kind.
> I believe you have two very fine officers to help you on each side of the work, and I know you will always have the blessing of the Great Teachers of the world.[4]

Much later Krishna would disregard these words, which were the very core of Raja's motive for taking on what would be his life work and for his devotion to it. Krishna would inaccurately claim that *he* had asked Raja to help him.

By May all of India is shrouded in insufferable heat and Rosalind, still suffering from a recurrence of urticaria, was relieved to board ship for England. Mrs Besant had been given a stateroom with private bath which she asked Rosalind to share with her. She would awaken Rosalind early every morning after first drawing her a bath and then urge her out so she could work in privacy on her manuscript, *India: Bond or Free?* Rosalind kept her face covered with a scarf to hide the blemishes made by urticaria, which led to a rumour among the European passengers that those dark young men had some nefarious hold over her. To avoid further gossip she had to show her face and declare that she was a free and willing passenger in the company of Mrs Besant.

A Left Turn

On their arrival in England, Mrs Besant wanted Rosalind to prepare to go to Cambridge to take a degree in political science. Rosalind was somewhat dismayed at the idea, but agreed to study French and prepare for the other necessary entrance requirements. She was staying with Miss Dodge, who took an immediate liking to her and arranged for her to be tutored by Miss Ellison, the headmistress of a girls' school.

One day Miss Ellison invited Rosalind to bring Raja for tea and told Rosalind afterwards that she would get quite as good an education by marrying him and giving up Cambridge. One can hope that they were both discreet enough at the time not to pass on this comment to Miss Dodge or Mrs Besant, although the day would come when the latter would welcome their engagement for other reasons. In any case, Rosalind was not ready for such a commitment, fond though she was of Raja.

When he returned to England that May, Raja had to face the task of organizing the Star Camp in Ommen. Although the primitive arrangements of the previous year were to be much improved, all camp members were now asked to do a share of the work, cleaning their own rooms and washing up dishes. Being accountable for the running of a large camp naturally subjected Raja to criticism from some camp members who were not accustomed to doing their own work or taking such orders. They compared Raja's efficacious manner with the gentle and undemanding Krishna.

This was the beginning of a lifelong role for Raja: he would be the whipping boy for any dissatisfaction that centred on Krishna's activities. It was not conceivable to most people that Krishna could be anything less than perfect; yet someone had to be blamed for the muddles that quite often occurred because of his actions. A few years later an enthusiastic follower told Krishna he would like to give money for a golf course at Ommen and Krishna said, 'What a good idea! Go and talk to Rajagopal.' It might have occurred to Krishna that he himself should have consulted Raja before giving any opinion to the eager donor. Raja greeted the idea with a forthright lack of enthusiasm, wondering what possible purpose a golf course could have for a few weeks of camp. The problems it would create were obvious, but the man went off saying that Raja was a most unpleasant fellow.[5]

Meanwhile Mrs Besant, disturbed by the dissensions within the society, wrote to Leadbeater from London on 17 June 1926 a compellingly frank and decisive statement of her moral and spiritual position in the face of the innuendo and gossip that had prevailed at Adyar.

She reaffirmed the tie between herself and Leadbeater, precluding any misunderstanding. Evidently she had not been aware of the extent of gossip at Adyar during the Jubilee which she now held responsible for preventing what should have happened, namely the 'coming'. Jinarajadasa had written to her that Krishna did not believe her words at Ommen concerning the 'coming'. Mrs Besant had first confronted Krishna after their arrival in London and he had explained his confusion over Leadbeater's evident disbelief and the differences he perceived between his two protectors. Above all, Krishna had been distressed by the gossip and assigning of labels. Avoiding labels would be a central theme in his talks as would a distrust of experiences – meaning occult ones.

Mrs Besant, however, remained steadfast in her own convictions that her words had come directly from the King (of the Occult Hierarchy) and that therefore there were only three possibilities if this were doubted: first, that she was lying; second, that she was deluded; and, third, that she was as sure of her directions as ever. If she was wrong about this, everything she had received would come under question. She would have misled many people who had trusted her and would feel compelled to retire from public life. She totally rejected this last possibility, saying that she would continue to follow any directions she might receive, but that all this did not affect her relationship with Krishna, and she did not mind being doubted. She had told Krishna that it might be best if she did not go to Ommen that year, but he insisted that she must. She replied that then he must risk what she might say.

Without reproach she commented that she had tried to speak of these matters with Leadbeater at Adyar but he had always been too busy with his books. While she had usually deferred to him on occult matters and admitted his superiority in that domain, she did not doubt her own experience when it came directly from the great ones. If Leadbeater had not always been able to confirm this, it was perhaps that some directions had not come his way. She urged him to recognize that this was an exceptional time when courage was more important than caution, and she reaffirmed her faith in the 'coming'. None of them should stand in the way of that great work. She begged him once more not to allow factions to divide and confuse the young.

The letter was a striking revelation of Mrs Besant's courage, integrity and loyalty; and, above all, of her capacity for deep and abiding love. These qualities would not be diminished, even by the baffling shocks she would soon receive from Krishna.

When the 1926 Ommen Camp started on 23 July, it was ready to accommodate over two thousand people from all over the world. Almost everyone moved into the tented grounds in the pine woods a mile away from the castle. Krishna, Raja and Rosalind stayed in Eerde Castle. Krishna was having occasional very mild recurrences of the 'process', which he now wanted Rosalind to mother him through. As before in Ojai, he clung to her like a small child and with characteristic naiveté she failed to find in his touch anything beyond the need to be mothered.

The fire-lighting ceremony to the God Agni was performed by Krishna and Mrs Besant when she arrived just in time for the camp opening. Krishna gave, as yet, no sign of the iconoclasm that was to come. But this camp and the gathering preceding it at Eerde Castle in early July saw a basic change in Krishna's message. There was no more reference to 'the Path of Discipleship'. Instead he urged that each find his own path and law and listen to his own voice. In a series of talks, given to a few invited persons before the large camp opened, he spoke of the kingdom of happiness which is to be found within each individual.

Most of the crowd had no inkling where this new turn would lead. Some felt the difference, although they still saw it as a fulfilment of the prophecy that the Lord had indeed really come.

At the opening camp-fire talk, attended by two thousand people, many were certain that the Lord Maitreya was speaking through Krishna. Others were less sure. James Wedgwood (a Liberal Catholic Bishop and close friend of Leadbeater) whispered in Mrs Besant's ear words so alarming to her that she asked Raja to drive her and Krishna back to the castle the moment the meeting broke up. Raja, some years later, wrote an account of that

extraordinary evening when A.B. told Krishnaji in his room at the Castle that it was a great black magician whom she knew well who had spoken through him. Of course I knew, though it was A.B. who said this to Krishnaji, it was really Wedgwood who claimed he saw it. I remember well his whispering something to Amma towards the end of the talk. Wedgwood was sitting next to her and I was sitting next to Wedgwood. As soon as the talk was over she had me bring the car; and quickly ushering Krishnaji into it, she and I drove straight to the Castle with him. She then came to Krishnaji's room. I was with him then and I went out because I saw she wanted to speak to him. I was waiting outside when, in just a few minutes, she came out, and she put her hands on my shoulders and said, 'My dear, everything will be all right, do not worry.' I was puzzled and thought that she meant that Krishnaji had been somewhat physically shaken, for he certainly was in a daze. I then said goodnight to her and went back to Krishnaji, who was sitting on his bed looking much amazed. He then told me what Amma had told him about the powerful black magician. Krishnaji said that he had told Amma that if she really believed that, he should not talk anymore at all, at which she was very disturbed and distressed.[6]

Wedgwood would raise the black magician whenever he found Krishna's words heretical, but Mrs Besant never again suggested that he was in the hands of the dark forces. Nevertheless, for her, the question of Krishna's consciousness was far from resolved.

10

Bypassing the Masters

While Krishna's new direction was unsettling to some and exciting to others, Mrs Besant in her old age and with her mind very taken up with the movement for Indian Home Rule and the troubles she correctly foresaw for India's future, was more and more confused by him. She was also, as we have learned from her letter of 17 June 1926 to Leadbeater, trying her utmost to reconcile the factions in the society and still allow Krishna to go his own way. At the end of that summer she was sufficiently upset by the differing factions around her to consider resigning as President of the society, but she decided instead to make an unscheduled visit to America. For years Krishna and Nitya had wanted to show her 'their' Ojai valley. Perhaps she sensed that it would now be sad for Krishna to return to the place where they had last been together and where Nitya had died.

Among the passengers on the SS *Majestic*, bound for New York, was a group of actors, including Lillian Gish, John Barrymore and members of the New York Theater Guild, who exhibited polite curiosity about the strikingly handsome young 'messiah'. There would always be an interest in Krishna among the Hollywood film set. This casual shipboard encounter would lead to occasional further meetings. Some years later John Barrymore, on a visit to Arya Vihara, went so far as to suggest that Krishna would make a good film actor portraying the life of Buddha. This remark, tossed out as it happened when Barrymore was in his cups, seems to have made a surprising impression on Krishna. He later claimed he had been offered the part at five thousand dollars a week and knew he could always have made a living that way if he had to.

In spite of the glamorous competition for limelight on board, Mrs Besant and her party were greeted with a barrage of innuendoes from the press on their arrival in New York. *Gentlemen Prefer Blondes* was currently running with great success on Broadway and this added colourful spice to the press stories in which Rosalind was romantically linked with Krishna as the mysterious blonde in his retinue. Mrs Besant suspected that an old adversary in the early days of the Theosophical Society, Mme Tingley, might have started the rumours.

At this point, no doubt to Mrs Besant's relief, Rosalind and Raja decided to announce their engagement. Raja had convinced Rosalind of his love for her and she had felt a deep affection for him even while Nitya was alive, but she still had certain reservations about marrying him. His increasingly serious nature and sometimes depressed temperament worried her, as did his habit of working all day and most of the night in his total commitment to 'the Work'. But that summer, walking on Wimbledon Common, he had eloquently assured her that he would change if she married him.

Krishna kept himself aloof from the large step his two close friends were about to take. His manner toward them both was cool and withdrawn, but he offered no overt indication of his opinion at that time, quite unlike his attitude towards others who had married or announced engagements and received the full blast of his horror. When he heard his old friend Marcelle de Manziarly was engaged he had responded that she was a fool and might just as well commit suicide.

Perhaps he looked on Raja and Rosalind's engagement as a matter of expediency, done for his sake, to stop the rumours and not something of their own choosing. Or perhaps he did not take it seriously.

When Mrs Besant heard that Orientals could not become American citizens and that American women who married Orientals would lose their citizenship, she was so outraged that she asked them to call off their engagement, which they did. It is ironical that England should have been less bigoted in this respect. (It was not until after the Second World War that Raja obtained US citizenship.)

For Krishna, who had been away from Ojai for nearly a year, their arrival was full of sad nostalgia. Arya Vihara was the place where he and Nitya had been most happy together and the place they had considered their home. He felt his brother's presence strongly, especially in the front bedroom where Nitya had died.

Life in California was austere. Arya Vihara still sparsely furnished with only fireplaces for warmth. Krishna slept up in Pine Cottage, Mrs Besant, Raja and Rosalind in the large house, which Rosalind ran with ease after her year in Sydney.

One evening after dinner they were all assembled in the living-room at Arya Vihara. Krishna was leaning against the fireplace and started to explain to Mrs Besant how his consciousness had now merged with the 'beloved', something more than the Lord Maitreya, in fact possibly the Buddha. Raja remembers the distress on Mrs Besant's face as she tried to comprehend this new concept which was not at all part of the plan intricately laid out to her and Leadbeater by the Masters and in which she so fervently believed.

Afterwards, walking with Krishna back to Pine Cottage as he did every evening, Raja too felt very disturbed by the discussion he had just witnessed. He had accepted Mrs Besant's and Leadbeater's view of Krishna as a vehicle for the Lord Maitreya, but not as a merged consciousness. This distinction was quite naturally of great importance to Krishna. Being 'one flame' with the Lord is preferable to being merely an available vehicle, even if the result appeared to be the same to his enraptured audiences.

Worried as she was by this change in Krishna's perception, Mrs Besant concluded that she would have to accept whatever he said. She had really put herself in this position by her unfailing outward loyalty to him, though between her and Leadbeater there had been moments of grave doubts which tended to be overruled by her love for Krishna. This love was soon further demonstrated, for when his plans to go to India with her in November had to be cancelled due to a painful swelling in his breast, resulting in the doctor's firm orders that he must stay in Ojai, she decided to remain there with him for the winter.

She never fully resigned herself to his 'blending of consciousness' theory. But at the same time, she gave him her unflinching public support and did her utmost to reconcile the two views.

[she reviewed] the development of her and Leadbeater's original theory of the taking over of a human body by the Teacher, and [told] how in London recently she had modified this theory in accordance with modern psychology to allow for 'dual personality'[1] and had now come to think that there would not be 'a going out and a coming in . . . but a thing far more inspiring . . . a blending of the consciousness of the Christ with the consciousness of His Disciple', a 'taking of the manhood into God.'[2]

The state of Krishna's consciousness was not absorbing Mrs Besant's entire interest that winter. She was also embarking on a serious real estate venture. One day she had been taken to the upper valley to see a tract of land, purchased the year before for the Order of the Star. However, Krishna and Raja had found the rolling hills unsuitable for a campsite. Besides there was no water. As Mrs Besant sat on the land under the grove of eucalyptus trees she had a very strong 'vision' or conviction that this would be the perfect centre for the future sixth sub-root race. She and Leadbeater had for some years seen California as a fertile area for this new generation with an advanced consciousness to develop. It became of the utmost importance to her to appoint trustees who would preserve the land for the right moment. When this moment would come or what type of activity would manifest itself was left sufficiently vague to allow for many possibilities. But she suggested any number of potential uses ranging from agricultural enterprises to schools and communities to film-making, all in the interests of strengthening the forces of peace and the spiritual as well as physical and intellectual progress of mankind.

She envisioned a natural link under the guidance of the Masters between the work of the world teacher and the community that would eventually flourish in Happy Valley. But each would be separate in entity and location. She and Krishna agreed that she would give the Order of the Star a cheque for the upper land, which would cover whatever money had already been raised for its purchase. The Order of the Star could then acquire a more suitable site for the Star camps that had been found at the other end of the valley. Mrs Besant named the land Happy Valley as she said it reminded her of a beautiful valley in the Himalayas. She also had in mind that state of being that Krishna had called the Kingdom of Happiness.

Among the original trustees of Happy Valley, were Raja, Sara and Robert Logan, an eminent Philadelphia couple, and Louis Zalk, a Duluth businessman. No one, Mrs Besant least of all, could have foreseen that two years later Krishna would sever his ties with all organizations, the Masters and their plans for him. In his defection he would take with him many of the subscribers who had pledged themselves to help pay off the heavy mortgage on Happy Valley. Many other contributors would be hit by the Great Depression. Thus it would fall primarily on the Logans and Louis Zalk to keep afloat financially this beautiful but empty acreage. Happy Valley would remain serenely undisturbed for the next twenty years, waiting for Mrs Besant's vision to shape into reality.

There was to be another pre-camp gathering at Eerde Castle in July 1927, which Mrs Besant planned to attend after her round of European lectures. At the last moment Krishna privately persuaded her not to come and, as usual, she complied with his wishes although she was puzzled. Krishna must have known then what he was going to say at Eerde and known that it would have been more difficult for him to say it in her presence. Possibly he wanted to spare her hurt, but nothing could have hurt her more than the way he handled this request.

Mrs Besant unexpectedly then asked Rosalind to stay with her in London. Rosalind had become very close to her and did many small personal things which Mrs Besant had come to find a comfort, such as brushing her hair and driving her. In Ojai the previous winter Mrs Besant had come to rely on Rosalind for night driving especially, saying she felt safest with her at the wheel. But this change in plans was a terrible disappointment for Rosalind, who had been looking forward to seeing all her old friends. She had also come to look on Krishna and Raja as her family and knew she would be desperately lonely without them. Yet she would not have dreamed of arguing with Mrs Besant or even of showing the least reluctance. Miss Dodge must have realized that for a young woman of high spirits to be left in a household of elderly ladies for the summer was not too exciting a prospect. She did everything she could to make up for it, arranging theatre tickets and parties and escorts, none of whom interested Rosalind. These occasions, in fact, gave her a life-long distaste for English upper-class society and a distrust of wealth. When Miss Dodge, who then, reportedly, had an income of a million dollars a year, wanted to adopt her, Rosalind declined, not only out of loyalty to her own mother but because she had an innate fear of so much wealth. Miss Dodge nevertheless showed her great fondness for Rosalind by setting up for her, as she had for Krishna and Raja, a lifetime trust.

While Rosalind was convinced that Mrs Besant wanted her presence for comfort, it is more probable that as the rumours linking Krishna romantically with Rosalind were again in the air, now that her engagement with Raja had been broken, Mrs Besant had decided to keep them apart for the summer. When she finally went to Holland she left Rosalind behind in London. 'Even among Theosophists . . . there were strong rumours that Krishna was actually in love at the time and that Mrs Besant had to exert heavy pressure to remind him of his duty as a celibate . . . the girl named was . . . Rosalind Williams.'[3]

Mrs Besant had another forewarning of Krishna's increasingly independent thinking. On a quick trip to Paris, where he spoke to the Esoteric Society, he referred to the Masters as 'mere incidents'.

Meanwhile in Ommen Raja and Lady Emily were busy changing the name of the *Herald* to the *Star Review* (since the world teacher was now officially here, *Herald* was no longer an appropriate name), and with Krishna's full approval, they drafted new objectives:

1   To draw together all those who believe in the presence in the
world of the World Teacher.
2   To work with him for the establishment of His ideals. The Order
has no dogmas, creeds, or systems of belief. Its inspiration is the
Teacher, its purpose to embody His universal life.

Both George Arundale and Jinarajadasa were in hearty disagreement
with the idea of the merging of Krishna's consciousness with that of
the world teacher. This was to place Krishna, who was in their opinion
still a disciple, too close to the Lord. This controversy would never be
effectively resolved. While under Krishna's sway, Jinarajadasa might
appear to concede. But he would later revert to his own opinion. His
undying love for Krishna in spite of this very great difference between
them placed him in a difficult position. He saw in Krishna's view
the destruction of the whole Theosophical plan of the brotherhood,
the Masters and 'the Path', which he now felt Krishna was trying
to bypass.

But Krishna was not deterred by any of these opinions. A few days
before Camp was to open he addressed the host representatives of
forty countries. He maintained that his consciousness was merged with
his beloved, by which he meant all of creation. He went further in
recommending that his listeners give their attention only to the truth,
not to outer forms or authorities. He did not deny that he was the world
teacher, only that he had ever said so. Nevertheless, in his reiteration
of being one with his beloved the audience was certainly led to believe
that he had attained a very lofty level and that it was his desire to help
others to the same attainment.

During Mrs Besant's stay there were no evident divisive incidents.
As soon as she left, however, Krishna spoke to a special Service Camp
session in which he went even further; so far, in fact, that no printed
record remains, leading some to speculate that it was later suppressed
because of Mrs Besant's disapproval. But several witnesses clearly
remember that he claimed he had never read a Theosophical book
and could not understand Theosophical jargon nor had any of the
Theosophical lectures convinced him of their knowledge of the truth. If
this were true, one wonders how Krishna justified keeping these attitudes
from his devoted Theosophical protectors for the past fifteen years.

The effect of this statement on Mrs Besant was powerful. Back
in London Rosalind remembers a cablegram arriving. She saw Mrs
Besant's face blanch as she read it and then the suddenly old woman
withdrew to her room and did not emerge for three days, refusing to

eat. Rosalind had never seen her ill, indeed Mrs Besant's reputation for incredible physical stamina was legendary.

Mrs Besant knew that many Theosophists were as badly shaken as she was and she wondered if Krishna's present spirit was destructive. This view of the dichotomy of Krishna's consciousness, reinforced by his own words and actions, would follow him for the rest of his life.

In London, Rosalind had become so noticeably lonely that Miss Dodge urged her to telephone Raja in Ommen. His response to this communication was to turn up the next day with a sprig of orange blossoms in his hand. That romantic gesture dispelled any lingering doubts Rosalind might have had.

They talked their plans over with Mrs Besant, who said she wanted to give away the bride and to have the wedding in London before her return to India. She immediately went to her calendar and picked a date, 11 October, ten days after her own birthday. Neither the deep concern she was wrestling with over Krishna, her busy lecture schedule, or all the work involved with her plans to return to India, prevented Mrs Besant from giving time and consideration to Rosalind's wedding. It was to be a large affair, in St Mary's Liberal Catholic church, following a civil ceremony a week earlier on 3 October 1927 at the Registrar's office.

Although he could easily have planned to, Krishna did not show up for either of these occasions. He was in London for Mrs Besant's eightieth brithday on 1 October, but claimed something important drew him away to Paris; possibly his sittings for the bust being made of him by the great French sculptor, Bourdelle. Perhaps he just abhorred the idea of weddings, but Rosalind felt keenly his disapproval toward both her and Raja.

The arrangements for the wedding were completely out of Rosalind's hands: the guest list, her bouquet, her white velvet gown. No loving mother could have planned it all with more care. Mrs Besant asked the chauffeur to circle for what seemed to Rosalind an eternity to allow the traditional tardiness of the bride of five or ten minutes, while a very nervous young groom waited at the altar.

What came next for the newlyweds was less a honeymoon than a lecture tour which Raja was to give throughout Europe. Afterwards he and Rosalind returned to Ojai and Arya Vihara, their home for the next forty-five years.

Meanwhile Krishna returned to India, as planned, with Mrs Besant. Here she did not allow her confusion to show itself to the public. She appeared at least partially to have accepted Krishna's view of himself, for she granted that his consciousness had blended with a fragment of the world teacher. While Krishna was not about to content himself with a 'fragment', George Arundale begrudged him even that, feeling that his own knowledge of the Lord made it unlikely that Krishna had even that fragment.

Leadbeater more or less kept his own counsel at this time, treading the narrow ledge between Mrs Besant and Krishna on the one hand and George Arundale and his faction on the other. Krishna had the impression that Leadbeater was totally behind him, even 'reverential' toward him. But others witnessed that 'Leadbeater privately wished that Krishna would "leave us alone to go on with our work" and was declaring that "the Coming has gone wrong." ' [4]

Krishna was to become increasingly hostile towards George Arundale, although always claiming that it was George who had feelings against him. Rukmini declared later that her husband George had no personal grudge at all against Krishna, indeed had once loved him and would have continued to do so had Krishna not turned on him. But he did see Krishna's behaviour at that time as destructive for the society. [5]

It soon became apparent that Krishna did not have as much influence either on Leadbeater or on Mrs Besant as he might have hoped. They suddenly launched a new vehicle in the shape of the world mother. And who was to fill this role? None other than Rukmini! Typically, memories and memos of the time often differ.

> As Rukmini Devi recalled it, she had no warning of what was to happen . . . when I interrogated Krishnamurti himself about the whole World Mother affair, he blurted out, 'Oh, that was all cooked u—' before he caught himself in the realisation that he was admitting to a recollection of events in his early life which he later came to deny he possessed . . .
>
> What was going on in the mind of Rukmini Devi Arundale while these remarkable things were happening to her is almost as fascinating a tale as what was going on in the mind of Krishnamurti when he realised the role for which he had been selected. A direct answer, however, is possible in her case as it is not in his, because she frankly and generously told her story to me one evening as we sat on the lawn of her bungalow on the bank of the darkening Adyar River, whereas Krishnamurti sitting cross-legged on the floor of his bare room on the opposite side [of the river] insisted that he had forgotten his early

life as the result of his final breaking with his past in the Theosophical Society.[6]

But the world mother was an even shorter-lived project than the world teacher. Rukmini herself never felt an inner direction toward the role and was instead to turn her considerable talents toward humanitarian and artistic pursuits which would make a great contribution to her country.

Krishna, no matter what his later memories or non-memories may have been, did not take kindly to this new vehicle. He did not want to be dragged into this new business any more than he had wanted to be involved with the apostles incident. He blamed George for the whole affair. It was reasonable for him to have assumed that George was heavily involved in the world mother programme, but it had been initially Leadbeater's idea. The whole situation hardened Krishna in his determination to make a complete break with the society.

11

Finding the Way

As Rosalind had originally suspected might happen, Raja did not change at all. He gave little time to his marriage, then or in the future, but he did stay with her in Ojai that winter, busily arranging for the first Star camp to be held in May on the new land, purchased the year before. Bath-houses and a cafeteria building were being constructed, water lines, septic tanks and electricity laid in and tenting sites cleared. A staff of workers had to be arranged for and funds raised. For all this Raja was responsible. This was the beginning of his close and long friendship with the Logans and Louis Zalk, all of whom were very helpful in the Star Camp organization.

Raja was also to form a close relationship with his mother-in-law Sophia and his sister-in-law Erma, both of whom loved him. Sophia had the same fastidious nature and habits as Raja. In some ways they both understood his nature better than did Rosalind, and when it came to food, they would cook what he liked rather than what he *should* eat, unlike Rosalind. In her increasing interest in nutrition, Rosalind would become more and more determined to eat what was healthy. Nevertheless her frugal and practical nature served their lives well, for not only was frugality necessary but something they both agreed was morally important, as they assumed, perhaps incorrectly, that it was important to Krishna.

Ojai in May is dry and balmy. The rainy season months are behind. The fields not yet burned by summer heat are soft gold, contrasting with the dark green leaves and ancient gnarled limbs of the oaks. Nestled against a hill, a grove of these trees formed a natural amphitheatre. Below the Oak Grove were the widely spaced bath-houses and the cafeteria building, low whitewashed structures in a barren treeless field. Tents were erected in the flat land. The daily camp schedule allowed time for rest but not restlessness, for meditation but not boredom. There were morning and afternoon lectures, plays, or music – and a camp fire every evening after dinner. Krishna did most of the lecturing, singing, and always lit the camp fire. An eyewitness at the first Ojai camp recorded her impressions of that week.

The spirit of the camp was extremely delightful, even though the whole 900 people arrived on Monday, and there was all the confusion of getting people to their tents, getting workers to prepare the dinner and serve it. Everyone fell right in line, all had their dinner without any confusion and everyone arrived at the camp fire with promptness, happiness and the wonderful feeling of having come home to a big family reunion . . . We sat down on our blankets next to someone we had never seen before, but we felt at one with them right away . . . to me it was a very great miracle, the fact that 900 people gathered there together all of one mind, one thought, one big family, radiantly happy, all one in the great upliftment that prevailed all through camp week.

During the meetings . . . Krishnaji . . . never sat in one place very long . . . moving three or four times . . . We felt he did this because when he stayed in one place several people would not pay attention to the lecture at all . . . but would whisper among themselves about him . . . always while listening to another lecturer he gave a great deal of his attention to the chirping and singing birds in the trees . . .

At one of the meetings Mr Jinarajadasa was asked to give his ideas as to the World Teacher in Theosophy. I don't think it was planned that Krishnaji was to speak but he came to the back of the platform as Mr Jinarajadasa finished and asked if he might say a word . . . with a mischievous smile on his face and said, 'I have been taking notes,' at which they all laughed – so did he. Then he went on to say that Mr Jinarajadasa had said so and so and that was not the way he wanted it understood, he said, 'I am going to bring [him] on the blanket when I get home.'

It is such a pleasure to see the love that vibrates between Krishnaji and Mr Rajagopal – they are both such slight, slender, sweet boys; so full of life, joy and happiness, and always speak to each other with great love and understanding, it just fills one with happiness to see them together. Of course Rajagopal is all attention to Krishnaji's wishes but there is not the slightest touch of servitude. Rajagopal is very handsome, a keen, bright eye, very boyish but you can tell by his talk that he is very powerful.

One wonders if there were any at that camp who might have lifted themselves long enough out of their euphoria to consider the humiliation that Krishna's words had inflicted on his old tutor Jinarajadasa. It is evident that the controversy about Krishna's blending of consciousness was still going on and that Krishna was now strong and clear about who he was. But it was still an emotional issue, as can be seen from the question and answer session on the second day of camp.

'You say you have no disciples, no followers; are you ungrateful to the Theosophical Society for what they have done in organizing and working for the sole purpose of furthering your coming?' This distressed him [Krishna] greatly, it just seemed to wring the very heart blood out of him. He simply answered, 'Is the rose ungrateful to the rose bush, is the branch ungrateful to the tree?' When he closed this meeting he said, 'I hope I can be with you tonight, but I am so tired and weary. Don't think I am making excuses, but this beating up against the blank wall of prejudice and personalities is so very hard and tiring . . . you ask one thing and do not listen to what I say. You . . . put your own interpretation to my words without letting them enter your inner self.'[1]

This would be a frequent complaint of Krishna's to his audiences for the next half century.

At the end of May, Raja and Krishna went to Europe for the summer Camp at Ommen. Rosalind stayed at home to allow her sister Erma to go to Europe and to Ommen for the first time. They felt one of them should be with Sophia, and Rosalind would also have to fill in for Erma with Mary Gray. Raja would not be returning to Ojai until October. These long separations were to become the pattern of their married life.

Judging from the letters Erma wrote home that summer to her mother and Rosalind, this trip was a rare and exhilarating experience for her in every way. It was Erma, with her interest in Theosophy, who had led Rosalind on to her present path. Now Erma would meet and make friends with the people in England and Holland who had already so warmly befriended her younger sister. Busy as he was, Raja made an effort to give Erma a good time in London before the Camp.

A few weeks later Erma wrote to Rosalind and Sophia from Eerde Castle:

It is great fun to be at the tables and hear people from Poland or Russia talk in their own language to each other and fluently change to French or English. This is certainly a great attempt of international understanding if nothing else.

Tennis matches are on every afternoon and many play on the fine courts. Others go bicycling and walking . . . Mr Mac Bean, etc all think Raja very wonderful. He has accomplished tremendous things here. Winifred told me last night that she has learned much working this past week for him and that no one in the work can have the faintest conception of what a careful administrator of money he is.

Fenn told me that one is forced to grow rapidly here, one sees a great change in all . . . Eerde itself is wonderful and one feels in complete touch with nature. I am sure one can travel quickly here if it is within to do so.

Evidently Erma was not among those Theosophists or devotees anxiously awaiting the world teacher; for Krishna's basic thrust that summer, opening the way for the total dissolution of the Order of the Star, seems not to have alarmed or confused her, although she remained in most respects a devoted Theosophist for the rest of her life.

Eerde   *July 11*
There is not the slightest doubt in my mind that we are enjoying the greatest privilege in the world.

We meet in the meditation room at 11 o'clock. This morning Krishnaji was answering questions. The wisdom he uses is beyond anything I have ever experienced and he makes the goal of Truth so real, so necessary to attain. When asked about the Order of the Star, he says it is useful as a bridge to enter the Truth, but as quickly as it ceases to be the bridge . . . we must break up the Order. That we must develop beauty and purity and truth within, unfold the life within, which so shines without that we become the bridge to that life so others might come and cross.

I had a short walk with him yesterday and told him that I, too, wanted to cross the ˙ream to the other shore he was talking about, but how to find the way. He said, 'You will do it,' that strength and will were necessary to break the fetters and advised me to go into the woods after the meetings. Someway I can be freer with him and more nearly myself than with anyone else. One thing he said this morning was that the sap did not concern itself with whether it was to express as leaves or flowers, but fulfils its own uniqueness. He said that hope and truth were not the same and seemed to think that hope created a barrier to truth.

The whole event I consider the greatest privilege of my life and feel so grateful that I am experiencing it.

99

Mr and Mrs. Leopold Stokowski, the Director of the Philadelphia Philharmonic Orchestra came today. All these people have fascinating histories and are splendid to know intimately. All are devoted to Krishnaji and now there seems to be a blending and deeper understanding among all.

Raja is very busy and I see very little of him. He works late hours.

. . . I suppose the apricot season is just about finishing up and things have been very busy at Ojai.

Much love to my darling mother,

ERMA

(Stokowski too must have heard about those apricots, for a year or so later he called on Marvel, Erma's sister in Ojai, and asked if he could come by for a piece of her famous apricot pie.)

Erma had the opportunity to make what would be lifelong friends at Ommen.

Marvel will be interested to know that Mrs Hastings's grandfather was Josiah Bailey who endowed Swarthmore College and her uncle built Wharton Hall. She comes of an old Quaker family and knows all Philadephia society. She said her grandfather had the best occult library in America and because she was so interested in it when she owned it, her husband burned it in the early days of married life. Now he believes these things and they are very devoted . . .

She was amazed at her bill which she considers astonishingly small, so she gave Raja $500 toward the tennis court and promises him something every month; because she thinks him wonderful. (I paid about $65 for the month.)

She says Philadelphia would be shocked to see Mr Stokowski going shoeless into the meditation room. He played a lot of his trial records for us the other night and they were wonderful . . .

Love to all from

ERMA

P.S. J. K.'s definition of a cultured man is: 'A cultured man is he who is absolute ruler of himself, who is not dominated by passing feelings, but who is dominated by intuition and who does not demand anything from any individual.'

He says there is a creative faculty without form (with which Mr Stokowski agrees) which is the ultimate stage but that the creative faculty expressed in form is the beginning. 'Life must take form to function, but form is not all there is of life.'

100

... he says that truth or life cannot be stepped down or translated into forms, creeds, beliefs or ceremonies, the minute that is attempted, it ceases to be truth, that we should come to fulfilment through ourselves and in the living of our lives becomes life itself and thus the bridge which others seeing the example may cross to that truth.

... Krishnaji has been very well lately, playing volley ball etc. Everyone is very enthusiastic about him and his talks. I know I am quite changed and would not have missed this summer's experience for a great deal.

One can only hope that Krishna himself, by the end of the camp, realized that there were many there who were willing and trying to follow his message. He had felt in the early summer that people were antagonistic to what he was saying, perhaps picking up from certain Theosophists a bewilderment at his new direction. Reports from the camp did not bring comfort to poor Mrs Besant, whose health continued to decline, both mentally and physically.

Neither did the Theosophical rule of never gossiping always hold fast. It was somewhat disconcerting to Raja to be told by several people that they heard Rosalind was going to have a baby. Erma wrote home inquiring:

Eerde   *August 2*
Dearest Mother,

Raja came to me and asked if I knew anything about the rumor that Rosalind was to have a baby. He could not believe that she would not have told him. I told him that several people had asked me and that I cheerfully denied it, having believed Ros would have told us, if so. But now Mrs C.J. [Jinarajadasa] tells Raja that Max Wardall told her it was so and was quite apparent. Of course I would be glad if it were to be and so would Raja. But this is a funny way to find out such news if it is true.

In haste,
ERMA

The rumour was not true. It would be three more years before I, their only child, was born. But Raja had other concerns that summer.

Krishna was ever widening the gap between himself and the Theosophical Society. There were many who could understand and sympathize with him on this issue even if they could not understand what he was saying. Some could extricate themselves from the emotional and spiritual muddle that this alienation was creating and some were left in total confusion. For, on one hand, Krishna was declaring that there should be no authority; yet on the other he had insistently and dramatically portrayed his own new condition as being united 'with the flame' and having the 'vision of the mountain top', which seemed to place him in a position of ultimate authority, nor did he specifically deny that he was the world teacher. If he had been willing quite simply to step aside or step down from the height on which Leadbeater and Mrs Besant had placed him and stand as a mere human being on his own philosophy, a great deal of present and future confusion could have been avoided. But then, of course, he risked losing everything the Theosophical Society and individual Theosophists had willingly given him – the Order of the Star, the castle, the land in Ommen, Ojai and India, and most important, a sizeable international following. He claimed he did not want followers which, perhaps, he did not equate with the audiences who would fill his camps and lecture halls for years to come.

To please him Mrs Besant had closed all the Esoteric Society chapters throughout the world, stating that Krishna was the teacher and ought to teach – no one else. But this victory would be short lived. After a short time Mrs Besant re-opened the ES. Her health was failing, she was losing her memory and she was stranded in the midst of an increasing conflict.

While Krishna had been struggling with the Theosophists, Raja had been struggling with his personal perception of Krishna and the internal frictions that had arisen around him within the society. Unlike Krishna, who appeared to consider himself entitled to all that had been given to him, Raja felt, and always would feel, a deep gratitude and duty toward his benefactors, no matter what differences might arise. Just as Nitya had been upset by Krishna's behaviour toward Mrs Besant and Leadbeater, now Raja felt a similar distress. Some of the ideas that were emanating from Krishna were indeed remarkable and Raja fully recognized this. Yet, not having the mentality of a blind devotee, he was able, sometimes to his discomfort, to see the often extreme bifurcation in Krishna's private behaviour and his public message. Knowing that Raja saw this did not endear him to Krishna; especially since, as the years passed, Raja would be more outspoken with Krishna when these instances occurred. But Krishna also seemed to recognize and rely upon certain characteristics in Raja: enduring loyalty and commitment, and a capacity for love which once awakened was never withdrawn, no matter how hurt he might be.

When Krishna returned to India with Mrs Besant after the 1928 Ommen Camp, Raja returned to America, where he was joined by Rosalind on another lecture tour.

The tour included Cuba, where they met a fashion designer, Mme Barrero, who was quite impressed with Rosalind's ability to design clothes, especially sportswear, and suggested that there be an affiliation between them. At that time Rosalind could not see how such a career would fit into her life.

Raja had planned to give about thirty lectures in as many different cities but after nineteen he called a halt and, without giving the true reason, cancelled the rest of the tour. He felt simply that he could not go on talking about Krishna as the world teacher. He would remain caught between the commitment he had made to Mrs Besant with the promise he had made to Nitya, to help Krishna in his work, and his own awareness that Krishna was not the vehicle. Nevertheless he still had an inner conviction that in continuing with his part of 'the Work', editing and arranging Krishna's talks, he would be realizing not only his own *dharma* but also fulfilling the expectations that had been placed on him by Leadbeater and Mrs Besant. However, from then on he would stay in the background.

12

The Pathless Land

In spring 1929, Raja was again preparing for the May Camp in the Oak Grove when Krishna returned to Ojai exhausted. The talks were postponed. Krishna went with Rosalind and the Ingelmans to recuperate at Idylwild in the southern California mountains. Here, without preamble of the 'process' he turned to Rosalind for comfort from his exhaustion. In the mountains that he loved and under her care the pain in his head and his bronchitis were alleviated. Krishna, at thirty-four, could still arouse in a woman a mothering instinct usually reserved for a young child. When he sometimes came into her bed, Rosalind held him like a small sick boy, later innocently relating these occurrences to Raja, who accepted her words at face value. It would not have occurred to either of them or to anyone else in their circle to do otherwise.

Although he had cancelled most of his lectures that spring, Krishna still had the energy to discuss reorganization. Raja had come to feel that Krishna's new direction made the Order of the Star inappropriate and that a much simpler organization should be established instead. They spent hours each day talking over plans that would change everything, the Star publications, the nature of the camps.

By the time the Ommen Camp opened in August Krishna had moved inexorably toward the dissolution of the Order of the Star. He could now rest assured that Raja was firmly by his side to build the organization he would need for the future. He was hardly stepping off the cliff. The Order of the Star would be replaced by the Star Publishing Trust.

Now that Phillip van Pallandt was married and expecting a child, the Dutch Government wanted him to reclaim Eerde Castle for his heirs, as it was a historical estate. The following year Raja would have the complicated task of returning title and sorting out the financial entanglements that resulted from this exchange as many improvements had been made by the Order of the Star. The pine forest land with the rustic but quite comfortable huts was retained for the Camp.

Krishna could now retire from all his earthly responsibilities, continue to refuse ownership of property, and withdraw from all his trusts. He had found one man in whom he could have total confidence, to publish his talks, to raise money, to run the Camps in Ommen and Ojai, to travel with him and to ensure his unhampered freedom. If there would always be a discrepancy between his actual situations and the image he put forth, it did not appear to concern him. Yet his frequent references to himself as a beggar, without personal belongings or wealth, were much too literally expressed to be taken metaphorically. Krishna owned a series of expensive cars, the most fashionable clothes, and always had several houses at his disposal, not only figuratively but legally, whether held in title in his name or in trust for him is surely irrelevant. He would never publicly admit that he needed clothes, automobiles, travel funds, places to live, to talk and to rest. To acquire the money for all these things would be Raja's concern, leaving Krishna free to make his declaration of independence. That summer of 1929 at the opening talk of the Ommen Camp Krishna announced the dissolution of the Order of the Star and declared that 'truth is a pathless land', that henceforth he wanted no followers, and that his only concern was to set men free from the bondage of all religions, beliefs and fears, as he had set himself free.

'All conquering and all knowing am I, detached, untainted, untram-melled, wholly freed by destruction of desire. Whom shall I call Teacher? Myself found the way.' Those lines, rooted in Krishna's mind nine years before, came to fruition in this talk.

Yet Krishna was still speaking to a predominantly Theosophical audience, present there by invitation. There were many who found his words confusing – even alarming. They had been waiting for eighteen years for the world teacher to appear and now Krishna had told them to 'wait for someone else', he had nothing to do with it. It is unlikely that anyone was sufficiently intrepid to add up the time, energy, money and hope that had been riding on him for all those years, now dashed in one very eloquent hour.

Whatever confusion and heartache his words had inflicted on Mrs Besant, she once again revealed her own greatness of spirit as she publicly supported Krishna by stating:

the very absence of an organisation might appeal to the more intel-ligent people who think out their own 'Great Truth' . . . My fundamental belief in Krishnamurti as the World Teacher makes me more inclined to observe and study rather than express an opinion on one whom I consider far my superior.[1]

Privately she would remain confused about him for the rest of her life. Publicly her motherly love for him appeared to support her faith that he would ultimately fulfil the role for which he had been chosen and nurtured for the past twenty years.

Krishna and Raja both attended Mrs Besant's eighty-second birthday celebration in London on 1 October. This occasion united her not only with her children but also brought together amicably, for that one evening at least, the factions in her 'spiritual' family. Her birthday message to the world reflected her continuing hope for world and individual harmony.

> If every one of us will work, strenuously and continuously, until each has purged his heart of every trace of resentment against every person, who has, he thinks, injured him, we shall then find, perhaps to our surprise, that Peace is reigning over the whole world.[2]

Krishna continued with his own theme, not peace but liberation; liberation of human beings from the fetters of their own beliefs and fears, and liberation for him from the role set upon him by the Theosophical Society.

Three years earlier, in 1926, Mrs Besant had encouraged Krishna's flowering interest in education by making him the President of the Theosophical Educational Trust. The TET had come into existence as part of Mrs Besant's plan to free the entire Indian educational system from its domination by the British, who were trying to denationalize all Indians. For this purpose, under various trusts, Mrs Besant raised money, bought land and started many schools and colleges throughout India. Long before Krishna's presidency of it, the Arundales also had travelled all over India to raise money for the National High School in Adyar under the TET. This school, run by Theosophists, had flourished.

When Krishna decided to resign from all organizations in 1930, he resigned also from the TET. This dealt a serious blow to all the schools under the trust. His followers, who had been helping, also lost interest and the trust could no longer function. He wanted to sell the school land in Adyar for which Mrs Besant and the Arundales had raised money, and transfer the school to a tract of land near Madanapalle which one of his followers had found for him. This school was then renamed Rishi Valley. Much the same procedure was followed with the school in Benares, later called Rajghat. Eventually a Bengali lawyer discovered that the transfer of the trust to Krishna's ownership had not been legally enacted. Thus the TET was still alive and could be revived by interested Theosophists like George Arundale, by then President of the society.[3] It is not difficult to imagine the ill-feelings that must have arisen during all these transfers and negotiations.

If to some people Mrs Besant appeared confused in her statements about Krishna, Leadbeater viewed her in a different light, as seeing more eye to eye with him regarding Krishna's role as the vehicle. Leadbeater pointed out to George Arundale that Mrs Besant was careful in her statements at the school to make clear that the manifestation was only partial, that Krishna was only the *vehicle* of the world teacher and that members should not be limited to studying only Krishna's writings, although she did request that they be included in their programme. Leadbeater went on to say that Mrs Besant did not approve of Krishna's intolerant and exaggerated statements any more than he, Leadbeater, or Arundale did, but neither would she obstruct him, feeling that they each had their own work and should not interfere with one another. According to Leadbeater Mrs Besant allowed that Krishna should show a certain fanaticism in order to make a strong impact on his public.

However, Krishna was no longer concerned with Leadbeater's opinion. He wrote to Mrs Besant in February 1930 reiterating his confidence in his own direction despite the opposition of Leadbeater or a million others.

The protectorship was over. It was not made an open issue, but there was now a definite estrangement between Leadbeater and Krishna, one which would never heal. Ultimately Krishna would express the opinion that Leadbeater was evil.[4] His teachings were now undercutting Leadbeater and many of the other Theosophical leaders. Their effort to maintain their positions by explaining that the coming had gone wrong and that Krishna no longer belonged in the society was, in his eyes, an open declaration of war. Leadbeater was to become more and more assertive that the coming had gone wrong, and even go so far as to suggest that if it hadn't been for Mrs Besant's certainty, no one would have paid much attention to Krishna at all. Although he had been the one to discover the young Krishna, he had very soon become open to the possibility that he had made a mistake. Now he appeared to be convinced.

When, in 1930, Krishna resigned from the Theosophical Society, Raja did not follow him in this formal step and was to retain most of his close friendships within the society in spite of Krishna's increasing antagonism. Later this would become a sore point between Krishna and Raja.

Raja's and Rosalind's lives were so full of people, travel, idealism and work that it would have been a wonder if they ever had time to stop and take stock of their own relationship. They were separated for long intervals and even when they were together they were seldom alone. One or the other of them was usually with Krishna, for it had long since been recognized that he should not be left on his own and they were always conscious of their promise to Nitya. Yet there was the inevitable strain of having too many people around, those who invited themselves and those whom Krishna inadvertently invited – then wished he hadn't.

Rosalind's interest in fashion design did not wane. This talent served her well in making her own clothes and sometimes a sweater or shirt for Raja. In the summer of 1930, following an invitation from Mme Barrero, whom she had first met in Cuba, she went to Paris to attend the fashion openings. It was typical of Raja that he never put down another's interest, no matter how removed it might be from his own. Throughout their life Rosalind would follow many pursuits, each with great eagerness; he always encouraged these ventures.

Krishna was also in France at this time, where his difficulties with the Theosophists did not seem to interfere with his success. On 23 October 1930 Rosalind wrote to her mother, Sophia from Paris.

> Evidently Krishnaji gave a marvelous lecture in Strasbourg and the papers gave good reviews. They said that except for Maurice Chevalier, Krishnamurti was the only one who could attract thousands. He read his lecture in French . . .

Along with the teas and receptions that they all attended in Paris, as well as art exhibitions, and lovely weekends in the country house of Mme de Manziarly at La Tours, Rosalind was aware of the Depression. 'We hear on all sides how everyone is financially hard hit in last week's stock exchange. Conditions are bad all over the world. I expect California is better off than anyplace.'

Rosalind had a more personal worry that month in Paris. She found that she was pregnant. Rather than feeling delighted as she normally should have, for she and Raja had been hoping for some years to have a child, she was in despair. Krishna had recently been reiterating his old view that none of those close to him should have children but must keep themselves free and pure for 'the Work'. That she was driven to consider having an abortion in Switzerland must be taken as an indication not only of her despair, but also of her initial willingness to be guided by Krishna's attitude; and one might wonder why she felt she could not discuss her predicament with the person who should be most concerned – her husband. She might have guessed that Raja would be totally opposed to such a course. Fortunately for me, whose future was at stake, Rosalind on her own suddenly felt an abortion was all wrong, no matter what Krishna would say, and decided to keep her baby. However, she had gone through a considerable amount of stress over the whole situation and on this she would blame a very difficult pregnancy.

On first hearing her news, Krishna displayed the same displeasure that he had shown when she married Raja. It was a reaction Krishna showed to anyone close to him who tried to pursue a life apart from efforts on his behalf. More than one person of talent was driven to abandon a promising career – fortunately not all succumbed. In this case, another reason may have been an emotional reaction he had at the thought of them having a child. When Nitya died Krishna had assumed that Rosalind would then be closest to him. Her marriage to Raja had probably been a shock that he had to endure in isolation. For them to have a baby was at the very least a further affront.

The serene Sicilian town of Taormina, perched above pine-fringed coves of pellucid water, under the volcanic shadow of Mount Etna, was still a very special place to Krishna. Here he and Nitya had been sequestered in 1913 during the guardianship trial between their father and Mrs Besant. Here he claimed to have seen the Lord Buddha. Taormina exudes romance and mystery, from its streets bordered with small shops of unaffected charm, to its ancient Greek amphitheatre and the ever-present Mount Etna, sometimes clad in snow and sometimes in sulphurous fumes, its spluttering flames licking a night sky.

Krishna, Raja and Rosalind came there in late autumn, out of season, with few tourists – leaving them in happy solitude. In this setting whatever resentment Krishna may have felt about Rosalind's pregnancy dropped away.

It was he who helped her tenderly through the first months of discomfort. He believed himself to have healing gifts and, whether or not this was true, he certainly never shirked the attempt to bring comfort to the ill. Raja on the other hand was of a squeamish nature, fainted easily at the sight of blood, and having a low threshold of pain himself, identified too readily with another's affliction. But those six weeks were a rare period of closeness and sanctuary between the three of them.

In December Rosalind went back to Ommen while Raja accompanied Krishna to Greece. Krishna was bowled over by the Parthenon. Although it was unusual for him to become so ecstatic over man-made beauty, he used to tell me how he had fallen to his knees and kissed the soil when he first saw it. He found Greece altogether a stimulating experience and his talks, if the size of the crowds are a measure, were an overwhelming success. He said later that he was even told that if he stayed they would make him the mayor of Athens. Krishna had a tendency to invest such comments with more significance than was intended and they sometimes went to his head. The loving, mystical nature that had been his at Taormina took a quicksilver turn in Athens. He and Raja had been put up in the Grande Bretagne hotel, and it was here that they had their first major confrontation. While the memory of what led to it has dimmed, the scene that followed was never erased from Raja's mind. Krishna had gone back upon confirmed arrangements which put Raja in a very bad position with their hosts in Athens. Raja was so exasperated at once again bearing the brunt of antagonism that rightfully ought not to have been directed at him, that he said to Krishna, 'You ought to be exposed.'

Whereupon Krishna had laughed and replied, 'Go ahead, try it, who would ever believe *you* against *me*?'

Of course he was perfectly right, as many similar incidents throughout the years would corroborate.

It is difficult for those of us not inculcated with the concepts of *karma, dharma* and reincarnation, to understand exactly what motivated Raja to give his life so unstintingly to the work around Krishna, as well as to the man himself. He had agreed to take on a task and with his sense of perfection he would let nothing distract him from giving it his total concentration. That the task would have difficulties beyond his imagining was beside the point. He did not doubt that Rosalind was firmly at his side in spirit and that they were bound to this common purpose. Even so, throughout the next thirty years there would be occasions when he felt he could take no more and would offer to leave. But Krishna would prevail upon him to stay and would go to any length of apology, written and verbal, to make things right again. Of course there was no real right, nor could there be. And the scenes and despair would become more and more intense over the years.

Both Raja and Rosalind wanted their child to be born in America, and they were planning to sail back together in good time. This was to be one of the rare occasions when Raja, perhaps still smarting from the episode in Athens, had allowed himself to leave Krishna, who had taken a brief side trip to Romania, where he had been invited by the Queen. Just before sailing for America, Raja received a cable that Krishna had been poisoned. The Queen, suspecting a plot, had him taken off the train before the scheduled stop, but even so he suddenly fell deathly ill. (Many years later, in 1946, the doctor who had treated him in Romania showed up in Ojai during another serious illness and confirmed this story.)

That night in Ommen Raja, sometimes in tears, paced the floor until dawn, torn between his two responsibilities – to go to Krishna, who might be dying, or to accompany his wife, still in a frail condition, to America. He went to Romania and was not to see my mother or me until I was six weeks old.

Rosalind, once back in America, was in the loving circle of her family. She was also surrounded by dear friends, with one of whom, Beatrice Wood, she had agreed to start a clothes designing business. Now she had to tell Beatrice that there would be a slight postponement of their plans.

'Don't worry,' she said, 'as soon as the baby's born I'll give it to my mother to take care of and we'll carry right on.'

Beatrice's scepticism about this solution turned out to be justified, for when Rosalind saw her baby she told Beatrice she could not possibly hand me over to her mother.[5] This was perhaps just as well for Beatrice, who then added ceramics to her other artistic talents and in this medium later became a world-famous artist.

Raja had sent Rosalind a list of Indian names that he liked and Rosalind chose the name Radha for me. From that time Raja would leave most decisions concerning my upbringing to my mother, while standing in the wings to be sure all was well. He told Rosalind that he would intervene only if he felt something was going wrong.

In July, after a very difficult childbirth, Rosalind's recovery was complicated by a bad sore on her back which, aggravated by the nurses' carelessness in the hospital, became infected and had to be removed immediately. It was found to be malignant and the doctor told her that this was the most serious form of skin cancer and that she would only live from two to ten years. She never told anyone this news (until she told me forty years later). But for the next few years she did not doubt the doctor, who had also advised her not to have any more children as another childbirth would be even more difficult than her first.

Raja returned to Ojai in September. He arrived at Arya Vihara late at night and Rosalind excitedly hurried him in to see his new baby. She concealed her disappointment when she saw that he was far more excited to tell her about the world's economic situation and America going off the gold standard. She did not then appreciate that Raja would continue to turn to great financial advantage his observations while travelling. He seemed to have a sixth sense about investments. In 1929 he had warned his friend Louis Zalk to sell out of the stock market. Louis had the greatest respect for Raja's karmic past as well as his present capabilities, but had wondered what a young Hindu could tell him, a successful American industrialist, about the stock market. His own Theosophical background, however, persuaded Louis that he should not totally ignore Raja. He sold half his holdings. When, a short time later, that half was all he had left, he acquired a lifelong confidence in Raja's financial acumen.

That night Rosalind paid no more attention to Raja's words than he did to his baby, but when I suddenly opened my eyes and looked at my father with a smile, he was quite overwhelmed. His next reaction, which Rosalind remembers came at that moment or shortly after, was much more difficult for her to understand. Raja remarked that now they had their baby there was no more reason for them to live as man and wife. It may have been that he still retained an orthodox Theosophical attitude toward marriage, that sex was only for having children, or it may have been a poorly timed quip (of which he was capable) not meant to be taken literally. Neither of them had a tendency to discuss their private thoughts, being perhaps too surrounded by so many other people's personal problems. In any event there was at this point a vast gap in understanding between them, for Rosalind took that comment, which Raja would forget having made, at face value and felt rejected as a wife. Whatever the factors involved, a side of their marriage that had never been too satisfactory was brought to an abrupt end. The strong and affectionate friendship between them would remain intact, but Rosalind would feel more and more that her marriage was not complete. When she later asked Raja for her freedom, he expressed a determination, on principle, that they should not separate, partly because they had a child, but mostly because he felt an obligation to Mrs Besant, who had presided in person and in spirit over their wedding.

Rosalind thought she faced an early death and would have to leave behind her young child, to whom she wanted to give as good a start in life as possible. Yet she was still full of life and high spirits and the eternal optimism of the young, who see death as a remote abstraction. She wanted the most out of what life she might have left to her. When Raja said they could maintain their independence within their marriage, she took him at his word.

PART TWO
PERSONAL MEMORIES

Truth is a Pathless Land
(1931–47)

13

A Cuckoo in the Other Bird's Nest

During my early childhood Raja was in poor health. He had a series of operations between which he had to spend much time travelling on behalf of the work he was doing, editing and publishing Krishna's talks, and organizing the immensely complicated camps for thousands of people, at Ojai in the spring and at Ommen every summer.

Although endowed with a fine physique and natural fitness, unlike Krishna who was compelled to spend a great portion of his life building himself up physically, since his youth Raja had avoided any of the precautions that would ensure continued good health. He disdained exercise, drank too much coffee, led irregular hours and ate sporadically, either too much or too little. He may well have been put off by the almost ritualistic adherence to physical health measures that Krishna insisted upon for himself and tried to instil in those close to him and by Rosalind's insistence on a proper diet. But Raja had displayed a rebellious disregard for his health long before meeting either of them, as warnings in early letters to him from Leadbeater testify.

When Krishna returned to Ojai in October 1931, and first saw me he surprised Rosalind by asking, 'Do you think it is Nitya?'

He took me on with a fierce protectiveness, hovering like a lion over my crib and never allowing any stranger to touch me. It was he and not Raja who did all the things that most fathers of that era left to their wives or nurses.

Rosalind divided her time between Krishna in Ojai and Raja, who was recovering from a sinus operation, in Hollywood. Neither man was left alone in her absence. Erma and Sophia took care of Raja and one of the Star workers, Hazel Crowe, who lived in a small guest house behind Arya Vihara, unobtrusively provided Krishna with his meals when Rosalind wasn't there.

Besides the two men in Rosalind's life there was me, a few months' old baby to take around with her and care for. It must have been easier for her in Hollywood, in a well-heated house and with a mother and sister to help. Arya Vihara still had no heat, only the fireplaces, and the

115

cold, dark winter mornings in the large empty house were not entirely pleasant. Krishna, however, was a warm and loving companion to her and did his best to be helpful. He liked to tell me in later years exactly how helpful he had been, changing my diapers, rocking my crib while Rosalind had an afternoon siesta, giving me oil rubs in the warm midday sun, being a true Indian amma or nurse, at least so he felt. There is no doubt that he must have spent a considerable amount of time with me for since my earliest memories he filled a special and unique place in my heart, not as a parent but certainly as much more than a nurse. I understood at a very young age that the depth and scope of affection in our circle was not related to a kinship of blood or legal ties.

Officially for most of that winter of 1931, Krishna declared himself to be in *samadhi*. A reporter had asked him if he were Christ and he replied that he was – in the true sense; a somewhat puzzling admission in one who wished to discourage followers, some of whom, including Lady Emily, were beginning to wonder if his life were an escape from responsibility, for he managed to live always in beautiful places without facing the sort of problems that those who work hard to support their families must face.

Krishna replied that it was not an escape to avoid plunging into unnecessary relationships, jealousies and ways of life. He had deliberately avoided the entanglements of family, along with the necessity of earning a living, though he still believed he could have made a lot of money – even as a beggar. This disclaimer of family existence would have baffled any objective observer of his life over those next few months.

Spring came and with it the Ojai Camp. Suddenly Arya Vihara was full of close friends, the excitement of hopefully uplifted spirits waiting for Krishna's words. My mother slept in the large front bedroom and I in an attached glassed-in porch. Raja did not share these quarters when in Ojai, but had similar rooms facing the lawn, separated by a long back hallway. Krishna still slept, as he always would, in Pine Cottage. Arya Vihara returned to monastic quietude at night, with Raja working as was his habit well past midnight in his office, guests and devotees departing at an early hour.

Krishna was particularly elated after his first talk that spring. There would always be great ups and downs in the flow of his magnetic power. Some people would come away from his talks shaking their heads in wonder, unsure what he had actually said but quite bowled over by it. Sometimes just one sentence would strike an individual and open for him a vital new insight. But Krishna always knew when a talk had been particularly inspired. Even if he said afterwards, as he usually did, 'I don't remember anything about it, how was it?' we could tell by the glow on his face, the private smile, that he knew exactly what he had done and how his audience had taken it. As he grew older his energy would lapse after a few hours and he would need to be alone for a long rest, but when he was still young he was often too stimulated to be alone. It was almost as if another self had awakened or come to life in him.

Rosalind remembered that first talk in the spring of 1932 for a reason of her own. She remembered his excitement and restlessness when they returned to Arya Vihara. He was full of laughter and sparkle as he went off to his cottage, but when the big house had settled into darkness he came back and into her bed. It was not comfort for a sick child that he was seeking now.

What followed then assumed all the force of the inevitable, though at the time it took her by surprise. Yet she came to realize that he had been playing the role of her own child's father for some months and had lavished on her all the care and solicitude of a passionate and fond husband – a role from which Raja appeared to have withdrawn, enabling Rosalind to slip into a love affair that would last for more than twenty-five years.

Assuming that he was aware of the condition of Rosalind and Raja's marriage, and allowing for his unconventional attitude toward marriage in general, that its vows had little meaning to him, Krishna's actions are understandable, but not excusable in the context of his relationship with Raja, who had given his life to helping him. Nor were they excusable in the context of the chaste image he continued to project and was careful not to tarnish, although it meant living a *sub-rosa* life. He would continue to affirm publicly that true love does not distinguish between human relationships but is boundlessly there for everyone. Yet privately over the coming years, he would frequently and eloquently declare his love to Rosalind and insist that 'what is between us is the most important thing in our lives'.

The miracle is that so few, if any, seemed to have suspected what was going on. That this 'perfect' being could have such a relationship would have been a *reductio ad absurdum* to the Theosophists, who would have been shocked enough had Krishna entered into a legitimate marriage, and the new non-Theosophical followers would continue to place him on a celibate pedestal. But there was at least one exception, Mme de Manziarly, who in 1938 heard her daughter Mima say, 'How charming and sweet, the way Krishna loves Rosalind and helps her with Radha,' replied, 'Hmmph! A cuckoo in the other bird's nest.' Mima Porter told me this in 1984, explaining that when her mother startled her with such a comment she pushed it to the back of her mind and did not think about it once until future events reminded her.

Rosalind, too, had a natural aura of innocence which protected her throughout her life from suspicion, at least among her closest friends. Even Raja suspected nothing until he was actually told twenty years later. Yet the discomfort and sense of isolation that he would feel increasingly to be his lot might well have been spawned in this shadowed area of their lives.

At the age of thirty-seven, Krishna had experienced his first sexual relationship, and, it is reasonable to believe, with someone he had secretly loved for many years. The new and joyful exuberance that he often expressed in those years was naturally taken by his followers to reflect his transcendent spiritual condition, an expression of the enlightened mystic, rather than of the happy lover.

In those early days, their times alone together were few. Rosalind remembers one summer night, as she was sitting with Krishna on the roof at Arya Vihara and looking at the starlight on his face, how she was struck by the beauty of him as he told her of his love for her. She had always been deeply moved by poetry and he was a natural poet.

Yet, when one loses through death a young, idealized and unrealized love, it can stand in the way of a complete love with another. Rosalind would always feel that Nitya had been her special love; but that love had never been consummated by so much as a kiss and would remain a romantic ideal. Her love for Raja had been based on a solid bond of friendship and perhaps she had not been totally dismayed when her marriage was re-established on that basis. Krishna provided all that was lacking in her marriage, physical love and the warm, attentive companionship that she had not found with Raja.

While she and Raja would always feel a profound respect for each other in their sharing of ideals and values, the trivial mechanics of daily life had tended to pull them apart. She was a morning person; he worked late and slept well into the morning. She was active and he was sedentary. They did not share the same sense of humour. None of these things alone was enough to destroy a marriage, but added to their lack of physical love created a considerable void. As the years passed Raja would become more and more the far point of the triangle.

Krishna and Raja returned to India in December 1932. They had not seen Mrs Besant for two years. In spite of all the dissension between him and the Theosophists, Krishna was greeted warmly with garlands and a welcoming committee and invited to lecture on the Compound. Mrs Besant was in a sad state. Her memory was failing badly, but she knew him and Raja and showed them great affection. Krishna felt quite out of place now at Adyar, asserting that they did not want him around. According to Rukmini, George Arundale had told Krishna he was very welcome at Adyar, but if he could not refrain from making fun of the Theosophists and being generally disruptive he should leave. Krishna interpreted this as a definite shutting out and would continue to make a point of this.

Throughout my childhood I would hear antagonistic comments about George, not only from Krinsh but also in a milder way from those in our circle who aligned themselves with Krinsh against the Theosophists and also from those like the Logans who remained Theosophists but still had a critical though never unkind attitude toward a few individuals. I suspect that all these attitudes stemmed from Krinsh's strong assertions that George Arundale was responsible for his banishment from Adyar. They never saw that this exile was brought on by his own behaviour and was in fact self-imposed.

One day Jinarajadasa took Raja aside and mildly reprimanded him for letting Krishna get so out of hand.

'Who am *I*', Raja replied with some annoyance, 'that I can tell *him* how to behave?'

Jinarajadasa then told Raja it was a pity he should go on with Krishna. 'If you would leave him and come back to Adyar, we would make you the Vice-President here.' I heard these same words, in retrosopect, forty years later when I first met Rukmini's brother, Yagna, at Adyar.

'We Theosophists lost a valuable leader when your father went with Krishnaji,' he told me. 'He should come back, even now, to Adyar.' But it had already been too late in 1932. My father was too committed a man.

When Leadbeater came from Australia to be with Mrs Besant at her deathbed, and then fell ill himself, he heard that Krishna, on his last visit, had referred to those at Adyar as exploiters, people who influenced others for their own purposes. 'Am I an exploiter?' the old man asked Rukmini, who was taking care of him.[1] Leadbeater died the following year with his question unanswered, at least by Krishna, who never saw him again.

In April 1933 Krishna and Raja took their final leave of Mrs Besant. She died five months later and for the next fifty years Krishna would not set foot in Adyar. With George Arundale as the next President, his ties with the Theosophical Society were completely severed. His memory of a past so heavily dependent on Theosophy was, he claimed, wiped clean. This claim was fundamental to his interpretation of the free mind which had been evolving since his rejection of his role as the vehicle. In order for the mind to be liberated, there can be no psychological memory of all the sticky miseries that society imposes on those who seek respectability. Total loss of memory also entitled him to a claim of originality in all his teachings, yet they bear a marked similarity to many of the Upanishads and the teachings of the Buddha, in both of which he was thoroughly well versed in his youth at Adyar. Of course there are those who will say that there is only one truth and the truth always sounds the same.

In the summer of 1933, Rosalind took me with her to Ommen, where she met Krishna and Raja, returning from India. As usual, Raja was totally absorbed in his work and also suffered intermittently from painful bouts of rheumatism. But there were many friends around who took a special interest in me, and Rosalind had a plentiful supply of helping hands.

Even at Ommen, Krishna would sometimes ask Rosalind to join him in his cottage and, although she complied, it made her nervous. Secrecy was much more in his interest than in hers, yet he seemed undaunted by the possibility of discovery. His attitude was realistic. One day Annie Vigeveno, a camp member, had been asked to go to Krishna's cabin to clean it. She assumed he was out, and was sweeping up the sitting-room when she heard Rosalind and Krishna talking in the bedroom and remembers feeling a little surprised at some of Krishna's uncomplimentary comments about people. She was not otherwise disturbed by the situation, assuming Krishna must be getting a massage from Rosalind; she did not allow any other possibility to enter her mind. She admits she would have thought it all very strange had they been anyone else.[2]

Rosalind did not feel guilty towards Raja for she felt he had given her symbolic freedom. She evidently had not concerned herself about Krishna's feelings of guilt, if he were capable of such. That summer something moved Krishna to write a letter to Raja which he first gave Rosalind to read. She found it beautiful and was touched by what it said. In it Krishna explained that he loved Rosalind and her baby and wanted to take full responsibility for them. And privately to her, he said they would be married and go and live on some island. She is certainly not the first woman in the world to have heard those words, and it is an indication of her naïveté that she gave them any credence

A Cuckoo in the Other Bird's Nest

at all. When Krishna returned from this mission, he said that Raja had hurt him by laughing in his face and brushing aside the whole idea. Raja might well have asked how he proposed to take care of anyone else when he could not even take care of himself. Krishna must have made it clear to Rosalind that there would be no such alternative, as living openly together without marriage, and Rosalind too felt that their sexual relationship was their own business and not that of the world at large. She saw Krishna as a man and a lover before she saw him as a world teacher; she had always had trouble seeing him in that role. It was perhaps the very fact that he was not remarkable to her that made it possible for her to love him – and for him to love her, in the way in which he did.

Rosalind did not question at this time that Krishna really *had* given Raja the letter. That Raja never spoke to her about it and behaved toward her exactly as before, with no apparent reaction, might have made most people wonder – yet it is characteristic of Rosalind to have overlooked this and merely to have assumed that Raja was not upset by what he had learned, and had quietly accepted it. When I questioned Raja fifty years later he was certain there had been no letter (if there had been it would undoubtedly have been found in his archives for he never threw away the slightest scrap). Raja remembered only a vague remark by Krishna, which he took as one of his quixotic ideas, never guessing the true nature of his and Rosalind's relationship. Because Krishna had known Rosalind first, and because Raja recognized that there was a special feeling between them that existed before his marriage, he felt that it was not his prerogative to question a relationship which he assumed to be quite innocent.

When the talks at Ommen were over, Krishna was scheduled to go to Norway. Raja, still very involved with business at Ommen, could not accompany Krishna. So, quite naturally, Rosalind went instead, leaving me in the care of my father and some very devoted ladies at Ommen, Anneke Korndorfer and Annie Vigeveno. That was the first time my mother had left me except with my grandmother. It was implicitly understood by those around Raja and Rosalind that their lives were dedicated to a high purpose which involved taking care of Krishna and for this reason it is unlikely that anyone questioned these arrangements. The love affair continued in Norway more ardently than ever.

On returning to California in late summer, Raja helped Erma and Sophia to buy a house on Gower Street below the Hollywood foothills. He established the Star Publishing Trust office on an adjacent property.

This neighbourhood bordered the land of the former Theosophical headquarters and was still heavily populated by Theosophists as well as those devoted to Krishna. Raja spent more and more of his time in Hollywood, content with the companionship of Sophia and Erma, as well as numerous friends. If he was unconsciously aware of the odd-man-out position that was his at Ojai, he would have found it psychologically painful to bring the implications to the surface. Such a recognition would have involved a departure from his commitment not only to Mrs Besant but to himself and place him and his work in an untenable position, both publicly and privately. He was well aware of many contradictions in Krishna but had for some years been convinced of Krishna's friendship toward him. To Raja friendship assumed a reciprocity of loyalty and affection, too deep and too strong to require affirmation, and, like Mrs Besant who was herself too truthful to always perceive the untruth in another, Raja was blinded by his own high ideals.

Rosalind's letters to friends at this time give evidence of the closeness of the three of them and of the structure of their lives, strange in conventional terms but evidently not to any of them. I doubt if they ever wondered what other people thought. But then they didn't have to because within their own extensive circle they were above reproach or criticism. To all appearances they were living a charmed life, full of interesting people, travel and acceptance in any kind of society they chose. But none of them had the usual attitude toward society. All three of them were non-conformists and disdained the very idea of being considered 'respectable'. Indeed Krishna considered the desire for respectability the prime root of unhappiness.

14

Childhood in the Sage Garden

My earliest complete memory is of lying in my crib at Arya Vihara and smelling smoke. I sensed rather than saw the shape of a figure through the window but saw clearly an intermittent red glow like a fire ember. I was in the front bedroom, my crib near the open screened window, for it was a warm dark July night. The dining-room seemed a vast distance away – beyond the living-room and the large entrance hall. I could hear adult voices and above these I called for my mother, who came quickly as she always did, for I was not inclined to false alarms. But that night she did not notice the smell of smoke (she had never had a keen sense of smell) and thought I was imagining things when I described the glowing light. I doubt anyone had ever had the effrontery to smoke in front of Krinsh, so I had probably never encountered a cigarette or cigar. The next night I called again and this time my mother believed me. The others believed neither of us. My mother told me many years later that she had decided if no one believed us and she became convinced I was in real danger she would have taken the car and run off with me. I suspect both my father and Krinsh would have considered her hysterical had they known what was going on in her mind. But the Lindbergh kidnapping only a few years before was still a tragic horror story in many a young mother's mind and my mother was aware that in Krinsh's large public there were a few who were not so balanced. Only one friend, Major Dev Meyers, finally took the trouble to look under the window, where he found cigar ashes. He watched for several nights and eventually caught the man, a poor transient with a Peeping Tom record.

Aside from that one, my childhood memories are an unchronologically woven tapestry of lovely places and loving people. The memories of these people cluster like iron filings around places, without reference to time and give no more weight to the living than to the dead.

Foremost were the Logans, who drove across the country from Pennsylvania twice a year in a big Packard with a silver owl sitting proudly on the front. They came for two months in the spring and again in the autumn and our lives were closely intertwined. Rosalind had first met Sara Logan in 1926 in India. Almost immediately they had developed a very close friendship.

Sara always wore flowing white dresses and shawls and had silky white hair, and penetrating blue eyes softened by a gentle smile. Robert, or Mr Robbie as we all called him, was more formidable, at least to a small child. He dressed with exact appropriateness for the occasion, with knickerbockers and visored cap for golf and hiking, white ducks for badminton, and velvet trousers and jacket for dinners at Arya Vihara. Robert and Sara bought the former guest house behind Arya Vihara with its three or four acres of land and two small cottages. They called the big house Saro Vihara and furnished it with Indian rugs, pottery and baskets which they collected each year as they drove through the reservations.

Robert Logan was a direct descendant of James Logan, the Quaker secretary of William Penn. Ironically James Logan made his fortune in furs while Robert's father, Sydney Algernon Logan was one of the founders of the Anti-Vivisection Society, to which he left his fortune. Robert went even further than his father as an animal benefactor. He was also a vegetarian and he and Sara campaigned against the use of leather products or furs. They had found many kindred spirits in the Theosophical Society, but Robert's ardent pacifism was an ideal passed down through the Logan Quaker heritage.

While Robert in his later years would say that Sara had the type of beauty that becomes deeper with age, he often liked to describe a moment in his youth at a débutante ball in Philadelphia where two of the most beautiful women he was ever to see were standing as young débutantes at the top of the staircase, Carolyn Hastings, a stunning brunette, and Sara Wetherill, an equally stunning blonde. They could not have imagined at that moment that they would one day share an interest in Krishnamurti.

Robert was born into circumstances which enabled him never to have to work, but with his Quaker background he was expected to attain a profession and at least for a while to prove he could live by it. He and Sara had once lived in a walk-up, cold-water flat while he practised law in New York and ate forty cent lunches at Delmonico's. He had joined the Players' Club and in later years told stories of his encounters there with the elderly Mark Twain. Eventually they moved to the nearly two-hundred-acre estate near Philadelphia, which they called Sarobia and which Sara's father had given them for a wedding present. Robert gave up the law and became a gentleman farmer and scholar.

Childhood in the Sage Garden

He also wrote fine poetry, translated the Divine Comedy into beautiful English, sculpted, and managed his stock portfolios. Eventually both Sara and Robert turned away from society to pursue a humanitarian and spiritual path. They also helped to promote artists and actors and, before their involvement with Krishna, supported a summer stock theatre at Sarobia. They housed innumerable people in need under their roof, some elderly and displaced who stayed permanently.

Behind the lawns at Arya Vihara was a bricked patio, with a trumpet vine trellis, tiered rock work, and a rectangular lily pond, all of which had been given by Sara, who loved to design gardens. She also made a croquet lawn below the terrace and, although she did not play, she had a concrete badminton court built on the edge of the orchard.

One Easter my mother brought me a small duckling. That it was missing an oil duct almost led to fatal mishap for both the duck and me, for it was unable to waterproof its feathers. Every time it went in the pool it sank. With my three-year-old logic I thought it simply didn't know how to swim. I persistently tried to keep it afloat. As I couldn't swim either, it was a good thing that there was always someone around. The duck and I would both plunge headlong towards the bottom of the pool. One day Mr Robbie thought he was seeing me trying to drown the duck for he did not understand about its oil duct problem – indeed at that moment none of us did.

'I clearly saw her trying to drown the poor thing.'

'Oh no! Radha would never do that. She was trying to save it.' My mother replied braving his anger in my defence. But no amount of explaining by my mother as to my motives, which she at least understood, could assuage his anger at me. Mr Robbie would never tolerate any kind of cruelty or even thoughtlessness to animals and in his view children were often the worst offenders and not really worth knowing until they were taught to be civilized. Perhaps under the influence of Sara, he tolerated me better than most and we would one day love each other very much, but for three days he wouldn't talk to me or to my mother because of her defence of me. By the greatest of luck, only a few days later, he read in a magazine about a missing oil duct in another duck and most graciously apologized. When it came to squeezing frogs or srogs as I called them, even Mr Robbie had to recognize that I was only guilty of an overwhelming love for these creatures and with great patience he eventually convinced me that I should show a little less passion toward them. I loved Sara, who unlike Mr Robbie was never strict and spent a great deal of time entertaining a small child. Her own daughter, Deborah, who was about my mother's age, was tragically separated from Sara and Robert in those years. But that was a story I would learn about later.

There were many people around us who had suffered tragedy and had found comfort and renewal in Krinsh's words. Some understood that a path starting with doubt and leading to enquiry and search was in itself the goal; that there was no answer beyond the direct and immediate individual experience towards which Krinsh in his talks tried to clear the way. The Logans were among those who had bridged the ravine between Krinsh and Theosophy, as had my aunt Erma. They seemed to find no contradiction in the Theosophical precepts of universal brotherhood, alleviating suffering and Krinsh's view that freedom lay in an unconditioned mind free of past thoughts, memories and beliefs. Whether or not they believed in the Masters and the occult areas of Theosophy they would have found irrelevant to discuss.

Much as I loved being with my grandmother in Hollywood and missed her in my long absences from her, life at Ojai was better. My cousin David, Grace and Willie's son, lived there. He was just a year younger than me and we were as close as brother and sister. He spent most of the time at our house when we were in Ojai. I have often wondered what life was like for David when we weren't there, for his world became so centred around ours. His father Willie managed the ranch and David and I used to follow him about and ride with him on the tractor. We were probably a colossal nuisance, but he never made us feel that. Willie was immensely strong and could easily carry both of us, each tucked under an arm. No matter how tired he was or how long his day, his laughter always came easily, bubbling up through his sturdy chest like clear spring water.

Willie Weidemann was the son of Frederick Weidemann, a famous opera singer in Vienna in the early part of this century. As a young man Willie often sang in the chorus of the Vienna opera. One of his brothers followed in the father's footsteps to become an opera singer himself. But not Willie. He turned against the high living of pre-First World War Vienna, vowing to himself, and he never broke this vow, that he would not touch alcohol. He went to Agricultural College in Denmark, got his degree in grass and grain agronomy and then took off for America, where he found a job training horses in South Dakota. Eventually he made his way to Ojai, where he worked with Marvel, Rosalind's and Grace's older sister, on her chicken ranch. There he first saw Grace when he helped her from the rumble seat of a car. It was love at first sight. In time Raja asked him to take charge of the orange grove at Arya Vihara and the Weidemann family moved there into one of the houses on Mr Robbie's land next door. Raja needed Willie's help in the office as well, and Willie, with his ability to learn anything to perfection, became not only business manager but Raja's trusted friend and confidant.

Although he was at the core of all of our lives, Willie never had any interest in the philosophical side of life around Krinsh. He helped in all the financial and practical matters, the mailing lists, the books, even sitting behind the table to sell the publications at the talks. He told me once many years later, after he had retired, that the reason he had no interest in what Krinsh had to say was because he had witnessed early on the great discrepancy between what Krinsh said and what he did. Willie never commented on this to anyone as he did not consider it his business but quietly made up his mind that he would find his own path, as he always had – and indeed as Krinsh himself publicly recommended.

In those early years neither was I in the least interested in what Krinsh said publicly. It was a wonder to me how several thousand people could sit spellbound by his words. His private behaviour was more intriguing. I also sensed with gratitude that his actions often drew on himself the attention and the irritation of my parents which might otherwise have fallen on me. Krinsh's habit of eating only half of everything annoyed my mother. There were halves of bananas, apples, pieces of biscuits or toast always left for her to dispose of. Nothing was ever thrown out or wasted so someone had to be found to eat the other half.

My mother too had her own way of being irritating. I think she was by nature a gambler for she loved to take chances. She was lucky almost always in the outcome and won at games of luck. Once on an ocean voyage, Sara had staked her in a bridge game and Rosalind had returned the stake tenfold. This luck was particularly irritating to my father, who seemed to have very little luck of his own. He was painfully meticulous about everything, a trait in itself annoying to some of us, yet he was constantly plagued by the serious consequences of others' errors while my mother sailed through such misfortunes without even noticing. Her luck would show up often in her driving. She certainly would have deserved some of the tickets she never got although she was always an excellent driver and never had an accident. She would not allow enough time for anything but still managed to get it all done and arrive almost on time (she considered a consistent ten minutes late on time for her). Krinsh was always consulting his Patek Philippe gold pocket watch, given him by Mr Robbie, to emphasize her lack of punctuality. Krinsh was never late for anything (unless it was due to my mother).

Dish washing was often a cause of considerable contention between her and Krinsh. First she stacked and balanced the dishes in the sink in such a way that they should have inevitably toppled over – but never did, a habit we attributed to her gambling spirit. She then rushed through the washing in a slap-dash fashion while Krinsh and I dried. He would search for particles of food and hand back the plate. Irritation increased on both sides and the whole routine became underlined by excited, half-joking half-angry chatter. My father had long since departed for his office. He felt no obligation whatsoever to join in this particular chore and looked on such skirmishes as intolerably petty.

His causes for irritation with Krinsh seemed, even to me, more serious. Krinsh loved to promise things to people. He could never say no to a request. Sometimes he would even offer to loan money. Of course he had no cash and no bank account either. I doubt if he ever wrote a cheque in his life. Krinsh had no concept of money. A thousand dollars meant no more than twenty. My father would then either have to write the cheque or explain to the supplicant that there were no funds for loans. Even I realized that money was scarce throughout my childhood. My mother ran the household on a strict budget, made all my clothes and Krinsh's and my father's shirts and pyjamas. I learned very young that it was best never to ask for anything, but neither did I feel the need to do so. Life at Arya Vihara was fun. We didn't need toys or expensive diversions.

Mary Gray's School of the Open Gate was still next door to Arya Vihara, although Erma no longer had anything to do with it. David and I both went there, but my attendance must have been somewhat irregular with all the travelling we did in those days. It was Krinsh who usually got me ready for school and taught me how to tie my shoelaces in the English schoolboy manner, with one end looped under so they never came undone. We also polished our shoes together every afternoon before dinner. In spite of all this emphasis on shoes, I never really liked them and as soon as I had a choice wore sandals or went barefoot. Krinsh himself usually wore his Indian sandals or sneakers around Arya Vihara. When I was very small he called me Tum-Tums. Happily he modified this to Kittums by the time it mattered and it remained that ever after. He made an earnest effort to share with me his interest in learning languages and we would have a regular half-hour of French Linguaphone records every morning before school. He was not a good language teacher for he failed to give me any indication of whether my pronunciation was improving. He would only say, 'No, no, not like that,' and the lesson would end with a tolerant smile that was far from encouraging. The same method was applied to my yoga lessons and I have found both these disciplines particularly difficult ever since. But of all my adults Krinsh was definitely the most fun. He was never cross or strict, always loving and usually willing to play.

Arya Vihara was its own island; we never heard what the rest of Ojai thought of it. But there must have been those who wondered who we were and what we were up to. We were not even part of the Theosophical community, which Krinsh firmly eschewed in those days. But nothing about our life seemed peculiar to me, even later when some of my school friends hinted that it was. Of course, in the early days most of my companions were the children of Krinsh's followers so I had no problems. He always joined David and me and our friends on the lawn for hide and seek. I was very proud to say that as well as a Mummy and Daddy I had a Krinsh, which was something no one else seemed to have.

Wild animals played a frequent part in our life. One day Krinsh brought home three baby opossums whose mother had been killed by a car. We fed them with a medicine dropper and they hung by their tails from the wire cage top, in time growing large enough to send on their own way in the world. I realized that wild animals were only visitors and not permanent members of our household, but I became keenly attached to them nevertheless. We once found a baby skunk in the garden and it became a pet for many weeks; more affectionate than our cat, it snuggled against my neck and I loved it, odour and all. One morning it was gone from its little house set on an earth bed in the patio. The skunk odour was strong around the house all night. We could see the traces of its tiny feet digging from the inside and the large marks of its mother's feet digging from the outside to reclaim her lost baby.

My father loved animals but he was also very fastidious and did not enjoy my little ducklings running over his bed or a puppy wetting his office rug. Only then did I encounter the irritation that he sometimes turned on Krinsh, yet I was never intimidated by him, for there was a reasonableness in his anger and it always subsided as soon as the cause for it was removed.

There were constant visitors. One who had a very special place in our lives for over fifty years was Blanche Matthias. She was a fine poet, an art critic, and had a great talent for bringing together good combinations of people. She extended her warmth and generosity to three generations of our family. Blanche had been introduced to Krinsh before I was born by Mima Porter, the eldest de Manziarly sister, who was now the widow of an American. She was the only one of the de

Manziarlys to marry. Blanche wrote her recollections about this first meeting with Krinsh:

> My friend led me through a large citrus grove, past a good-sized house, to a small one-room 'shack'. I was asked to remove my shoes, and leaving them outside I went alone into the shaded room. Waiting there, sitting quietly on the floor, was the most beautiful being I had ever seen. He was as shy as I was and I do not remember one word of our conversation or if we spoke at all.
>
> I left him with the certainty that there was something in life I had not suspected. Something other than writing and music and art – something other than Christianity and white skins.[1]

It was Blanche who initiated a series of summers in Carmel. There she introduced us (really Krinsh) to her friends; the poet Robinson Jeffers, the writer Erskine Scott Wood and, the photographer Edward Weston among others. Blanche also arranged and provided for our accommodation.

On 17 July 1934 Rosalind wrote:

> Darling Blanche,
>
> Yesterday we all decided considering many things that if it would really suit your convenience we would rather come to Carmel in September . . . Krishnaji thinks Raja should have a month free from work first so that his mind will be fresh for the book they are going to do in Carmel.
>
> . . . As to rooms: you are all much too kind in your arrangements but we do not really need so many rooms. If Krishnaji has his bedroom and one other room where they can work we thought it would be better if we were all together in the hotel – otherwise I could never be with them and help them if the baby were alone, asleep, etc. So if I could have a room for baby and me, Raja a room, it would be perfect. Please do not do this if it means turning anyone out of the hotel . . .
>
> Much love from us both,
>
> ROSALIND

The hotel referred to was Peter Pan Lodge in the Carmel Highlands which, unhappily for the many who loved it, burned down about thirty years ago. We were to spend many summers there.

Rosalind could not have known when she wrote this letter that her and Krishna's rooms would be adjacent, each with its own little balcony and that Krishna would take the tremendous risk of jumping Errol Flynn style between the two to come into her room at night.

In view of this, his apparent concern for Raja being rested and in good frame of mind to help with the book shows how comfortably Krishna situated himself in the middle of that marriage. He also displayed a father's protective instinct toward Raja's baby. One night carrying me down the stairs at the Lodge, Krinsh slipped and fell and everyone present noticed, and commented for years after, how he protected me at any cost to himself.

Vivid memories of Carmel still linger; Peter Pan Lodge and Wendy who ran it – Tinkerbell the cat, the seagull with a broken wing that we tried to repair. Every night there was clear potassium broth for dinner with a bit of parsley floating in it and iced celery and carrot sticks. I don't remember what came after, but undoubtedly they went to great pains to provide good vegetarian fare.

It was very much Krinsh's and my mother's time together. I can see him sitting on the edge of her bed and massaging cold cream on to her face. She always dressed well and carefully and took care of her face and hair, but had she not done so he would certainly have seen to it that she did. He must have been very strong for he carried me everywhere when I got tired of scrambling after them over the rocky points and tide pools of Point Lobos and the pine-sheltered trails on the hill behind Peter Pan. Where my father was on these occasions I do not know. He is not part of my memories in Carmel. Those summers that he came there with us, he must have spent mostly in his room working on manuscripts. It would have been uncharacteristic of him to accompany Krinsh, my mother and me on our walks. Evenings, too, he would have been working alone in his room after they all retired and early mornings he would, as was his custom, sleep late having been up working half the night. It is Krinsh that I remember vividly, laughing often, particularly when he was with my mother. Our world then seemed flooded with joy and gentleness – and love.

15

Beyond the Garden

Although Raja had some devoted workers in the Hollywood office he ran a one-man show and made himself responsible for every detail of its multiple facets. Managing the various trust funds, keeping accounts, figuring taxes, procuring visas, arranging Krishna's itineraries and talks in half a dozen or more countries, were all tasks that Raja refused to entrust to anyone else. But above all these in importance was the meticulous editing of Krishna's manuscripts and verbatim talks. Therefore, I saw very little of my father. His hours were not adapted to a child's. He usually got dressed at mid-morning, often skipped lunch, put in a brief appearance for dinner, and worked until four in the morning. He seldom came to Ojai at all, preferring to stay in Hollywood with my grandmother and Erma. Erma admired him tremendously and used to wonder why my mother seemed to enjoy the company of so many other people when she was married to a fascinating man like my father. Of course she never had an inkling about Krinsh. To have known that might have broken her heart, or then again she might have encompassed such knowledge within her broad philosophical outlook.

In early 1935 Rosalind discovered she was pregnant. She had been sternly warned that another childbirth would threaten her life. To Krishna's obvious relief, she decided not to have his child – for reasons of health rather than discretion. She went to an osteopathic friend in a town east of Los Angeles. Only Krishna knew about this. He was very compassionate and comforting, getting her on and off the bus, but not offering to accompany her. Only he could understand the need for care she would have for the next few days. She was quite ill but her family attributed this to a mild attack of appendicitis, to which she was subject and from which she recovered without medical help. If Krishna felt any compunction for his responsibility in her ordeal, he did not show it beyond being kind and loving; not even by taking more care in the precautions he assured Rosalind he was using. (Realistically, it is hard to imagine how the erstwhile world teacher could have come by these pre-cautions or how she could have been so naïve as to believe he had.)

Beyond the Garden

Sophia was not as blind as everyone else appeared to be. They had all been together in Hollywood for an unusually long time, under Sophia's quiet observation.

'You should be wary of Krishna,' she told Rosalind, 'he could ruin your marriage. Why don't you ask Raja to take you and Radha away – even to South America?'

Sophia was not a meddler in the slightest degree, even when it came to her daughters, but she loved Raja very much as a friend and as a son-in-law. Her insight, for she had been told nothing and was never to be told of the actual relationship between Krishna and Rosalind, might have startled Rosalind, but after her recent ordeal she was in no mood to go off with Raja to a foreign land or to leave Krishna, to whom she was after all closest at that time.

Raja had his second sinus operation in late January 1935, and as he still needed time to recuperate, he remained in California while Rosalind, Krishna and I went to New York to the Logans, where talks were scheduled at Sarobia. Photos taken at this gathering document on film the love that Krinsh's face could reveal when he looked at my mother. One wonders again how those hundreds of onlookers failed to notice – or perhaps they did and their comments, if they made any, never reached our ears, but I think that very unlikely.

I did not like getting into trouble and very seldom did, but that year at Sarobia I once again fell foul of Mr Robbie. There were at least twenty cats who had the run of the whole house. I knew better than to affront Mr Robbie's favourite Pack Wack, huge and irritable and always sitting on his desk, glaring at interrupting little girls. But one day I found a tiny kitten all alone in the garden and carefully picked it up to return it to its mother. I had seen the mother pick it up by the scruff of its neck and it hadn't looked too happy about that. I thought the tail would be better. Suddenly Mr Robbie bore down on me and, taking me firmly but not unkindly by the hand, delivered me to my mother. By then he was furious and scolded my mother even more than me, again not believing her when she tried to explain that I meant no harm. I remember feeling comforted that she would defend me, for she was generally the strictest person in my life, though I never remember any harshness. It is certain that no one would have thought of laying even the mildest hand on me. Indians were culturally opposed to disciplining small children and the high-minded Westerners among my adults refrained, not only because I was ostensibly being raised by Krinsh, but because I believe my Indian features evoked an image of the suffering Indian masses. Anger retreated before their compassion. Of course my mother suffered from no such cultural delusions and would put me in my room to think about my misdeeds, a punishment I found quite mortifying.

For the most part, some of my happiest memories centre around Sarobia. The Logans loved *Alice in Wonderland* and had made a chess-board garden with a Humpty Dumpty sitting on the wall above it. Sarobia also abounded in strange and wonderful living characters. There was the artist Blossom Farley, an old man whom some took to be a bit off, but he knew how to gather edible mushrooms and lived in a little cottage behind the mansion. Sometimes he saw brownies and fairies sitting on his mushrooms. I never saw these, but I did learn from him to find the tiny turtles emerging from their eggs and to listen at night for the screech owl that sounded like a witch laughing. The big house had dozens of clocks, most with chimes, all set to ring harmoniously in succession. Mr Robbie spent the better part of each Sunday winding and setting them. In this task I seemed to be his welcome companion.

Krinsh was at his happiest when surrounded by small groups of intelligent and serious listeners. Everyone at the Sarobia gatherings was there by invitation, unlike the camps at Ojai and Ommen. The atmosphere around Krinsh was charged with many elements, but in those days it was particularly charged with a sense of love – usually unsentimental and undemanding with a few unwelcome and quickly discouraged exceptions. It was my mother's unfortunate duty to deflect from Krinsh those probably unbalanced and positively pestiferous devotees who inevitably turned up wherever he was.

In late March, Raja and Byron Casselberry, a friend and helper, having joined Krishna on the east coast, sailed for Rio de Janeiro and Rosalind returned to California with me. It was on this South American trip that Krishna wrote Rosalind a series of his most tender love letters. The habit of writing to her every day, as had once been his habit with Lady Emily, would continue through all their separations.

Strangely enough Krishna was also able to focus his attention and his affection on Raja. His relationship with Rosalind did not seem to affect his behaviour toward Raja. He accepted Raja's love and commitment toward him without question. Just as Lady Emily had noticed a 'divided personality' and Mrs Besant, with quite different implication, had granted him a dual consciousness, one day both Raja and Rosalind would wonder if Krishna were in some way more than one person. But their questioning was still far off. At this time, Raja merely struggled to keep his equilibrium in the face of Krishna's changeable personality, which led to serious misunderstandings between them and with others. Quarrels due to what Raja remembers as Krishna's frequent lying and undercutting of him, Krishna's agreeing to proposals behind Raja's back, and making promises that could not be kept, became so severe after several months in South America that once Krishna, who could only take so much criticism, slapped Raja. This was not the only time that would happen, but it was the first. Before the tour, already cut short, was over, without explanation to anyone, Raja left Krishna in the care of Byron Casselberry, who was translating the talks into Spanish. Even Rosalind was not informed of Raja's sudden change in plans. On 5 August 1935 she wrote to Blanche Matthias repeating Krishna's explanation:

> Dearest Blanche,
> . . . Krishnaji, himself made up his mind to cancel the Central American countries as he felt there was very little use in going to each one of them for only a week. That is the only reason they are returning earlier. In Rio he stayed for two months and the first few weeks were spent in discussing all the old ideas of Theosophy, before he was able to say what he had to say.

One might surmise from this letter that whatever problems lay between Krishna and Raja were exacerbated by Krishna's dissension with the local Theosophists. Nitya's estrangement from his brother ten years before was now reflected in Raja's disapproval of Krishna's critical attitude toward those who still made up a large part of his audience. Krishna had convinced himself that it was the Theosophists who had turned away from him and cast him out of Adyar. The Theosophists saw him as having left them in a strange limbo. They had been told that no matter what he did they should follow him because he was the world teacher, and they wondered where to turn when he rejected that role. While Raja sympathized with Krishna's criticism of many Theosophical beliefs, he felt that those who were left in this state of confusion deserved more patience and understanding than Krishna was willing to give them.

When I was still quite small, we spent a good deal of time in Hollywood. My mother had a full life there, playing tennis and going to parties, often leaving me with my grandmother. She was very good to my grandmother, driving her several times a week to visit her elderly lady friends, and the three of us went shopping together on Fridays at Bullock's Wilshire and had lunch in its tea-room. There were also weekly lunches with the Ingelmans, with whom Krinsh always stayed when in Hollywood. Hilda had a great fat black cat and a large garden behind the house with beehives, which provided all of us with generous amounts of honey. She was always telling me that she was the first person to have ever seen me, even before my mother had. The Ingelmans, with no children of their own, made me feel I was a good substitute. I adored them both, with their lovely melodic Swedish accent and incredible kindness. I do not believe that in their eyes bad people existed. Everyone who came their way seemed to be loved and dear to them. They addressed both me and my mother as 'little darling'.

My aunt Erma was included in this circle and so was Louis Zalk, for whom she now worked. He had lost a child some years before and had never recovered from the grief of this loss until he met Krinsh, who, he felt, gave him back his ability to enjoy life. Everyone could see that he and Erma were very devoted to each other.

Rosalind's friendship with the Van der Leeuws had led to a deep interest in architecture with considerable exposure to the Bauhaus movement. She had seen the Van der Leeuws' exceptional modern factory in Rotterdam. Kees Van der Leeuw had introduced Rosalind to the young Austrian architect, Richard Neutra, who had moved to America in the 1920s.

Rosalind was fascinated to see Los Angeles through their eyes, especially the site for the new University of California campus in Westwood, of which Kees and Neutra were both very critical. With their Bauhaus taste, they disliked the old-fashioned neo-gothic brick. Rosalind asked Neutra to design a small flat above her mother's house on Gower Street, so that she and Raja would have their own quarters when they were in Hollywood. Neutra and she became good friends, although they had vociferous arguments about colour, the one aspect of his taste with which she was in disagreement. Neutra was to comment later that she was the one client with whom he could not always have his way. But the apartment was a great success. Raja now had privacy when in Hollywood, where he mostly was, and they could give parties on the large terrace without imposing on Sophia and Erma down below. They were, after all, both still in their early thirties.

During the past few years Rosalind had also become friends of the German movie director William Dieterle and his wife. One day we were invited to their house to meet Keiro, the famous palmist who had forecast many eminent futures with remarkable accuracy. He had predicted a decade earlier that the Prince of Wales would never be King of England. The Dieterles had taken palm prints of Krishna, Raja and

Rosalind and shown them, scattered among others of their friends, to Keiro, who immediately picked those three from the pile and said, 'Who are these people, for I have never before seen three hands so strongly linked?' There were no names on the front side of the prints and when he discovered who they belonged to he wanted to meet them all, but Krishna and Raja were still in South America.

Keiro told Rosalind that she had a sign on her palm that indicated a possible injury or death from a jealous woman. He said Mrs Besant had the same sign and that in ancient Egypt girls with such signs were put, for their own safety, in temples. 'I would not be surprised to pick up a paper one day and see that you had been murdered, the same might have happened to Mrs Besant.'

Mrs Besant's life had ended peacefully at Adyar two years before and Rosalind was not unduly alarmed by this gloomy prophecy. But Keiro also told her she would soon be asked to take a long flight and that she should refuse to go for the plane would crash. When we returned to Gower Street there was a cable waiting for her from Raja asking her to meet them in Mexico. Fortunately for her, his quarrel with Krishna must have occurred right after he sent it. Another cable soon arrived cancelling the plan. Perhaps because Rosalind wasn't on it, there was no report of a plane crash.

Dev Meyers, the same friend who had rescued me from the Peeping Tom, was so impressed that he went to Keiro for a reading too but suffered a grave disappointment, for Keiro said practically nothing. When Rosalind privately questioned the palmist and explained how disappointed her friend had been, Keiro said he had indeed seen a great deal, that Major Myers would die in a few years in a plane accident. He never told people such news when it was inevitable. Several years later, Dev crashed flying alone in an Air Force plane.

In 1935, again through Kees, Rosalind met the newly arrived German actress Luise Reiner, who asked Rosalind if she would help her with English as she particularly liked her accent. This would mean spending a lot of time with Luise; it seemed for a while that we were all one family for we were together almost every day. Luise took me around with her to the studio. As my dark hair matched her colouring much more than Rosalind's, the rumour spread – and Luise did nothing to deny it – that I was her illegitimate daughter. I knew nothing about the rumour and would scarcely have understood it, but I found the stares I received from Luise's movie crowd more disturbing than the stares around Krinsh, though my natural shyness found more refuge in his reticence than in Luise's evident enjoyment of publicity.

Luise too wanted to be read by Keiro and was dismayed on being told that she would go straight to the top and win more honours than anyone in Hollywood ever had and then fall like a rocket to the bottom. (Luise won three Oscars in a row and then disappeared from the Hollywood scene as well as ours.)

Also that year Max Reinhardt came to America to make a film of *A Midsummer Night's Dream*. William Dieterle was the co-director. The cast was a most improbable mixture: Mickey Rooney, Olivia de Havilland, Dick Powell and James Cagney. To these Dieterle wanted to add me as the little Indian Prince. My father was in South America, so he had nothing to say about it. But my grandmother, who seldom expressed disapproval except where my welfare was concerned, was very much opposed. Fortunately for my mother the problem was gracefully resolved when I came down with tonsillitis that appeared at first to be mumps. But Mr Dieterle allowed us on the set to watch the filming.

Hollywood was a world apart from Krishna for both Raja and Rosalind. With her looks and elegant style in clothes (most of which she made herself), her Indian husband, and Indian-looking child, and close association with an Indian sage, she presented a certain exotic appeal which was not lost on the Hollywood of that era. The Dieterles were more than acquaintances and she enjoyed many years of close friendship with them. Every Christmas they sent their chauffeur to Ojai with a carload of Christmas presents for me, all of which Rosalind passed on to less fortunate children without my being aware of this excessive bounty.

Through the Dieterles Rosalind met other Hollywood personalities, including the film music composer William Blanke and director John Sturges, most of whom had swimming pools, much more rare in those days, and into which I invariably fell and had to be fished out.

Rosalind's former tennis days stood her in good stead too for she found new friendships through this sport with, among others, the composer Arnold Schoenberg and the screenwriter Dorothy Arznar. Dorothy introduced her to Galka Scheyer, a woman who was to have a considerable influence on Rosalind, for she encouraged her to take up painting.

Galka had come to America in 1924 to introduce both the paintings and the ideas of the 'Blue Four' artists, Feininger, Jawlensky, Kandinsky and Paul Klee, already well known in Europe. She played a considerable role in awakening American taste to modern art. I had my first painting experience with her and thoroughly enjoyed her method of putting water colours on already wet paper, allowing the paint its own freedom of design. Although she preferred to teach children, she was convinced that Rosalind must paint and was then sufficiently impressed by her work to keep many of Rosalind's paintings in her collection. She loved her sense of colour and if Neutra had done anything to shake my mother's confidence, which I doubt, Galka would certainly have restored it. I remember Galka as short, wide and large-headed with red hair and the loudest voice I had ever heard. Her forceful and loving personality can be seen in the following excerpts (not chronologically placed) of her letters to Rosalind during the ten years of their friendship until Galka's death in 1945.

Dearest Rosaline,
   Since I am anxious for you to continue to paint with me I have arranged to have the grown up painting class on Fridays. I expect you to come if it is possible for you . . .
   I hope you will start *soon*. You are an artist and they are born to create and not only have duties to care for others . . .

Dearest Rosaline,
   I find in my book by Huxley *Means and Ends* (*Ends and Means*) notes of following pages in the back of it.
   Page 4, 44, 48, 158, 113, 313, 214, 278, 296, 309, 318, 361, 362.
   I marked them in disagreement. So if you like read them and see what you think about them.
   It was lovely at your house. We enjoyed it *very* much. You are a darling and you are very much loved by us and by me because I need to know that you exist . . .

Dearest Rosaline,
   Today I'm writing to tell you the tiny Puff, the smallest and favorite of the two dogs, is staying with me with the purpose to go to Radha when she comes back. I want her to have that dog. It is half the size of all the others, vivid and lively and I think it is waiting to go back to Radha and therefore pretends not to grow up and stay a small baby. I really have not the heart to give that dog away. As I said I want Radha to have it, except you would be really opposed to it. If you think because you move around so much, it would bring difficulties, I do not believe so. You can always return the dog to

me and Radha can have the dog with the understanding as she had before that it will be for the time she will stay in Ojai. Let me know if you agree to this.

Our travelling during those years was indeed extensive and probably for this reason, as Galka feared, I did not get the little Puff.

Beatrice Wood often attended Galka's classes too. I called her Beato – a nickname that became her signature on her pottery. She and my mother would remain close for the rest of their lives and she eventually moved to Ojai right across the street from Arya Vihara. Beato was profoundly interested and influenced by what Krinsh had to say, but was not drawn to him as a person as she was to both of my parents. She dressed in an exotic and colourful manner, with loads of heavy silvery jewellery, full skirts and large hats, all of which was in strange contrast to her very distinguished 'main line' accent. Beato, later to be called the 'Mama of Dada', knew everyone of interest in the art and theatre world. Even when she ultimately achieved fame as a foremost ceramicist, Beato remained a charming and utterly unassuming person, full of wit as well as a vivid and true sense of what was real.

Raja too had his circle of friends in Hollywood, many the same as those of Rosalind, but some more special to him. He was a first-rate chess player and this gave occasion for many evenings out. The amount of social activity meant neither of them really suffered from loneliness in their often separate lives. Though basically shy, Raja had a charmingly naughty streak that delighted his friends, especially Beato, who felt she had learned from him the importance of truth and of striving for perfection. But Raja's jokes often seemed to shock Rosalind. This naturally dampened Raja's fun and too often their evenings out together ended in disharmony.

Rosalind adjusted easily from her life in Hollywood to the equal amount of time she spent in Ojai when Krishna was in America. As the office work was at that time all centred in Hollywood, it was difficult for Raja to get away. This left Rosalind to run Arya Vihara and see to Krishna's welfare while he was in Ojai.

Krinsh had returned exhausted from South America. Rosalind had not been told of his quarrel with Raja so she had no reason to feel caught in the two men's conflict. She only knew that the steady flow of letters from Krishna had reaffirmed his love for her. In late winter of 1936, the three of us without my father went to Carmel for a month's rest, staying as usual at Peter Pan Lodge. Winter in Carmel is even more beautiful than summer, for the weather is clear and enormous waves rise and crash over the rocks at Point Lobos. The sea-lions bark and the sea is deep sapphire.

It was not long before Rosalind was again pregnant. This time the decision as to what to do about it was taken out of her hands. One day in Hollywood Krishna and Raja had one of their more terrible arguments in front of Rosalind and Sophia. Rosalind was not involved and can no longer remember what it was about, but she was highly distressed that the two men would shout at each other in front of her mother. They must have forgotten her presence for it was very rare for either of them, but especially Krishna, to expose this side of their relationship to anyone. Leaving me in Hollywood, as she sometimes did, Rosalind and Krishna left that evening to drive back to Ojai. She had been deeply shaken and upset by the quarrel and was convinced that it was the cause of her losing on the way to Ojai, in an isolated field, this second baby with Krishna. He was, as usual, tender, kind and loving and helped her as best he could.

It took some time, however, for Rosalind to recover fully from this ordeal and Krishna remained solicitous throughout the spring. He insisted that she should not over-do it, that she get enough rest, and he spent time reading to her to keep her quiet, and he played with me. Of course I did not understand what was wrong with my mother, but I remember sharing Krinsh's concern.

This much loving care was rarely to be enjoyed by Rosalind. She had strong physical endurance and a high threshold of pain. She never cared for her own comfort, yet had to adapt to living with and caring for two men of extreme physical sensitivity. She always had a remarkable ability to discard and forget what troubled her, to see the world as she wished it to be. However, when faced with recalling an actual memory she could bring it back fully but seemed to set herself apart as though it were another person who had lived through it. It may be that she simply had a remarkable capacity for acceptance of certain things like pain and death as natural and inevitable circumstances. She still had Krishna's love and their relationship would continue unde-tected. For the most part the three of them contained their contentious moments in a private realm. In these earlier years they all felt a very real bond of affection. It was this bond that made them subject to idealization by both friends and strangers. Rosalind wrote a letter to Blanche which reflects a period of harmony at yet another gathering at Sarobia.

LIVES IN THE SHADOW WITH J. KRISHNAMURTI

June 28 '36

Dear Blanche,

You really should have been here it has all been so lovely, and everyone seemed to enjoy it so much in such a deep sense. Also the discussions which were held every other day, were the best I have ever heard. Krishnaji gave two splendid talks in New York and three here. They were corrected and sent off the next day. Rajagopal said they were well done too. Altogether there were five talks and so many have said they have never heard him speak so well before. I think so too. In a few days we sail.

At five years old I was sailing to Europe for the second time. The Ommen Camp was an exciting place for me. Krinsh sometimes let me sit next to him in the big tent where the discussions were held; while it was hard to sit there the whole time, I believe I managed to do so. There were other children about, but mostly I was, as usual, in an adult world.

Sometimes those two summers at Ommen mingle in my mind and I am not certain to which one specific memories belong. There are visions of the Indian sisters of the Sarabhai family taking long hot showers in the communal shower room at the end of the hall and my fascination at their graceful winding in and out of their saris.

I remember the great white house called Henan in which we stayed, surrounded by people who lavished on me the love and gratitude they felt toward Krinsh but were unable to express directly to him because of his precept against devotees. My mother waged a constant battle to prevent me from becoming spoiled.

There was a little seat attached to the back of Krinsh's bicycle for me. Krinsh biked me around the beautiful pine-forested grounds, past the barn with little piglets and the fat pink sow – probably my first sight of that species, Eerde castle with its moat and swans, the camp fire circle in the sand dunes. I had been sternly warned never to take my feet off the foot rests. One day curiosity got the better of me and I lifted my right foot off the rest. It was instantly caught up in the spokes throwing us both off the bicycle. My heel was cut to the bone. Krinsh was adept in a physical crisis. I can remember feeling no fear and much comfort as he carried me back to my mother. I was laid up for some time after that, but was showered with attention from the scores of followers in the camp who were much concerned with the well-being of a creature so close to Krinsh. Attention was not my sole prerogative for long. Sara Logan was suddenly stricken by a severe attack of appendicitis and needed care. She was to die a few years later from complications resulting from the ensuing surgery.

After the camp, my mother had flown to London with Krinsh for a short rest, leaving me again at Ommen with plenty of ladies to help my father look after me. I can remember one morning awakening in my crib, which was covered with a white net, and seeing a large red rose lying over my head. I do not remember feeling sad, just looking at the rose and knowing it was there instead of my mother.

It had been an exhausting session for my mother, trying to keep a laid-up child happy and to look after the seriously ill Sara. She was confined to the house and had even missed the lectures which had been attended by nearly a thousand people. She was also depressed by the cloud of impending war. Like Mr Robbie, she had pacifism in her genes and was proud of her grandfather, Carl Waldo, who had risked being stoned on the street corners of Buffalo to speak against the Civil War. Along with others of her generation, she had believed the First World War would end all wars and her father's friendship with Woodrow Wilson and his serving on Wilson's Peace Commission had heightened her optimism. It was now evident that peace was fast sinking beneath one horizon as war rose over another.

Those times were rare when I was left with my father. I remember them as very special. From him I learned a different sort of knowledge than from Krinsh. My father taught me to tell the time, to use numbers, and to take an interest in good handwriting. He read me stories from the Indian Jataka tales and from the Bible. His gifts to me were usually books. We never played hide and seek, but we played indoor games like Chinese chequers. He did not care what I ate or when I went to bed and put very few demands on my behaviour as long as I did not disturb anyone. It was he who somehow instilled in me the importance of being truthful and the undesirability of hypocrisy.

After one of his operations he had lost feeling in his right hand, which made it difficult for him to do many things – braid my hair or tie shoelaces. By sheer will power he did not let it affect his beautiful handwriting.

When my mother and Krinsh returned from England we all had a holiday in Villars in Switzerland. We stayed in a charming old hotel, at which a solicitous devotee, who had obtained a miraculous cure at the Bircher-Benner Clinic in Zurich, had already established herself. She showed the cook how to make Bircher muesli, a then unknown nutritional marvel and persuaded Krinsh that we must all eat it every morning. To this day hotels all over Switzerland and even the Peninsula Hotel in Hong Kong serve muesli.

After this unusual breakfast, Krinsh and I took walks every morning, watching the cows with varying sizes of Swiss cow-bells going to pasture. Krinsh would rub his head with pine needles because he thought it good for his hair. (Later he would discover he was allergic to pine needles.)

Our association with Krinsh led to encounters with an incredible variety of people. Some accepted us merely as part of his entourage. Many became close friends of us all or one or the other of my parents or myself for reasons that extended beyond Krinsh's sphere.

Among them was Molly Berkeley, an American from the Lowell family, who divorced an American husband with whom she was bored and later married the Eighth and last Earl of Berkeley, whom she had met at a country weekend in England. Her hostess warned her that there would be a guest who did not like Americans. This guest, Lord Berkeley, arrived, saw Molly across the room and came straight over to meet her. He said, 'I have a question to ask you.' He was suddenly interrupted and didn't have another chance to talk to her that evening. A few weeks later they met again at a hunt and he was impressed by Molly's superb horsemanship. He asked her to dine with him and at the end of the evening he reminded her of the question he had been about to ask when they first met.

'I'd like to ask it now,' he said. 'Will you marry me?'

'I will,' she replied, 'but you will have to live in my little cottage in Santa Barbara, California, because I cannot live anywhere else.'

As a peer whose ancestry went back to the Norman Conquest, Lord Berkeley was known to have thought it beneath him to entertain the King and Queen of England, whom he called 'those Huns'. He said that, of course, he could not live in Santa Barbara. So they parted. When Molly arrived back in America, she was met at the ship with great bouquets of roses and a cable declaring. 'I cannot live without you. I will live in Santa Barbara.'

They spent a few summers in what she called her cottage but which was in fact a sizeable villa on a hilltop above Montecito. Lord Berkeley had it painted a dreadful shade of Kelly green, his hunting colour. As he wished to give large dinner parties starting at nine in the evening and in the style to which he was accustomed, and as it was not possible to find staff in Santa Barbara who would fulfil these exacting demands and hours, Molly found it increasingly difficult to live there. In 1939 the war in Europe prevented them from returning to America and Molly offered the house to us; we lived there for six months.

Beyond the Garden

I never met Lord Berkeley, but my mother stayed at Berkeley Castle before I was born and played chess with him every evening. When I visited the castle as a tourist many years later I hoped that my mother, always a vegetarian, had not been told of the ancient custom of throwing cows' carcasses down a pit in the prisoners' wing to asphyxiate the inmates by the stench; or of the horrible death of Edward II, who failed to be asphyxiated in time. People with Theosophical backgrounds who pride themselves on being sensitive to vibrations would not rest easy in Berkeley Castle.

We remained friends with Molly until her death in Assisi over a decade ago. On a last visit there she told me how, with one short sentence, Krinsh had helped her. She had complained to him of dissatisfaction with her life: the great castle in England to run, the villa in Rome, it was all too much with the servants and entertaining. 'Either leave or put up with it,' he told her, and that was all it took to enable her to settle down peacefully with her husband until his death. Alone during the war, she was bombed in London and was left for two days buried in a cellar. She became a Roman Catholic after that and retired to Assisi, her final home. An American priest was there the day I visited her shortly before her death. Suddenly she turned to me and said, 'Krishnamurti has more wisdom in his little finger than the whole Catholic church put together.' I shall never forget the priest's expression.

In 1936, after Villars, Sara Logan joined us and we all stayed with Molly in her villa in Rome. I remember a great dining table with a footman behind each chair and things being handed to me before I knew I wanted them.

My parents were quite convinced that summer of the great danger to civilization. My mother did not know it would be our last summer in Europe for many years, but she must have sensed it for I can still remember her taking me to the Sistine chapel and impressing Michelangelo's paintings on me as if I might never see them again. I returned twenty years later, but I still remember that first viewing most vividly, especially the hand of God reaching toward Adam.

As children have their own sense of the important, I remember equally well my first giraffe, which I saw in Rome Zoo, commenting, to the amusement of my adults, that its eyes were like Rukmini's but its legs were like Krinsh's.

We were taken to tea one afternoon at the castle of Count Orsini, the last of his line. I promptly disappeared down a spiral staircase into the dungeons, causing consternation to my parents, but evidently not annoying the old Count for he gave me a carved wooden dog-clock which still ticks intermittently.

Sara Logan sailed back to America with my mother and me. We passed the rock of Gibraltar, another landmark that was thoroughly impressed upon me. The voyage was so rough that Sara and I were the only passengers on deck. One day a careless deck-hand left open the guard rail at the rear of the ship. He had failed to notice one little girl and a lone lady who had survived the rough seas to wander up on deck together. I eluded Sara's attention for a nearly fatal instant and hung fascinated over the open drop to the churning waters above the propeller. The *Conte di Savoia* was a very large ship and I must have been several storeys above the water. I never forgot Sara's calm but firm grip on my arm as she pulled me away from the precipice and led me, without a trace of anger, to safety. She was too fair to blame me but I can now imagine the fright I gave her. It was on this voyage, left solely in her company, that I developed a still deeper attachment to this person who had taken both me and my mother into her heart as her own family. She would be my first loss and one I would never forget.

H.P. Blavatsky

Annie Besant, aged forty-two

Charles Webster Leadbeater

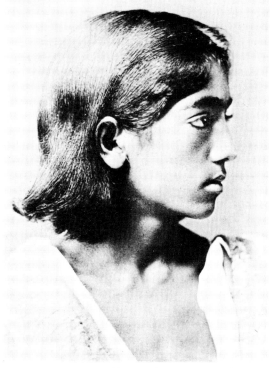

Jiddu Krishnamurti, 1910

*Krishna with his brother
Nityanandam and Charles
Leadbeater at Adyar in 1910*

*Mrs Besant with Charles
Leadbeater* (STANDING),
Krishna (SEATED RIGHT) *and
C. Jinarajadasa*

Croquet at Wimbledon, 1911: Nityanandam (LEFT), George Arundale, Krishna, and Mrs Besant (CENTRE)

Jinarajadasa with D. Rajagopal, 1913

Raja aged eighteen

Raja at Adyar, 1919

Rukmini, 1919

Rosalind aged twenty-one in Hollywood, 1924

Nityanandam and Krishna, place unknown, 1925

Raja and Krishna at Arya Vihara, 1925

Mrs Besant and Krishna at Ommen, c. *1930*

Krishna in London c. *1929*

Krishna, Charles Leadbeater and Mrs Besant at Adyar in the late 1920s

Raja, Radha and Krishna in
Los Angeles, 1932

Radha, Raja and Rosalind in Hollywood, 1934

Krishna, Rosalind and Radha at Point Lobos, 1934

Krishna and Rosalind at Sarobia, 1935

Krishna, Rosalind and Robert Logan at Sarobia, 1935

Radha and cousin David,
c. *1936*

Rosalind and Radha in
Hollywood, 1936

Radha and Jinarajadasa at
Ojai, 1934

Sarobia, 1937: (ABOVE LEFT) *Sara Logan, Rosalind and Radha;* (ABOVE RIGHT) *Raja, Radha and Rosalind;* (BELOW) *Krishna addressing a gathering*

Krishna with Robert Logan at Sarobia, 1937

Arya Vihara, 1939: Radha and Rosalind with Jerry-bo

At Lady Berkeley's villa in Santa Barbara, 1939: (ABOVE LEFT) *Radha and Krishna;* (ABOVE RIGHT) *with Maria Huxley;* (BELOW) *Raja and Radha*

Life with the animals at Ojai, 1938—40

The war years at Arya Vihara
photographed by Beatrice
Wood: (ABOVE LEFT) Krishna;
(ABOVE RIGHT) Rosalind with
Tina; (BELOW) Willie
Weidemann and Krishna

Krishna in 1946 after his long illness

Krishna and Aldous Huxley at Wrightwood, 1947

(FROM LEFT TO RIGHT) *Aldous Huxley with Radha's dog, Desdemona, Krishna, Igor and Vera Stravinsky, Maria Huxley, and Radha, 1949*

Lili Kraus

Krishna at Point Lobos in 1953 with Coco, baby Tinka and Radha

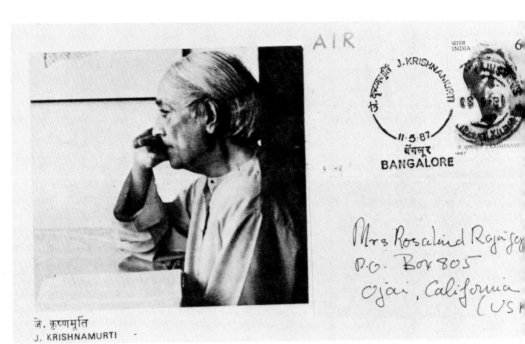

Krishna, from an Indian first-day cover

16

Sages and Shadows

Although Krinsh was certainly the magnet that attracted people to our lives, there were a few, like Sara and Robert, who turned their main focus on Rosalind. Robert was like a father to her and did much to replace her own father whom she had left when she was sixteen. Much as Sara loved and admired Raja and Krishna, my mother remembers her saying that women should not live in dependency on men and that she was going to see to it that some day Rosalind would have financial independence. At the time Rosalind paid no attention to these comments. Years later she would understand the seriousness of Sara's intentions. Before she died, Sara asked Robert to honour in his will her wish that Rosalind would inherit a sizeable portion of their estate. They both had faith that she would do something worthwhile with her life, independent of Krishna or Raja.

Sara built an apartment for Rosalind on the second floor of Arya Vihara. She thought Raja's rheumatism would improve if he slept on an upper level, but her main purpose was to provide them with more privacy than the downstairs of Arya Vihara afforded. Sara did not realize that Raja and Rosalind were living separate marital lives and she certainly did not realize that the apartment with its front and rear outside staircases would grant Krishna even greater opportunity to visit Rosalind in Raja's absences from Ojai. Nor did I ever mention to anyone those frequent early mornings when from my bedroom window I saw Krinsh, in the white raw silk nightshirts that my mother made for him, creeping up the stairs with a flower in his hand. Those were their times together, early mornings and sometimes late evenings, after I was supposed to be safely tucked away in bed.

In the summer of 1937 my mother and I went east, first to the Logan's summer place in Winter Harbor and then to Sarobia to meet my father and Krinsh, who were arriving from Europe.

The Winter Harbor house was a large, typical New England summer house. There was a sloping green lawn to the bluff above the rocky beach. We had blueberries every morning for breakfast, freshly picked from the surrounding woods. My mother and Sara spent hours putting together puzzles or playing chess while I roamed about the gardens, often following Mr Robbie doing those chores he so assiduously set for himself.

The Logans believed in self-sufficiency and they ran a household with minimal servants. Guests washed their own dishes and helped with the cooking; even if they were European princesses, of whom there was one in the house that summer. I cannot remember why she was there for no one seemed to know her very well, but the Logans were already beginning their era of hospitality to the displaced fugitives of fascism. This particular Princess was pretty but in my six year old's opinion, spoiled. She had no idea how to wait on herself. She and my mother played tennis together while I sat on the sidelines and struck up a friendship with an elderly gentleman who later insisted my mother bring me to tea in his Park Avenue apartment.

Sara and Robert were abruptly called away to California by a crisis in their daughter Deborah's life. The Princess took advantage of our hosts' absence to insist that my mother and I move out of the room Sara had assigned us. She claimed it was more suitable for her. My mother complied without hesitation for her nature was such that she never felt comfortable with anything that anyone else coveted, but Sara was indignant when she later found out.

The Logans' tragedy centred around Deborah, their only child. Eighteen years before, when she was not quite twenty years old, Deborah had fallen under the influence of a doctor of sorts, a hypnotist who had induced Deborah to marry him and adopt his daughter, presumably in the hope of acquiring the Logan fortune. This man had had two previous wives, and Deborah claimed the last wife had died an unnatural death. She told Sara that she had even been forced to help dispose of the dismembered body, but the whole story was so improbable and grisly, so alien to everything in their lives, lives which tolerated no form of killing – even a fly – that Sara could not decide whether Deborah was hallucinating or had been hypnotized by her husband in order to bring her under his control. If the story were true she knew that to open an inquiry would create a horrible scandal and do worse damage to Deborah. She was afraid to tell Robert, fearing that his pacifism might be overridden by his anger against a man who had so used his daughter. The worst of all for Sara to bear was that it was her own interest in this doctor's unorthodox medicine that had led to his meeting Deborah and inducing her away from her parents to California. It is an indication of her love and confidence in Rosalind that she told her alone the details of this story. Rosalind bore the burden of that terrible secret in silence for over forty years. Sara and Robert succeeded finally in rescuing Deborah from the clutches of this man, only to find her so badly damaged that they despaired of her ever recovering from the mental breakdown which she suffered that summer.

In the midst of her tribulations Sara took the time to write to Rosalind just after she arrived in California.

Fri. P. M., July 30th, 1937

Dear Rosie,

I do hope you are having breakfast in bed and resting, a real rest – and some tennis . . . I saw Deborah twice! It is very terrible! I cannot be sure she knew me. Got Dr White [Deborah's husband] to sign for her at a private hospital. She is to see no one and they do not want her to even have me go in to see her but of course I simply had to . . . They say it is a kind of mental case that never gets well or kills – she is strong physically. If I could only be with her I feel it might help at some offhand moment, but, as Rob says the Doctor is very fine, is tremendously interested in the case and White's queer ways and that she for the 1st time in all these years is out of his house and influence. That is some hope that she might at least be free of his pull . . . The Doctor says this phase lasts from three weeks to four months and the following stage of reaction and depression indefinite time in years – but I never give up and yet look for nothing to take refuge in. Without last year at Ommen I assure you I could not have witnessed this corner of the vortex with such quiet and calm . . .

Of course, I understood very little of this at the time but put together bits and pieces of adult conversation later. A great part of my diversion as a child was listening in on adult conversations. We seemed to be surrounded by people who had intense and often interesting problems and I very early found out that if I remained as 'quiet as a mouse' as I was often told to and never interrupted, my presence was overlooked. I often overheard much more than anyone intended I should.

At the end of that summer, Krinsh and both my parents and I prepared to drive across country in our new Lincoln Zephyr, which they had bought at factory price for only nine hundred dollars. It was silver-green with two doors, one wide front seat for the three adults and a small rear seat for me.

149

Sara gave us a picnic basket with red and white plastic dishes and cutlery to match, all of such good quality that I still have them. Motels were just beginning to sprout up around the country, not the luxurious type of today but sparsely furnished individual bungalows. We always picnicked on the road for lunch. It being still in the Depression, we were often joined by a hobo, to whom my mother would offer at least a hard-boiled egg, cooked on a camping stove in the motel, before setting off each morning.

I cannot imagine how we all survived that trip, cooped up for weeks in a one and a half seat car. I do not remember it as a happy time but neither do I remember any particular 'scenes'. It was an unusual thing for all of them to be doing. They never took long journeys for the fun of it and perhaps this came close enough to a pleasure trip for them to do their best to behave toward each other as well as they could. It was the first time I was acutely conscious that when others weren't around all three of them at once were too many. Everything was more pleasant when they came in twos.

Krinsh wrote a thorough report to Mr Robbie about the trip shortly after we arrived back in Ojai, giving all the technical details about the car, its fuel consumption, powers of acceleration in the mountains, and the fact that he gave it a daily bath all across the country. He was quite ecstatic about that car. When it was his turn to drive he took off at alarming speed. Once, that is, that the engine had been perfectly broken in according to a timetable he had established.

Krinsh prided himself on having been taught to drive by Miss Dodge and Lady De La Warr's chauffeur in their new Rolls-Royce. In those days, the Rolls-Royce Company provided a specially trained chauffeur with the automobile. Krinsh learned a system of driving that was supposed to save the brakes by always rolling to a slow stop, never riding the clutch, varying the engine speed every ten minutes and above all 'watching out for the *other* fool'. This sounds sensible when combined with moderate speeds which were essential on English country roads, but it also presupposes a limit on speed with which Krinsh did not bother. There are some people who are thankful to be alive in spite of having ridden with him at the wheel. My mother, on the other hand, prided herself on having driven a car from the age of twelve and a motor-boat before that. Her grandfather was the first man in Buffalo to own an automobile. It was she who taught my father to drive, though it was his bad luck on one of his first lessons in Britain to rear-end a Scotsman and knock off his fuel tank. Both Krinsh and my mother frequently expressed slightly scornful criticism of Raja's driving.

Even my father, however, had fewer accidents and near accidents than did Krinsh. There was also the problem of car sickness from which my mother and I suffered. Cutting corners and keeping a steady foot on the accelerator was essential, which Krinsh did well enough but my father tended toward jerkiness, abrupt stops and swishing corners. All this did not lead to a completely harmonious three-thousand-mile drive.

The sight I found most impressive was the Carlsbad Caverns. Having been read *Tom Sawyer* and *Huckleberry Finn* by Mr Robbie that summer, caves held for me a graphic interest. Krinsh, on the other hand, was not the least impressed by the caverns and he wrote to Mr Robbie saying he greatly preferred Boulder Dam. Perhaps, as he himself suggested, my adults were just tired the day we saw Carlsbad, for that was uncharacteristic of Krinsh, who was always extolling the works of nature over those of man. Perhaps he was impressed by the fact that an astute guard at the dam sensed among us an important personage. However unlikely it might be that he knew exactly who Krinsh was, he gave us an exclusive private tour. For some reason long forgotten we skipped the Grand Canyon altogether. Of course they had all seen it before I was born.

Mr Robbie took the trouble to write to me en route. From then on he wrote me weekly letters whenever we were separated.

Miss Radha Rajagopal,   *October 21, 1937*
Hotel Paso del Norte,
El Paso, Texas
Dear Srog, [Mr Robbie's nickname for me after my mispronunciation of frog]
   I wonder how the Zeppelin is flying along and whether you have heard any srogs along the wayside saying 'Brek-ek-ek-ek Co-ax Co-ax'.
   We have been missing you all very much even Pack Wack [his big fat cat] has been asking where his scroggy friend has disappeared, and the wind says it is hardly worth blowing over Sarobia when there are no badminton birds to blow about.
   I enclose cards for Krinch and Daddy.
                         Much love from,
                                   MR ROBBIE

We had been invited to visit Frieda Lawrence in Taos, New Mexico. Frieda had been at Arya Vihara the year before and wrote to Rosalind just before we started out from Sarobia.

Kiowa Ranch, San Cristobal, N.M.   *12 Oct, 37*
Dear Rosalind,

We are looking forward to your coming, come as soon as you can because of the weather. You know we are so high and you might find snow. Tell me if you would all like to meet people or rather have a rest – It has been so very lovely, the mountains superb, with aspens turning yellow and the red oak and dark pines.

So we will look for you about the 26th. I won't forget you are vegetarians.

With kindest regards,

FRIEDA L

(and from me Angelino)

Anyone who knows Frieda's story will of course recognize Angelino as her lover at that time and later as her husband; D. H. Lawrence had died seven years before.

I was delighted to be in a private house once more after the weeks in cramped motel rooms, eating food cooked on a camping stove. We were given a guest cottage and could make our own breakfasts but ate the other meals with Frieda. She was plump and red-headed and very warm toward us all and I felt comfortable among the assorted animals, including a small pig, who came and went freely through the house. I soon gravitated toward the barn, where I found Angelino milking the cow. He was a large man who laughed easily, too easily. I disliked him at once, an unusual reaction in me. I could not understand his remarks as he leaned his head on the cow's stomach and yanked at her teats, nor can I remember them now but I felt uncomfortable and retreated in silence back to my family.

In a letter to a friend in Europe, Maria Huxley beautifully described Frieda's household and Taos. The Huxleys, whom we had not yet met, but would shortly after our return to California, had just left there a month before we arrived.

This place, I mean Taos, 20 miles off and where we never go, is a nest of scandal and quarrels. Frieda has been, and still is so affectionate and generous and warm-hearted that I do not want anything to come back to her which could be misinterpreted . . . the quarrels with her and Mabel Luhan who wanted to steal Lawrence's ashes from a childish little chapel Frieda built over them here . . . The desert . . . begins four miles from us . . . pink on the barren soil, grey with the sage-brush, bright green in the irrigated oasis and the black cracks which are the turning banks of the Rio Grande . . .

Sages and Shadows

Frieda's life is extraordinary. She lives in such a primitive way that we can hardly understand it. Angiolino built her a concrete house . . . and the sitting-room is hung by all Lawrence's pictures. But the heart of the house is a large kitchen which has only a wooden range which heats, or rather tepids, a little bath water and which must be lit for every cup of tea. The easiness might be called messiness, the milk which comes . . . from a pretty Jersey cow is around in all forms of creams, and butters, and sour creams, and milks and what not . . . there are also the pig-bowl and the cat-bowl and the dog-bowl; many things to horrify me and shock me; yet she is essentially clean if you can imagine that; perhaps because she is a blonde. My greatest horror is to be asked to meals; it is then taken for granted that I do the washing up – I arrive with my rubber gloves – but the mess is such that if there were a heaven I deserve a bit of it for every washing up I do. Meanwhile there she sits, talking of Montaigne or Buddha or Mabel Dodge [Luhan] . . .

Frieda is continually visited out of the blue by vague friends or strangers; they want to see Mrs. D. H. Lawrence, and though she complains she lets them. Then they bring her cakes and think they have paid her for her trouble.[1]

(The chapel was still there when in 1972 my husband and I and our children visited the ranch, now run by the University of New Mexico as a writers' retreat. Lawrence's ashes are in a simple urn inside. Outside, under a marble slab inscribed with her coat of arms and full German title of Baroness von Richthofen, lies Frieda.)

The affront to Maria's fastidiousness by Frieda's housekeeping would have been fully shared by the two Brahmin men in her wake if they had been exposed to it. But Rosalind was adept at establishing, even at the expense of tact, the standard of cleanliness they would expect.

That autumn, soon after our return to California, we met Aldous and Maria Huxley, who were renting a small apartment near my grandmother's Gower street house.

Maria, like Sara, immediately saw Rosalind for herself, apart from her connection with Krishna and Raja, and loved her for herself. She also fully understood the complications of life with a 'great man'. She admired Rosalind's skills and practicality and there was soon much sharing and pooling of their respective abilities.

In spite of her closeness to Sara Rosalind didn't confide in her that most essential part of her life – her relationship with Krishna. It is hard, looking back, to believe that this profound and yet worldly woman would not have recognized exactly what was going on. Perhaps she did but was far too sensitive to intrude in an area of Rosalind's life where she had not been invited.

Sara never failed to take time to write to Rosalind and to stay in close touch with her. Sometimes she wrote every day. She wrote the following letter on 11 January 1938 a couple of months after our drive across America. She had evidently witnessed some incidents while they were still at Sarobia.

> I have thought much of your problems as they are or as I imagine them to be, personally I feel we cannot do more than accept people, as they are; and let them be themselves – and no matter how close, let them find with others what we cannot give them. Every man needs spoiling by some one, he must think well of himself at any price. The more he doubts his ability to stand alone, the more he will protest it. A man, like a woman, does not so much want a fuss made over them, as much as to feel their wives or husbands do not belittle them, hurt pride is often at the secret of many otherwise congenial friendships. Marriage or love as it is known is supposed to give no cause for such a state, so people look out for this, independence from it as a sign of weakness in the one and insult to the other – marriage be damned as it is expected to be!! It takes a great indifference in both male and female, as to what other people think to get the happy companionship that joint interests affords. It's seldom what the husband thinks of the wife or the wife of the husband that causes the trouble, but the wonder of the man if he is made to seem small in the eyes of the world or the wonder of the woman if she is supposed not able to hold the affections of her husband! Pride or fear of pity or of censure wrecks many a pleasant enough hand in hand fight through life. Why a husband and wife feel privileged to tell each other what they think of each other I do not know: yet it is not a thing that can be hidden, it is made quite real by words about it yet nothing is as hopeless as being put into a pigeon hole, and watched as soon as one tries to sneak out unobserved. I hope Raja has a car of his own, and can get someone to ride with him who thinks his driving, as well as everything else he does, is perfect – This will help a lot. No doubt it's stupid to get married just as stupid to get unmarried . . .

Whatever else it may have been that set off this treatise on marriage from Sara, it is certain that during the few weeks we were all at Sarobia after buying the Zephyr she would have witnessed the criticism of his driving that Raja suffered from both Rosalind and Krishna. She obviously recognized that Rosalind and Raja's marriage had difficulties; both Sara and Robert had had love affairs in the course of their marriage without destroying that part of their relationship they both most valued – companionship and love based on a deep mutual respect. She would have understood a love affair in another's marriage if it was based on honest understanding between the two married partners. She would not have understood hypocrisy.

Sara's troubles with Deborah continued. She had brought her daughter home to Sarobia after eighteen years of estrangement. Although Deborah's health improved remarkably under her mother's care, irreparable damage had been done to her. In her frequent letters to Rosalind, Sara expressed her depressed as well as her happier moments.

Dear Rosie . . .

. . . no doubt happier days have been and may be for me and others, there is no sense of comparison present, it simply seems enough that the damp heat of yesterday, broken by a thunderstorm in the evening has dramatically and marvelously made way for the blissful happy air of today. New-cut grass, June roses, fragrant honeysuckle fill the air.

This AM Rob neat and dapper with the kerchief border protruding just the proper degree from the breast pocket, took himself to lunch and golf at the country club and I was conscious of a greater serenity and happiness than I felt he had before this last trip west. It has left him happier, freer, something lifted. Perhaps to me it has also done something but not of the nature my friends and family evidently would feel themselves or expect me to feel – when they say 'How happy you must be to have your daughter with you' but I have no sense of accomplishment . . . The burden and anxiety of her immediate danger are, in a way over, but my heart perhaps always holds too much of the useless refrain. It's 'heavy with the world's . . . woe', as the Buddha said in some special moment of more depression than happy compassion: if compassion can be happy! Out of the frying pan into the fire! What frying pan and what fire! who can say – but surely some frying pan and some fire. It needs must be so, until we are enlightened and out of bondage to illusion and love of power. How much of a . . . revelation this lasting assurance of the blissful state may be; how much a weary plodding through life and death, how much a clearing of the atmosphere created by the two great beasts of mind and body that the inner man may make a clear free get away, I do not know. Surely the rose seems to have no battle with illusion to attain its fullness. As we are nature's products only to this point and here the real self-conscious hassle begins; to what indeed can we look for help . . . the warmth of the sun is a factor in the opening of the rose, perhaps Krishnaji could if I did not create my own shade aid me . . . In short how, ere it is too late for this body are we to handle our rudders so the ship rides free with the wind? A mere man may teach me to steer a boat, no one may teach me to handle the vessel of myself. Deborah has a headache and is, I hope, asleep. At times I am overcome by her clear thinking and dynamic energy. I am so glad you feel drawn to her. She is most balanced and happy by nature. It seems we are to constantly be reminded that action comes from some sort of illusion; things, even tragedies, heartbreaks, narrow escape from being murdered or worse still from murdering, looked at in the light of an old familiar lamp or under a tree of our youthful days with one we love, all suddenly is as if it had not been . . . and we wonder that such days of strife were of such import at the time. Yesterday as Deborah put on a hat she had got 18 years ago, she recalled the feel of its soft velvet that she had felt the day she wore it first. 'Mother how is it, he might have killed me! There was a moment I would have gladly killed him, yet the touch of this velvet and all is suddenly as if it had not been and life is back where it was 18 years ago.'

Right or wrong I assured; life is indeed dangerous, perhaps our consciousness needs must know the dangers that our own latent fears and impulses create. They lie near the surface and so we learn wisdom and compassion, caution and the equality of our likeness to those about us . . . It is all intensely, momentarily interesting if we can be keen to our reactions.

In this last year of her life Sara's letters indicate that she suffered often from depressing thoughts. World events in that year were giving cause for depression as many of those Americans travelling abroad were to find. Sara wrote her feelings to Rosalind on 19 June 1938 about a friend's report from Europe just before she herself was to leave for the Ommen camp with Deborah:

when people get to the sailing port . . . one doctor to every 8000 people . . . no money to just sit by till their turn – the hope of leaving. The fear of not getting away and hunger besides. A few men so cruel to so many, and the whole world helpless to help. It's too much to contemplate. It makes one really ill and heartsick. Yet history repeats itself and will ever do so . . . What is to become of the world and its poor stupid and horror loving people as well. There can be no end to it all.

On 3 August 1938, Sara began a sixty-page diary letter for Rosalind, who would not be at the Ommen Camp that year; this would be the last camp ever held there. Sara's diary is quoted in part here as it gives a vivid account of the effect of Krishna's talks on one perceptive individual, struggling with intense personal problems, while adjusting to and trying to help a daughter who had been lost to her for eighteen years. Sara was neither a devotee nor a sentimentalist. She found much personal help in Krishna's words and recognized that what Krishna gave to his audience often went beyond words. He transmitted a highly charged energy that could awaken within the individual a capacity to confront the depths of his being. Not everyone responded to this force. Some felt it, then turned it back into an adulation of Krishna rather than applying it to themselves. Some complained that he offered neither method nor guidance, leaving them to struggle alone. 'Those', he would say, 'completely missed the point.' Krishna seems to have struck a chord that was already well-tuned in Sara. She listened to him in her own independent way.

Aug. 4

K. opened his talk without preliminaries saying words were futile – and through them it was difficult to understand another. He or we could not meet in a friendly basis if we looked upon him as a teacher and he could not meet or understand those here with isms or propaganda to expound . . . It would be a waste of his time to discuss these things – please leave all our propaganda and problems behind. Few are living wholly in their great and burning desire to live or act after their own manner and fullness. We must find out what we really are and live it in action. To find this out we must catch ourselves in the act with intelligent choiceless awareness . . . He spoke of the necessity of great love of morality –

. . . I feel tired, and as if since 1934 there was nothing to be done about anything. From then on though anxious about Deborah, felt it was Rob's job to carry on, since for me it seems finished which is absurd. Nothing is ever finished . . . but as if this life and birth were done; and held for me in this body no more interest and no desire for rebirth. Perhaps if I felt I could get over with this wheel here and now I might find renewed effort possible – but my only hope of any degree of enlightenment must now come not through action, but through giving up – utterly and completely – but this seems as if it must come from some sort of frustration of which I am not aware or hardly conscious – which at my age and after 10 years of studying Krishnaji's books as well as himself and my own reactions a rather futile 10 years of introspection, certainly for me, the more the mind and intellect and desire for knowledge enter into it all the more stranded I become and farther from that deeper inner happiness of unobstructed flow of life. Deborah and I were recalling together K's talk. It seemed to mean more to her than to me. She is more attentive to words, more literal – she says perhaps I am looking at too many angles and depths and degrees of meaning as he talks and so miss much of what he is saying which was interesting in the light of Amma [Mrs. Besant] saying she questions instead of listening, and then questioning.

To Deborah K's reference to lying fallow was an inspiration, that it was good and necessary. To me plowing, sowing, reaping and lying fallow were all a weary process with nothing of the spirit. She thought I argued myself into pessimism which she felt was really foreign to me . . . I do not know. Glad at least to see she lives fully in the minute.

Frid. Aug 5

Met Rajagopal. He is anxious for fear Deborah will get involved in some unfortunate acquaintance and situation. He is very wise – she certainly seems anxious to make contacts why I do not know and surprisingly interested in people's names and getting them placed in some way in connection with us. Several things often make me feel she is still W's [Dr White, Deborah's ex-husband] agent in some way – but this is her, not my affair. Raja said he was trying to save me any more unhappy situations through her and I should keep an eye on her but I really cannot though am only too glad to be with her . . . Raja is so often right I am glad of his warning of not too much freedom for her here where he feels there are many undesirable 'pick-up' possibilities for her. It would be only too natural if she should in her happiness at being free from White want to go on some bat or have some burst of self-assurance and self expression with those about her.

Aug 6th

Last night I thought much about my selfishness, in being so much alone – the petty annoyances of the constant 'excuse me's' 'thank you's'; tried to discover why the habit of being alone should result in a sort of frustration . . . Finally after a refreshing nap to find myself much happier, freer and willing to have no time to myself at all. This is something. Now I must understand why it is that having someone stand over one, gesticulating, dynamic, repeating again and again the same thought, explanation, narrative about things or people one is not interested in, makes me embarrassed and nervous. I shall call on my affection and realize I should be or am interested in what interests her. Its all great fun and I am really so happy to have her here with me, and she so dear, and grateful for all that life brings her. It is good for me to learn from her and how another's mind works. I find mine stops! I am impatient of ways to ends when perhaps only the ways really matter.

This A. M. Krishnaji spoke so wonderfully, so clearly and it seemed to me for the first time hopefully of our ultimate fulfillment of happiness and reality. He spoke of nationalism and internationalism and asked us to think upon it deeply – our unfriendliness in camp over national, political, financial or social barriers.

'We may all, you and I, all be bombarded and killed. So the burning question is political and national. What are we going to do about it? Nationalism results from a habit, a prejudice, from egotism, or belief, in God being on our side. This has been led up to by the habit in meditation. Those who meditate rely on a habit to get them somewhere – a habit is stagnation, will never lead to truth. If you meditate find out why you meditate. Those who do not had also better find out why they don't. I do not say I am for or against meditation . . .

I would suggest that for the next twenty-four hours those who were in the habit of meditating give it up for just that time. To think these problems over, not to gossip to visit but to alone think, deeply – after the conflict, the struggle, in the following calm might come the miracle fulfillment, not to look for it or expect it, but it lay if at all in the silence after the struggle.'

Yesterday then, he meant as Deborah thought – It might come only in the lying fallow after the tilling. I went too far in the idea, feeling discouraged that after the lying fallow there was again only the poor farmer preparing for his next job.

So I am left as one who does not meditate. Deborah thought it might imply it would be good for those who did not, to try – I am not sure of this . . . I had meditated and repeated mantrams and taken part in vocal incantations, and the result was a power, as of another using me – my voice was resonant, full of assurance, the power was strong though not ungentle like a prayer answered and it made me feel perhaps that I was to use it for something and I wished to do nothing with it, not to be a leader, a power in the E.S. service through which it came . . . I did not believe in rituals, people got foolish – sanctimonious about them . . . I had asked for power and it had come. It was wonderful but it alarmed me so I had given up meditation but not quiet thought; concentration; which I think more safe, intelligent and not, a retreat, or what K. might call an escape.

What was extraordinary about Sara is that, having felt this 'power', she preferred to relinquish it, unlike so many who would use such an experience to promote their own spiritual importance.

Aug 10

Deborah seems to be making friends with many people, she seems quieter, less jerky and dynamic, if not happier – more thoughtful.

Today K said one must be 'as spontaneous in fear, as in love'. In an earthquake or a calamity when there is no escape something surely happens – only the real is left to us.

I feel that what K is talking about is much simpler than all this discussion, but suppose I am not simple enough . . . I sometimes feel this awareness is like sorting buttons or carding wool. It takes constant diligence . . . K thinks to keep notes . . . or to write to friends is to keep one's self in one's own ideas and nitches – certainly it often is to seem wiser than we are or to want to share, or show off but about the notes I write am not yet sure if they hurt or help so will have to think that out – am sure I shall never re-read them so perhaps its a waste of time to write. By putting reactions down he may feel we crystalize them and refer to them when we once having eliminated something need surely not go back to it. I notice when he writes a letter or poem he does not make many comparisons – just the bird singing.

Aug 12

I feel deeply happy like the silent currents at the bottom of the sea and if my mind and attention is drawn to the surface I do not leave my depths but bring it to the surface as things happen. I cannot solve problems but when alone am happy with the flow or stillness about me in which one loses ones self without desire to do so. It is indeed spontaneous and soon as I find my mind trying to analyze it it goes . . .

I can see that all this writing is indeed quite useless, a waste of time, for to put on paper what one gets out of camp is not a help or the real thing.

I met K at the mechanic shop where he had his tire pumped up. He looked a bit worried or anxious or tired, asked him if he was tired he said no and it occurred to me there might be many people he had tried to help and certainly did not – some a little but none enough and among them Rosie [Rosalind] I thought and I have been anxious for her health for a long time. In 1936 would not say what the trouble was which made me feel it was really serious with her and I felt at Ojai K. tried to keep her quiet, unexcited, not overtired, early to bed, so did not go to play chess in P.M. as she wanted to do for fear it would keep her up and create a sense of competition which I do not care about if it ever comes to that. Lay awake a long time last night wondering if D. [Deborah] and I could join Rosie at Ojai and Radha – keep house, D. could cook until Raja came in late October to be with her. He tells me she wants an operation for something – some pain. But I do not think it the appendix as he intimated. It comes too quick and severe to be put off till he arrives as he said he wrote her to do . . .

When she was in Ojai in the spring of 1936, Sara had evidently noticed Rosalind's condition. She did not know the cause, but Krishna, who did know, might well have been wondering here at Ommen, two years later, if Rosalind was again pregnant or had suffered another miscarriage. 'K. paid us a visit. Felt there was something he wanted to talk about – felt anxious about Rosie but asked him nothing about her . . .'

At the end of Camp Sara expressed her wish to come to Rosalind if she were having an operation.

August 22nd, 1938

Dear Rosie,

. . . Rajagopal told me you were contemplating an operation for the appendix or something and he had written you if possible to wait for his arrival in L.A. . . . will you really truly let me know dear Rosie if there is any way or place that Deborah and I could help you or be with you to give you a real rest and look after you a bit, so you can get built up before the operation. We know you enjoy being with us both. This is not the question. The question is if we can be of use before or after Raja arrives. Our idea was we might help with Radha or your mother. Do not want to bother or complicate anything . . . let me know if I can help personally or a bit financially . . .

Always lovingly,

SARA

Whatever had been the matter with Rosalind was set straight by the time Raja returned and no more was said about an operation. Sara did not come to California that autumn. On 13 October 1938 from Sarobia, she wrote her last letter to Rosalind.

> this afternoon I picked a few leaves, glowing in mild golden stillness of an embracing sun and sent them to you. By the time they reach you they will be dry and wrinkled. They are only a forerunner of the promise of the fall. The camp meant much to me. It was a stirring one. At one time in Ojai I was impatient of it all and tried to forget it. I think now my state of health was at bottom of that spell. You were dear and asked me to come while you and K. read, and to share his thoughts with me, and I would have none of it. Impatience got in my way of enjoyment and gentle questioning – what queer creatures we are and how hard to know ourselves. One learns to value these unhappy feelings and long after an impulsive something has cropped up and it is recalled suddenly out of a clear sky and one says, now I know, this shows me what was back of that day.
>
> I am glad you are feeling better. It will not be long as time goes till we are all together again.

Goodnight,

SARA

Sara died six weeks later. Rosalind felt she had not fully appreciated her friendship with Sara until after her death. She had not expected this loss to be such a blow to her. They had shared so many attitudes and so many interests; building, puzzles, chess, painting. It was only when Sara was gone that Rosalind realized what a tremendous support this deeply affectionate friendship had been.

From then on Robert took up a correspondence with Rosalind which was very regular on his part, though not so on Rosalind's, who always considered herself a poor letter writer.

Dec 8, 1938

Darling Rosalind,
    Your very dear and understanding letter touched me very deeply. I know how dearly you loved Sara.

162

Sages and Shadows

I too felt as you did about her pulling through because she had pulled through several times before but her heart was weak and gave out.

I am quite sure that although she fought gamely to the end her ego had really decided to go on, feeling that when she got Deborah back she had paid off a karmic debt and was free to escape into a larger and truer world and be free of the irksome limitation of her troublesome body.

Deborah was perfectly splendid through the ordeal and the funeral but I am very sorry to tell you the bad news that the strain was too great and she has broken down and is in a nearby hospital after trying to kill herself.

Faithfully,
ROBERT

I too felt Sara's loss deeply. After she was gone Mr Robbie no longer seemed the formidable person to me that he once had been. He was the only person I knew who liked the Sunday comics and when he was in Ojai, I would head up to Saro Vihara right after breakfast on Sunday mornings and spend an hour or two absorbed in two sets of comics. They weren't available at Arya Vihara because, out of frugality, we didn't get a paper at all. Anyway the comics were frowned on for me, but Mr Robbie never gave me away. I think, intellectual though he was, he believed they represented an important sector of American culture as did the radio programmes 'Hopalong Cassidy', the 'Lone Ranger' and 'Charlie McCarthy'.

If he was stern with me for mistreating an animal he could be just as stern with my mother for mispronouncing a word, or eating peanuts in the car or singing a song like 'Mama's little baby likes shortnin' shortnin'', which he could then never get out of his head.

But he could write letters straight to a child's heart, mostly about his or our animals. Once Sara was gone he retreated more and more into this world of animals and he welcomed those who could share it with him. He remained actively involved with the Anti-Vivisection Society, various human rights and animal welfare groups, and the many individuals whom he never turned away in their need.

The autumn, shortly before Sara's death, Blanche Matthias had invited us to a dinner she was giving in the Town House Hotel in Los Angeles for the famous Indian dancer Udai Shankar. The dinner followed his performance and the dessert, a sculptured palace in different flavours of exotic ice-cream, regrettably made much more of an impression on me than the dancer; even though the ice-cream never thawed enough for us to eat it.

A few weeks after this memorable evening, Rosalind wrote:

Dec 12, 1938

Dear Blanche,

It was so nice to have your letter and thank you also for the enclosed letter from Shankar.

It was a great shock to hear from Mr Logan that Mrs Logan has passed away. You know how fond we were of each other and her passing leaves me with a great sense of loss. I did not know I felt so deeply for her and I was unprepared for anything like this to happen to her . . .

When next I see you I want very much to discuss with you about taking Radha to Shankar's new school. Raja is never very keen about my taking Radha and living in India as he says the climate is so bad but I want to very much.

This letter is characteristic of my mother who could turn in a sentence from her grief and shock back toward her zest for life. Yet she felt sorrow intensely. I have seen it often in her face, her blue eyes with their innocence fill with silent tears as she bit her lip and gazed away out the window. Then it would pass – brightness would return. My father attributed this changeableness to her being a Gemini – an explanation that she disliked.

Raja had long ago lost any desire to live in India; he returned only because he had to accompany Krishna and to see his mother. At that moment he was also pessimistic about the future of the world and thought it sensible for us all to remain together in Ojai.

But Rosalind was restless. She had missed the past two summer camps in Ommen. And Sara's death had left a great gap in her life. My father usually seemed unaware of or unconcerned with the daily routine of our lives and we saw him at most for dinner. But sometimes he was alert to a particular discontent and then made an effort to be more of a companion – even to the extent of walking with us. There was a steep climb behind Arya Vihara called Twin Peaks. One day my parents and I did the four miles to top. Such occasions of my father's companionship were rare enough that I remember each distinctly.

On 20 June 1939, came another shock from Mr Robbie. It was written coincidentally on my mother's birthday.

Sages and Shadows

Dearest Rozzie,

Deborah was buried today. She eluded the nurses and hanged herself Sunday night just when the doctors were feeling much encouraged about her recovery.

The last few times I saw her she seemed so completely normal and clear thinking that I began to think she might be able to shake off this obsession of self-destruction and come back to Sarobia . . . However I never really counted on her recovery for I felt the real damage had been done years ago and that Sara's death only brought on an acute attack. The tragedy really occurred twenty years ago when she fell into Dr White's clutches and it is better to have her gone than to have her spend her life in confinement and under a cloud of depression and fear.

Robert had always claimed not to enjoy babies or very small children but after two such terrible losses in one year, which he bore with outward stoicism, he adopted both my mother and me as his closest family.

I should like very much to have a picture of you and a picture of Radha or one of you both if you have no separate ones. If you haven't had one taken with Radha you should do so before she begins to shoot up and get gawky . . .

I miss you both very much for you are both close to my heart.

Affectionately,

ROBERT

Because of the war in Europe the Berkeleys could not make their annual trips to Santa Barbara and in 1939 Molly had offered her 'little cottage' to us more or less indefinitely. It was seldom that my father came over. That summer he went on his own to Europe, leaving my mother and Krinsh to enjoy Molly's offer. Molly's house was a castle to me. I delighted in the silver wallpaper in the master bedroom and the sunken black marble tub. There were servants' quarters and lovely grounds that came complete with an Italian gardener. His lunch, consisting of a raw egg, carefully pierced at either end, sucked out of its shell, and gulped down with his homemade rootbeer, fascinated me.

At first Rosalind had been appalled by the size of the house and decided to decline Molly's offer, but Maria Huxley loved it as it was very Italian in design and situation. She persuaded Rosalind to accept the house and showed her how to close off much of it and thus cut down on the upkeep.

165

Mr Robbie, who even through tragedy, had not lost his light touch wrote:

August 29, 1939

Dearest Rozzie,

I am so glad you and Krinsh are roughing it so successfully in Lady Berkeley's little shack! I should love to be there with you.

I wonder if you could send me the negatives of three of the snap shots you sent me so I could have them enlarged?

One is the picture of you sitting on the railing and looking a good deal like a young girl graduate dreaming of Clark Gable.

The second is of Radha and Krinsh . . . and the third is of Radha, you and Beato . . .

We had many visitors, among them Jinarajadasa and the Huxleys, who came quite often, and sometimes brought their friend, Bertrand Russell. Russell was spending that year in Santa Barbara having, like Aldous Huxley and Christopher Isherwood, decided that England was not just then a fertile place for pacifists. At least he found kindred spirits among us though each of our group had his own very individual approach.

In Santa Barbara Rosalind found she was pregnant for the third time and now, somewhat recklessly, considered having this child. She loved children and had always wanted more. The threatened cancer had not returned and she had more or less forgotten all about it. Being thirty-six, however, she realized the risks of a pregnancy were even greater than before and was therefore partly testing Krishna when she told him her feelings. He certainly made it clear that he didn't think it a very good idea for them to have this baby. He didn't go so far as to put into words that she must have another abortion, but he never needed words to make his wishes clear, and again she got on the bus alone, he solicitous and loving as ever and giving her the same tender care when she returned.

17

A Garden of Peace in a World at War

Krinsh was by far the most rewarding person to play pranks on. The sour lime tree in the orchard bore fruit with juice that looked exactly like the juice of an orange. Whenever I served this to Krinsh for breakfast he gave a wonderful performance of surprise and shock. Putting frogs in his bed met with equal success. The row of acacias leading from Arya Vihara to Pine Cottage was on a route travelled by Krinsh at regular intervals throughout the day. As he was a person of precise routine it was easy for me and my cousin David to know just when to hide in a tree with a small pail of water ready to dump on his head. He never scolded us for inflicting this considerable inconvenience on him and he never failed us in reacting exactly as we hoped he would, sometimes pretending he knew just where we were, holding his large straw hat over his head and running – only to have guessed wrong.

That the peculiarities of our family did not make me in the least self-conscious was due largely to my mother. She had a way of making things turn out for the best, at least where I was concerned. When I mentioned once that all my friends had turkeys at Thanksgiving time and why didn't we, she came home one day with a pair of turkey chicks. It didn't occur to me until much later that this was not the usual way to serve up turkey. By dubious fortune the chicks grew into a male and a female and when the time was right Mrs Turkey devoted a great deal of effort to egg laying. Even the gobbler became distraught by her obsession with sitting on endless batches of eggs. Finally he turned to me for comfort. The huge bird, who weighed as much as I did, would hop on to my lap and put his strange wattled head on my shoulder. Indeed he so loyally attached himself to me that he slept on the railing at the top of the outside stairs by my room and no one dared to go up there without his permission.

When at length his forty offspring grew to full size the whole flock would join us on our afternoon walks up the road toward Thacher School; bad luck for any of the few cars that wanted to use the road at that hour. There were heavy rains that winter and in one storm the bridge at the bottom of the road washed out and the one above us was about to go. If that happened we would be cut off from the village. There was a good deal of concern among the adults; the turkeys and I joined them near the bridge watching the water rampage over the boulders and eat away at the pilings. The turkeys tilted their heads and peered over the bank with amazement.

My friends came to watch our turkeys, whose favourite pastime was tobogganing down the back of the Lincoln Zephyr, which was moulded in one sleek slope from roof to bumper. If Krinsh felt annoyed that his regular polishing and care of the car was futile, he never showed it. After the next Thanksgiving had come and gone our turkeys were still happily running around the garden.

When I was very young I was spared the uglier of life's realities. One summer we departed for our usual stay in Carmel. On our return to Ojai all the young turkeys had gone. I sensed it would be a mistake to insist on knowing what had happened to them. I was told they had gone away as there was no one at home to look after them. It was Willie, of course, who always dealt with that side of life, usually sparing everyone else the details; however, I had heard him grumble occasionally when Mr Robbie complained about the gopher traps. 'You can't have it both ways, if you want a good orchard, you have to get rid of the pests.' Not long after that, coyotes made off with Mrs Turkey and my gobbler. That was my next loss after Sara, and as all children in time must do, I was beginning to learn that grief is an inevitable part of life.

Happily two goslings followed quickly on the disappearance of the turkeys and soon grew into two enormous geese. Eggs began appearing, fortunately from them both, so we were spared the problem of any more gaggles of fowl. The eggs made delicious omelettes and the geese seemed happy not to have to spend their time sitting on them. Instead they became fierce guardians and attacked all those they disliked, though their idea of friend or foe was never clear to us. They particularly disliked ladies in stockings. I am sure there were those who felt they were failing in their spiritual advancement if geese so closely associated with Krinsh picked on them with such outraged contempt.

My grandmother's health was failing in 1939 and Rosalind made frequent trips to Hollywood to help Erma take care of her. Krinsh then became my guardian as well as playmate, seeing that I ate properly, dressed neatly for school, and showed responsibility for the animals. He was always protective and I felt completely safe with him, but David and I often took advantage of his indulgence toward us.

Dearest Mummy,
    The other day Krinsh and Davit and I all took a little walk and found a dead snake on the road. We wanted to take it home. But we did not want to carry that smelly thing all the way home so Krinsh said that he would and when we got home we put the snake in the garage and when Grace came down to bring the paper she saw the snake. Then she began to scrime for she thought it was alive . . .

No doubt it was again Willie who had to dispose of the smelly snake.
But when it came to thought, Krinsh was another person. The gentle easy-going nature disappeared and he could be as fierce with me, if I asked or said something he thought stupid, as he was with his audiences in the Oak Grove or at the small Sunday discussion groups at Arya Vihara. I tried hard not to arouse this side of him for I found it most discomforting and felt tender pity for those poor questioners who recklessly laid themselves open to his scorn and impatience by asking stupid questions. The pained look on his face should have been enough to quell curiosity in the most determined seeker of truth, yet they tried again and again. 'What about life after death, reincarnation, and belief (or disbelief) in an ultimate reality?' Imagine when I came along and asked if he believed in fairies like our Finnish cook did!
'That', he said, 'is like the three blind men and the elephant. The one who feels the trunk claims it is a tree, the one who feels the tail claims it is a rope – '
I don't remember what the third claimed but I got the point and never dared ask the next question foremost in my mind – did he believe in Santa Claus? In time, as I grew older I realized that the very word belief was not a question of *what* but of *why*. Why we wanted to believe anything revealed our own psychology. It was important to observe and experience; ourselves as well as the world around us, without labelling or judging. Neither had Krinsh any regard for an accumulation of facts or knowledge and if I had been solely under his influence I would have considered education a colossal waste of time.
Either for better or worse there were other influences on me. My father taught me to read and write and do arithmetic and geography long before I went to school and I treasured these times with him. Erma came up from Hollywood almost every weekend and she taught me to love books, history and nature. David and I would walk in the Ojai

hills with her and learn the names of all the sages and grasses and rock formations. She had a lovely singing voice; as a little girl I always wanted her to sing me to sleep. Erma said of herself that she was an observer. She never sought to be the centre of any situation but was content to watch without criticism the goings on around her. I have never met anyone who was more of a joy to be with than Ermie. Capable of profound philosophical discussions, she also had a delightful sense of humour. Krinsh called her Sister Erma, a pleasant familiarity that she enjoyed. She was always different in her political views from the rest of my adults, more conservative, and stood up to them very well with her arguments, even against Krinsh, for she knew a considerable amount of history which she had taught herself. Erma, like Sara, was one of those rare women who grow more and more beautiful with age.

And then there were the Huxleys. Aldous and Maria came to Ojai frequently. Even though Aldous was blind in one eye and could see very little in the other, the intensity of his interest made him seem to have keener sight than those of us with perfect vision. He was never overbearing with his knowledge and with childlike delight – like Krinsh – he would squat down on the grass with me and play with the geese (which he named Toddleiums and Susielums, names soon reduced to Toby and Susie by Mr Robbie. (The fact that Toby was a lady goose was disregarded.) I was too young to be in awe of Aldous. I have a clear vision of him, on those weekends, sitting on the lower lawn under the large pine tree, typing a book. First, *After Many a Summer Dies the Swan*, one of whose characters he said was loosely based on my mother, but he would not tell her which, although he seemed surprised that she didn't recognize herself. When he asked her how she liked the book she said, 'Aldous, I'm sorry but I can't honestly say I liked it.' 'Good,' he said, 'it was not supposed to be liked.'

Maria had a little Pomeranian called LouLou that went nearly every-where with her. She was not altogether an animal person, being of the same super-fastidious nature as my father. Yet it was she who one Easter, when we went to tea at their home in Los Angeles, presented me with a baby goat. My mother took this unusual gift in her stride and we took the goat back to Ojai, where eventually it was my job to milk it, although it was never my favourite animal. Aldous shared our family's love for animals and he and Maria had both become vegetarians since their arrival in America. This was a bond between us all, as was an affinity for nature – particularly in Krinsh and Aldous. On their long walks they would observe together, Aldous knowing all the names in Latin and English of flowers, shrubs and butterflies. Krinsh, generally disapproving of labels, but seemingly fascinated by Aldous's ability. Their minds approached nature from such opposite paths and yet they found harmony in each other's company. Aldous quoted a German philosopher who once said the greatest joy is to pick your nose while watching the sunset; Krinsh would say just watch, don't remark on it or try to hold the beauty in your memory or it will be lost instantly.

I loved going to the Huxleys. Something exciting always happened around them. Once a rather mixed group of us including Bertrand Russell with his sons, Aldous and Maria with their son, various Hollywood personalities, plus Krinsh all went for a walk in what was then the back country – the hills of Los Angeles. Signs were posted everywhere against smoking or fires and we were all scrambling illegally under barbed wire fences, crossing private land and defying 'no trespassing' signs. That was all right but then the Russells all started smoking. That was not all right, even with Aldous who understood by then the hazards of our California dry season. But nothing deterred them – until a deputy sheriff appeared with a drawn gun and was ready to arrest the lot of us. 'Sure and I'm Bob Hope,' he said when someone tried to explain that none of us were criminals, in fact 'There is a famous writer, there a famous actress, and there a famous philosopher' – however he let us go after a good scolding about the cigarettes.

Dinners at Arya Vihara, even when we no longer had a cook and my mother had to do everything herself, were formal in comparison to the rest of the day. I can still picture my mother, in a long dress she had made of Indian silk, at one end of the table with Krinsh at the other end in a curved high-backed chair. When Mr Robbie or Aldous was present, she gave up her place to him with Krinsh always sitting at the far end. I never remember my father sitting at either end.

Everyone, even Krinsh, deferred to Mr Robbie. There was something beyond his age that inspired this. After dinner we played poker dice with Mr Robbie's beautiful Chinese eight-sided ivory dice or Monopoly, at which my mother excelled. Even Krinsh played occasionally, always looking a bit pained, but I am sure he would not have played if he had not enjoyed it, for he never did anything he didn't really want to do. In her autobiography, Beato described those evenings and how they struck some people not in our immediate household.

Friends in Hollywood were excited whenever I went to Arya Vihara and asked me to listen carefully to everything Krishnamurti said so that I could report back to them. At first I went to Ojai expecting to hear talk of 'higher' matters, and was surprised to hear conversations that revolved around Rosalind's vegetable garden and the cow . . .

I longed to discuss such things as the third aspect of the Logos, or the coming of the Sixth Root Race, but conversations usually dealt with human affairs and the activities were unpretentious and ordinary. In fact, everyone loved games, especially Monopoly. One night Rosalind, who was a real shark at real estate, got everybody's holdings and even bankrupted Krishnamurti. I sat there paralyzed with boredom when Krishamurti, catching my distant gaze, suddenly threw up his hands and said: 'Beatrice has no idea what this is about and never will. Don't bother with her anymore.' I was enormously relieved to withdraw myself from the encounter, which went on for three more hours![1]

It was seldom that Krinsh became involved enough to stick out a game that long. He most enjoyed games which required no thinking whatsoever. He would never have dreamed of playing chess. Most often, promptly at nine o'clock, he would leave for his cottage after having pulled out and carefully consulted his Patek Philippe.

Mr Robbie had a Patek Philippe also and he and Krinsh compared their watches daily to the second. They tuned in to the government time service in Virginia every Sunday on my father's short-wave radio. I used to wonder how, in our kind of life, the exact time could matter so much. I could see where the second hand was important to Krinsh in his Yoga breathing exercises but not the hour hand. Perhaps perfect punctuality was a remnant of Leadbeater's upbringing.

Although my upbringing seemed strict to me in comparison to that of my friends, this strictness applied more to behaviour than activities. There were relatively few activities in that time and place that could lead to serious trouble. In the eyes of all of my parents, lying was the worse offence – no other misdemeanour could equal it; it was always better to tell the truth and take the consequences. I interpreted this to mean that I did not have to volunteer confessions that were not asked for. Probably the naughtiest thing (and the most dangerous) that David and I and an occasional friend did was to swim in the reservoirs on the adjacent ranches. These wonderful large pools of only slightly slimy green water nestled in the foothills and were used for irrigation. The slippery sloping sides could be treacherous when little wet feet tried to climb back out and drowning was not at all an unlikely possibility. None of these dangers, of course, meant a thing on a hot summer day. One of my earliest disillusionments came when I confided one day to Krinsh –

only after he had crossed his heart and hoped to die if he betrayed our secret – that we had swum in the reservoir, although one at a time so that the other two could help the swimmer out by lowering down a pair of blue jeans to grasp hold of. We had thought this eminently sensible and above criticism, at least from him who appeared to be always on our side in our pranks. He did even then seem to be on our side and offered not even the mildest scolding. I shall never forget my overwhelming sense of betrayal when my mother called me in and confronted me with this escapade, admitting that Krinsh had told her. At that moment I lost my trust in him. I did not wonder then why he had chosen to break his word rather than to take an adult stance and deal with this small matter of discipline himself. He might easily have explained that the situation was far too dangerous to indulge in childish secrets and that he must be sure I would never do it again. I am sure I would have disliked this approach but it would have preserved my confidence in him. I was never to trust him with a secret again or with any small personal problem that arose in pressing urgency in my adolescent years. From then on I went to the person I would always look to in serious moments – my father.

In September 1939 Raja returned from Europe, after stopping in Detroit on the way to California to pick up a sporty Cadillac convertible. His new car was received by Krishna and Rosalind with no more enthusiasm than his driving. Krishna displayed the same contemptuous reaction as in 1924, when Raja turned up with a Buick. Rosalind felt it was inappropriate for Raja to own a Cadillac. As it had been stripped of its paint by a sandstorm while crossing the desert, Raja was persuaded to turn it in for a blue Ford Coupé.

Before leaving Holland Raja had desperately urged his Dutch friends to emigrate to America. He was convinced by what he had seen on a side trip to Germany that as soon as the bumper German crop was harvested, Hitler would turn westward and eventually march on Holland. Only one family, the Vigevenos, believed him and with their three children and valuable art collection, left everything else behind and sailed on what was to be the last boat to America. After the war Annie Vigeveno would learn that forty of her German relatives had died in concentration camps.

I was shielded from most of the horrors of the war. My mother saw to it that I heard none of the news broadcasts that Krinsh and my father listened to every night. Fearing that the future held grave uncertainty, she wanted my childhood to be normal and happy for as long as possible. At the same time I was encouraged to be aware of individual misfortune. There were plenty of people around us who had suffered from the war long before America's involvement.

One day while we were in Hollywood, I was invited by myself to the Ingelmans' for lunch. There I met another guest, a large and very morose French painter called Guy Ignon. I learned that he was a refugee from France who had jumped ship in New York and swum ashore, miraculously making his way to the West Coast. John and Hilda Ingelman were trying to help him get papers and work, for he was practically starving. Gloomy as he was, I took an instant liking to him or perhaps felt it was in the tradition of our family to invite such a person home to tea, which I did. He may have been somewhat surprised at a very formally presented invitation from a nine-year-old girl, but he did show up the next afternoon and my parents took him on. They introduced him to the Vigevenos who, though recent immigrants themselves, had already established a successful art gallery in West Los Angeles. Ignon's fortunes changed from then on and he always looked on me as his little mascot. He painted my portrait, which my mother bought although she never liked it, for Ignon had painted me with enormous eyes holding all the suffering in his own heart and more besides. Even after he married a lovely young wife and had a son, he still looked morose.

In spring 1940 my grandmother Sophia died. She had just undergone a successful gall bladder operation and was recovering well in the hospital when her doctor went off duty and forgot to warn the staff that she was fatally allergic to certain medicines. When these were inadvertently given to her, she instantly declined. With the doctor's permission, Rosalind took her home to Gower Street, where she and Erma nursed her until her death a few weeks later. During this time Aldous and Maria came every morning and sat quietly in the living-room, not expecting to visit or talk but just giving her their quiet support.

Erma describes this time in her diary:

We are really going through a great experience, and Theosophically speaking, Mother must have some pretty good karma since she looks very beautiful in her fading gradually and when the release comes she will have doubtless been separated from all the denser matter and be fully released just as we would all like to be. Dr Norris seems very pleased with Rosalind and me for the way we are taking care of her, since she is kept immaculately clean – and we have established a quiet

174

peace in the house, it is almost like a sanctuary now, so all is well in accordance with our beliefs – if we may call our ideas that.

Erma always managed to balance gracefully between Theosophy and Krinsh.

I was at school in Ojai the day my grandmother died. I remember suddenly putting my head down on my desk and knowing she was gone. When my mother came to tell me I said I already knew. I felt her loss keenly for in her last years my grandmother had put her whole focus on me and given me, among other things, her love of music. After her death Christmastime was never again the special occasion it had been while she was alive, for it was the one time of year she came to Ojai. My mother and I, David, my aunts and Willie would stand around the piano, which my grandmother still played beautifully despite the arthritis in her hands, and would sing Christmas carols. My grandmother sometimes inspired Willie to sing 'The Ode to Joy' from Beethoven's Ninth Symphony, remembered from his youth when he sang in the chorus of the Vienna Opera. Of course, Erma's lovely contralto added much to these occasions. I had heard of the musical evenings in Buffalo and, despite the richness of interests and people in our lives, I still missed being part of a musical world. It was gone completely when my grandmother died. No one could play the piano. Krinsh disliked the very idea of Christmas and made us all quite uncomfortable about it; and all the underlying tensions in our house seemed to be squeezed to the surface by this now empty celebration.

But what Krinsh lacked in Christmas spirit he made up for in small daily rituals; the early morning flowers for my mother and the single beautiful rose, fragrant with morning dew, on her birthdays. He told me one should never smell a flower before it is given in order not to detract anything from it.

Robert, sensing Rosalind's fatigue after Sophia's death, wrote to her in May 1940.

> I am adding $100 to the check so that you and Radha can go to Sequoia or Yosemite or somewhere for a couple of weeks of change and rest; you certainly need it and must have it.
>
> With much love,
>
> ROBERT

My father also recognized how tired she was; in June he took us to Sequoia National Park, in the High Sierras, in his Ford. As we entered the park we saw a bear in the middle of the road. To my surprise and my father's distress, when I offered her a piece of chewing gum, she showed her lack of appreciation by leaving a deep claw mark on the running board. The wild park animals in those days had not yet been spoiled by human beings, although feeding bears was forbidden as we were soon told. This was the beginning of annual summer treks to Sequoia, which continued through the war years.

In 1940 an early autumn gathering had been planned at Sarobia. My mother went with Krinsh, this time leaving me in Ojai as I was about to start attending the private and progressive Ojai Valley School. My father was left alone in charge of me with Mrs Kaarna, our cook. It was a happy time for me, but must have been hard for him.

Shortly after her return to California Rosalind wrote to Blanche:

Dearest Blanche,
Raja looks thin and tired as he is working hard . . . Since being home I have had Radha three weeks in bed with the flu and I have never seen her so ill before. It is the first time I have ever had to call a doctor in for her. Over six hundred people in Ojai had the flu. Krishnaji was in bed a week with a slight bronchial disturbance and I have never seen him in bed for over a day or so before. They are perfectly well again and chipper than ever . . .

Rosalind's comment about Krishna's health is interesting in view of the continual health problems he was said to have in his earlier days. Actually he was very sound in those years and almost never caught colds or flu, suffering only from allergies that caused some minor swelling around his eyes and occasional coughing.

One day while my mother and Krinsh were still at Sarobia I looked out of the dining-room window, which opened on to a long verandah running the full length of the house. There I saw pacing up and down, a giant. I ran to Mrs Kaarna who, since she believed in fairies should know if this were indeed a giant. We called my father who let him in and discovered that he was only the very tall husband of Iris Tree. Iris, along with this husband, Count Frederick Ledebur, her son Christian and the whole Chekhov troupe of actors who came with her to Ojai (many of them pacifists, like Iris), would add a new dimension to our lives, particularly my mother's and mine. They became a part of our lives separate from Krinsh (who always acted slightly disapprovingly of Iris). Although Iris, like the rest of our greater circle, faithfully attended his talks, Krinsh was not the reason that Iris and her crowd had settled in Ojai. They had their own very full and colourful lives and soon started a repertory theatre.

A Garden of Peace in a World at War

Familiar as we were with Hollywood, live theatre was for me a new and wonderful experience. Iris Tree had been born to it. Her father, Sir Herbert Beerbohm Tree was knighted for his greatness as an actor and was particularly famous for his portrayal of Malvolio in *Twelfth Night*. Queen Victoria, as she touched her sword to his shoulder, had repeated the lines from that play: 'Some are born great, some achieve greatness, and some have greatness thrust upon them.' Thanks to the Chekhov players, Ojai would be favoured for many years with first-rate performances of Shakespeare, Chekhov, and many other classic plays. Iris would also give wonderful parties, to which Charlie Chaplin and other movie actors came.

Maria and Aldous had been old friends of Iris's in England and had sent her to see us when she thought of settling in California. In Rosalind's absence, it fell to Raja to help Iris. He had already disrupted his usual routine to take care of me but, as we can see from the following letter, he found time to effectively help Iris. It was typical of him to take considerable pains in such instances, in ways of which few people were ever aware.

Dear Mr Rajagopal,
  It was so kind of you to have taken such trouble about me and the house and I am most grateful –
  Please forgive me for having bothered you with it all when you are so busy with many things. But I loved the place and was relieved to get settled with the boy there – always, having set one's heart, it is hard to turn it away again . . . perhaps Mrs Grey (*sic*) will soften about the dog. It was a great pleasure to have met you and I thank you for all your hospitality and courtesy . . .
                              Yours sincerely,
                                   IRIS TREE

Iris had fine blonde hair cut in a page-boy style which she rinsed with carrot juice to preserve its colour. She had large violet eyes and a mischievous smile. She could mimic anything from an egret to Maria Huxley's charming, heavily inflected Belgian accent. Iris never mimicked people to their faces, as she said that would make them self-conscious. Neither did she ever mimic Krinsh in front of us, although I suspect she often had a good time over that too.

While my father enjoyed her company he found her extremely unfastidious habits distressing. He was once prevailed upon by my mother to give Iris a ride back to Ojai from Los Angeles. She often travelled with an array of animals. He met her on the designated street

177

corner never suspecting, until it was too late, that he would also have to transport a large Nubian goat in the jump seat of his tiny, pristine Ford Coupé.

Iris was a creative cook and willing to serve up delicious vegetarian fare, but her kitchen left something to be desired. Displayed in casual array on the shelves and counters were open cans of cat and dog food, paint, unwashed dishes and Iris's latest poem. At one dinner my father found himself half-way through his spaghetti, which he had been politely swallowing in spite of a bitterness that he could not identify. Suddenly, Iris remarked with a hearty laugh that she must have used linseed oil as she was refinishing her desk and had poured it into the olive oil bottle. It was some time before he could be prevailed upon to return there for dinner.

Iris generously gave me a puppy from the litter of her rare and beautiful white German shepherds. This was to comfort me for the loss of my first dog Jerry-bo, given by Maria and named by Aldous. Jerry-bo had run off and disappeared while we were living in Molly Berkeley's house.

My pets were still a perpetual problem; trips to either Sequoia, Santa Barbara or Hollywood made care of them difficult, although geese, ducks, possums, skunks and chipmunks had all proved easier to handle than a dog. Aldous named the German shepherd puppy Babs (after Elizabeth Barrett Browning). When barely full grown, she ran on to the road in front of Arya Vihara and was hit by a motor-cycle. My screams and her howls of pain brought Krinsh and my mother running. Krinsh then demonstrated his own considerable physical courage and fortitude, for he allowed the poor dog to comfort itself by gnawing on his fist. Babs was taken to the pet hospital and put into a traction harness in the hope of restoring the use of her back legs. As always at such moments, Mr Robbie offered to help.

June 1st, 1941

Dearest Rozzie,

The extra $75 on the enclosed check is to help out . . . with the Sequoia cabins or with the hospital expenses for Babs or whatever you think best.

Please write once in a while and let me know how you all are and about poor Babs and Krishnaji's visa etc, etc. After all, you know, you are about the only 'family' I have left.

Much love,

ROBERT

A Garden of Peace in a World at War

(One of the persistent problems that Raja had throughout the war years was renewing Krishna's visa which he did successfully, though sometimes needing some influential help.)

Krishna, my mother and I went off to Sequoia as usual that summer, as Babs would be confined to the hospital for some time. Iris followed us with her entourage soon after writing this letter:

Ojai   17. VI.41
Dearest Rosalind,
     Late night in our valley, just home. The rivers are drying up and the green is burning, but there are still flowers on my estate and geese in yours. I think of you all with joy, Hollywood was Babylon and 'deletante living' without thought or love.
     Party at Marion Davis in the gold and white Versaille they built for her on sand . . . poor little milkmaid, calling her guests in like cows to the stable, does she care if she is watched by Greuzes and Gainsboroughs? Champagne, Venetian goblets, gossip, decay and furtive terror with the waves beating so near – But who am I to preach, for there I sat enjoying my superior feelings . . . ah well . . . what else? – Earl Carrols vanities. Ninety naked ladies of exactly the same pattern in patriotic brassieres, smiling and kicking in perfect time to a deafening orchestra while the audiance watches and eats and drinks at the same time. So there is progress . . . what else? . . . nothing beautiful or gay? yes, the Gipsies, the fiddle, that forgives everything . . . what an exquisite instrument, what companionship between it and the player and the listener what concentration set free into what ease and joy –
     I have no fiddle and the typewriter wont spell. This is the season of the ants.
     On saturday maybe I shall go look for you in the big trees, bringing Boon and the dogs and so much love. Please don't have gone and don't be disturbed and at the same time don't have forgotten me . . . I hope you like it all and are happy. If you see a cabin please tell it to wait.

Yours,
IRIS

P.S. Babs is a little better.

The arrival of Iris and her family was a welcome change for me. Now instead of playing by myself all morning, reading or feeding chipmunks and deer, I had friends who would take me along on their horseback rides, make lovely camp-fire picnics with Iris's antics and mimics and pantomimes for entertainment. And there was her son Chris (Boon), older than me, but never showing impatience at being trailed after by a pigtailed ten year old.

There were also, each summer, one or more devotees; single ladies who discreetly took a cabin far from us and were content to get one daily glimpse of Krinsh as he walked to the village for the mail. Peeking from under his large straw hat, I could see he knew they were there watching, but he never acknowledged them for he was supposed to be in retreat. For Iris and the Huxleys and certain friends 'retreat' was modified, although no one ever dared be quite as funny or naughty when Krinsh was around, even Iris.

After we had gone back to Ojai, Iris stayed on and wrote:

Goodbye and greetings to you – come back soon to the trees – they are dark now, full of shadows and bears and its a bit homeless in our village of one-night-cabins all about to start down hill –

How is it in the valley and what did you take down with you? – you left a lot up here – food and tasks and many things not on the list –

> Come back to the rivers –
> Come back to the meadows
> they will spring green again,
> leap again – flower, faun,
> waterfall – come
> back to the trees,
> light silence, murmuring bird –
> But wherever you are
> it all goes with you –
> from the tops of the hills – whether you
> come back or not – and
> love from us.

IRIS

When we returned to Ojai we found poor Babs had not improved, but she quietly died before the decision had to be made to put her down.

Before there was any certainty of America entering the war, Rosalind had arranged with a friend in England to send over thirty British orphans whom she planned to care for at the unused Star camp buildings until the war was over. Just how was not totally laid out, but would have been dealt with no doubt with her usual practicality. At the last minute, with the orphans nearly aboard and papers and sailing all arranged for, the British government cancelled the project, deciding the voyage would be more hazardous for the children than remaining in England. Rosalind then diverted her efforts to producing food for our household and a good part of our immediate community of friends and fellow pacifists so, as much as possible, to be self-supporting and no burden on the world's food supply.

Life soon became nothing but heavy work, particularly for my mother, with Krinsh and me helping a great deal. We bought a gentle, tame cow which I named Iolanthe. Willie showed us how to milk her after extracting a promise that he would not have any further involvement. He alone knew what having a cow meant. He also warned and was proved right that it would cost more to feed that one cow than to buy milk in the store. But cost was not the chief object and even Willie did not know then how welcome her butter and cheese would be in the coming period of rationing. There was a plentiful vegetable garden, all planted according to the latest US Department of Agriculture pamphlets. Rosalind had sent for these, along with instructions on cheese making and dairy procedures. We had beehives from which we extracted honey. Every summer the fresh fruit was dried under screens on the roof and sent along with other produce through the agency of CARE to Europe. There was endless canning of tomatoes, beans and fruit. Fortunately for Iolanthe, Krinsh developed an allergy to her for she didn't like the feel of his chronically icy fingers and would turn her head around to glare at him and invariably plop her foot in the milk pail. So milking was out of the question for him; instead he gathered the cowpats and tossed them on the compost heap and hosed out the barn in his high rubber boots. My mother and Krinsh worked the vegetable garden together. We even tried a hydroponic garden which an Indian friend of ours, called Sharma, had just developed for the US Navy. Krinsh was supposedly spending most of his day in retreat but actually he seemed to prefer, or felt an obligation, to hang about my mother during the long hours of heavy work. I milked the cow every morning before breakfast and then again before dinner. Although I went to a private school, I took the public school bus and Krinsh never failed to walk with me to the road where the bus stopped. He waited discreetly behind the rock wall until he saw me safely off. When the bus returned me in the afternoon I watched the tip of his straw hat moving along behind the wall until I met him at the driveway. He never embarrassed me by showing himself, nor did he upset my sense of independence by making me feel his presence was anything but companionable. Krinsh always took an afternoon walk when there wasn't a badminton game on. He tried to coerce my exhausted mother into going along and sometimes we all went with the cow in tow. She liked to graze along the road in the grassy season and this saved on the cost of alfalfa. Maria and Aldous turned up one day with a large barrel-shaped butter churn. Thereafter, making butter became a regular routine. Frieda Lawrence sent an encouraging letter:

Dear Rosalind,

I want to send you my greetings because it is a pleasure to think of you these days and all of you & your goodwill, when the world is so full of bad will –

A woman brought me the life of Krishnamurti by Ludowic Rebault and I was so very interested in Krishna's fight with those dumb theosophists! Always the same story! It reminded me so much of Lawrence in another way – and the things Krishna says are much like Lawrence. All big men have really the same ultimate source of the vision, only each in his own individual way.

Maria wrote some time ago that you made butter & it is a success. I hope you are all well; it is a joy to think of a child like Rhada [sic] to have so much love.

My kindest greetings and wishes to you all –

FRIEDA

Being a pacifist in that era was a considerably less popular position to hold than it is today, especially when the fascist atrocities began to come to light. When confronted with the question: what alternative to war is there against such evil forces? the answer might be much the same as that of a doctor of preventative medicine being asked to cure a terminal lung cancer patient. Solutions based on certain medical or moral philosophies must begin at the source, before the disease has started and progressed to a critical stage. The doctor would have told his patient to stop smoking years before and the pacifist would be constantly alert to alleviating the causes of war. Unfortunately those in power throughout the world are seldom, if ever, pacifists.

Robert Logan and Aldous Huxley, on either side of the Atlantic, had striven hard and eloquently to offer peaceful solutions to the alarming rise of fascism in the early 1930s. They had very similar philosophies. In his pamphlet *Case for Constructive Peace*, Aldous wrote in 1936:

182

A Garden of Peace in a World at War

War is a purely human phenomenon. Animals kill for food . . . fight duels in the heat of sexual excitement . . . Man is unique in organizing the murder of his own species. War is *not* a law of nature. The old saw about the survival of the fittest is obviously nonsensical – active warfare tends to eliminate the young and strong . . . aerial warfare kills indiscriminately . . .

The whole philosophy of constructive pacifism is based on a consideration of the facts of personal relationship between man and man.

There are men who profess to be pacifists in international politics, but who are tyrants in their families, bullying employers, or unscrupulous competitors . . . [It is not] possible for a government to behave as a pacifist when the individuals it represents conduct their affairs in an essentially militaristic way. Constructive peace must be first of all a personal ethic . . . Means determine ends . . . the only right and practical policy is one based on truth and generosity.

Aldous went on to lay out a practical plan through a conference of the great powers to deal with Mussolini's aggression against Abyssinia and to try to settle some of the injustices of the Versailles Treaty. After which he continued:

The greatest immediate sacrifices . . . will have to come from those who possess the most. These sacrifices, however will be negligible in comparison with the sacrifices demanded from us by another war. Negligible in comparison even with those which are at present being demanded by the mere preparations for war.

And with the full impact of his enormous eloquence, he concluded: 'One generous gesture on the part of a great nation may be enough to set the whole world free.'[2]

Ojai was to become a haven for pacifists during the war. There were many faces of pacifism among us but Aldous, Mr Robbie and Krinsh all believed that peace must be a clear issue within an individual before he could publicly promote it. Also they recognized that during the fever of war political pressure was no longer feasible.

Rosalind had her own very strong tradition of pacifism and was in no sense simply following along with Aldous, Mr Robbie, or Krishna when she wrote to Blanche her feelings about the darkening scene in Europe.

Dearest Blanche,

. . . I am so afraid of all the movements that are being started to try and make peace in Europe. They seem to close our eyes to the things that are happening here and might easily lead us into war. Considering that we are supposed to be rank idealists I sound very realistic, don't you think? I think if some of the heads of government were a little more realistic they would try and find some other solution than war for their problems. People are so taken up with the outside chaotic problems that they have no time to know what living means . . .

The inevitability of war was coming ever closer, and again Rosalind wrote to Blanche, her tone even bleaker than the year before.

Feb 14, 1941

Politically everything seems more and more confused and I wonder if we will ever know the truth about anything? The more one tries to have an open mind the more everything seems to go right through it and one is left with nothing at all. One can't see very far ahead can one?

And then on 9 December 1941: 'Now the conflagration is complete. If you come out to the coast you had better come to us here. The world is mad.'

Early in 1942 Raja sold the Star Trust office in Hollywood and moved all the work to Ojai. Jon D. Davidson, the architect, who was designing a house in Ojai for the Vigevenos, designed a small apartment for Raja over an office and fireproof room situated in the orchard next to Krinsh's Pine Cottage. Raja had no inclination to move into the ménage at Arya Vihara. He appeared only for dinner at the big house, never for lunch; sometimes Krinsh took him a breakfast tray.

My father had always remained behind the scenes and seemingly enjoyed that spot. But he had never liked being referred to as Krinsh's secretary or manager. Neither did he like being asked by countless old ladies what Krinsh ate, when he meditated and other personal details. Nevertheless he had always shouldered this nuisance side of his life as part of his work.

It was a bit much when he was blamed for Krinsh's misdemeanours. Once my mother and I were having tea with an elderly lady in Santa Barbara and Rosalind mentioned that Krishna had been caught speeding on the way down from Carmel. 'Oh no!' she said, 'It must have been Rajagopal. It couldn't have been our dear Krishna.' My father had not even been in the car. Another incident that had particularly galled Raja occurred a few years before in India. He and Krishna were being accompanied to the airport by their very wealthy and elderly host, who, as he said goodbye to Krishna, pressed into his hand a large wad of money. Krishna dropped it on the ground as if it had been a snake. He said, 'I don't handle money, give it to Rajagopal,' leaving it in the dust for someone else to pick up.

Yet in spite of their quarrels, Raja's affection for Krishna never seemed to waver. His isolation and pessimism increased, but everyone in our circle seemed pessimistic in those war years. (Aldous would sometimes arrive in such a state of gloom that Maria would beg us to leave off all war talk for a few days.) Raja enjoyed much of that part of his life that he could keep separate from Krishna and Rosalind. He was a person who was most content when working and was fortified in this attitude by Willie, who fully shared it.

Willie Weidemann was probably the person closest to Raja, who had taught Willie to do all the accounts and book work connected with running the ranch and Star Publishing. He and Raja shared a similar sense of humour, which included seeing American ways through the eyes of the foreign born. They had many laughs over the latest popular songs like 'I've got spurs that jingle jangle jingle ' and American idioms and dialects. There was a couple called the Hawkins who had come out from the dust bowl of Oklahoma. They helped with the orchard and the housework. Both Raja and Willie soon adopted many of their phrases like, 'Everything's did that oughta be did', and 'Go straight down there and don't turn no whichaways.'

We still managed to get up to Sequoia, despite the petrol rationing during the war. We only went to the village once a week and perhaps once a month to Santa Barbara. Thus we saved enough coupons for the one long drive to the Sierra.

My father spent just a few days each summer at Sequoia, finding a ride up and returning with us to Ojai. He was markedly not conforming to Krinsh's quite rigid daily routines. He always had his own little cabin, as did Krinsh, while my mother, David and I shared a bigger one where we did the cooking. I would visit my father in his cabin every morning and he read me the story of Amos or some other prophet or saga from the Bible, probably because the Bible was provided by the Lodge and there was nothing else to read except magazines with terrible war news, from which I was protected. A few years later when the Modern Library brought out a translation of Dostoevski's *The Idiot*, Krinsh brought it to the mountains and, in turn, it kept us both busy. I lay on a fallen giant sequoia near our cabin and read all morning, giving him the book in the afternoon.

Each summer we took long walks in the High Sierra, capped by a final strenuous hike for which we had spent our entire vacation getting in condition. My father would arrive from Ojai a few days before this exploit and refuse to get out of bed all day. Krinsh would do all he could to persuade him to exercise, but without the least effect. When the morning of the big hike came, my father was up and ready with the rest of us. Much to our surprise and Krinsh's mixture of annoyance and amusement, he beat us all to the top of the peak and back (a twenty-mile round trip) without any evident ill effects, more than could be said for the lot of us, including Krinsh. Whether he did this deliberately to annoy or was just functioning on his own track we never knew.

One summer in Sequoia, a few days before we were going to leave, we found a tanager with a broken wing. My mother crocheted a delicate sling for her and very soon the little bird was so tame that she would sit on our fingers and let us hold her up to the windowpane to snap up live flies. We had to take her back to Ojai with us as her wing was still far from mended.

Our habit was to leave late mid-afternoon to avoid the valley heat and arrive in Ojai about ten at night. We usually carried a picnic supper as Krinsh hated eating in restaurants, but this particular time we had neglected to do so and were forced to stop at a little café in Bakersfield. None of us, not even my father, noticed the sign on the door which stated that the establishment reserved the right to refuse service to anyone. We certainly looked no worse, in our blue jeans and sneakers and with Krinsh in his straw hat trying not to be recognized, than any of the other patrons of that rather grimy diner. We were taken for migrant farmers or *braceros*, or whoever else the café owner decided he had the right to refuse service to, and were asked, not very politely, to leave. Even the little bird perched on my finger did not soften him. Standing somewhat in shock outside the door, we heard a gentle voice say, 'I witnessed that. It is disgraceful and I feel ashamed for my town. I insist that you let me take you all to a decent place for dinner.' We could hardly refuse and followed the man to a fancy restaurant with white tablecloths which welcomed us, blue jeans, bird, vegetarianism and all. It turned out, surprisingly enough, that even in Bakersfield Krinsh had been recognized.

A Garden of Peace in a World at War

The little tanager became one of our most loved pets, and although the wing never healed well enough for her to fly, she seemed to enjoy her life in our care. Our cat Minnie exhibited extreme jealousy towards the bird. We were careful to keep her locked in the house when we had the bird outdoors. One afternoon Ignon, our French painter friend, came for tea. He, among all our friends, had a special love for the bird. Suddenly, out of nowhere, Minnie sprang, grabbed the bird and dashed out of reach under the house. I was heartbroken; Ignon was so furious he swore he would kill the cat if he could lay hands on her. Minnie knew enough to keep out of sight for over a week. But she lost a great deal of our affection.

Before the Japanese residents in California were interned, Rosalind had ordered seventy-five newly hatched chicks, the last batch that would be sexed as eggs by the Japanese, who were said to be the only people with the ability to tell from the eggs which were to be hens and which roosters. My mother, Krinsh and I drove to the train station in Ventura late one night to pick up our precious cargo and brought the little chicks home to the coop that Krinsh and Willie had built. There was not one rooster in the batch. We soon found that a rooster was necessary to keep peace among the hens and scare off the weasels. We added a big iridescent black cock of the walk called Hercules. Every Saturday, Krinsh, David and I scraped out the chicken coop. Krinsh seemed to take on the most menial chores with a hearty enthusiasm. I collected the eggs and fed the chickens and in the process made pets of all seventy-five hens and Hercules, who dominated their lives. Several hens had a name from Greek mythology, which I was studying in school at the time, and I claimed to know each one by her voice.

Soon egg production was going full tilt and we even had a surplus to preserve in vats of lye for the lean season. Eggs were sorted and cleaned and sold to neighbours and devotees, who probably thought they had special qualities, as it was known that Krinsh helped in all this.

There was such a demand for our produce that we bought another young cow called Tina, who had been an orphan and hand-fed by bottle. She was so well-bred that I could bring her into the living-room and she never once misbehaved. Neither did Hercules who, with one or two of his privileged hens, ate their dinner in a common bowl alongside the cat under the kitchen stove (usually while my mother was trying to cook dinner).

Just before dinner was also the favourite hour for Norbert Schiller, the Austrian actor and poet, to arrive. He had built his own round stone house down the road, and would walk up to Arya Vihara and right into the kitchen with his goat. The goat nibbled on the tablecloth or Krinsh's straw hat while Schiller produced a very smelly goat cheese from his leather pocket for our meal. This was indeed most generous of him for he lived almost solely on goat cheese and the mustard greens and avocados which he picked from our orchard. Eventually he would prosper by getting character parts in films. In those days no one in Ojai prospered, nor did they appear interested in doing so. Money played but a small part in any of our lives.

Although he was sympathetic to our endeavours, my father took no active part in the farming at which we worked so strenuously during the war years. He kept himself busy in his office, but Krinsh, prevented by the war from his customary travels, would probably have been bored and restless without all his chores.

Life on the farm got harder. The two ranch hands were drafted, leaving only Willie who, as manager, was exempt. The initial excitement of getting the enterprises going wore off a bit and the endless realities of labour and the demands of the animals became all we had time or energy for. Yet with the world in the state it was, we felt exceptionally fortunate.

Rosalind worked from six in the morning till after dinner each night. In addition to the farm work she still made my few good clothes and my father's and Krinsh's good shirts and nightshirts. Most of the time we wore blue jeans and denim shirts, except my father, who stuck to his old English grey flannels.

Eventually we were allowed to provide agricultural labour for two young conscientious objectors who came to stay at Arya Vihara and help there as an alternative to war duty. One of them, Bill Quinn, had gone to Harvard and was deeply influenced by Thoreau. In fact, he was far better at quoting Thoreau than wielding a pitchfork, but in time his gentle ways won over even the cows. Life at Arya Vihara suited him perfectly. He had a fondness for the animals which was a requirement in caring for them as the two cows, all seventy-five hens and Hercules were my personal pets.

Rosalind did her best to keep up a correspondence with her closest friends. To Blanche, in November 1942, she wrote: 'We are well and busy. A friend who has not seen Krishnaji for months says she has never seen him look so blooming. So now you will be able to put down the New York rumors of death and illness. Raja is one moment seemingly all right and the next not so well.' The false rumours had brought wires of condolence about Krinsh's supposed death.

A Garden of Peace in a World at War

Mr Robbie, ever faithful with his letters, must have been one of Rosalind's prime diversions during these years. He had a light touch in everything, even in expressing his strong feelings about the war:

Jan 5, 1943

Dearest Rozzie,

Aside from the cold and the rationing and the taxes everything is better – better than next year! Mabel [his secretary] and I have reserved passage on the American Airlines for L.A. and hope that the O.P.A. and the W.P.B. and the Japs and the Germans will not prevent our going . . .

Aug 25, 1943

Have you read about the 'Big Inch'? the 24 inch pipeline which has just been completed from Texas to Pennyslvania and New Jersey. It has broken twice since it was completed last week and thousands of acres only a few miles from here have been ruined and the Nesharminy Creek and the Delaware River have a scum of oil on them which has killed thousands of fish. Nice going! And now the only man in the Cabinet – Sumner Welles – has been fired because old lady Hull and the Southern voters thought he had too many brains.

Sept 23, 1943

Dearest Rozzie,

Beato recently wrote quite incidentally something so nice about you and so cleverly phrased that I must share it. She said: 'I have not seen Rosalind nor Rajagopal since you left. I long for a glimpse of Rosie, she has the power to dispel with such quick immediacy the thickness of everyday life.'

That is a gem of a sentence and in your case, dear, it is true. How are you and Radhi and Raja and Krinsh and the cows and the bees and the chickens? Don't feel you have to write, but a line is always appreciated.

I too put my oar in the pacifist cause by volunteering my father to counter-argue a *March of Time* newsreel on India that had been shown in my school. Even at eleven, I was outraged by the broadside attack on Gandhi and asked the headmaster if he would invite my father to give a truer picture. This he willingly did and then asked me for a little background on my father – a tall order which I simplified by saying, 'When he was a little boy he was so poor he stood around garbage pails to catch the crows to eat.' I have no idea how this image of my Brahmin, vegetarian father could have entered my imagination or what mischievous impulse came over me. Just before Raja had to give his talk the headmaster asked him if he had really lived on crows as a young boy. My father was so baffled by this question it is a wonder he could talk at all, but he did and, much to my pride, so brilliantly explained Gandhi's actions and philosophy that not only the headmaster but most of my friends changed their attitude toward India – in spite of my crow story.

The old days of beautiful pergolas and roses and lily ponds at Arya Vihara vanished with the war and the need for all our effort to go into productive activity. As Mr Robbie observed:

> *Jan 6, 1944*
>
> . . . I am sorry about the pergola which Sara took such pleasure in building. I should have been glad to help repair it but I suppose Willie, Raja and Krinsh felt that it was of little use and should be replaced by something that would bring in a return . . .
>
> Please forgive me for dragging you into this S—— affair. I don't know what she has in mind and doubt if she does either so I tried out the formula for success in Washington: 'Shoot the bull, pass the buck and make seven copies of everything!'
>
> Love,
>
> ROBERT

Mr Robbie was referring to an unbalanced lady who had been troubling him over her fixation on Krinsh, wanting Mr Robbie to intercede on her behalf.

As is to be expected around people like Krinsh, there was never a shortage of unbalanced people; most of them quite harmless but some creating a good deal of consternation. One could only hope that, as Aldous put it in one of his later talks, the lunatic fringe did not become like a Spanish shawl where the fringe is greater than the shawl. In some instances Krinsh exacerbated the problem by not dealing with them decisively in the first place. A few were bordering on the dangerous. One of these cases was a supposedly crippled and semi-bedridden woman who lived down the hill from Arya Vihara. She wrote several pitiful letters to Krinsh and he finally agreed to go and visit her, which he then continued to do regularly. One day I answered the front-door bell to find a stout unkempt woman standing there on her crutches.

A Garden of Peace in a World at War

I immediately guessed her identity, which was confirmed when our cat Minnie, who herself had become slightly demented after the bird incident, took one look at the woman, arched her back and hissed. I felt my elders should have taken this as a serious warning, but they did not do so.

Another day my friend Ellen and I, walking in the hills, saw this woman charging down the path with her crutches tucked under her arm. I told Krinsh I thought he was being deceived. My mother began to receive anonymous letters threatening terrible consequences if she did not get out of Krinsh's house. Finally Mr Robbie was accosted by the woman, who threatened him with her crutch. This was taken seriously. Thanks to the unorthodox co-operation of the post lady (who gathered and delivered the mail in her Model A) my father was able to prove where the letters came from. After much difficulty, legal action was taken and the threatening member of the 'fringe' banished from the state of California.

One of our harmless members of the 'fringe' seemed fairly normal by day but on moonlit nights would wander up and down the road in front of Arya Vihara with her long white hair streaming down her back, chanting Krishnaji-i-i-, Krishnaji-i-i. My mother had made a dressmaker's form which probably accounted for the rumour started by this woman that Rosalind kept a skeleton in her closet. That papier mâché form of my mother must have terrified the poor moonstruck lady, but perhaps it taught her to keep out of other people's closets.

Although I had been strictly brought up by Krinsh not to indulge in beliefs (which had effectively done away with fairies, leprechauns, Santa Claus and God), I was astonished one night to discover that ghosts fell into another category, although just what category I was never to discover. I sensed already that ghosts might not fall in the realm of belief. But no one in our family had ever mentioned them in the realm of personal experience either. Once I saw a startled look on Krinsh's face when I matter-of-factly stated that I had seen Nitya's ghost in the hallway. There was something in his expression that forbade my making further play of this, which was all it had been. I knew that Nitya had died in the front room but he was in some ways alive to me even though I had never seen him. My mother had spoken of him often and of her times with him, reading poetry and singing, and I had picked up some of her nostalgia. He was seldom mentioned by Krinsh or my father.

One evening at dinner my father said that for the past three nights someone had been entering his fireproof room, which was double-locked and impossible to break into. The metal door made a peculiar clang when it shut, no matter how careful one was. Each night he had investigated and found no sign of a person. 'It must be a ghost,' he said. My mother looked annoyed by the story and put no credence in the idea of a ghost, which she was determined to lay to rest. She did have some anxiety that it might be a person, one of our 'fringe' perhaps. Krinsh suggested that the three of us, without telling Raja, take turns keeping watch all night from his veranda, which overlooked Raja's office. Of course, I thought the whole thing a great lark and felt sure that was indeed all it was until, when it was my turn to keep the watch, Krinsh said to me in utmost earnestness,

'Kittums, remember this: a ghost can never hurt you. It can only make you think it has hurt you.'

At first, I was inclined to assume he was only adding a little spice to our adventure, but when I looked at his face I knew he wasn't joking. He was really nervous about leaving me alone out there. Nothing whatsoever appeared that night and the next day we asked my father if he had heard his ghost. Most disappointingly he replied that there had been no sounds all night. So the mystery was never solved, but the sounds never recurred.

The war was nearing its end, and reports came from Europe that were more and more horrifying. Not until then had Annie Vigeveno known that over forty of her family had died in the gas chambers. Ommen had been used by the Nazis as a concentration camp. Some friends had died and some had survived, but Ommen would never be the same and Krishna would never return there.

Mr Robbie wrote, 'I am sorry too about Mrs Vigeveno. I am afraid Germany earned her fate by allowing a crazy fanatic to dictate her policies and alienate from her the whole common sense (even if largely hypocritical) world.' And in reference to a smaller private war, he commented, 'Did you know that George Arundale has repudiated – for himself at least – Co-Masonry, the L.C.C. and the E.S.? He says the only essential teaching of theosophy is brotherhood; too bad he didn't think of that sooner.'

18

Wrightwood

The Huxleys had a home in the Mojave desert in a small spot called Llano. There was nothing but a curve in the road and a sign to distinguish Llano from any other spot in that vast stretch of piñons and Joshua trees. Aldous began to suffer from bronchial trouble there and in the course of their frequent explorations they had discovered a mountain town between the desert and Los Angeles called Wrightwood. Aldous was much relieved by the mountain air. But poor Maria detested the village, found the houses ugly, and the altitude made her slightly ill. She called herself a desert rat and Aldous a mountain squirrel and never came to like Wrightwood; but with her characteristic concern for Aldous's well-being, she cheerfully accepted an impractical and badly made house and all the difficulties involved in living in such a remote place in wartime.

Late spring 1945 found the world still in the throes of terror and chaos; the future was far from clear. The first atomic bomb had been detonated, even though it was afterwards admitted within scientific circles that there was no absolute certainty the whole atmosphere would not be ignited by this experiment. Aldous was one of those few who saw so clearly at that moment the future consequences of such an experiment. With the details coming to light of the concentration camps on the one side and the results of fire bombings of much of Germany on the other, and the plight of refugees all over Europe, there was some reason to believe that much of the world had run amok.

Using affectionate persistence, the Huxleys prevailed upon us to spend the rest of that summer in Wrightwood. As usual, it was the three of us, my mother, Krinsh and I who made this move. My father would drive up from Hollywood or Ojai for an occasional weekend. Maria, in her letters to Rosalind had begged that we pretend to like Wrightwood, even if we didn't, to make Aldous happy.

We found them painting their house, Aldous smeared from head to toe, valiantly wielding a paintbrush. To us, the village was charming enough, not Alpine or with the overpowering stillness and magnitude of Sequoia, but we did not share Maria's dislike.

Wrightwood is dry, austere, without the attraction of water or the accompanying noise of water sports. Years later when I had seen the Himalayas, I felt the affinity here. The silver earth was studded with pine and fremontia, small clumps of lupin lingered that first summer and the Indian paint brush in occasional bursts of deep orange nestled by mica-flecked rocks.

We saw the Huxleys every day – either for tea at their house or for dinner at ours. Rosalind and Maria each tried to help the other in her own way. Maria included us on many occasions when interesting people came up to see Aldous, for she understood that Krinsh particularly seemed to need these encounters. Maria began a hope chest for me, although I was just a child. I still have the lovely Belgian linens she gave me then. Preparing food and running large households, something of a hardship for Maria, was fairly routine for Rosalind, so she often provided the meals for the whole crowd. Thus our lives, though in different houses, were linked by mealtimes and also by walks, a daily routine for both Aldous and Krinsh, accompanied by whoever could keep up with Aldous's long stride, which was easily matched by Krinsh's fast one. These were the occasions of their most serious talks together, and I would glean particles of profound utterance as I drifted between them and Maria and Rosalind with their, to me, more intriguing talk about friends and family.

There is one evening that first summer that still stands out in my memory. Raja had come up from Hollywood and after dinner the three men remained in the living-room, while Maria, Rosalind and I retreated to a bedroom to chat about lighter matters than we suspected the men would indulge in. Through the thin wall we could hear and distinguish their voices, each with his unique, clear British accent and beautiful pitch. Like a string trio, themes picked up in turn, never interrupting each other, they played out a conversation that rose and fell in sonorous tones in a minor scale, gradually winding down to a dead silence that lasted many minutes. Overcome by curiosity we crept into the room to see what had befallen them. Three pairs of eyes were bent on the floor, faces sombre, each lost in a private gloom into which they had so harmoniously talked themselves. It was the middle of August 1945.

Finally the war was over, but like Aldous, Krishna and Raja and many others who had insight towards the future, Mr Robbie saw the darker side of victory.

Wrightwood

Dearest Radha,

We are of course tremendously pleased that peace has come but there isn't the same thrill as there was when the last war ended for then everyone was full of hope that there would be no more wars and this time we merely rejoice that this war is over and the next one not yet begun.

And a month later he wrote to Rosalind, 'The Atomic bomb seems to put the last nail in the coffin of Christian civilization. If only Genghis Khan could have had the use of it he could have killed 180,000,000 people in one year instead of only 18,000.'

Before that summer ended Krishna and Rosalind had been shown the cabin at Wrightwood which Krishna was to name Greenwood Gate. They stood together under the great three-hundred-year-old oak tree that is still there and both felt certain this was the right cabin for us. It had been built of whole logs nearly a hundred years before by the first forest ranger in that area. In the 1920s a wealthy lady from Beverly Hills had added, in the same style, bedrooms and bath, hardwood floors and other comforts, before she lost everything including the cabin in the Depression. There was a wistaria-covered porch and beautiful stone patio. A surrounding forest of pines sheltered the cabin from the sun, which Krinsh so detested. Aldous, on the other hand, always sought all the light he could find and thought our cabin sombre though charming.

Using a small sum left to Rosalind by Sara Logan, Raja, with considerable trouble, arranged the purchase. There had been a flood the winter before that had washed away several houses but went right around this one. Its elderly owner had been on her knees all night praying for survival. A good part of the mountain had come down in an avalanche of late April snow followed by heavy rains. Raja had to wait for an act of Congress to allocate funds for the reparation of the dirt dam between us and the wash, before the property could be released for purchase.

(That was just the beginning of tribulations for us and the cabin. Following her vision that this cabin would have a long place in our lives, my mother gave it to my husband and me twenty years later, urging us never to sell it. To this day we are glad we haven't, although there were times when we were sorely tempted. There was another flood just after it became ours, causing us to remove twenty truckloads of silt from the house and the garage. The cabin is standing on the tail end of the San Andreas fault, on target for the worst earthquake of the century. But our family has enjoyed it along with its resident carpenter ants and bumble-bees for the past forty years.)

Wrightwood marked the end of our annual treks to Sequoia. Our time was pleasantly intertwined with the Huxleys. Maria and Rosalind shared their domestic problems.

My dearest Rosalind,

I missed you at Wrightwood but I found out much usefulness for both of us and this is to impart it . . . I found excellent men to do urgent things; regulate oil stove . . . new locks. In fact quite important details. And I found that Mr Steele though slow is wonderfully conscientious, willing and capable. If you need him for stoves or electric light or gas or anything don't hesitate. I found that your friend of Australia, Harry may become very useful to all of us as an odd-job man. He seems honest and certainly cheap. He talks too much . . . 60¢ an hour. He is sorting apples for you and leaving them there. They are rotting . . . There is a Mrs Strott who lives near the apple orchard . . . we heard the bells of her cows, near the little lake, when we walked. I had her once. I think she may be very useful and go to you if you insisted that you needed her – 75¢ an hour. Tell her I am your friend. I believe she rather enjoyed the work with different sort of people – Oh dear, how hard some people work. She is happy because she had six 'wonderful boys'.

We shall arrive late on Friday morning and pass by your house hoping to arrange a walk or something else.

The days were warm and last night was the only one I spent there . . . I slept atrociously on what I had thought was a divine bed which took me all day to prepare for Aldous. So I shall have to think up something else; the difficulty is it must be seven feet.

The departure was dramatic under a darkening sky, the first flakes of mixed snow and rain and a howling wind. When I reached the desert a pretty moon seemed ironically to watch my hurrying car; so I slowed down and enjoyed the radiant peace while the clouds crowded our hills. And so I am home and happy. I go to town tomorrow. It will be wonderful to meet and I have made some cakes. To send to Europe as you suggested. Eight pounds for them and the rest for us when you will please come to tea. One batch turned out like toffee but your family is sweet about my misfits so I am keeping them for you! Good night my very dearest. May I say that I am more fond of you than ever and that it is a very happy feeling to be so fond of someone. I hope you are well. Your family has my loves [sic] too. Make sure they all have warm clothes. The cold has a slow creepy strength which suddenly has paralysed one and the face is green and the nose is red and the hands clumsy – and yet that is where we choose to live.

When late spring came we moved to Wrightwood for long periods, taking carloads of produce from the ranch and returning every few weeks to replenish supplies.

In between major reprovisioning in Ojai, we made weekly trips to the Safeway in San Bernardino. Very occasionally, we could persuade Krinsh to go to a movie down there with us. He refused to go to romantic films, but enjoyed Westerns. Whenever there was a kissing scene he covered his eyes in horror and said, 'What rot!'

While this attitude may have been perfectly understandable to his devotees, it seemed somewhat inconsistent to me and probably even more so to my mother.

I was now fourteen – no longer a small, unobtrusive child. While they never made me feel *de trop*, I sensed they needed to be alone, especially in the mornings when Krinsh went into my mother's room where she often would have taken her breakfast tray to bed. This was a small treat which she particularly enjoyed when away from all the ranch chores. I was not interested in their conversations any more.

I wandered off by myself up the wash through the waves of desert heat marbled by wafts of fog-cooled breezes. Sometimes a friend from Ojai came for a visit. But our household seemed strange to most of them and I felt easier left alone, to sketch, to read among other things an old edition of *War and Peace* in four leather-bound volumes that I brought from Arya Vihara. In that edition the English was interspersed with long passages of French which I could not get through without Krinsh's help. Sometimes I swam in the local pond or practised the piano in the local schoolhouse. These were my summer mornings and I was perfectly content with them. We always rested after lunch and then went to the Huxleys for tea, and a walk. Or they came to us for dinner and an evening around the huge stone fireplace, built so long ago by the forest ranger. There were no telephones so plans were made from one day to the next.

Greta Garbo came for the day and I trailed along the Blue Ridge behind her and Krinsh. She was easily as beautiful as her legend. She was without a trace of make-up, except perhaps on her lashes. The only evidence of vanity was an anti-wrinkle plaster between her eyebrows. Her hair was straight. She wore a straw hat and pants. She asked 'profound' questions of the 'Indian Sage', questions parried, averted, unanswered. Deepest blue eyes glanced up under those famous lashes to test his imperviousness, or was she genuinely ingenuous? Who could ever say? They were two such private people. I just hoped she didn't notice the look Krinsh threw me as he often did when I was there to witness some particular embarrassment, as though I could somehow cast back a little sympathy. I could feel his question, 'What am I to do with this?' Yet I also knew of his secret yen for the world of actors and popular renown. He had a peculiar affinity for it and had once told me, 'I would like to write just one big Broadway hit, just to see how it feels,' or sometimes it would be 'Just one best-selling detective novel.'

There was a picnic with the Huxleys and Stravinskys also on the Blue Ridge at an altitude of 8000 feet. My mother, as usual, had brought food for everyone and laid it out while the rest of us walked. That day someone or something persuaded Krinsh to take a sip of wine and he suddenly fell back off the bench in a dead faint. Everyone except Rosalind was alarmed. She knew how easily he could faint. In such company Krinsh always looked a bit aloof and outside the circle, except with Aldous and Maria with whom he felt perfectly at home. He showed affection for Aldous, but maintained the usual formality with Maria that he reserved for all women, seldom using first names, preferring Madam or Signora. No matter how eminent our guests were, it was still Krinsh who was always the centre of attention. The more he appeared to retreat from this position, the more it encompassed him. There was something in common between him and Greta Garbo in this. We had witnessed her attempts at incognito when shopping in Beverly Hills which never failed to draw attention to herself. Everyone knew exactly who she was.

One day we were invited to tea at the Huxleys to meet a psychologist, his wife and secretary. I was sitting next to the wife and suddenly noticed a complete change of expression, although she seemed to be attentive to our conversation. A moment later, her original demeanour returning, she asked me to repeat what I had just said. Maria explained to me later that she was a split personality, just like the woman in the true case history of the film, *Three Faces of Eve*. But in this case both personalities were compatible and helpful to each other. I never forgot this extraordinary intimate glimpse of that unusual woman.

Even in Wrightwood there was always a lot of work to do. We did almost everything ourselves. Krinsh decided it would be nice to have a rose garden. Perhaps he missed the one that had been taken out years before at Arya Vihara for wartime economy. We planted a row of roses along the wall above the driveway. The soil was basically rocks of serpentine and mica, grey and infertile and much digging and mulching had to be done. Eventually the roses did very well. He and Rosalind also made a small bathroom down in the garage. A local plumber installed the fixtures but they did the tiling and painting themselves. This bathroom was for Krinsh, who slept in the living-room and liked to get up very early.

When we returned from an afternoon walk one day there was a large rattlesnake curled comfortably on the mat by the kitchen door. Krinsh was not lacking in courage but it was my mother who had the knack of dealing with difficult creatures. With gentle urging from a broom and a firm voice she told the snake to remove itself and find another home. She was surprisingly persuasive and the reptile slowly uncoiled and moved off into the brush. We didn't see it again. To my knowledge, my mother never killed or harmed anything. In this she was like Mr Robbie, who had once remarked to Beato when she was about to swat a fly, 'Let it live. It values its life as much as you do yours.' Beato never again killed anything either.

My mother also had her own ideas about politics. Even Aldous could not influence her on issues about which she felt strongly. She had grown up in a politically oriented household. Her father had been a state senator with a strong socialist bent and the family had weathered many campaigns. During the Alger Hiss trial, there were many heated discussions about his innocence. My mother was certain he was not guilty, but thought, in any case, he had not received a fair trial. Everyone else tried to argue her down, not because they thought Hiss was guilty but because her certainty seemed to them irrational. Although Krinsh had always maintained that if a person were not liberal in his youth he would be mentally ossified in his middle years, next to my mother he definitely sounded politically conservative, but when my Aunt Erma was present, who was not only a staunch Republican, which she saw as the party of Lincoln, but also allowed herself on occasion to sound pro-American and mildly nationalistic, Krinsh would remind her, sometimes quite sharply, of the importance of not thinking in terms of nationalism and ideology. Krinsh was not a political thinker but lumped both religious and political ideologies in one trash bin. All leaders were on the wrong path, politicians, teachers, experts of any kind were to be eschewed. This was helpful for adults with overly encumbered minds who were seeking freedom from their conditioning, but for young students hoping to get educated, it was not helpful. It took me quite a few years to overcome the feeling that what I was being told in the lectures at college was anything but nonsense. I would find myself reflecting the supercilious attitude that I had so often seen Krinsh put on in the face of intellectual power. While I was never permitted by any of my adults to make derogatory or even personal remarks, Krinsh occasionally did so, perhaps unwittingly or somehow stirred to an inner exasperation. It was seldom this happened, but I remembered him saying after a long walk with Aldous, 'His mind is like a wastebasket.' I am sure Aldous would never have suspected that Krinsh would make such a comment.

I look back now on those years at Wrightwood as the last of our happy times together with Krinsh. Both my parents had occasional quarrels with him, but they were of the same nature as they had always been – usually because he had lied about something. My mother asked him once why he lied and he replied with astonishing frankness, 'Because of fear.'

In some ways Rosalind's psychology was so simple. She thought once a fault was recognized and admitted all you had to do was decide to stop it. She never recognized the complexity of Krinsh's problem until it was too late. My father, on the other hand, tended to make everything so complex that he became mired in his own speculations.

There was still a great deal of love: between my mother and Krinsh, from my father to Krinsh and possibly from Krinsh to my father, though of this I am still uncertain. I never had any doubt of the love I had for each of the three of them and which they all had for me.

19

A School is Born

When, in 1927, Mrs Besant had bought the Happy Valley land and entrusted it to the Happy Valley Foundation, whose members she had chosen, she told them they had centuries in which to work. By extending her vision over such a long range she alleviated the impatience that might have arisen in her trustees to see instant marvels arising in Happy Valley. This, however, did not alleviate the problem of meeting the annual payments on the $90,000 mortgage with which the property was encumbered. That onerous duty fell largely on the Logans and Louis Zalk. They issued regular appeals for pledges to help clear title. Those loyal to Mrs Besant, those who shared in her vision of the coming sixth sub-root race, answered the call for help until the Great Depression fell upon the world. Then the Logans and Louis Zalk were left with a considerable financial problem, for they also were affected by the crash. For the next twenty-five years there would be a running correspondence between Robert and Louis about their joint responsibility. This exchange began in Robert's usual wry tone in October 1930.

> Dear Louis,
>
> Of course I will help you out as you request but really I do not quite understand what the situation will be, to whom payments will be made and by whom records kept and receipts sent.
>
> Enlighten me a little in words of one syllable . . . I remember we had a meeting . . . at which everybody was elected trustee and then immediately resigned and was replaced by everybody else.
>
> . . . believe me, with all good wishes,
>
> > Faithfully,
> > ROBERT

This tone of informality should not belie the competence and dedication of these two men in their efforts to bring to fruition Mrs Besant's vision. Had they not believed so firmly in that, they would have found the task too trying. The only source of income on the land was a walnut grove which sometimes helped to pay the taxes and mortgage and was managed by a tenant farmer, the original owner of the land. There was a steady stream of people, mostly Theosophists, who hoped themselves to be a part of the new sixth sub-root race or at least wanted to be there ready to welcome it. Fielding these inquiries was a duty which fell to Robert.

June 22, 1935

Dear Louis,

I quite agree with your letter about not considering any colonizing plans until we can hold a real meeting of the trustees.

As I have had to answer a good many criticisms and enquiries lately . . . I inclose copies . . . of some of my answers for your comments.

Dear Kahuna,

As for starting colonization, there is certainly no 'no Theosophist need apply' attitude on the part of the trustees; there is only . . . a desire to be very sure of not making some wrong venture when the land is still under a substantial mortgage. A failure now would make it almost impossible ever to get the mortgage paid off or reduced to safe proportions . . . meanwhile it could do no harm to submit to Louis Zalk some practical plans and suggestions toward first steps in colonization.

Dear Mrs S——

You are quite at liberty to change your pledge or cancel it altogether . . . As for the colonization of Happy Valley, the trustees have no other thought in mind and would certainly not have made all the efforts they have had to make for seven years to reduce the heavy mortgage from $90,000 to $43,000 if they had not been dedicated to the ultimate accomplishment of Dr Besant's intentions.

T.S. members are sometimes too ready to criticize each other's efforts without a clear understanding of the facts and I hope when you hear further criticism of the Happy Valley Foundation . . . you will ask the critics to send in some helpful suggestions instead.

By 1941, the Happy Valley situation was basically unchanged except that the mortgage was being reduced and the land therefore still intact. There were still as many ideas as to what the land should be used for and who should do the using as there were people, both within the foundation and on the outskirts – to say nothing of the 'fringe'.

There was also a claim (later proved to be unfounded) by a Theosophical member against Happy Valley for a school in lieu of a former loan, about which Robert commented:

September 12, 1943

Dear Louis,

If Miss S. should depart for Shamballa [the home of the king of the occult hierarchy believed to be located in the Gobi desert] before the time comes either to found a school or repay the money, there would probably be no controversy at all; . . . it all seems to rest on Dr Besant's two letters and the minutes of the Happy Valley.

. . . To my mind it is not so much a question whether or not we are trustees of the $12,400 for the purposes of a school as whether we can avoid having Miss S. at Happy Valley in any capacity. I am not very clear as to what a Sixth Sub-race person should be but I feel very sure he must be of quite a different type from Miss S. Or any other rigid educationalist.

Faithfully,

ROBERT

P.S. We might turn it all over to Miss S. and merely amend our charter to read THE UNHAPPY VALLEY FOUNDATION.

Whether answering the proposals of over-zealous Theosophists or members of the 'fringe', Robert politely but firmly maintained the trustees' intention to steer clear of all the rigid and, in some eyes, nonsensical aspects of Theosophy such as initiations and the consequent hierarchical attitudes which he and Sara had never embraced. Mrs Besant herself had not included these aspects in her concept of Happy Valley's future.

Robert and Louis were both among Krishna's closest friends and contributed heavily to what was now called Krishnamurti Writings Incorporated or KWInc, instead of the Star Publishing Trust. But Krishna still maintained an aloof distance from Happy Valley. He had divorced himself from this enterprise before Mrs Besant even had it off the ground. He was finished with Masters, the sixth sub-root race and with Theosophy in general, at least at that time.

As soon as the war was over, my mother wanted to start a large community vegetable garden in the lower valley, mostly to provide work for the Japanese who had been interned during the war. It was a token drop of help in the face of such disgraceful and unnecessary injustice as they had suffered but she felt strongly about it. Raja, who thought it was not a feasible undertaking, dissuaded her from the garden; but he did arrange to hire a Japanese couple, who came to live in the smaller of Robert's cottages behind Saro Vihara. Ishi worked in the orchard and garden and Mrs Ishi helped in the household. If they had bitter feelings they kept them to themselves and showed us always a courteous and cheerful demeanour.

In 1945, Robert and Louis went into another partnership which would provide the seed bed for the first enterprise of Happy Valley. They bought the old Star Camp bath-houses and cafeteria building and the acreage around them from KWInc and were planning to remodel the bath-houses into apartments. There were murmurings of the possibility of a school, murmurings which Robert had intuitively foreseen some years before. Although nothing definite was being decided along these lines, it was in the back of both their minds that if there should be a sudden need, the apartments would be available until more permanent structures could be built on the Happy Valley land fifteen miles away.

December 17th, 1945

Dear Louis,

I have your letter of December 11th and note instructions to Willie about bath-houses 3 and 2 . . . If anyone swims out of these bath-houses with a clear mathematical picture of my two-thirds and one-half and your one-half and one-third, it will be Albert Einstein. No one else would have a chance!

Faithfully,

ROBERT

The nucleus that would start the school was forming. A retired philosophy professor from Vassar, Dr Guido Ferrando, had moved to Ojai Valley during the war and had given several series of lectures on the American transcendentalists and on the Divine Comedy. He had also entered into many discussions on education with Krishna, Rosalind and Aldous Huxley. His ideas for a Socratic method of teaching fitted in with many of Krishna's ideas but were more specific and applicable: term papers rather than formal examinations, small classes arranged in a circle with a flow of questions and answers between the pupils and the teacher. Pupils would learn from asking questions and discussing rather than being lectured to. The emphasis would be on learning to think and there would be no barriers between different disciplines but an integration of subjects as well as cultures into a world view.

Rosalind had been for some years a member of the Ojai Valley School Board which had originally been based on Edward Yeomans's precepts of non-competitiveness, in classroom and sports, tolerance and a free and open mind; similar educational principles to those which Krishna later formulated.

There was a need in the valley for a co-educational high school, especially at that moment. The ninth grade class, which included me, was about to graduate from the Ojai Valley School. I well remember the concern we all had as to where we would go next. Most of us, having spent four or five years in a very progressive school, were not enthusiastic to finish our high school days at the public school. All the other schools in Ojai were for boys only. A ready-made tenth grade to start with seemed an opportune moment to lay the first cornerstone of a long-hoped-for reality. Rosalind had been invited on to the Happy Valley Foundation a few years before, largely due to Robert's faith, which he had inherited from Sara and was joined in by Louis, that she would accomplish something important if given the chance. At that time, Rosalind was unaware of this confidence in her, but was to be sustained by it in the ensuing years.

It was Mr Robbie and Louis Zalk who made the school possible financially. They leased for a dollar a year the old cafeteria building, to be used for the school house. This was the beginning of their long role as chief benefactors of the school, just as they had been of the Happy Valley Foundation.

Rosalind was rapidly caught up in the practicalities of starting even a small school. Providing equipment, housing, classrooms, kitchens and budgets fell to her, in addition to discussing the ideology of the school with Aldous, Raja, Krishna, Dr Ferrando and many others who had hoped for years to be part of such an undertaking. Robert and Louis remained largely in the background of these discussions but as trustees their undiminishing correspondence revealed their deep concern. They both believed the school should reflect Mrs Besant's educational ideals, based on the brotherhood of man and that all the future trustees should be chosen with this principle in mind. In the midst of the war Robert had emphasized these views.

The Happy Valley must be a nursery for that true peace which can only come through understanding and good will, through sympathy and not through domination . . . [it] is the opposite of the conception of mechanization and regimentation, which has been dominating the world of business and politics, and creating not only the war, but the war of daily life.

In these words Mr Robbie was in accord with both Mrs Besant's ideals and Aldous's as expressed in *Case for Constructive Peace*.

It was agreed between Krishna, Raja and Rosalind that Arya Vihara could be used that first year as a temporary living quarters for the boarding students until the bath-house remodelling was completed. This was only because Krishna was planning to leave for Australia in the summer of 1946, and to be away for a year, the first time he would leave America since the war had begun. He had never been confined in one place for so long and his restlessness was showing. Although he had had the summer trips to Sequoia and Carmel, he must have missed the large gatherings for his talks in Ommen and India. He had talked in Ojai only once during the war, in 1944.

That summer of 1946 Krinsh, my mother and I returned to Sarobia for the first gathering since 1940. This proved to be a fertile hunting ground for prospective students of the Happy Valley School. Rosalind made the most of the opportunity. It was here that she urged Catherine Sloss to send her son out to California. In part because of her interest in Krishna and in part because of the school situation in Birmingham, Catherine went home sufficiently convinced to persuade her husband that it was a good idea. Little did they realize that Jimmy, then only fifteen, was to emigrate more or less permanently to California.

A group of eminent Freudian psychoanalysts had invited Krishna for a discussion session to Washington, DC after the Sarobia gathering. Dr Benjamin Weininger had organized these Washington sessions and had invited us to stay in his Maryland home. These meetings were a new experience for Krinsh. Here he was not among his old followers who found every word and every sigh he uttered something to cherish and remember. Men like Harry Stack Sullivan and Erich Fromm were quite sure of their ground and their vocabulary, from both of which Krinsh tried to dislodge them. He tried to insist on dropping old conditioning, thought, knowledge. While some of them felt they had come up against a blank wall and needed a new frontier, what Krinsh called professionalism in their vocabulary became a frequent stumbling block. The whole session, whether successful in terms of closer understanding or not, was arduous for Krinsh.

A School is Born

He had relied emotionally for the past fourteen years on Rosalind's total attention and enveloping care being projected toward him. She fully understood that he needed the devotion and commitment of those close to him no matter how detached he liked to sound. While he did everything to encourage her to take on the school, he realized that he had lost her undivided focus. During our stay at the Weiningers, with a strange sense of desperation Krishna came to Rosalind's room at night. He had not shown such indiscretion for a long time and it made her very uncomfortable.

At Arya Vihara we still had the cow and the chickens, which the Ishis had cared for in our absence, but for which Rosalind was still basically responsible. One day the rooster Hercules did not recognize my mother when she came to feed him and his hens. Her face was blocked by the large pan she was holding. He rushed at her and jabbed his spur all the way through her foot. Fortunately, no infection resulted, but the wound was very painful; it was typical of her to have no hard feelings towards Hercules.

The week the school was to open and all the boarders were to arrive, Rosalind, unstable still from her foot wound and the long-ago effects of a ski injury, slipped on the back steps. She broke her ankle, which had to be set in a cast to the knee.

Many of the students had never experienced the joys of farm life, Jimmy Sloss among them. The day after he arrived, the cow went into calf-birth, and, as the calf was coming feet first and had to be turned, it took all the help available. With my mother laid up, Willie, as the head midwife, feeling that I, a young girl should not be present, called on Krinsh and Jimmy to help. His mother believed she had sent her son to Ojai to be under Krishnamurti's enlightening influence. But Jimmy, who did not even know that hens could lay eggs without roosters around, who was not too sure just how milk got from the cow into the bottle and had never seen anything being born, felt this was quite a startling though edifying introduction to Ojai. In spite of the novice midwives, all went well with the calf and Tina provided good milk throughout the school year. Not long after that our eccentric cat Minnie decided to have her kittens on Jimmy's bed.

Suddenly Krinsh became desperately ill with high fever and kidney pain. As my mother was on crutches and nine pupils were living in Arya Vihara, it was a crisis. Krinsh would allow no one but my mother near him. She moved him from Pine Cottage to the front room in the big house, where she had nursed Nitya before he died. There she undertook to nurse Krinsh night and day, at the same time somehow managing to run the household and oversee the organization of the school.

As she found crutches impossibly cumbersome while feeding and sponge-bathing Krinsh, she had to crawl around the room, dragging her encased leg. Even in a semi-delirious state, Krinsh insisted that there be no other nurse and made her promise if he became unconscious that in no event would he be taken to the hospital. He was convinced he would surely die there. He refused also to have a doctor, but Hugh Keller, a friend and chiropractor, checked him every day. It was Hugh's professional opinion that Krishna's illness was entirely due to his celibate life which, he thought, had affected the prostate gland. If she had been capable of such feelings at that moment, this diagnosis might have caused Rosalind a fleeting moment of amusement.

Aldous and Maria, as they had done when Sophia was dying, came very often and sat quietly in the patio, giving their loving support. They felt Rosalind was in a very bad position with her promise to Krishna and would be severely criticized if anything should happen to him.

One particularly critical night, while my mother stayed by Krinsh's side, my father and I paced up and down the driveway under the brilliantly starred Ojai sky. I shall never forget the love he expressed for Krinsh, saying our lives would be so strange and empty without him. He could not have guessed then that it would not be death that would cause that emptiness for him. That time had not yet come when they would no longer be close. In spite of difficulties, there had always been a tie, which even Keiro, by whatever means, had recognized, for better and for worse.

Eventually a urologist was consulted at the Sansum clinic in Santa Barbara. He diagnosed that Krishna had nephritis. After intensive care for over six weeks, Krishna slowly began to recover and entered into six months' convalescence. Of course, all his travel plans for that year had been cancelled, but there was no way to cancel the use of Arya Vihara as a dormitory. It was imperative to keep everyone quiet during the worst of his illness. We all sat in the living-room in the evenings, doing our homework as quietly as if we were in a library or monastery. We were allowed to play classical music softly on the phonograph. That young people from diverse homes could be so co-operative and, with such good will, show spontaneous consideration was an unexpected precedent in those first formative months for a school that was based on precisely such ideals. Some of the pupils had never heard of Krinsh, some were Theosophists, a few were children of his followers.

A School is Born

As Krinsh got better, the young people in the house did not seem to bother him. He had grown a beard and would sit about in his bathrobe and look over our activities with increasing interest. He came out occasionally to chat especially with Jimmy, for whom he had a particular affinity. Jimmy already had the clear mind of the mathematician he would become. Some were too shy to speak to him and others not shy at all. I believe his recuperation was enhanced by this mingling with young people. We all felt his quiet observation of us and in part returned it. He had often said that to help someone with a problem all you had to do was understand it without judgment, to see it clearly, and in time this understanding would be transmitted to the other person. His non-verbal self was at its best in such circumstances. To have had the opportunity to experience that directly was worth a hundred of his lectures.

Thanks to Louis and Robert the financial end of the school held up in spite of a ratio of twelve students to eight teachers. There was a great deal of enthusiasm for the project. It seemed that finally Mrs Besant's vision was shaping into reality, even though the school had not been built on Happy Valley land. Although no one realized it then, it would be another thirty years before the school could move there.

The walnut ranch was still the only source of income for Happy Valley and it just barely paid expenses each year as the correspondence between Louis and Mr Robbie showed:

October 31st, 1946

Dear Louis,

I have your letter of the 29th in regard to the proposed expenses on the Happy Valley Nut Factory.

Our trouble in blowing the nuts off the trees will be greatly exceeded by our trouble in blowing the other nuts off the land as soon as the Fifth and Sixth Races begin to move in.

Financing the school was to become an ever-increasing problem. Fortunately, Rosalind was adept at finding ways to economize; both men appreciated that quality in her while they recognized that she sometimes became overly optimistic in her expectations of people.

November 13th, 1946

Dear Louis,

I think you must have heard from Rosalind about employing F——
to build the dormitory. Rosalind was at first too enthusiastic and is

now perhaps a little too disillusioned, but anyway I will be quite content to have Neutra or any other Neutral architect you may choose.

Rosalind and Krishna weathered the first year of the school, but their relationship had undergone a change. Nursing him had put an emotional and physical strain on her. Perhaps they both felt that they had been too closely confined during the past seven years. The heavy work during those war years had taken much of Rosalind's vitality. She had begun to feel Krishna's constant presence and needs taxing. She welcomed the thought of a little space and time apart from him.

The school rested heavily on her shoulders, although she had no official title and never took a salary. Dr Ferrando was not able, due to age, health, and lack of experience to run the organizational end, although he was a wonderful figure at the helm and in the classroom. Rosalind also had to oversee the converting of the bath-houses into dining-room and dormitory space for the second year of the school. There were now too many students to fit into Arya Vihara. For Rosalind, the school had become, and was to remain for twenty years, an eighteen-hour-a-day job, as Robert was among the first to notice.

August 1947

Dearest Rozzie,

   Don't work too hard nor worry too much . . . last year we had 12 pupils and no dormitory and this year we shall have 12 dormitories and no pupils which makes a perfect average . . .

The dormitories were finished in time for the opening of the second year, leaving Louis and Robert with still more mortgages to pay off. They were indeed the angels behind the scenes. Louis wrote to Robert in January 1948:

Dear Robert,

   . . . I note your fear as to my getting to heaven through the Happy Valley back door. My idea of heavenly developments on Happy Valley would be if we raised forty tons of walnuts this year and got about thirty cents per pound. But so far we are very short of rain indeed. There was an Indian chief who came to town from Oregon the other day, and he caused a very minor sprinkle in Los Angeles. I hope that he is still actively dancing around a spot in the ground and that Old Man Coyote will hear his invocations.

A School is Born

Now for spiritually minded people, it is a shame that the subject of money intrudes itself at every point. You know that together we owe $4000 on a mortgage on the second building. I am intending to clear up my share sometime this year since I do not like the smell of mortgages. I venture to say that you feel the same.

. . . may I suggest in the spirit of the deep friendship between us, that both of us, in our Wills, protect the future of the School – just in case Karma uses the actor's wooden hook and yanks us away from the stage before we meet?

PART THREE
DENOUEMENT

Lost in a Pathless Land
(1947–86)

20

The Shadow Deepens

In the autumn of 1947 Krishna, fully recovered, left Ojai on his first trip abroad since before the war. Raja went with him as far as England and stayed in Europe until the following spring while Krishna went on to India. Rosalind remained in Ojai, absorbed by the school.

Krishna was to remain away for a year and a half. He had never lost his attachment to the country of his birth and in the last seven years he must have yearned for it. Yet from the moment of his departure from Ojai and Rosalind, he resumed the correspondence with her that had been a daily routine in his absences before the war. His letters continually reaffirmed his love for her and the importance of their relationship; letters which Rosalind seldom answered, for she did not look on them as a form of correspondence but as a need in him to communicate his inner thoughts to someone close. He did not expect her to write and in fact urged her, as he often did me, not to bother.

Soon after his arrival in Bombay, Krishna met a very beautiful young woman, Nandini Mehta, who was married to a Bombay businessman, and her sister Pupul. In May, he went with these two sisters to Ootacamund. In their presence, for the first time in twenty years, the 'process' recurred. Except for one time in Ojai when he had wanted no one, Krishna had always wanted a woman to help him through the 'process'. Nandini would not be the last. This recurrence was very similar to those of the past; weeping and calling for his mother, the pain in the head, the strange voice, widened eyes, different face and a general plea for care of the body. And as in his Theosophical days, there was evidently no question raised by those present of a psychological or physical disorder.

In April 1949 Krishna returned to Ojai. It had been the longest separation between him and Rosalind since they had met in 1922. At first it seemed that their relationship would continue as it had for the past seventeen years, surviving his long absences before the war and the close confinement during it. They seemed happy to see each other. Involved as she was with the school, he gave her support and advice in her new work. On her side, she managed to get away from Ojai for the spring holidays and go with Krinsh and me to Wrightwood.

I had grown up with the knowledge that my parents had a peculiar marriage and I had always felt, and on several occasions had even observed, that the true marriage in our house was between my mother and Krinsh. This never bothered me in the least, perhaps because I was too young to judge. And I was brought up to 'judge not'; Aldous used to say that was one of the most important precepts in the Bible. Anyhow by that spring I was deeply absorbed in a love of my own.

From the moment he had arrived to attend the school in the autumn of 1946, Jimmy Sloss and I had felt a bond which some of our Theosophical elders described as the meeting of 'old souls' but which we took more prosaically for falling in love. Neither of us had the background to be flattered by this reference to old souls. Hopefully if we had, we would have had the sense to realize that it was our proximity to the charmed circle, rather than any merits of our own, that drew forth such conjectures. It would be a source of happiness and reassurance to us both that we would have in the future such wholehearted approval from both immediate family and close friends, for we would marry very young. There would be a few years of separation after Happy Valley School, however, before we came together for good. Jimmy went off a year ahead of me to college in the east. In June 1949 I graduated from the Happy Valley School and was looking forward to going east to Swarthmore College where I had been accepted, as had my cousin David. I was still surrounded by loving adults both within the family and without. Mima Porter gave me a beautiful long satin dress that my mother and I had fancied in a shop window in Santa Barbara but felt was not affordable. My mother spent the summer in Wrightwood with Krinsh and me, making my college wardrobe.

Most unexpectedly, a few days before my departure, Krinsh handed me a hundred dollar bill to buy a warm coat in Philadelphia, the first material gift I had ever had from him. And Iris Tree wrote for me the following poem:

> For Radha
> Wherever you go
> Wherever the winds blow
> May there be singing
> May there be flight
> Of clouds alight
> And wild birds winging

The Shadow Deepens

Wherever the winds rest
And the birds come to nest
To you the dove –
On you through the winds stirring
Through the blind darkness living
The eyes of those you love.

While my adolescent self-centredness had largely insulated me from the realities of that summer, I could not escape noticing a new tension between my mother and Krinsh. It was not happy tension but one which led to quarrels quickly suppressed by my presence. It would be more than twenty years before I knew the cause.

At first Rosalind had found her relationship with Krishna ostensibly unchanged. He seemed eager to return to the intimacy they had shared before his illness. But once he called her by Nandini's name; a name which at that time she did not know. She tried to convince herself it was just a vague and befuddled slip of the tongue. But when this happened again with the same name, she was perturbed. It had not occurred to Rosalind that disloyalty could enter into this relationship. For the reasons already mentioned, she did not consider herself unfaithful to Raja, just as she would not have felt betrayed by any liaison that he might have made. But where Krishna was concerned, at the very least she would have expected to be informed if he were interested in someone else. As her suspicion grew she finally questioned him. He denied absolutely that there was anyone else in his life or could ever be anyone but her. Rosalind was not as gullible and naive as she had once been, and the vehemence of his denials made her all the more suspicious. Later she would claim it was the uncertainty more than his suspected disloyalty that upset her. Over the years she had come to realize that Krishna was not always a truthful person and as he himself had told her that his lies stemmed from fear, she tried to reassure him that there would be no difficult consequences whatsoever if he would just tell her the truth. She said she could accept if he were in love with someone else and they could go on being friends, but she could not endure being deceived.

Over the years, fear and its origins such as death, ambition, insecurity, had been important themes in Krishna's talks. It had always struck me that those problems he talked about with the most profound insight were those problems he struggled with in himself. Others have thought this too, but then wondered, as I did not, how he could speak so knowingly about sex and love.

Krishna's adamant protestations of fidelity to Rosalind were considerably undercut when, six months later, after he had returned to Europe, the following article appeared in *Time* magazine.

REVOLT OF A DOORMAT

Among the great fads of the 1920s [was] . . . Jiddu Krishnamurti . . . a long-haired young Indian seer whom Bernard Shaw once called the most beautiful human being he had ever seen. The Theosophist Annie Besant had adopted Krishnamurti, and was freely predicting that he would be a new messiah. He was more modest. 'I may or may not be the second Christ – I don't know,' he once said. 'I don't want people to look up to me, to worship me. Most people are dumb anyway.'

Bunkum & Nonsense. Almost as if to prove it, thousands of disciples – mostly women – used to gather to listen to his lectures on 'truth and love' . . .

Two years ago, close to 50 and still handsome, Krishnamurti returned to India and relative obscurity . . . Last week he was in the news again, involved in one of India's rare cases of marital dissolution.

After nearly ten years of marriage, the wife of a Bombay textile millionaire, Bhagvandas Chunilal [sic] Mehta asked for a legal separation. She testified that Mehta beat her, locked up her medicines and used insulting language. Then Mehta took the stand with his side of the story. His wife had become a disciple of Krishnamurti. She had heard him call the sacred Hindu wedding verses 'bunkum and nonsense'. At another lecture Krishnamurti said to the males in the audience: 'Do you know what your relationship with your wife is? We all know this relationship – sex, nagging, bullying, dominating, the superficial responses of marriage . . . If you are dominant and you make her your doormat, you say: I am happily married.'

As a result of listening to such teaching Mrs Mehta's attitude toward her husband had changed sharply. 'Before she was always strong, but good,' said Mehta. 'Afterwards . . . she became aggressive . . . I had come to the conclusion that under the guise of teaching, Krishnamurti was running after my wife.'

Resentment & Rupture. Declaring that her eyes had been opened by Krishnamurti's teachings, Mrs Mehta had told her husband she would live a celibate life and had moved into the dressing room. Judge Eric Weston . . . denied Mrs Mehta's petition. He dryly observed: I do not think there is any room for doubt that the teachings [of Krishnamurti] suggesting revolt of the wife from her

doormat position must have had their effect upon her mind . . .
This led to her refusal to carry on marital relations with her husband,
which must have caused considerable resentment.'[1]

Rosalind knew a side of Krishna that was undreamed of by Raja. She
could read between the lines and believe that Mr Mehta might have some
truth on his side. Raja's only concern was to protect Krishna from such
notoriety. He went to considerable pains to persuade *Time* not to go on
with this story. It was the first unpleasant publicity since the 1920s. It
was quite disconcerting to him that the moment Krishna took off on
his own he had become embroiled in such an unsavoury situation.

Rosalind noted the obvious inaccuracies in the article while believing
that Nandini was a passive and innocent party. She realized it was quite
possible that Krishna had become infatuated without his affections being
reciprocated – at least in kind. But she was still convinced he had not
been truthful about his own feelings.

In spite of the trouble Krishna had landed in during the previous
year Raja again refrained from accompanying him to India in 1950.
Krishna had often been the subject of various rumours, unfounded in
even a grain of reality. Rosalind's suspicions would not have occurred
to Raja. Besides, he had a lot of work to do in Ojai. The three of them
planned to meet in Europe in the spring.

When Rosalind arrived in London, her first trip there since 1936, she
met up with many old friends some of whom, like Kitty Shiva Rao, had
just come from India. She heard innuendoes that had been circulating
about Krishna and his new friends. She was deeply disturbed and was
further convinced that Krishna had refused to be truthful with her; for
his letters, in which he supposedly described to her every detail of his
life, did not correspond with what she heard. According to these reports
he was not always in the place that he claimed to her to be and Nandini's
name was frequently linked with his. Krishna never mentioned her in
his letters to Rosalind. There was no one with whom Rosalind could
discuss her distress. For many years she had carried that secret part of
her life with ease for it had been relatively happy. Now in her misery
the burden was becoming unbearable. She lost weight and was unable
to shake off a feeling of malaise that had started on the transatlantic
voyage.

Rosalind went on to Paris, where she was to meet Raja arriving from
California and Krishna arriving from India. On his arrival in Paris on
3 April Raja found her staying in a miserable hotel and immediately
moved her to a better one. He was shocked by her appearance and

state of mind. When she started to tell him the stories she had heard in London about Krishna, and her conviction that he was involved, at least emotionally if not physically, with another woman, Raja was puzzled by the depths of her distress. He could understand his own distress at the probability of more notoriety, if Rosalind's suspicions were correct. In his efforts to protect Krishna he would have put himself in the position of covering up for him and this sort of hypocrisy was highly repugnant to him. Then suddenly, in her frustration, the whole story of her relationship with Krishna burst out. It was a tremendous shock to Raja, to learn of the duration of the affair and particularly to hear of the pregnancies and subsequent abortions. Looking back on that traumatic discussion, Rosalind clearly remembered Raja's shock, and then her shock at realizing that he had not known what she had assumed Krishna to have told him in that letter long ago in Ommen, a letter Raja had never seen.

Krishna arrived in Paris the next day. He was staying as usual with old friends, the Suarés, in their lovely apartment overlooking the Eiffel Tower. For years Carlo Suarés had been translating Krishna's books into French. Both he and his wife Nadine were devoted to Krishna and they were also very fond of Rosalind. It was difficult to keep her distress from them. She told Krishna that she had to have a long talk with him, that she had something important to tell him and asked him to meet her for a walk. They walked for hours along the Seine, he enchanted by the lovely spring day in Paris; she seeing nothing as she told him what she had revealed to Raja.

Krishna was at first horrified and then angry, but after a while he agreed to do as she asked, to talk to Raja about the situation. She felt it was up to Krishna to make his own peace with Raja. Krishna promised to do this, but whenever Rosalind asked him if he had yet done so he put her off with some excuse. It was not the sort of confrontation he would welcome, any more than he had been able to forewarn Mrs Besant privately of his defection from Theosophy. Raja, however, assumed from the way Rosalind had talked about her affair with Krishna, that it was now over. He felt the most profound sympathy for her and in no part of his heart held her to blame. He would always see her as a victim, but Rosalind did not feel victimized. The fact that she had given Krishna so much of her life and her care did not enter into her thinking. She harped on one thing only: knowing the truth, and nothing Krishna said convinced her she was getting it.

Rosalind returned to America on 19 April and visited me at Swarthmore on her way back to Ojai. I knew then that she was very unwell but was given no hint as to the cause and assumed it was from purely physical origins.

When the spring term finished, I met my father and Krinsh at Sarobia to spend a few days with Mr Robbie. It was there that one morning I overheard a terrible quarrel between them. Fortunately we were on a floor to ourselves, Krinsh staying in what had once been Sara's bedroom. My door was open and I heard all they said, the gist of it being that Raja was once again threatening to walk out for good. After many sharp exchanges Krishna begged Raja to stay and he agreed to admit in writing that many times over the years he had lied to Raja and betrayed him in ways he refused to discuss but that he would never do so again. My father eventually calmed down, but lines of unhappiness were etched even deeper in his face.

The three of us went to New York, where a friend had loaned us her vacant apartment. I kept house during Krinsh's talks at Town Hall. Willie had come from Ojai to handle the book sales at the talks. As always, when surrounded by friends and followers, there was an appearance of harmony. Indeed peace seemed to have been restored. There were some pleasant times together, dinners with all the de Manziarly sisters, my father laughing and teasing in his old way and Krinsh joining in and sometimes remarking as he often used to that 'Rajagopal is in very good form and full of jokes.' It would be many years before I would appreciate the depth of my father's power of forgiveness. When I asked him years later how he could have gone on in his relationship with Krinsh, he replied simply, 'What else could I do? If I left him suddenly there would have to be some explanation. Should I have exposed him and Rosalind and brought all that trouble on her and on her work in the school? No! I went on with my end of the work and hoped he would behave after that.' But of course he didn't. Things only got worse.

Raja became more than ever convinced that there were 'two Krishnas', the one who could speak with such insight about the human condition, and the other shadowy Krishna who could deceive and betray a man upon whom he depended and then beg his forgiveness without any intention of rectifying matters. Perhaps it was easier for Raja to accept that there were these two Krishnas. Some day Rosalind would arrive at a similar conclusion.

After the New York talks Raja went directly back to Ojai while Krinsh and I flew to Seattle to meet Rosalind, who had driven up from Ojai with friends. Krinsh was to give a series of talks there, but first we went for ten days' rest on the reclusive Orcas Island. In those peaceful surroundings, whatever tensions there were between Krinsh and my mother seemed to subside. Perhaps by sharing with Raja the burden of her distrust of Krinsh, Rosalind had found it possible to regain her own equilibrium. Back in Seattle for the talks, one day she and Krinsh saw a beautiful little white Ford convertible in a show window and phoned Raja to ask him to buy it for them, which he did.

Krishna had decided to take a year of retreat in Ojai, ostensibly to recuperate from general fatigue, but in fact he made a tremendous effort to heal the rift between himself and Rosalind. On the surface, everything began to appear much as before. Perhaps Rosalind allowed herself to half-believe him or at least to push aside her distress, a tendency she had when things became too difficult.

Raja meanwhile buried himself even deeper in his work. Aldous had introduced him to his publisher at Harper & Row. For many years this would be a fruitful and vital connection for Raja. He had spent the past few years preparing manuscripts for publication as Aldous had been encouraging him to do. Krishna showed not the slightest interest in this project and would not even look at the manuscripts, but he urged Raja to carry on, saying that was his part of the work and he had no wish to be involved in it. Perhaps because of his commitment to this new project, Raja was able to live with the hurt of Krishna's deception. He also allowed himself to assume that the relationship between Krishna and Rosalind was over as he understood Krishna to have implied. Could he really have gone on with his association with Krishna if he believed otherwise? Years later he told Mima Porter that he would have understood people falling in love, that was only human, but he could not understand Krishna leaving him in darkness all those years, while living a life so contrary to the life which Raja had believed he wished them all to live. Perhaps it is the loss of free choice in deciding one's own course of action that is the worst aspect of being deceived. It seems unrealistic, knowing the fearfulness in Krishna's nature, to have expected that he could level with Raja. Raja, however, never saw himself as an intimidating person. He had always tried to do everything Krishna wanted and in the way he wanted it, talking over the details of their lives with great thoroughness. That Krishna was actually agreeing to things he didn't want would have been hard to guess, yet that is what he would later complain of. That winter all three of them made an attempt to return to some sort of normality, if anything about their lives could ever be called normal.

Raja wrote to Rosalind, who had again gone east to spend Christmas with me at Sarobia.

The Shadow Deepens

Jan 13, 1951

Dearest Rosalind,

Sorry not to have written to you before. There really wasn't much to say from here. I still strictly mind my own business, and am very busy with it.

The arrangements you made are working out very well. K. is busy with his gardening. I think he wants to be an expert in growing roses and all sorts of flowers. He seems very well and quite well fed, at least, so he says.

I hope you are having a really restful and interesting time, and that you are feeling all right. When you see Mr Robbie, please give him my dearest love . . . and of course a big kiss to Radhie.

All my love, darling,

RAJA

My frequent weekends with Mr Robbie at Sarobia meant the most to me in those two years in Pennsylvania. He suffered a stroke during the second year which left him quite immobile, and I would sit with him in his sunny study downstairs, from which the intimidating Pack Wack had long since departed, and talk over my term papers. I treasured those times with him, for his mind was as clear as ever but his patience more mellow.

After two years there, I had come to feel Swarthmore was not the right place for me and when the term was over I decided I would transfer to a college in California.

After driving across America with David and our two aunts, I walked happily into the living-room at Arya Vihara to find my father and Krinsh engaged in yet another confrontation. My father was glaring in angry silence while Krinsh, in evident frustration, was pummelling him on the chest. After my nine months' absence, they scarcely took time off to greet me. I drove down to the school in search of my mother and was warmly greeted by a new member of our household; through Iris Tree a large silvery mocha poodle called Coco had found a home with Rosalind. As soon as I walked into the main hall, Coco, about whom I had heard much but had never met, rushed up and licked my face. My mother, observing her dog's acceptance of her daughter, said she had never done this with anyone else. Coco would prove to be a new and much-needed bond in our family.

When Krishna returned to India in that autumn of 1951, Raja decided to accompany him. His mother was getting old and he wanted to see her again. He wanted also to see for himself what was going on around Krishna in India. He went ahead to Europe by train and boat and was to meet Krishna, who preferred to fly, in England.

Whatever Raja's disillusion with Krishna, his affection for Rosalind had not diminished as his letters to her show.

Chicago   *Sept 13, 1951*
Dearest Rosalind and Radha,
    I felt very sad to leave you both and feel very homesick.
    Thank you both for a really nice restful time I had at Wrightwood. You will be back in Ojai tomorrow and I'll be in New York. I am going further and further away.
                      All my love to you both, Darlings –
                                                                    RAJY

And a few days later:

Rosalind Dearest,
    It was so nice talking over the phone with you last Saturday. You did not sound too well. I do hope, darling, you will be sensible about yourself & take good care in every way –
    I shall write to you often, & don't forget to send for me should there be any emergency –
    Is Krishna's knee better – I hope he will rest properly till he has to leave. Give him & all my love.
                      With dearest love to you,
                                                                    RAJY

It took Rosalind a month to answer:

                                                          October 31, 1951
Darling Raja,
    The time goes so quickly that I find it hard to write every week as I see you do.
    In Hollywood we both went to Dr Lupica and I must say I like him very much; he has been very helpful. K did his immigration business with Willie . . . After we returned to Ojai K got his back dislocated and we had quite a time with it . . . The Huxleys were here last weekend and we took him back last Monday to Dr Lupica and he fixed it and strapped it and it is slowly getting better. I was quite worried if he would be able to go off as he was quite crippled from it. Dr Lupica said it is partly due to old age and he would have

to watch it. I hope it is all right while he is with you in London . . .
The school work seems to take all of one's time and energy and I
am trying to get things in a condition where it will not always be
like this.

No matter what their emotional state they both were aware always
of their responsibility for Krishna's well-being, and this continued to
be a primary link in their relationship with each other. There was also
frequent mention of Coco.

Rosalind's involvement with the school and the people around it
was becoming ever deeper. Lili Kraus, the great Hungarian pianist,
had come the previous spring for the Ojai music festival; Lili became
one of the pivotal points in Rosalind's life, not only because of the deep
affection between them, but also because of Lili's generous sharing of her
enormous talent with the school. She would soon be staying for several
months at Arya Vihara with her husband, Otto Mandl. (Rosalind later
arranged for Lili's favourite 1916 Steinway to be brought to Ojai for
Lili's use on her annual visits.)

Aldous and Maria still came regularly and Aldous was now on the
school board. The school took its motto *Aun Aprendo*, ('I am still
learning') from the graduation address he gave there. The philosopher
Gerald Heard gave several talks, as did Alan Watts, the well-known
writer and lecturer on Buddhism, who later sent his daughter to the
school. A letter from Alan Watts to Blanche Matthias dated 16 March
1951, gives his impression of his first encounter with Ojai.

Dear Blanche,

I thought I would . . . thank you for your introduction to Rosalind
Rajagopal. We met again at the end of our stay in L.A. and her husband
guided us up to Ojai.

I must say I am enormously impressed with Rajagopal. I don't
know when I have met such a thoroughly integrated person, at once
so relaxed and so keen in mind . . . and it was a rare pleasure to enjoy
the company of such an amazingly natural human being – especially
after meeting, in L.A., so many would-be philosophers, each with
a separate axe to grind.

We visited the Happy Valley School, and I had a very interesting
hour's talk with the children. Quite a group! They are wonderfully
alert and free without being offensive, and I like the atmosphere of
the place very much.

Most sincerely,

ALAN

There was a lengthy list of eminent visitors in all fields who added an exceptional cultural depth to the school.

Being physically close again that whole year in Ojai had done much to heal the breach between Krishna and Rosalind, at least in Krishna's mind, as his letters to her would show when he left. He told her that the struggle had brought them inwardly closer, that she must not let sadness or anything else come between them and that she was and always would be in his heart – that they were together in their love.

His letters reveal the physical wrench he felt at leaving her and are a series of impassioned pleas to maintain their relationship at all costs. Yet his words reflect, along with his love, a physical and psychic dependency on her. He feels her sitting next to him on the plane and sharing with him the drifting clouds and the blue sky. He says they have been through too much to let anything happen to this inward closeness. He also admonishes her to take regular walks as much for Coco's sake as for hers and to brush and feed the dog properly.

When Krishna met Raja in London he reported back to Rosalind, writing of Raja's cheerful spirits, 'There's a briskness about him which is nice.' He also assured her that of all the dogs he encountered in the park Coco was the aristocrat. And finally he promised that everything would be all right and he would not be influenced then or later. He wrote her a few paragraphs every day and mailed the letter after a week or so, a pattern he would maintain in his absences for the next fifteen years, though the absences would become more frequent and longer.

Rosalind had asked Raja to try to meet Lili Kraus and her husband in Paris. Lili sent Rosalind her fresh and entirely innocent description of this first meeting.

Darling Rosalind,

You must have served our Lord in many lives in many ways to His great joy and satisfaction to have been granted the incomparable privilege to share your life with two such creatures as Krishnamurti and Rajagopal, a Saint and an Angel, a fighting angel at that.

Never will I forget this sign of true friendship and love which enabled us to see 'him' what must I call him, this pure light, this heavenly serenity, this sweet child with the grace of a fairy prince, the politeness of a knight; the wisdom of another, the only real world; this diamond, flower, bird, butterfly – all in one; promise and fulfillment, all in one; this living miracle which goes among us by the name of Krishnamurti? Do, darling Rosalind, tell Rajagopal, when you write to him, our deepest thanks; do also tell him that we found him so sweet in his fierceness! You see, by rights we had no business to see K at all, as we had no permission of the police. The airfield at Orly for transit flights is . . . a border only and the passengers are not allowed to overstep it . . . Mme Suarés had permission and was therefore entitled to have tea with them in that restaurant. But we couldn't get in there. So Rajagopal brought K in to a 'no man's land', which the police allowed us to enter too and that's how we met. I am sure it wasn't at all easy for darling Raja to arrange all that – and he was so sweet and angry because they made such a fuss for really nothing. We saw them for about 15 minutes; an unforgettable, incomprehensible eternity of keenest, rarest happiness, indeed, there could not possibly have been a more auspicious, more promising omen for our Ojai stay, for our association, than this meeting. K spoke so warmly, tenderly about you and about our future in our joint work at the school, as if he would have read my own thoughts!

Darling Rosalind, thank you for your . . . settlement of the matter. A rock rolled off our chests . . . You will be as happy when you hear the piano as you can't possibly imagine! . . .

Love and all good wishes.

Ever,

LILI

While Krishna kept up his repeated reassurances to Rosalind from India, we can infer from Raja's first letter, he had his own troubles.

Madras   *December 11, 1951*
You must have had all the news from the usual Source about the flight from London and what has been happening here since we arrived on the 24th of November. Krishna had a slight fever but he is all right now. I also had something or the other for a couple of days . . . I saw Raja [Jinarajadasa] once or twice. He is quite cordial, though seemed quite surprised that the Happy Valley Foundation is still continuing and doing excellent work. He asked me a hundred questions in a rather supercilious manner. I also saw Rukmini and her Schools . . . I have seen my mother and family too. She has grown very, very old, can't hear or see very well. Except generally in many ways conditions here are worse than I imagined and I certainly feel

quite 'lost'. I hope you are well and are taking good care of yourself and not forgetting the promise to write or cable me should anything turn out to be serious with you.

All my love,

RAJA

Ever since Krishna's defection from the Theosophical Society there had been an estrangement between him and Jinarajadasa. While the two Rajas had maintained their early affection, the politics involved caused some strain.

Krishna meanwhile kept on with his daily letters to Rosalind, evidently confident that she was pacified and accepting his reassurances. He said, 'a molehill was made into a mountain and now even the molehill has gone. Be assured everything is all right.' He also commented on Raja's talk with Jinarajadasa but left himself out of it. He said Jinarajadasa was overly upset about things that happened twenty-five years ago and should be more ready to forgive.

In the early 1930s, under the Star Publishing Trust, a substantial house on six acres had been built for Krishna to stay in and to house the work which continued even in his absence. The place was called Vasanta Vihar and was across the river from the Theosophical Compound at Adyar. Krishna would walk along the river in the evenings, on rare occasions accompanied for a short distance by Raja. Continuing alone beyond the Elphinstone Bridge toward the sea, Krishna avoided, with great deliberation, setting foot in Adyar. He had sworn he would not return there after Mrs Besant died. He made a continual issue of being unwelcome and locked out from the apartments she had said were to be his for life.

Raja did not share these sentiments and often went across to Adyar for a pleasant evening with his friends or a musical performance. Sitting home alone at Vasanta Vihar, Krishna faithfully reported all this to Rosalind, adding cryptic comments about the lust for power in the name of the Master, building schools and organizations, obvious references to the Theosophical activities at Adyar.

Just before Christmas Raja had a letter from Rosalind telling him that an examination had determined she needed major surgery. She intended to go ahead without him or Krishna there. She wanted only to have Erma and me with her. Raja and Krishna both reacted with worry and solicitude about her health:

The Shadow Deepens

Darling Rosalind,

By the time this letter reaches you, you'll have been through it all – and I shall be thinking of you, loving you, and praying for your quick recovery & safe return home. So very sorry that this had to be when I am so far away – but everyone there near you, loves you & would have done everything to make it all bearable and easy – Please do not plunge back into school activities and worries.

All our love, Darling,

RAJA

Krishna's letters indicated that he had been given no advance warning by Raja about the operation. Once he found out, he told Rosalind he had sat all day and thought of her, loved her and, with Raja, prayed for her. If all this were true one can visualize a rather touching scene of the two men together on one side of the globe, drawn close in their common concern for the woman they both loved on the opposite side.

In this same letter, Krishna allowed himself to be distracted from his concern for Rosalind by his annoyance with her over an accusation she had made. He objected to her use of the word, infatuated, regarding his feeling for Nandini. Yet in an oblique way he admitted his attraction by arguing that the word 'infatuated' was still too strong. He claimed it was only a flutter, if even that. But Rosalind would continue to have unwitting indications from friends that he was lying to her still.

Krishna portrayed to Rosalind an amiable and close relationship between him and Raja; praising his work, his advice and showing concern for his occasional illnesses. He also expressed his irritation when he felt Raja did something foolish like taking a hot bath and then sitting under a fan. Of course, Krishna related, he got another cold. This cold led to fever and several days in bed requiring Krishna's nursing.

In spite of Krishna's concern for Raja's health, as usual Raja cured himself in his own way and not at all as Krishna would approve. Each of them considered the other a bit foolhardy in their care of themselves. And in their separation from Rosalind, both their bouts of illness became more frequent.

Rosalind Darling,

I have not been able to write to you during the past 3 weeks, as I have been in bed with constant fever, not high, and a racking dry cough – & headache – K must have written whatever news there has been. I been thinking of you constantly and . . . I am still anxious.

What about Lili Kraus – If you really think it wise & would like to have her & her husband stay at A.V. with you, & thereby make things easy for you in connection with your work, I won't be in your way – I know you will do whatever you think best & wise, especially knowing anything I have said or not said has been because I have only thought ahead, of you & your welfare, about which you have not yourself thought or considered, sufficiently or at all.

Dearest, take good care of yourself, you are a very precious person, and you must get well for everybody's sake & especially for Radha's & mine –

All my love to you,

RAJA

When Nandini and Pupul came to Madras, Krishna no longer tried to keep their visits a secret from Rosalind. Instead, along with his explanation that there was no more 'flutter' at all, he enclosed a perfectly circumspect note to him from Nandini requesting an interview. He also stated that he had shown Raja the note and that Raja enjoyed the company of the sisters and was the one who invited them often to lunch and for evening outings. Krishna was starting to use Raja as a blind, on one hand leading Rosalind to believe that it was Raja who showed an interest in being with the sisters, when in fact Krishna made arrangements for Raja to go somewhere with Pupul, leaving Nandini behind. Raja was in an uncomfortable position, aware of what was happening but unable, without showing indiscretion, to do anything about it.

The situation became more uncomfortable for Raja in Bombay, where he and Krishna stayed on their way to London. Here they were the guests of Ratansi (the rich Indian with whom Nitya had once hoped to go into business). Krishna continued to lay the blame for any contact with the sisters on Raja. One day he arranged for Raja's absence from the house by urging him to take a long and tiresome train journey to the outskirts of Bombay to visit an old friend. Krishna wanted the field to be clear for an important interview with Nandini's father-in-law, who wanted him to persuade her to go back to her husband. Krishna reported this to Rosalind and admitted that he had insisted Nandini be there too and had then told her it was her life and not his and up to her to make up her own mind. He closed the letter to Rosalind with the usual reassurances of his love.

Raja wrote from London a week later. He was always extremely careful about putting anything in writing, especially to Rosalind, whom he believed to be rather careless about leaving letters around. But when he returned to Ojai we would hear how upset he had been by the situation around Krishna, the way of life in India, so contrary to the relatively austere and quiet years in Ojai. There had been devotees too in Ojai, but not often in the house, and certainly not in Krishna's bedroom, where in India they frequently gathered while he ate and dressed.

Rosalind Darling,

I hope you received the short note I sent you from Bombay just before we left. We have been staying quietly at Mrs Bindley's, she is very kind, the house peaceful, & the food good. K gets just what he wants & has been quite well. I want to be alone & quiet for a couple of months & sort myself out, I need to badly after my visit to India – can't write about all this to you & you will understand I am sure. About July or so I shall slowly return to Ojai. K had better go to Wrightwood for May & June, I think he ought to be quiet & alone, & not get involved in Ojai activities. That's my feeling & you & he will do whatever you think best – After July he may want to give a few talks in Ojai before returning to India in September via Europe, as he wants and plans to do.

I hope you are better now tho' I hear you are again overdoing school etc. Please, please take good care of yourself. At least you won't have me round your neck in any way.

I was delighted to hear various accounts of your announcement of Radha's engagement – Hope they are both really happy about it.

All my love, Darling,

RAJA

Please do not leave my letters about. I feel nervous to write.

That February of 1952, Jimmy and I asked Rosalind to announce our engagement at the school's Valentine party. My father had written to me from London:

Dearest Radha,

. . . I shall write to him [Jimmy] soon and tell him how glad I am about him and you. It is good to hear that you feel right about him and really happy . . . When are your exams?

Don't work too hard, just enough . . . unless you really enjoy your studies. I only hope that you intend to complete college both of you & get your degrees – you need not do brilliantly but it would

be wise & good to finish what you have begun. I hope Jim feels that
way too. Of course I am very happy about you, darling, and I love
you always very dearly . . .

All my love to you, darling

DADDY

Krinsh also gave his blessings, still addressing me as Kittums. He
said he was really so glad, very glad and happy about me and Jimmy
but it wasn't a great surprise for he had thought, all along, it would
be that way.

And I believe he really had from the very first.

With Raja's approval, Lili Kraus and her husband Otto Mandl had
been spending the past few months at Arya Vihara. Raja understood
how much this meant to Rosalind, even though he worried that as
always she was overdoing it. Krishna would not normally have minded
this arrangement, but he would later feel that Lili and Otto were part of
the obstacle to his returning which Rosalind unexpectedly raised. On
the grounds that her health was still not back to normal and that the
strain of closing the school for summer was very great, she asked that
he wait until June to return to Ojai. This had never happened before
and it evidently did not occur to Krishna that he himself might be the
cause of strain on her and that she wished to get through her school
year without this added burden. He acquiesced in her request but made
mournful allusions to the gloomy weather in London – that his hands
were so cold he could hardly write, and nostalgic allusions to California
in the spring, hoping she saw the beauty of Ojai and rejoiced. While
Krishna would never have stated any resentment about Lili being in
Arya Vihara, there is an occasional subtle reference to her presence
there and a hope that this was not the cause for Rosalind's fatigue.
Rosalind knew Krishna well enough – and he knew she did – to get the
message that he was unhappy at being kept away from Ojai, having to
walk round and round in a dreary little park (although there are larger
parks in London which are very beautiful in April) and go to boring
movies with Raja. He was distinctly out of sorts.

She suddenly changed her mind, relented, and as far as Krishna was
concerned everything was well again. The nearer the time came for
them to meet, the more loving his letters became and India and those
he had left there seemed to recede utterly from his thoughts, at least
those he expressed to Rosalind.

Once back in Ojai Krishna appeared to be quite charmed by Lili, as
indeed who would not be, and he even made a point of sitting in the

232

patio when she practised the piano to show how much he enjoyed her playing.

In addition to being one of the greatest pianists of our time, Lili was one of the most extrordinary people we had met. She had an intense beauty, and a vibrancy of spirit that not only flowed through her playing but warmed all those in her presence, and this quality never diminished, not even in her last days of life.

When the Japanese took Singapore and subsequently Java, Lili, her husband and children were on a concert tour in the Dutch East Indies. They were incarcerated in a prison camp for three years; for the first year she and her husband were separated from the children. A vindictive Dutch woman, threatened by severe beating for having had an affair with a Japanese officer, declared that Lili was a spy, thus she was put into the subterranean cells of the Kempe Tai, the equivalent force of the Gestapo.

Dr Mandl forced his way seven or eight times to the offices of the Kempe Tai, maintaining that whatever charges were to be made could only concern him, since Lili was totally apolitical: an artist and a mother – nothing else.

One of Lili's co-prisoners told her husband that the guards had threatened to cut off her hands. Fortunately, just in time, the camp was visited by a high-ranking officer who had once heard her play in Tokyo. Not only did he avert this unspeakable tragedy, but he saw that she had a piano and reunited the family, though he did not release them. They lost almost everything material in the war, but Lili's existence was not dependent on material things as she would prove. When she left Ojai after her stay at Arya Vihara, Lili wrote to Rosalind:

> You remember after having met Krishnaji and Rajagopal in Paris, I wrote to you saying, how well you must have served the Lord to be chosen as their life's companion. Having had the never fading joy of living with you all these months I can understand so easily why you should have been granted that privilege. I will not make you blush and wince and wiggle by telling you of all the virtues which make the very air round you sweet for me to breathe; let me just tell this much, that in all hours, days, weeks we spent together never once was my intention, taste, desire in discord with yours, not on one single point. All you wanted, or did, or thought, or felt, or planned I found good, right, reasonable, lovable in perfect harmony with my reactions. So that now, being away I am there, living in you, as it were, except, my poor sweet love, that all such

burden, work, problems, difficulties as doubtless have to be coped
with are left for your shoulders to bear, like always. I only having
the picture of you living in Arya Vihara with beloved Krinsh and
beautiful, incomparable and ever unique Coco . . .

I embrace and kiss you with all the tenderness and love of my
heart.

Ever,

LILI

And Lili's husband, Otto Mandl, also expressed his gratitude for their
stay in Ojai:

June 7th, '52

My dear Friend Rosalind!

People tease me for being an optimist – But even so I had nearly
given up hope that in this life of mine I would still be able to find
a place where I can put my roots in the ground . . . We both feel
without hesitation or doubt that we have found our home, our new
and lasting home in your nearness, whatever roof you may ultimately
choose for us in Ojai valley. The loving care you bestowed on us, the
full confidence and its echo, the deep understanding you had for our
needs and wishes, this and much more for which I have no words
but an unfading memory, cannot have been a passing phase . . .

I will in London and Paris . . . search for every gleam of hope, for
a solution of the Famine problem which seems to worry Krishnaji
as it worries Aldous. Oh, I know only too well, how Krishnaji (I
hear his words, his very fiery voice) will say: 'What is the use of all
your material remedies, your calculations, your statistics and your
planning, unless you can improve the heart of man?' Let me try just
the same, especially to improve my own mind, to see, think more
clearly, more lovingly, more detachedly.

One thing I found in your spiritual atmosphere, found it for the first
time in my old age: that the thirty or forty years, since my youth must
have made a rather bad old creature out of me – this I recognized one
morning, after having lived 3 weeks in Arya Vihara, when suddenly I
felt different, cleaner, unburdened, carefree, with a better conscience
toward my future; and like a revelation I knew: 'That's how I always
felt when I was 16, 19, 25!' I had lost the memory of it and I must have
been sliding down away from the 'Right Way' into an entanglement
of worries, of impatient efforts, of patching up weaknesses, of futile
vanities – and suddenly it seemed that fresh strength had been given

me to start anew . . . to see once more with a clear mind, to strive for truth, for unity with the universe, as I did 40 years ago.

I had no intention to tell you this when I started the letter . . . It may not be understandable to you, and still I would have hidden the most important thing that happened between us, had I not mentioned it. Yours with a happy heart,

OTTO

Lili and Otto were not the only ones to have these feelings about Rosalind. Most people who came to Arya Vihara attributed the healing atmosphere there solely to Krishna, but not all of them. Beato also, would one day express her feelings about my mother.

As I think of friends who influenced my life, I know that your mother has meant more to me than anyone else. I doubt if I could have hung on had I not met her, for I was in deep confusion, and she lifted my orientation towards the spiritual life. Being near her cured me of fanaticism and false worship where the higher life is concerned, and though Krishnamurti's words meant a great deal to me, I understood more of what he said because she lived the actuality of his thoughts.

It started sixty years ago at a party when I saw her glance at your father with the most beautiful of smiles, as if the heavens opened and there was no evil in the world, and that glow from her has remained with me ever since.

There were times when in despair I went to her for comfort and her presence clarified the problem and lifted me into another dimension . . . My life has not only changed living near her, but in the darkness that comes down at times on most of us, she has been the light.[2]

That light was in danger of dimming. Even as close a friend as Beato could not see the cause of Rosalind's increasing unhappiness. It would have been difficult for many people to accept that anyone living so close to Krishna could have problems at all. Many years ago Raja had flinched when a devotee had given him a vigorous handshake. 'I have arthritis,' he explained. '*You* have arthritis when you live so close to *Him*?!' was the incredulous response.

Raja returned early in July to California to find his immediate family in a tailspin. Jimmy and I who had been engaged since February now wanted, for a very good reason, to get married right away. Not yet knowing the story of my mother's secret pregnancies, I was surprised to find that she took my news so hard. I looked forward most anxiously to my father's arrival from Europe and my expectations were not in vain. Raja was able to set aside his own worries enough to reassure us that all he was concerned about was that we really loved each other and wanted to marry. He would continue to support me through my final year of college, as he was anxious that I should finish, and Jimmy's father agreed to do the same for him so we had no immediate financial problems.

Our wedding was a happy occasion. Both family and friends had long felt that we were perfectly suited for each other and whatever tensions hung about somehow floated away that day. Even Krinsh who, to my knowledge, had never gone to anyone's wedding, was at ours and in his most positive and beneficent mood. Perhaps his attitude about such things had just mellowed, but he seemed genuinely happy about this marriage. John Ingelman performed the service for he and Hilda had been the first people to see me and I had always been exceptionally close to them. Because John was a priest in the Liberal Catholic Church the service would be that, as Rosalind's and Raja's had been in London, but both Jimmy and I insisted on certain religious phrases being removed which gave John considerable trouble with his bishop.

We honeymooned briefly in a charming cottage on the Santa Barbara riviera, belonging to one of Krinsh's elderly spinster devotees. She had offered the house to Rosalind and Krinsh for the summer.

Krishna still maintained his long-standing position of having no involvement with organizing or publishing his work. Raja had completed the editing of the first book with Harper's, a slender volume, *Education and the Significance of Life*, published in 1953, soon followed by *The First and Last Freedom*, with a foreword by Aldous Huxley and then the three volumes entitled *Commentaries on Living*. On these last, Raja finally allowed the publishers to include his name as editor. Both Krishna's notebooks and his verbatim talks needed meticulous and patient editing, which Raja had spent most of his time doing for the past twenty-five years. He had always kept himself in the background even though, from the beginning, Krishna made it amply and frequently clear that all publishing was entirely Raja's domain. Raja saw to the contracts and had an excellent working relationship with the editors, a relationship in which Krishna showed only the most cursory interest. He was to reverse this position drastically.

21

The Letter

Krishna's year of retreat in Ojai had done much to heal his relationship with Rosalind, but he still felt it necessary to convince her of his loyalty. Shortly before his departure from Ojai in autumn 1952, he gave her the pencil copy of a letter he had written to Nandini. He said he was going to carry the original, of which this was an exact duplicate, to deliver in person. This gesture of Krishna's did not mean as much to Rosalind as he might have hoped. She still remembered the letter he had written in Ommen, which she now knew had never been delivered to Raja.

Thinking that this was very likely to happen again, Rosalind told Raja that Krishna had written a letter to Nandini and asked that he see that it was properly delivered. She did not show him her copy and he was not aware of its existence.

Always afraid of indiscreet letters falling into the wrong hands, with Krishna's approval, Raja agreed to carry the letter among his papers for safe keeping until they arrived in India. There, unless Rosalind advised otherwise, he would give it to Krishna to deliver. While Raja did not wish to involve himself further in the matter, he hoped that the situation would be resolved as quickly and quietly as possible. He well understood the strain Rosalind had been under and sympathized, but her relationship with Krishna, in addition to the personal anguish it caused him, had greatly complicated his professional life. Now the last thing he wanted was to be caught in another triangle, that of Krishna, Rosalind and Nandini. He had tried all these years, as part of what he felt to be his duty toward Krishna and 'the Work', to protect both from the muddles and messes that Krishna too often generated around him. He did not regard this letter as a prudent course for Krishna to take and hoped Rosalind would encourage Krishna to drop the whole matter. Raja was wearying of these complications and would gradually withdraw more and more. He found travelling with Krishna and arranging the details of his life an increasing source of irritation.

From a later vantage point, one can see that the old cornerstone of their lives together had crumbled disastrously. But at the time they all failed to clarify between themselves exactly what the new cornerstone, if any, would be. Raja had believed that there was a bond of affection between the three of them that excluded none of them. The physical relationship between Krishna and Rosalind had upset the balance. For him or Rosalind to have become involved with an outside party would not have had the same impact on their lives. For Krishna to become involved with *anyone at all* was in contradiction to the chaste public image he himself had established and to which Raja had lent his trust. Raja felt that a severe transgression of this trust had taken place but that this transgression had ended. If he had read the letter, at least the copy that Krishna left with Rosalind (which may or may not have resembled the original), Raja would have realized that in Krishna's mind the affair with Rosalind was far from over. For in that copy of his letter to Nandini, Krishna stated that there was a woman in his life who had been there for more than twenty years and that such a relationship was not to be broken and he didn't intend to break it. He went on to apologize if his letters or conversations had given a misleading impression and advised Nandini not to build around false hope.

As usual, Raja left for London somewhat ahead of Krishna, from where he wrote to Rosalind before Krishna left Ojai to join him.

2nd October, 1952

Thank you for your very dear letter which I received on the boat just before sailing. I hope you are feeling a little rested. Please don't exhaust yourself. It is better to live doing little than to die doing too much.

That special letter is still with me, and I hope to hear from you definitely about it once again before anything is done.

London is bitterly cold and dreary. Please tell Krishna to be warmly dressed. Usually he likes to carry his overcoat on one arm and his coat on the other, and freeze and look miserable.

Please pat Coco for me, and tell her how much I love her. She is some Coco – one can't forget her easily.

All my love,

RAJA

Krishna continued with his daily writings to Rosalind. Ardent affirmations of his love for her were interspersed with descriptions of people and scenery and details of their daily existence. Kitty Shiva Rao and her brother-in-law Sir B.N. Rao, Indian Ambassador to the United Nations, were on the plane with them as far as Rome. They both stopped off in

The Letter

Alexandria to visit the Suarés, who had a villa there in addition to their apartment in Paris. (They would shortly, under Nasser, lose most of their money and all their holdings in Egypt). Krishna walked with Carlo Suarés along the beach in Alexandria while Raja slept. That Krishna's concern for his public image was as strong as Raja assumed it to be was graphically tested a few days later. There came what was for Krishna a nerve-racking episode. Ready to depart from Bombay in Cairo airport, they were temporary victims of the domestic tensions in Egypt. In customs every shoe and every pocket was felt and searched. Officials read all the letters that Raja was carrying but by some miracle missed the one intended for Nandini and also the one Krishna was in the process of writing to Rosalind and had not yet mailed. He mailed it from Bombay, expressing his resolve never again to be caught with such a letter on his person. He thanked God they hadn't found the letter to Nandini either. Before closing, he resumed the pattern of his previous letters from India, stressing Raja's close association with Pupul and Nandini, while he, Krishna stayed home alone writing to Rosalind, feeling her closeness and his love for her and asserting that all the ado about 'that other person' was faded and forgotten.

For the next four months Rosalind was given almost daily excuses for why the letter had still not been delivered to Nandini. At first Raja was the reason. Krishna claimed that Raja refused to turn over the letter saying it should not be delivered as it would cause gossip and involve him and Rosalind. Krishna assured Rosalind that he tried each day to bring up the subject and got nowhere. He said he would not give up, even if it meant writing another letter and sending it without Raja's approval. This he somehow never got around to doing. By mid-December he had a new excuse. Nandini's health was poor and Krishna was worried that she did not have the strength to read such a letter, so delivery would have to be postponed. After that Krishna and Raja went to Benares and from there, according to Krishna, it was not safe to mail the letter as the mail was easily tampered with.

Rosalind had long since realized that the letter would not be delivered and was too involved with her work to give it much more thought. In Krishna's absence the whole matter lost its significance. She made no effort to communicate with Raja about it. Later, Raja claimed he had long before handed it over to Krishna, there had not been those endless discussions and he forgot about it, never suspecting that he had been worked into Krishna's dissemblance. What had evidently occupied a considerable amount of Krishna's thought had been pushed to the background by both Rosalind and Raja. By February the subject was dropped for ever and no more was heard of the letter.

Raja's health was poor that year. Krishna thought Raja had strained something doing yoga, which he had been persuaded by Krishna to take up. He found it hard to swallow and developed an intermittent pain in his oesophagus. This would become a chronic problem with serious side effects and I would later wonder if the cause was not yoga but that there had just been too many things for him to 'swallow'. He gave only a hint of this in his letters to my mother:

Poona   *Jan 12, 1953*
Rosalind Darling,

I received the only letter, since I arrived in India, that you have written. I have been, I know, very remiss, and I am very sorry. Not a day has passed without my thinking of you with deep love . . . Please remember letters get lost here very easily, or opened & thrown away – So write guardedly & do not forget to glue and seal properly.

Of course I shall be there for Radha's graduation or even before – Hope all goes well – Thinking of you constantly with deepest love,

RAJA

Bombay   *March 1, 1953*
Thank you, Darling, for the 2 cables. The first one made me rather worried & then a few hours later came the good news. I am very happy, all is well.

How is the new Baby & how is her dear, darling mother? To think of Radhi with a baby girl. Incredible!! What name has the Baby? I wonder if Radha & Jimmy liked my suggestion?

All my love, always,

RAJA

[handwritten on the bottom of typed letter]

Things are not right for me here. I am afraid finally so. Well – That is the end of the long matter. However I shall go on –

Krishna made it clear to Rosalind too, in his own way that things were not right between him and Raja. He was justifiably indignant that Raja failed to inform him when Jimmy's and my baby was born. It was twelve days after the news had come, before Raja mentioned

240

it to him, a clear indication of estrangement, large or small, between them.

Yet another cause for conflict was on the horizon. Lady Emily wanted to publish *Candles in the Sun*, the autobiography of her years with Theosophy and Krishna. Once again Raja would be the scapegoat during the period of bitter controversy that would ensue.

22

Candles in the Storm

As he had promised, Raja returned to California in time for my graduation from Scripps College and Jimmy's graduation from Pomona in June 1953. The two colleges were adjacent and we had lived for the past year in a small apartment in Claremont. In July we moved with our baby, Catherine Anjali, to northern California, where Jimmy worked as a physicist at the Atomic Energy Commission for a year before we both went on to graduate school at Berkeley.

There was also another change in the family: Louis Zalk's wife had recently died and Erma and Louis were married that summer of 1953. They were in their late sixties and were to enjoy ten years of happily married life. We would remain very close to them both. Louis had always been a strong presence in our lives and his devotion to both Krishna and Raja had been steadfast.

Rosalind had been offered a house on the south edge of Point Lobos in the Carmel Highlands, and she and Krinsh spent a good part of that summer there, with us joining them on weekends.

At fifty-eight, Krishna still wanted the same physical relationship with Rosalind that had started twenty years before and which, in spite of the recent contentiousness between them, had not, as Raja believed, yet terminated. The house on Point Lobos stood in isolated scenic beauty, opening on to the State Park and hanging over a churning sea below. The bark of sea-lions was constant above the waves and the tide pools harboured an array of exquisite sea creatures. Except for our visits on the weekends, there was every opportunity for intimacy. On Rosalind's side, their relationship had become a habit like the habit of a marriage that is no longer good but not bad enough to struggle through an ending. But at times like this, away from the pressures of the school, she still felt resurrectional sparks of their old love and Krishna made every effort to fan these embers. He acted toward me as he always had and assumed a grandfatherly role toward Tinka (as we had nicknamed our baby). He was pleased that her middle name was Anjali, my father's suggestion, and explained that it meant in Sanskrit literally the space between the hands when held together in greeting, or infinite peace. I felt at times that we were once again the family we had always been, which expanded under the same tension to incorporate my father on his infrequent appearances. While Raja and Rosalind expressed deep affection towards each other in their letters, their personalities caused conflict in direct communion, exacerbated by the presence of Krinsh, who often went back and forth between them like a child intent on dividing and ruling. Ostensibly trying to make peace, the comments he repeated and the tales he told inevitably led to worse arguments. My father's disposition became more and more irascible and even his close friends began to wonder at this change, making it all the easier for Krishna in the near future to draw on their sympathy.

Krishna and Raja left again for Europe and India in the autumn. Krishna's letters began to express a more philosophical tone than they had in the past, but he still included his declarations of love. He entreated Rosalind to remain open to everything, including their love and to feel their closeness.

Raja was busy in Europe arranging foreign translations and copy-rights, and meeting with the editor from Harper's, who was in Rome. Krishna joined them in a tour of the Vatican and expressed to Rosalind his approval of Raja's efforts. For some time he would continue, in small ways, to assure Rosalind of this approval of Raja, just as he assured her of his love for her, as if he were anxious to maintain a status quo, to keep their relationships and their lives as they had always been. Sometimes he seemed to be chiding her, saying it was thoughtless and destructive to obscure their love by their behaviour.

Lady Emily had asked Raja to come and see her about a book she had written, but both his health, his own involvement in publishing, and an instinct that this was going to be a sticky matter, led him to defer this interview and he and Krishna went off to India without fulfilling her request. Krishna, however, wrote and asked that he and Raja could see the book before it went to press. Lady Emily took the trouble to send her manuscript to Madras with the hope that they would return it as soon as possible. She had a publisher and was naturally anxious to proceed. Krishna refused to look at the manuscript carefully, although he glanced at it peripherally and indicated to Raja that it should not be published.

Raja, who read it thoroughly, thought this was unfair to Lady Emily, that there were things in it that could be deleted to spare various people's feelings but that it was an important record of Krishna's development at a crucial era in his life, as well as the historical events around the

Theosophical Society. However, he felt his suggestions would be too involved to handle by correspondence and urged Lady Emily to hold up publication until they could all discuss it together.

Raja had the added complication of explaining Krishna's attitude, for Krishna refused to do this himself. It was clear that Krishna didn't want it published at all, but he would not be pinned down, claiming he had not read it, though he had obviously read enough to draw a negative conclusion. What had struck him was the inclusion of his experience under the pepper tree in Ojai. Lady Emily had been one of the privileged few to receive the full account typed by Raja in 1923 and she had included that in her book as well as many letters to her from Krishna, revealing his innermost thoughts about Theosophy, his protectors and other relationships.

In 1953, Krishna was as adamantly opposed to many Theosophists and their views, as he had been when he broke with the society. He had no wish to be reminded, or to have his public reminded, of his origins in the Theosophical Society. All this Raja understood – and he sympathized with much of it. He felt, however, that the book could be satisfactorily edited. He also felt that Krishna must speak for himself and directly to Lady Emily. Meanwhile Lady Emily was left hanging with the clear impression that Krishna was too tired to read her book and would let her know about it later. Raja had made the mistake of protecting Krishna by excusing the delay because of Krishna's fatigue. Much as Nitya had suffered over Krishna's treatment of Mrs Besant, Raja began to imagine the same situation for himself evolving around Lady Emily's book. He tried to get Krishna to take a clear stand. But Krishna characteristically insisted that he would neither approve nor disapprove, that Lady Emily must come to the right decision herself. In addition to this issue, which Raja correctly foresaw was to bring grief all around, the trouble with his oesophagus flared up again.

Life in India was complex for him emotionally. He was often caught between Krishna's new affections and enthusiasms and the consequent appearance of disinterest toward his old workers, who had devoted years to helping him. Krishna had always needed the association with famous, well-to-do and colourful people, while Raja was content to build his friendships among those who were loyal and conscientious and with whom he had a good working relationship; not very exciting, but he had never sought excitement or outward stimulation. There were the inevitable bruised feelings and rivalries endemic in most 'spiritual' circles. When Raja had believed he and Krishna and Rosalind stood together on a solid base of commitment to a way of life, it had been easier to cope with outside personality problems. His letters to Rosalind, only hint at the increasing depression which was soon to consume him.

Darling Rosalind,
     It has not been possible or easy for me to write often; my life in India these few months has been an exact repetition of last year's, nothing whatsoever new, same everything including the problems, but I have thought and thought of you, and you will have known that.

Unlike Rosalind, he could not and would not walk away from problems or pretend they did not exist. He was still determined to carry the responsibilities he had assumed nearly thirty years before. Nevertheless, he was feeling the need to withdraw from a close association with Krishna, although at this point their lives were still tightly bound together.

Rosalind too was undergoing some basic changes. More and more the school was absorbing her attention and becoming her whole life. Her energy, which had been severely tested during the war, had not regained its high level. Yet it was still vital. When Krishna and Raja were in Ojai, or when Jimmy and I came to visit, her outward activity was the same. She still ran the household herself, cooking meals at either end of a long day at school. Her focus, however, was obviously on her work. Her thoughts, as reflected in her conversations, were all related to the school. Her close friends like Lili noticed the change.

Today is the 24th of December
& it is the first free hour in which, at long last, I can go on with this letter . . . but I will never be able to say with words all that is in my heart. I am longing for you with soul and spirit; I already missed you grievously during our last stay in the Ojai. Somehow there was never time enough for the sweet, peaceful relationship; for the exchange of thoughts, ideas; for the beholding of the other's being in wishless, grateful wonder of a fulfilled friendship as it all happened in that unforgettable first sejour of ours in your house. But flowers do blossom differently every year &, as Goethe said 'and, oh, you will not swim in the same river for the second time'. But the river is all there, lovely & mighty, but changed, with new waters running through its bed. And you are there too, in the old-new sameness – & all this is as it should be . . . ever yours,

LILI

In Madras, Krishna was still taking his walks, gazing across the Adyar river at the Theosophical land where he had once been happy and which he was told was still beautiful. He would not break his resolution to never set foot there, but Theosophists came to his talks and he commented to Rosalind that they are not a thoughtful breed.

He wrote her repeated warnings about certain Theosophical Society members who had come to Ojai and were involved in the Happy Valley School. He was adamant that their influence should not enter into the school. He repeatedly insisted that she must speak in the assemblies and keep a tight rein on the general atmosphere, to create the right feeling of oneness and not leave it to others to interpret. No one reading his letters could doubt that he had a strong interest in the school, but just how strong was not yet clear. He evidently felt confident that Rosalind would transmit, without conscious effort, his ideas. He had insisted from the start that he wanted no official connection with the school. It would become clear in the future that he assumed he would have a pipeline to it through Rosalind.

In March 1954, Jimmy and I had our second and last child, whom we named Robert after Mr Robbie. My father found a moment of happiness in this news, writing to us from Athens,

Dearest Radha & Jimmy,

The day I received the news about Baby Robert I went to the Acropolis by myself and sat at the Parthenon and thought of you and Mummy and the newborn, and sent you from there all my love and blessings – It was such a lovely coincidence that I could be at the Parthenon that day – you can have no idea, till you see it, how beautiful it is – not only that but the Acropolis & all around it the sea –

I am sure that one day you will come here & see it all – That at least was what I wished when I had just heard of my dear new friend Baby Robert.

It is good that all has gone well, darling & I hope you are very happy. Please send me a snapshot of the baby & also of Tinka.

All my love to you Four,

DADDY

In Athens, the problem of Lady Emily's book was finally confronted, at least to some degree, by Krishna. He still refrained from making a positive statement about whether it should or should not be published. He used on Lady Emily and her daughter, Mary, very much the same technique he used in his lectures and discussions: to lead his listeners to his view while making them feel they were finding their own path. They were to be open, drop their preconceptions and their desires, and experience what he was saying. This procedure had mixed success when working with abstractions. It was totally disastrous when applied to anything so concrete as a book. He admitted now that he had read it very carefully, that it read very well. Only in talking it over together could a right decision be reached as to whether it should or should not be published, and that decision would not be his.

Raja had hoped that if he kept his opinions to himself Krishna would be forced to come to his own decision and make his opinion clear to Lady Emily. He soon saw that this hope was in vain. When they arrived in London, Krishna was reluctant to discuss the book at all and brought up no objections whatever with Lady Emily. He did show an interest and enthusiasm for the title, *Candles in the Sun*, the sun being the World Teacher in whose light all the candles (those who awaited his coming) were dimmed. This single approbation led Lady Emily and Mary to assume there were no further objections and they proceeded with the publication – little realizing that the storm had just begun.

23

Out Out Brief Candles

There were endless discussions that summer about Lady Emily's book, often in my presence, both in Carmel and Ojai. Like Raja, Rosalind felt that it would be unfair to ask Lady Emily not to publish it, but Krinsh had convinced her that the role she played in the 'process' incident, as described by Nitya, because of her connection to the school, would bring undesirable publicity to it. She suggested her name could be left out, but saw no reason to stop the book. Publication was scheduled for the autumn and Raja had been sent a next-to-final set of page proofs.

Seeing the manuscript in this format seemed to snap Krishna out of his detachment. He became actively opposed to publication at all, which surprised both Rosalind and Raja. Krishna insisted on writing his decision to Lady Emily, leaving no room for doubt as to his objections. She cabled back in distress, explaining the intolerable cost of withdrawal at this point and expressing shock at what she saw as his sudden *volte face*. Krishna persisted with his conviction that the book would do untold damage to him and his work and that no other consideration was important. Lady Emily and Mary found this demand so inconsistent with Krishna's attitude in London that they suspected it was Raja's influence which had wrought the change. This was totally erroneous and one more example of an inability in many people to place responsibility on Krishna for those actions they saw as less than perfect. Krishna could be extremely positive if not downright stubborn when he wished to be, a side of himself that he rarely displayed. If Mary and Lady Emily failed to get this impression in London, they are certainly not to blame. The intentional vagueness that Krishna wielded as detached influence too often caused confusion.

Raja disapproved of KWInc funds being used as financial recompense for the débâcle, reasoning that money collected for Krishna's work could not ethically be used for such a purpose. Neither was he in agreement with Krishna's attitude, but felt it was Krishna's responsiblity to work it out with Lady Emily. Krishna magnanimously offered to pay off the cancellation costs in monthly instalments out of his allowance from

248

Miss Dodge's trust. But Lady Emily declined to accept. Her family shouldered the financial burden alone. According to Mary the whole incident added ten years to her mother's appearance.

Towards Rosalind Krishna took on the role of a protective knight, assuring her repeatedly while in Ojai, and later that autumn in his letters from London, that he had done all this for her and that he would continue to see that everything was right between them. He was more ardent than ever in his pleas that nothing would ever come between them and that what they had together was more important than anything. He promised to make no more mistakes, to do no more thoughtless things and that there was no diminishing of his love.

He ignored the fact that Rosalind did not feel very strongly one way or the other about *Candles*, not even in so far as it affected her. He seemed to feel that the whole incident had drawn them closer, perhaps because he was for once in a position to protect her and to make her aware of it. Perhaps he was also anxious, because of Nandini, that the first occurrence of the 'process', with Rosalind in 1922, be kept private.

Krishna must have sensed that Raja was withdrawing from him. The controversy with Lady Emily had left new wounds between them, wounds unheeded for the time being but which would flare up in the near future.

Back in London, Krishna did his best to comfort Lady Emily – to the degree that once again she got the impression that he would not have minded all that much if her book were after all published. But on the same day that this meeting took place he wrote to Rosalind that *Candles* would definitely not be published *ever* and that he had told Lady Emily she must accept his decision, even to the extent of putting in her will that it would never happen!

Did Krishna himself believe he had settled the matter with Lady Emily in the way he described to Rosalind? Would Lady Emily have been shocked to have seen how casually, in his letter to Rosalind, he treated her distress, always confident that he could sway her to his point of view? Or was he aware of his inability to face any unplesantness; to offer a straightforward 'No' face to face? Lady Emily was not as taken in as Krishna might have imagined. She may have been powerless to take a stand against him, but she could be very clear-sighted. One day she would write to Raja: 'You have been the lamb on Krishna's altar.' Before she died she went even further. She said she knew Krishna was a congenital liar but that she would nevertheless always adore him.

24

India Revisited

For the past few years some of the happiest moments between Rosalind and Krishna had revolved around Coco, the exceptionally intelligent poodle which had come into their lives in her full maturity. Both Krishna and Raja understood that the way to Rosalind's heart was through her dog and in their letters they seldom failed to refer to Coco with great affection. What Rosalind considered to be a love match had occurred between Coco and a beautiful black poodle belonging to the opera singer, Lotte Lehmann. The expectation of puppies had created almost as much of a flurry as Lady Emily's book and Krishna was deeply disappointed that he must leave Ojai before their birth. His letters to Rosalind from London and later from India were full of advice and reminders for the care of the pregnant dog. Then in February 1955 he received the following letter.

Dear Krishnaji:
We have for you $1000.00 to be given to the Rishi Valley School. You may wonder how I am able to send you this amount. Will you please tell the children in your school that I sold my children to raise the money to give you as a token of my regard for you and for all you have done for me such as walking, brushing, feeding and understanding me. I think I must correct the statement that all the money was given for my puppies. There were actually some people who gave money NOT to have a puppy! This I know you will find hard to understand as I do. Hardly anyone could see my beautiful black puppies without longing for one. We have arranged it so you will see one when next you are here, and you can even have one of my grandchildren.
With a heart full of love as always,
COCO [signed with an inked paw mark]

Krishna attributed both the letter and its sentiments to Rosalind. His reply makes clear how deeply touched he was by her generosity to his school and he closed the letter by telling her he loved her very much. (Coco received no credit at all.)

250

India Revisited

Rosalind's dear friend Maria Huxley, died that same month. No one, most of all Aldous, had realized how ill Maria was. She had brought Aldous to visit us in Berkeley not long before and had even then been on radiation treatments for cancer, which she most ill advisedly suspended to take that trip. Her spirit masked whatever misery she was undergoing until the very end. For Aldous's sake, she insisted that everything be as usual. Rosalind had helped to bring Maria home from the hospital two weeks before she died and had remained as close to her as she could. After the funeral Aldous asked most unexpectedly if he could come right up to Arya Vihara. Being with him those few days was my first confrontation with such intense grief. We all, even my mother, felt absolutely helpless in the face of it.

Although Raja accompanied Krishna to Australia in 1955, he had no desire to return to India. At Ojai he could live his own rather hermitic life and go about his work without undue exposure to the annoying aura of devotion that Krishna appeared to encourage in the country of his birth. Rosalind, however, wished to see for herself the scene around Krishna in India and once and for all sort out her feelings. She left the Happy Valley School in the hands of her trusted Assistant Director and flew to Australia to meet Krishna, while Raja returned to Ojai.

She had not travelled abroad with Krishna since the 1930s. She had forgotten what to expect. There was a large crowd to see them off from Sydney, another to greet them in Djakarta during their brief layover to Singapore; nothing of course like in his Theosophical era, but so much more than in California. Fortunately at Singapore there was no reception committee. They stayed at Raffles Hotel and were able for one day to be ordinary tourists. At first Krishna balked at the idea of sightseeing but ended up enjoying it thoroughly, like a small boy who had discovered a new game.

Rosalind's diary for those six months indicates that she had a very interesting time, on which she reported at length for the benefit of the school children back in Ojai. At Benares they were met by a crowd from the school at Rajghat and taken to a beautiful house by the river. It seems they were plunged right off into the school problems, to quote from Rosalind's diary.

Tues. Dec 6: Foundation talk, Rao upset, all upset, crisis for Foundation members to know what to do.
Wed. Dec 7: Foundation meeting. Gurtugi suggests closing upper schools.

On these visits to Krishna's school she was often appealed to by the staff to help clarify what Krishna was saying and what he expected of them. She had behind her nearly ten years' experience in directing a school and was well aware of the psychological as well as of the practical problems. On the one hand Krishna would ask her to help, but he was impatient about her criticism of his habit of favouritism and his failure to acknowledge the honest efforts of those who were really keeping the school together. Rosalind could see that everyone in the school hung on his every word, although Krishna often criticized the staff for failing to understand his teachings.

In Delhi Krishna and Rosalind stayed with Shiva Rao and his Austrian wife Kitty. Shiva Rao, an early tutor of Krishna's at Adyar and Raja's first tutor in Benares, had remained a lifelong friend of them both. Rosalind also met many of Krishna's devotees and friends. She picked up subtle innuendoes about the Mehta divorce incident but could divine no actual facts. More and more, however, she sensed that Krishna had been far from truthful with her. In addition to her personal hurt she was concerned that Krishna might continue to be involved in scandalous repercussions, but no amount of discussion with him would clarify the issue for her.

In Delhi, Rosalind coaxed Krishna to go with her to visit Humayan's tomb and the Qutub Minar. In a letter to Rosalind a few weeks later from Madras, where Krishna had gone ahead, he told her it had been a beautiful day – he was glad they went together. And he added, as soon as she saw all she wanted to see, he hoped she would hurry down to Madras and they would again be together. He might have sensed that he was about to become ill. By the time Rosalind arrived in Madras, Krishna was very ill indeed. His talks had to be cancelled; Madhavachari was alarmed and grateful that she was there to take over nursing him. This kind man who was in charge of Krishna's household, talks, travels and general welfare in India was almost in tears with frustration and anxiety for Krishna was a difficult patient. Poor Madhavachari could not have foreseen the future times he would be left with an ill Krishna. Rosalind developed a great fondness for him during this stay. Later it upset her to see that, while Krishna always went first class, usually by plane, Madhavachari spent days on buses and overcrowded trains to save funds.

Rosalind found brief occasions while nursing Krishna to visit Raja's family. His mother was very touched that her American daughter-in-law turned up every day with a lotus blossom and played with her great-grandchildren.

When Krishna was well, he and Rosalind went to Rishi Valley for the month of February. There they encountered many of the same problems as at Rajghat. There were teachers' meetings, discussions, or Krishna's talks every day. Among others who complained to her was Krishna's nephew, for whom Krishna had found work at the school but who was not fitting in well with the others. There were charges of nepotism. Eventually, this nephew would become the principal.

March was spent in Bombay, again with discussions or public talks every day. Here, as had Raja, she found the numbers of devotees around Krishna both surprising and disturbing and got the impression that he did nothing to discourage it. She could not comprehend how Krishna could put up with this intimate idolatry while he ate his breakfast, dressed, and then had interviews or meetings before lunch. In Ojai he was so protective of his privacy. In spite of his attendants in Bombay he found time and opportunity not only to express his physical love for Rosalind, but also to arrange for his friends to take her shopping and sightseeing. He seemed most anxious that she enjoy this time in India in every way possible.

Rosalind had hoped that she would be able to meet Nandini and to feel out for herself exactly what the situation was. However, Krishna told her that Nandini was in *samadhi* (that exalted and egoless state of liberation in which Krishna himself had claimed to be long ago in Ojai), although she believed Krishna had deliberately arranged Nandini's inaccessibility.

Friends had planned a day's trip by plane to see the Ajanta and Ellora caves. Rosalind had come down with a cold. Krishna felt they should cancel the trip. But she was reluctant to cancel such elaborately made plans and insisted on going, accompanied by two friends and a somewhat reluctant Krishna. In the small unpressurized plane Rosalind suffered excruciating pain in her ear and was to learn later that her eardrum had burst. It was an altogether unpleasant day. The happy moments they had shared in the early weeks of this journey, sightseeing and revisiting old haunts, suddenly seemed very distant.

Just before leaving Bombay, however, Rosalind did have one brief meeting with Nandini at one of Krishna's public talks. Rosalind sensed a reserve in her that could have been no more than natural shyness. Krishna deftly avoided giving them an opportunity to talk. Rosalind realized the tension that Krishna felt trying to keep his two lives apart. Yet the hospitality shown her by Nandini's sister Pupul, and the brief moment with Nandini herself confirmed Rosalind's belief that Krishna's 'infatuation' had not been reciprocated. She had always regarded Nandini as an innocent figure in Krishna's deception. She could understand Krishna's attraction for this woman who was in many ways an ideal Indian beauty. She realized also that the nature of his relationship with Nandini, whatever it might be, was, to her, of secondary importance. It was what Krishna felt in his heart as opposed to what Rosalind considered the untruthful insistence that he loved only her that she found unbearable. Her repeated confrontations begging him to admit that their relationship was over and that he was interested in someone else were futile and met only with stony silence on his part.

On the whole Rosalind had been happy on this trip, for she loved India. But good as Krishna had been to her there, she was deeply disturbed by the contradictions in his life: the devotees and adulation which he appeared to enjoy on one side of the globe while decrying them on the other.

When Krishna and Rosalind arrived in Rome they were virtually penniless. Raja had failed to get the money there for them that they had expected. They were met by an old friend, Vanda Scaravelli, with whom they both stayed. Thus the situation was not grave, as Raja realized, but this oversight would be the beginning of much future conflict between Krishna and Raja.

Raja had always been the one to see to all the tiresome details in our lives. When Krishna and Rosalind had a 'bright idea' it was Raja who had to implement it – arrange to buy the car, the cabin, the sending of money to Krishna's schools and relatives in India. He had disliked being referred to as Krishna's secretary or manager. He felt his true responsibilities lay in the editing and publication of the teachings, the organization necessary for travels and, along with Rosalind, seeing to the well-being of Krishna. Raja's education would have enabled him to have many careers, from professor at a university, to law or politics. Neither he nor Rosalind had ever been devotees. They had both always been scrupulously careful not to interfere in Krishna's inner life. They tried to arrange for him the solitude and the simplicity of life that they had always understood from him to be his requirement.

During the best of their times together Krishna appreciated this arrangement. He depended heavily on Raja's judgment, not only in practical matters but also for his advice in the projection of his teachings. On many mornings before his Sunday talks, he would appear at Raja's door. They would spend a half-hour going over the questions that had been sent to him. He seemed to find, in Raja's presence, a reassurance that the words would come at the right moment. He used to describe to me his fear that one day he would sit there in silence before the audience with his mind empty. He never wanted to be with anyone but my father before the talks.

Leaving Krishna in Rome, Rosalind went to Paris for a week by herself. Krishna wrote her a long letter summing up the past six months together which he said, with a few exceptions, had been good. He said it had been beneficial for her to see the many beautiful things she had seen and the different cultures, as if she were a schoolgirl who had never seen such things before. Again he implored her not to let superficial agitation and emotionalism disturb the deep inner understanding and love that was between them. But he misjudged the change of heart that had finally taken place in Rosalind.

She met both Krishna and Raja in Stockholm. Here one day walking alone with Raja by a canal, she told him that she did not want Krishna to return to America. She wanted to be completely free of him, for a while at least. Her school work demanded she remain in Ojai, but Krishna could live elsewhere just as well. Her emotions, which had been ricocheting for the past five years between her lingering love for Krishna and her increasing suspicions of his feelings, finally pushed her into throwing out this bombshell, which much later even she would see as irrational and somewhat outrageous. Perhaps she was moved by an increasing consciousness of her own individuality, now that she had a separate life with the school. Perhaps part of the cause was her discomfort in continuing to live a secret life with Krishna while taking on a role which demanded a new concern for reputation. Before the school she had seen discretion as a necessity for Krishna rather than herself. Besides it is one thing to take risks for a happy love affair and quite another for one that is faltering.

Raja was caught in this conflict. It involved him, of course, as long as he was connected with Krishna. He felt Rosalind was being unreasonable in her demand, even though he understood her emotional state. But surprisingly Krishna agreed not to return to California.

However co-operative Krishna appeared to be at the time, there would be later repercussions that would fall on Raja's rather than on Rosalind's head. But judging from Krishna's letters to her immediately after, when she had returned to California, one wonders if he had taken Rosalind seriously at all or if he were just certain this mood would pass and that the love between them was ultimately inviolable. He wrote as though nothing had changed, asked after Coco, the school, and imagining how happy and excited everyone must have been on her return. He repeatedly assured her that she had his love as always and that only when one has lost love do things go wrong.

Mr Robbie died in Ojai that June of 1956. He was eighty-two and had suffered several strokes. He had wanted to go for a long time. One afternoon at his weekly tea party under the pergola behind Saro Vihara my mother was trying to cheer him by getting him to recite poetry. She said, how wonderful it must be to have so many beautiful verses in his head. He replied, nothing mattered any more, that he had been waiting ever since Sara died to die himself. It was difficult for Rosalind to be philosophical about Mr Robbie's death. It was a great loss.

Robert had left Rosalind enough of his estate to make her financially independent for life. This was something Sara and he had agreed to do years before, but it was unexpected and unlooked for by Rosalind.

25

Exiled

Jimmy and I were still in graduate school at Berkeley in 1956. He was working for a PhD in mathematics and I was for an MA in comparative literature. My father felt that a few summer months in Europe would be good for us and he gave us the trip. As our minds were very taken up with our studies while bringing up two small children, he also asked Willie to make the arrangements for us through a local travel agent. My mother offered to take care of our two children. My family continued to be very supportive in our life, but we had not been much involved in theirs for the past few years, witnessing only occasional conflicts on our rare visits to Ojai and in the summers at Carmel. All three of them had visited us – but not all at once. When Krinsh and my mother came to the Bay area together, he stayed with us and she in a hotel as we had a very small house. Krinsh showed an affectionate interest in our children and even babysat a few times, although this appeared to exhaust him and he would complain that American children were too well fed and hence too energetic. Sometimes we went to a good Italian restaurant in San Francisco, but the food never matched, in Krinsh's opinion, that of a Roman meal. Once we took him to a class on semantics by Professor Hayakawa, which Jimmy and I were attending. Krinsh made disparaging remarks afterwards, saying Hayakawa was shallow and unoriginal, but he was struck with some of the metaphors and repeated them later, for example, making the map (psychologically) fit the territory.

When my father visited we had a very good time with him, going out to restaurants and the cinema in San Francisco and having dinner with old friends like Blanche Matthias. I could see a new weariness in him, but he was quite cheerful around us and enjoyed the children.

My mother, if she came alone, usually urged us to go off on a little trip by ourselves and leave her with her grandchildren. Perhaps some contrary reflection from her own marriage had convinced her that it was important for young couples to have some time to themselves.

She was more than generous, considering her busy life, in providing us with these occasions.

In July, Jimmy and I flew to Copenhagen, where my father was waiting to greet us and launch us on our first grand tour of Europe. We did not know that Krinsh was waiting for us in Holland in order to spend a few days with us and accompany us back to Paris. Not until many years later, when I read his sad account to my mother of how we had never even called and he had missed us in Holland altogether, did I realize how badly the communication had broken down between him and my father. It was not an intentional oversight on Raja's part. He had been dissatisfied with the arrangments made for us by the travel agent and had spent a lot of time in Copenhagen re-arranging our trip. Krishna was simply not on his mind at that moment. But this was in itself a new attitude.

By the time we met both Krinsh and my father in Paris, the path was smooth and there was a harmonious tone between them and their old friends, who did everything to make our stay there memorable. We were ensconced in a French Air Force General's apartment in the École Militaire. A private military car and driver were put at our disposal. The General and his wife were followers of Krinsh. Mima was in town and we had lovely dinners with her, full of reminiscences of old times – better and happier times, no doubt, for Krinsh and my father. Yet there was a lot of gaiety and once more I felt surrounded by that strong aura of love that I had known all my life. I could not have guessed how frail were the bonds that were holding them all together.

I had a slight touch of flu and Krinsh sat with me in the General's apartment trying to pull the fever out of my feet, as he had when I was a child. He was distressed that I should miss any time at all seeing Paris, but he spent the afternoon with me wanting to hear about Mr Robbie's death; the last sad weeks when he could no longer speak or leave his bed, the last quiet moments with my mother there to hold his hand.

'Poor Robert,' Krinsh said, 'he hated to be pushed around and wanted to go.' By this he meant pushed around in a wheelchair. Mr Robbie was one person to whom Krinsh had never shown anything but deep respect, even behind his back.

Another friend of his and my father's, Nadia Sednaoui, a beautiful Egyptian girl, showed us the special jewels of Paris like the Chapelle de St Louis. Neither Krinsh nor my father would sightsee, although they were both adamant that we should see everything worthwhile.

Exiled

We parted company in Paris, Jimmy and I off to Switzerland for a few days' driving about on our own, Krinsh to spend the rest of the summer with friends in the Dordogne, and my father to Rome. By the time we joined him there he was again low in spirits and in health as though he had depleted the small reserve of happiness and vitality that had welled up those few days in Paris. Vanda Scaravelli, a person who would become very dear to both Jimmy and me, as she had been for years to my family, showed us all over Rome and then Assisi, Venice and Florence while my father spent most of the time confined to his hotel room. This was a pattern in his behaviour which was not totally unfamiliar. He had never been one of the crowd. Through all the excursions and holidays of my youth he had gone his own secluded way.

In Krishna's letters to Rosalind during the next year he appeared to accept her wish to be free of him, at the same time maintaining that his feelings for her had not changed. From India, he described a second trip to the Qutub Minar which he had visited with her two years before. The Qutub is a high iron pillar built of non-rusting iron. It was placed on its present site in AD 1052 but is thought to be two millennia old. It is the setting that is beautiful amid the rolling hills south of Delhi. There is a strong nostalgia in Krishna's words for the time they had gone there together and he wrote that she was with him too this second time. It is clear that he was not willing to let Rosalind slip out of his life. His needs had always been strong and complex and up until now she had filled them. It was against her nature to deprive anyone of care that she could provide. Krishna knew her very well, but he was not in tune with the slow change within her. He was aware that the different aspects of his personality could cause serious problems. He also relied on the infallible force of his own words. He believed that to tell Rosalind he still loved her was enough, whatever actions of his might persuade her to the contrary. On the other hand she had come to feel that 'actions speak louder than words'.

If Rosalind had found the exile of Krishna from Ojai a satisfactory, if temporary, solution, Raja had not. He still could not come to terms with his own position in the now fractured triangle. It had been one thing to forgive their intimacy, but now Rosalind's stand to free herself from Krishna had created a new problem. Arya Vihara was Krishna's home and he had every right to be there whenever he wished. Raja could not agree with Rosalind's request that Krishna stay away, yet he understood her feelings and his affection and sympathy for her were unwavering in spite of everything. He knew there must be some changes in his life, that he could no longer play a personal role with Krishna, a mixture of nursemaid and manager. He felt it was incumbent on him to sort out a problem which was not initially of his making.

In the spring Raja again set off for Europe. Rosalind had persuaded him to fly rather than take the boat, as he had always preferred to do. With her characteristic practicality, she had even advised him where to sit on the plane. One can see his state of mind from the few letters he wrote to her after his arrival in Europe.

> Have been quite laid out by the happenings before I left & feel very weary – but shall see what's going to happen – This is a miserable letter but will send it just to let you know I got here alright, tho' very tired. Am very concerned about you – all the time.
>
> Love,
> R.

Raja was supposed to meet Krishna – returning from six months in India, in Rome, but communications had again broken down, as Raja complained to Rosalind.

> There has been no letter or sign of anything from India. I have no idea of the situation or what is happening. Have you had any news from Bombay since I left Ojai? The situation is still the same in my mind and I don't yet know clearly how to set about it.
>
> I hope all is well with you and the burden is lightening in some way. Please send some news soon.
>
> All my love, dear,
> R

Elaborate arrangements had been made for Krishna to talk throughout Europe that summer. However, when Raja met him in Rome at the end of March whatever transpired between them resulted in all talks throughout the world being cancelled for the next year. Krishna gave his ill health as the grounds for this abrupt change of plans. The health of all three of them was certainly suffering from the conflicts arising among them. Krishna may have felt exhausted, but he could not exist for long without talking. It is also unlikely that Raja wanted the talks cancelled after he had gone to so much trouble to make the arrangements. Although one may infer from Raja's letter to Rosalind that he was seriously looking for a way to withdraw personally from

Exiled

Krishna, that he had not heard from Krishna for some time had greatly irritated him as there were always many questions about Krishna's plans needing answers. In writing to Rosalind Krishna expressed relief that the talks were cancelled. He said he was going to write to no one except her and Raja and would take a complete rest 'good for the body and the mind'.

Whatever talks he had with Krishna in Europe did not resolve Raja's problems as to his ongoing relationship with Krishna and the work:

> I am feeling a little better, but of course the various problems have not been even tackled yet. Hope you are all right and not totally exhausted. I am sure the rest at Carmel will do you good. I may come there for a few days while you are there . . .
>   All my love, dearest Rosalind,
>
>   RAJA

Raja was still torn between his sense of responsibility towards Krishna and his own need to get his head above water. Since the affair between Krishna and Rosalind had been revealed to Raja six years before, there had been no clear redefinition of any of their relationships. Krishna had never even discussed this with Raja, as he had promised Rosalind he would do. This in itself hurt Raja, for he felt the act of disloyalty to him had been Krishna's not Rosalind's. Raja, being unafraid of any human being, underestimated Krishna's fear of him, this fear being the probable basis of much of Krishna's behaviour, especially that involving deceptions, as years ago Krishna himself had admitted to Rosalind. But perhaps Raja's most serious difficulty was that in spite of everything, he still had a deep affection for Krishna and he still could not realize, or accept, the possibility that Krishna had none for him, if indeed he had ever had. It was this more than anything that would ultimately make it difficult for Raja to free himself.

Krishna had begun to complain to Rosalind more and more about his own health, and about the conflicts between him and Raja. He said he would not return to Ojai until they *both* asked him and added he was definitely getting old and could not stand all this.

Yet there was one last interlude of companionship between the two men. They went for a few days to Gstaad, Switzerland, which would later be a summer centre for Krishna. One can infer much by the fact that Raja made the effort to take long walks with Krishna every day; walks which must have relieved the sessions of talking that filled the rest of their time. One of these walks ended in the rain with the two ageing men slipping and sliding down a muddy path to see a lake, huddled together, arm in arm under Raja's umbrella.

Krishna seemed saddened by the gradual realization that their lives were pulling apart. He still reaffirmed his love for Rosalind. He told her he loved her and meant this with all his heart and he begged her to believe it. He admitted he had not made it all easy but reminded her, as he had said before, that she would have to forgive. He prayed everything would be all right, that everything ugly would be wiped away between them and that there would be peace and love. That was foremost, he said, and repeated that she was loved with all his heart and then asked for blessings on them all.

According to Krishna's letters to Rosalind, Raja and he appeared to have ended their talks amicably even if in Raja's mind many issues were still left hanging. Yet from this time on Krishna started a campaign to discredit Raja in a way so subtle that no one would understand just what was taking place. In order to understand one would have to see that his claims against Raja were false. Krishna had a surprising and largely unsuspected talent for long-range planning. He had demonstrated this talent in acquiring the schools in India from the Theosophical Society and on another level, in preparing himself all summer for those final treks in Sequoia.

Just after Raja's departure from Switzerland, Krishna wrote to Rosalind that he had gone into town to cash cheques for his train trip and the hotel bill. He made no mention of a shortage of funds which he surely would have done had that been the case. Yet when he was met by his hosts with whom he would again stay in the Dordogne, he complained that Raja had left him penniless with barely enough to pay the hotel bill. It would be several more years before Raja would comprehend the growing criticism of him, fanned by these deceptions, among most of his friends and associates throughout the world.

The summer of 1957, spent in Ojai, seems to have been relatively calm for Raja. Probably because for most of it he was alone. Rosalind was making it her habit to spend the summers in Carmel. But Raja's health was still bad and he hoped to get a check up at the Bircher–Benner clinic in Zurich before returning to India with Krishna in the autumn. That Krishna had little concern for Raja's problem was soon evident.

Dearest Rosalind,

I am writing this from Amsterdam and I telephoned Krishnaji from Hamburg. It was most distressing. He seems to be very anxious to go immediately back to India, even though I indicated to him that I would like to [spend] two weeks in the clinic in Zurich.

So we are going on the 6th. I think things are not as they should be. It is no use bothering you with all that. You have your own worries and I hope all is going well with you.

I shall do what I can for the best of all of us in India. I hope I shall be able to get back to California as soon as possible.

With much love,

Yours,

R

Contrary to the impression that Krishna was beginning to promote of being manoeuvred by a wilful man, it had always been and still was typical that Raja deferred to Krishna's wishes, even when it was difficult for him to do so. Krishna often acted as though he didn't care what he did or where he went, but anyone at all tuned in to him could easily discern his preferences and Raja had always gone to great pains to be sensitive to them. He tried to find people with whom Krishna would be happy to stay, as hotels were distasteful to him. He arranged for first-class air travel while he himself went economy. There was very little that was done without Krishna's endorsement, yet Raja's overtly secretive nature, his insistence on running KWInc in a very private manner between him and Krishna and two or three trusted individuals, eventually made him an easy prey to charges of domination.

Krishna did not intimate to Rosalind that there was any friction between him and Raja and they set off apparently on good terms for India, but there all the excuses and explanations about Nandini began once again. Rosalind had not asked for these reports and indeed was not interested in them any longer. She had given up hope long ago of hearing the truth and now preferred to hear nothing at all.

She sent Raja a list of people, mostly relatives of Krishna whom she had met in 1956 whom she proposed to help financially. As soon as she inherited from Mr Robbie Rosalind began to think of ways to give away her money. She would never feel comfortable with money and would always continue to spend very little on herself. She sent a sizeable sum to Raja's family as well and to some people associated with Krishna's schools. This generosity was to be implemented by Raja, although he questioned the wisdom of some of it.

On this, his final trip to India, Raja was spending a minimum of time with Krishna. Raja's mother would die soon after and he would not return again. She had been an important reason for his visits, but he had never enjoyed staying long in India.

He had turned over the European arrangements for talks and travel to Doris Pratt in the London office. He was still taking responsibility for the publications and the overall financial management, but had provided the London office with sums for Krishna's use in different countries.

Rosalind, who had never intended to be Director of the Happy Valley School for so many years, had once again started a search for a new Director. When Krishna heard of this he reacted vehemently: although she had, he wrote, been saying that there must be a new Director, fortunately that evil hour has so far been postponed. He thought it would be a calamity if another Director took her place. Why should he care? Unless he had indeed seen Rosalind as his pipeline of influence in the school.

In January 1958 Raja left Krishna in India, and resolved to do something about his health. The resolve seemed to bring him a fleeting lightening of spirits and sense of optimism:

Dearest Rosalind,

As you know, I wanted to go to some Clinic somewhere to see really what is what with me, and I have decided to go to Bircher-Benner Clinic for a few days, and maybe for a few weeks. I shall be returning to Ojai the latter part of March. I do not at all like the idea of being in a wretched Clinic but I guess I will do it – not so much for my own sake but for everybody else's sake.

On the whole everything is well with me in a strange new way.

With much love,

RAJA

But everything was not so well with Krishna in India. He still reported the details of his life regularly to Rosalind, giving exacting and reassuring accounts of his visits to Pupul and Nandini. He perhaps did not realize that she was never to read these letters carefully, sometimes not at all. She was impatient and busy. The school was becoming too much for her and she was not succeeding in finding her replacement. In spite of Krishna's admonitions she was still trying to do so.

Krishna, suddenly showing exasperation, asserted that he would not report on his activities with Nandini, that it was absurd and silly to do so. He also alleged that his letters might be opened for blackmail purposes and therefore he would henceforth write more discreetly.

Exiled

When he went for the summer to the hill station of Ranikhet, his letters, however, resumed their loving tone. He spent four months there in relative isolation, from which he seemed to benefit emotionally and spiritually.

Raja found at the clinic that his oesophagus problem was mechanical and incurable without surgery, so he decided to 'lump it and put up with the discomfort'. He remained in America for the next two and a half years. While he had no conflict with Rosalind, there was no more harmony between them than there had ever been. She had buried the shock of Krishna's disloyalty under her work. That she had intentionally distanced herself from Krishna did not mean that she wanted to get closer to Raja, not closer than she had been for these past twenty-five years. They were no more temperamentally suited than they had ever been. But a deep and affectionate friendship still remained between them.

Raja was still very involved with Harper & Row, editing and publishing books from Krishna's talks and from his notebooks. Krishna still showed no interest in being personally involved with all this, and seemed glad enough for Raja to continue this work. Krishna had decided a few years before to resign altogether from KWInc, perhaps as part of a short-lived impulse toward total retirement. Throughout the years Raja had suggested that Krishna settle down somewhere and let people come to *him*, but Krishna had disdained the idea. Now his faltering health prompted him in this direction, but after the months of isolation at Ranikhet, a part of him longed for a return to activity.

As Krishna was remaining in India for so long and quite out of touch, Raja had asked him to sign a document to facilitate the financial arrangements that were part of the contracts with Harper's and the European publishers. This document, stated in writing no more than had always been the implicit and often expressed understanding between them. It was only necessary now as Raja was dealing with outsiders. While he complied readily at the time, later Krishna would read a wholly imaginary, sinister implication in this request, or allow others to convince him of one.

When Rosalind had been at the Rishi Valley School two years before, she had already noted the increasing dissension between Krishna and the headmaster, Mr Pearce. Krishna was undercutting his influence in the school by appointing people of his choice over Pearce's head. At last Pearce resigned and Krishna reported to Rosalind that there was a lot of misery and upset in the school over this. His letter sounded as though it were all more of a problem that Krishna could cope with.

Pearce retired from Rishi Valley to Ootacamund, where he started the

Blue Mountain School. His wife told us sixteen years later that Krishna had broken her husband's heart by manoeuvring him out of the Rishi Valley School and he had not lived long thereafter.

Krishna also lost a very old friend that winter, one who went back to his and Nitya's youth. Ratansi, with whom he usually stayed in Bombay, died unexpectedly of a heart attack. Intensifying these events was the heat, fiercely increasing after the middle of March. Krishna wanted to get away from India, from the problems and from everyone; but Madhavachari recommended that he rest in Kashmir instead of going all the way to Europe. It was often hard for Indians to understand just how Westernized Krishna was and how he yearned for that other culture when cut off from it for too long. But he acquiesced and agreed to remain in India. In his letters to Rosalind there are frequent nostalgic references to Ojai, wondering if the valley was green and beautiful; life in India was becoming increasingly tiresome for him. But he would remain there for another year on top of the year and a half he had already stayed, his longest sojourn there since he had left in 1911. Neither had he ever been away from Ojai and from Rosalind for so long a time in thirty-seven years.

26

A Moratorium

In Ojai, Raja and Rosalind, for a time brought closer by their common problems, now seemed pulled apart by them. Their relationship was becoming more and more strained, in part because they did not agree on how to deal with Krishna, although they both wished to withdraw from his orbit.

It was in this atmosphere that Raja fell in love, almost against his own wishes. Annalisa Beghe was living in the Saro Vihara house, which Rosalind had inherited from Mr Robbie, and was assisting Rosalind in the school. Annalisa and Rosalind were friends. One day on a walk, in the spring of 1959, Annalisa turned impulsively to Rosalind and said, 'Raja and I are in love.' If Rosalind received a shock she gave no sign of it at the moment.

'I am so glad if he has someone special to love him,' she replied. Rosalind was well aware that Raja had been very much alone for the past twenty-eight years. The friendship between her and Annalisa continued. There were frequent dinners *à trois* when they discussed their situation, often with bursts of ironic humour. At least, in this relationship, everything was out in the open. But Raja was very hesitant to embark on another marriage. 'Why should I jump out of the frying pan into the fire?' he said to me one day while visiting us in Berkeley.

His attraction to Annalisa was understandable. She had never cared for Krishna personally although she was interested in his teachings. When she had first seen them both many years ago, before being introduced she had thought, 'Raja should be standing in Krishna's shoes.' She was Swiss-Italian, twenty-five years younger than Raja, beautiful and very feminine, also willing to show deference to him in a way Rosalind with her strong American independence could not have done.

I realized that my parents had never in my memory had a true marriage. I was not disturbed by this new attachment in my father's life. But I was disturbed by my mother's frequent depression during these years. I did not know then about the distress she had gone through over Krishna's disloyalty. Partly due to her own design she now had to make a life independent of the two men whose focus had been exclusively hers for so many years. And Coco, who had been her most loyal and loving companion, died that winter.

Raja too seemed more and more depressed; sometimes Annalisa would appear on Rosalind's doorstep in tears, asking for advice on how to help him. Rosalind was sufficiently alarmed by Raja's state of mind to write Krishna a letter of distress, appealing to him to come to Ojai immediately.

Krishna replied giving a string of specious reasons as to why he could not oblige. These ranged from lack of funds to the difficulties involved in procuring a visa, but he ended with a more credible objection; until he heard from Raja, as well, that they both wanted him to return, he would not do so. It was obvious that he had no wish to become involved in their present crisis. He warned Rosalind not to do anything 'drastic or irrevocable'.

Shortly after sending this letter, Krishna fell seriously ill. When he had recovered enough to travel he made plans to go to the Bircher-Benner clinic and then communicated with Raja about returning to California. His illness had shaken him and he wrote to Rosalind that the whole organism was rapidly disintegrating. However, this morbid alarm disappeared on his return to Ojai. Rosalind was determined that the disputes and unhappiness between them all must be resolved no matter what course their future might take, together or apart. It was her nature to want this and she could not accept its impossibility. She still thought she had some influence on Krishna. Krishna on the other hand was upset by Raja's intention to move away from Arya Vihara. It was often difficult to understand why Krishna so vehemently disapproved of certain things. Why should he care where Raja lived? He must have realized that without Raja's presence at Arya Vihara, it would be difficult for him and Rosalind to remain there alone together. Raja, for all those years had unwittingly provided them with an umbrella of propriety. Krishna was not yet ready to re-organize his life.

After lengthy discussions between the three of them, Annalisa keeping well out of it, Rosalind asked that they have a moratorium until the following year, during which time they would all agree to the following: there would be no more recriminations between any of them. The three of them would get along and leave everything alone – no changes would be made until they met the following summer. They would write every two weeks and discuss all plans together. But, most important, Krishna would agree not to give any large public lectures until the year was out.[1]

A Moratorium

Rosalind was not the first to recommend that Krishna lead a less public life. Many years before, Mme de Manziarly had told him bluntly that he should stop travelling all over the world in high style and settle down quietly in one place, letting those who wanted to hear him come to him. Krishna had taken offence at that suggestion and he ignored her after that. When she died, he did not send his condolences to her daughters, although it was she he had called on long ago to take care of Nitya when he was so ill.[2] It is most likely that Krishna found it easier to agree to and then ignore Rosalind's proposals than to argue with her.

Much as he had taken pains to give Rosalind the impression that he was protecting her interests in stopping publication of Lady Emily's book, he now made a great point of another issue; an issue which he created. This time Raja was the unmentioned but obvious object from whom Krishna wished to protect her. He wrote Rosalind a formal letter stating that Arya Vihara, from the very beginning, belonged to all three of them (and to Radha). Since Raja now had his own home (he had bought a house adjacent to the Vigevenos at the other end of the valley), Krishna wished to put into writing that whatever the circumstances in the future, Arya Vihara was to be the home of Rosalind and of Radha for their lifetime. He urged also that Rosalind never abandon and leave that property. He took the trouble to give a copy of this statement to Louis and Erma and asked them to witness that it was his wish. Rosalind was naturally puzzled by this insistence, as she was justifiably confident that no one connected with KWInc, least of all Raja, would expect her to leave and, if they had, she would not have greatly minded. Krishna was evidently assuming that Raja's involvement with Annalisa had alienated him from Rosalind and from her best interests, or else he was deliberately driving a wedge between them.

Krishna apparently regained much of his health and strength during the six months he was in Ojai. Rosalind had always known how to take care of him; and he had seldom been ill with her except for the one serious attack of nephritis in 1946.

From the first letter he wrote after his departure, Rosalind had every reason to feel assured that Krishna had taken the moratorium seriously and had agreed to her request about his talking in India. He promised he would follow in letter and spirit what they all agreed to. He also said he had written to Madhavachari to arrange only limited discussions and no public talks in India. He reminded Rosalind that her part of the bargain was to stay at Arya Vihara, although that had not been part of the moratorium agreement. He reiterated his concern that the school must remain the work of the Happy Valley Foundation and that Rosalind must be the co-ordinator and spirit behind it. He cautioned her not to allow experts, specialists and super organisers to swamp her.

His letters were now on a three-day instead of daily schedule. He explained that he did the same thing every day and it was boring to repeat. This was in no way a new circumstance. He complained that communications with Raja were still bad and he was not receiving replies about plans. Within a month the limited discussion groups had increased from sixty to a hundred; by the next month to two hundred packed in like sardines. Krishna was becoming annoyed by the terms of the moratorium.

Meanwhile Raja had cabled Krishna in India saying he could no longer arrange for the European gatherings and had turned over the management to Miss Pratt in the London office.

The summer had taken its toll on Raja. He would never again throw off the dejection he had almost dispelled two years before. In the late autumn of 1960 he left for Europe, deeply depressed, for six months on his own, purposeless and at a loss as to what to do with his personal life. He wrote to Rosalind:

Zurich   *Dec 6, '60*
Since I arrived here I have not been able to sleep at all nights, but as I am doing nothing, and know no one here, it has not mattered. I shall get adjusted to this coming away for no particular reason but to have a change.

To the above letter he received an affectionate response from Rosalind, who gave a rare admission of what she too had been through.

It was nice to have your letter & to know that you remembered your promise.

It has been a very busy time with the school, holidays & family otherwise I w'ld have answered it sooner. I feel that I can just barely survive as I am constantly harassed by a strange dizziness . . . I need a little more breathing space – a little more time as these last years have been a tremendous shock and strain. I will feel better to know that you are doing everything possible to get things right for yourself & let us hope that we meet in June in a good way. Always with dearest love and wishing you all the best,

ROSALIND

A Moratorium

But after four months in Europe Raja showed only a promise of improvement. He wrote to Rosalind what would turn out to be the last letter she ever received from him.

Geneva $\qquad$ *April 3, '61*
Dear Rosalind,

I have not felt like writing to anyone, anywhere and I am afraid I am forgetting how to write. There has been no news, I have been existing and trying not to think about anything or anybody. Hope I shall get a true perspective someday soon –

But I am glad to have been completely alone & away from my grooved life of 40 years nearly – & am hoping for the best.

How have you been, needless to ask, for you are not going to write & tell me the news.

Anyway I do hope you have had a complete rest from certain things & are feeling happy & well.

Shall let you know when I arrive in N.Y.,

Love,

R

Rosalind made the serious mistake of trying to change the date when they had all agreed, according to the moratorium, to meet in Ojai. She had forgotten how demanding the final weeks of school could be. It did not matter to Raja whether it was 15 or 30 June, as she now preferred. Krishna, on the other hand, who in the end had not heeded the terms of the moratorium at all and had made extensive plans for public talks in Europe reacted with an outrage Rosalind had never felt from him. He said he was not coming to hang around till she was ready, that she had work to do and so did he. Rosalind compromised quickly by cable with an earlier date.

When they all met at Ojai in that summer of 1961 the moratorium had solved nothing. Krishna was mostly interested in getting his teeth fixed. Raja had resolved none of his problems. He did not yet know that Krishna had begun entrenching himself with others who would eventually help him in a fight against Raja. Krishna picked his new circle very astutely for this purpose. But the time was not yet ripe and he was avoiding an open break. Krishna was then confident that Rosalind would never side with Raja against him.

For her part Rosalind wanted to be free of them both. She was weary and as depressed as she had ever been in her life. She did not want a divorce. However, she felt a divorce was right for Raja. As she

271

was categorically unable and unwilling to say anything against Raja, wishing to claim only incompatibility as grounds, it was necessary to get a Mexican divorce. This she did smoothly enough through a lawyer in Carmel. Raja and Annalisa were now free to marry. But this would not free Raja from the complex web around Krishna.

27

A House Divided

That summer of 1961 Jimmy and I and our two children moved to Santa Barbara, where we had just bought a house. Jimmy had joined the Mathematics Department of the University of California at Santa Barbara. We were so busy remodelling our house and settling in that we did not fully comprehend the gravity of my family's situation. Aside from a few unhappy scenes, we were not involved with the discussions that summer, except one which I remember vividly, although I was puzzled by it at the time. Just before he returned to Europe, on 6 July, Krinsh came over to Santa Barbara with my mother. I was in the middle of painting our bedroom and they urged me not to stop while they kept me company. Krinsh seemed to enjoy the lovely view from our window of the mountains. But the amount of work remaining still to do dismayed him. My mother had swept up a pile of plaster chippings left on the floor and then sat quietly on the bed. Krinsh remained standing. I could feel his restlessness.

Suddenly he said, 'Kittums I want you to clearly understand that Arya Vihara is to be Rosalind's home for her life and yours too.'

'Thank you for including me, Krinsh, but we have just bought this house and hope to stay here for a long time. Besides we cannot live in Ojai. Jimmy's work is here.'

'Just remember what I am saying, Kittums. If Rosalind should ever leave Arya Vihara I will not return to Ojai again.' Even then that seemed to me an empty threat, and rather pointless. I could not understand his urgency. It was not clear to me until later that he had convinced himself my father would try to push her out. He still saw himself and Rosalind as united against Raja.

Krishna wrote to her, just after he left Ojai, that during his last night there he awoke feeling a sense of cruel oppression, intrigue. Possibly he was suggesting that Raja had been taken over by the black forces. This attitude would circulate among his new friends in the near future, much as Wedgwood had claimed to have seen the 'black magician' in Krishna when he started to withdraw from Theosophy.

More and more Krishna refused to discuss anything with Raja, while claiming that it was Raja who would not answer his letters or talk to him. It is true that Raja's personality had become more abrasive. In addition to his disillusionment with Krishna there were new corrosions in what he had thought were old and loyal friendships. Even Erma and Louis had shown a new coolness toward him. In their case, though Raja did not realize it, this was due to his marriage with Annalisa. No matter how graciously Rosalind had accepted this marriage, Erma was torn between her deep and affectionate friendship with Raja and her loyalty to Rosalind. Although Rosalind did not admit even to herself such a reaction, Erma was convinced that her sister's pride had been hurt by Raja's new marriage and she felt a protective sense of indignation. She was ignorant of Rosalind's long affair with Krishna and would remain so until her death, therefore she did not have a true perspective on Raja's actions. But where other people were concerned, there is no doubt that Krishna's insinuations and subtle casting of doubt about Raja's performance and motives had eroded many of his relationships. For the past few years another problem had developed. An Indian doctor had suggested that a small drink of Scotch every day would ease the pain in Raja's oesophagus. India was a dry country and obtaining alcohol was no easy matter. Krishna managed to arrange a permit through his influential friends. He soon found that Raja was much easier to live with after an afternoon drink. This drink had became a habit, kept in moderate control. But it only added fuel to the rounds of criticism already turned against Raja. With a balanced diet that excluded alcohol, Annalisa succeeded in improving Raja's physical health. He continued to be depressed, however, as he began seriously to question the worth of his life's work.

At times, Rosalind still felt compelled to step between Krishna and Raja to try to keep communications open, and to jolt Krishna into seeking a reconciliation with Raja. This was a vain expectation; neither persuasion nor warnings would succeed.

In his insistence that Rosalind be given a lifetime interest in Arya Vihara, Krishna was pursuing an issue that meant very little to either Raja or Rosalind. Rosalind was entertaining hopes of one day living up on Happy Valley. Memories of happier days at Arya Vihara were not foremost in her mind.

Six weeks later Rosalind received a copy of a letter that Krishna had written to Raja. He stated that he would never come back to Ojai if Rosalind left Arya Vihara, that if anyone should leave it was he and Raja and not her. He suggested that Arya Vihara now be *given* outright to Rosalind and after the death of Radha be returned to KWInc. He demanded that Raja find some legal way to arrange this.

Raja tried to explain that a non-profit foundation could not give away property to an individual. A few years later, his solution, honestly based on what appeared to be Krishna's wishes, and one that met with Rosalind's approval was to give the house to the Happy Valley Foundation, of which Rosalind was a member, for her lifetime use. This would anger Krishna. Krishna may have sincerely felt that Rosalind needed his protection in her divorced state and that he was standing by her against Raja. But he would remain adamant that it should not be given to a foundation in which he had no part.

Since its inception, Krishna had kept himself aloof from the Happy Valley Foundation, now he suddenly plunged himself into the affairs of both the foundation and the school. He wrote a formal letter to Louis Zalk as the President, stating that Dr Besant had intended that the teachings be the major purpose of the foundation and that the school had been established to 'express these teachings as much and as deeply as possible'. He said that during his last stay in Ojai he had noticed that the school had wandered away from this purpose and that it must be guided back on to the course for which it was intended or it would slip into the wrong hands. He claimed to have to have heard this also from various parents and from James Vigeveno, a Happy Valley board member. James Vigeveno had been a devoted follower of Krishna since the early Ommen days. He was in a difficult position, trying to represent Krishna's wishes to Raja and now to the Happy Valley Board.

Since 1946, when the school was founded, Krishna had deliberately remained in the background and had refused to have his name used officially. Rosalind had often asked him to attend the board meetings, to speak at assemblies, and, in short, to be as involved as *he* wished to be; however, one thing he would never tolerate was sharing the limelight with *anyone*. There were many luminaries now involved peripherally and within the school, actualizing the basic principle that there should be no single exclusive influence. The first thing in the morning there were readings from a selection of philosophical works, suggested in part by Aldous, followed by silence and music. In sports, emphasis was on exercise rather than competition, and to discourage a competitive attitude no grades were given out to the students, just written reports. This policy stemmed from the educator, Edward Yeomans, as well as Krishna's teachings, and was intrinsic to the spirit of the school.

Krishna's memory, as stated in his letter to Louis Zalk, of the founding of Happy Valley and of the school is faulty at best and false in some cases. While Annie Besant saw a strong link between the Happy Valley and the world teacher, she did not consider the future development of Happy Valley as a base for his teachings exclusively but rather as a simultaneous flowering of the physical aspect of a spiritual ideal. He himself backed away from her ideal. She had paid him back for the land when he moved his campsite to the lower valley and he had never in all the years since uttered a hint that he felt future developments on Happy Valley would be connected to him. When he wrote ostensibly in impersonal terms of 'the teachings', meaning of course *his* teachings, he was assuming that these should be included in the sustaining fabric of the school, and they were. In his letters to Rosalind through the years, he had urged her to speak to the children regularly and to keep a firm hand on the school, feeling confident that through her his ideas would flow. Among these ideas was one that she took very seriously; there should be *no authority*.

If his intentions were quite harmless, one can only wonder why in 1960, during the sixth months that he was in Ojai, when he was still acting as if he were on close terms with Rosalind, he did not once try to give suggestions to her directly. Why did he work behind her back through James Vigeveno? Why didn't he come to her with the criticism he heard from parents? And why did he wait for three years, after his observations of the alleged shortcomings, to present *his* criticism? Louis Zalk answered this letter with considerable finesse, while pointing out certain clearly erroneous statements in Krishna's letter. This whole incident would be the beginning of Louis's personal disillusionment with Krishna.

> *19 August, 1963*
>
> Dear Krishnaji:
>
> I have been associated with the Foundation from its very beginning, notably during the first bleak fifteen years or more. It was a dead piece of land until Rosalind, with unstinting effort and devotion, began the school some seventeen years ago. We all know the extent of the great effort she has put into it. You, of course, were present and were a very great help indeed.
>
> I sincerely believe . . . that the only difference between James [Vigeveno] and me [is] in the method of bringing your teaching to bear in our school program so that it fully permeates our educational plan. Now who among the nearby critics of the school has the creative energy – sense of dedication and capacity – to properly present your teaching to pupils? I must ask the question, 'Would there not be a

great confusion which would seriously jeopardize our present school and fail of creating a school in harmony with your ideas?' Frankly, we are short of teachers who, if they have understanding of your ideas, could convey that understanding to the pupils who come to us. Can they awaken Truth in the pupils without first making assertions and generalizations? The present school is Rosalind's very life. To destroy it is to destroy her. Do we really wish this to happen? Knowing the goal of our school to be in harmony with your ideas, I cannot aid and abet that which would mark her destruction. In my long and reasonably successful business career, I have found that enthusiasm is not always accompanied by the capacity to devise channels for creative action. I have had the priceless privilege of listening to your ideas for something like 35 years and have not varied in my appreciation of their everlasting significance. In this background I suggest most earnestly and urgently when you are here next year that we have the privilege of discussing with you definite steps we can take to improve our methods. We would like to have a direct contact with you and not through interpreters and intermediaries, however sincere they may be . . .

With much love,

LOUIS ZALK

Louis was soon to find, as Raja had already found, that this was much too direct an approach to Krishna, who *preferred* to deal through interpreters and intermediaries rather than involve himself in debates.

Krishna's response to Louis was evasive about when he would return to Ojai and made no reference at all to his letter that had stirred up so much commotion. Rosalind had responded in her own way, insisting that Krishna either explain his criticism precisely or withdraw it. She was indignant that he had gone behind her back and discussed with members of the Happy Valley Board, as well as parents in the school, criticisms and proposals that he could have discussed with her. She felt he should know well enough from experience in his own Indian schools how easily an atmosphere of rebelliousness can sweep through a school and how difficult it is to quell it. She was convinced that he had now turned on her, as he had on Raja, and was using the school as a route of attack. Krishna responded with innocent denial that he had ever intended any criticism of her or the school and was only trying to be helpful.

Louis and Erma used to come to us for dinner in Santa Barbara every Monday night. During these visits he would sit and talk about the strange twist the path around Krishna had taken. Louis cast forth no judgments, but his kindly face was shadowed with bewilderment as to how a person could reach such heights in what he said and spread such confusion by his actions. He was also beset with problems in his own business.

'When your house is on fire, don't worry about the tiger in your kitchen,' he said. He wrote to Krishna:

30 October, 1963

Dear Krishnaji,

I have heard quite definitely from James Vigeveno with reference to the School.

I have been going through a very very difficult year in my personal affairs, in the effort to free myself from associations in the business world. These have been trying and painful – and my strength has been seriously depleted.

Under these circumstances Rosalind – and Jim and Radha have strongly urged that I let Rosalind discuss all matters of any nature brought up by James [Vigeveno] to relieve me of that much nervous strain.

Rosalind has been in association with you for over forty years – and I am sure she has knowledge of your viewpoint and ideas in Education – and can serve in this matter much better than I. I do hope dear Krishnaji that you will understand.

Always with love and appreciation of you –

LOUIS

In spite of his denials, Krishna had worked very hard on James Vigeveno and had chosen him as his emissary to both Raja and the Happy Valley Foundation. This well-meaning and honest man would have his eyes rudely opened before long.

The past year had been a sad one for Rosalind in other ways than her distress about Krishna's interference in the school. John Ingelman had died in February. And on 22 November 1963 Aldous died. After Maria's death nearly nine years before, Aldous had come to be a close friend and was still a frequent visitor at Arya Vihara. Rosalind had encouraged him to give his first series of university lectures at Santa Barbara in 1959.

He had modestly protested, 'I am not a speaker, Rosalind, I am a writer.' But she was so convinced by the one talk he had given at a Happy Valley School graduation that she continued to urge him. Before long he was offered more engagements than he could possibly meet.

A House Divided

One day he phoned us quite unexpectedly from the Santa Barbara airport.

'Radha, this is Aldous,' as if anyone could fail to recognize that beautiful voice! 'I have been invited to the Center for Democratic Studies, but no one has shown up to meet me.'

Before driving him to the Center, we took him home for tea and a walk, which he always enjoyed as much as Krinsh did. I noticed that some buttons were missing on his tweed jacket.

'Yes,' he said, 'my sewing isn't very effective.' There wasn't a trace of complaint in his voice, but I couldn't help feeling a deep sense of loss that Maria was no longer there as I tried to match the buttons and sew them on firmly. Maria had been an excellent mender and I had heard her comment quite unfavourably about young women of today who would throw out a good sock rather than pick up a needle and mend it.

Whenever we went to Los Angeles, we made it a point to see Aldous. He sometimes came for a simple lunch in the little Neutra flat on Gower street. We had never got to know Laura, his second wife, well. We realized very quickly that this marriage was entirely different from his first. Maria had taken total and exacting care of Aldous, always driving him herself, except on rare occasions when a trusted friend filled in. Now Aldous took buses and planes around the country from MIT to Berkeley by himself, staying in rooming houses or small hotels and opening a can of beans for his dinner. While this independence may have given him an appearance of new youthfulness, he was actually fatally ill. In the flat in Hollywood on one of our last times with Aldous he remarked on the strained relationship between Krinsh and my father and wondered with the kindest sort of interest what was going wrong. I could not tell him much then, but he said he hoped my father would not feel himself to be the target of the trouble. Aldous did not live to see how much of a target Raja would become.

In October Aldous was felled by the cancer which he had known for some time afflicted him. It had started as a lump on his tongue. By the time he considered an operation it would have meant losing his speech. Both he and Laura shunned this maiming. It might or might not have saved his life. The alternative treatments had not sufficed to stop the malignancy; he suffered great pain as the disease moved into his larynx and spine. Rosalind went to see him very often towards the end and rubbed his feet as he told her that brought him more relief than anything else. She had just returned to Ojai when she awoke the next morning and felt strongly that she must go back to Aldous. She got in the car and was driving over the Conejo pass on the six-lane freeway into Los Angeles when suddenly she saw herself surrounded by white light and could not see the cars or the highway. She assumed she had been in an accident and that this was what death was like, but then the light faded. She drove on, so intent on reaching Aldous that she thought no more about it.

Aldous and Laura had been living with a friend in the Hollywood hills since their house, with all his papers, had burned down in 1961. That morning when Rosalind arrived, Laura rushed up to her, saying that Aldous was dying. There was some commotion about setting up an oxygen tank and while waiting in another room, Rosalind heard about the assassination of John F. Kennedy but did not take it in, even when the doctor said not to tell Aldous about the President. Aldous could still talk clearly when she first saw him, but was very restless. When she offered to rub his feet he said he would prefer it on his tummy. By early afternoon he could not talk any more but could write on a pad. Soon after he was too weak to drink water and by late afternoon he was in a coma. When Laura asked if she should give him LSD, the doctor murmured to Rosalind that it didn't make any difference what she did as Aldous was too far gone.

When Maria was dying Aldous had whispered in her ear until the last, knowing that the hearing is the last sense to go. The words he used in his novel *Island* give a close description of those final moments. Rosalind attempted to use the same words as well as she could recall them.

Think of those lights and shadows on the sea, those blue spaces between the clouds. Think of them, and then let go of your thinking. Let go of it, so that the not-Thought can come through. Things into Emptiness.

Emptiness into Suchness. Suchness into things again, into your own mind . . . Let go now, let go . . . go on into the Light, into the peace, into the living peace of the Clear Light . . .[1]

Rosalind found the end 'strangely quiet, peaceful and beautiful. One was completely uplifted and full of awe and love – no tears'.[2]

It was not until that evening when she drove down to Hollywood Boulevard that she saw the headlines. President Kennedy had been shot, strangely enough, just when she had been enveloped in the light. Typically she never connected these two occurrences until it was pointed out to her.

Since Raja had married Annalisa, Rosalind had kept entirely out of his life. Her relationship with Krishna was becoming tenuous, with increasingly infrequent communications between them. He still professed not to understand what he had done to upset her and Louis.

As Jimmy was on the Happy Valley Foundation Board in 1964, he and I undertook to clarify the issue. We were planning to spend the summer on an extensive drive through southern Europe and were delighted to include a visit to Krinsh on our itinerary. He was staying at the Chalet Tanneg in Gstaad where he stayed every summer, thanks to Vanda Scaravelli's generosity. It was a lovely spot on a hill overlooking the valley with a winding road leading up from the town. Krinsh was alone in the house when we arrived in our new Volkswagen with our two children. Although Vanda was away, he had arranged with her that we could stay there. He helped us in with the luggage, graciously showed us our rooms right next to his, and offered us some tea. After three years' absence from him, his hospitality made me feel a little less than family but soon his old affectionate ways returned and everything felt very much as it always had, though the style of life was quite different from any I had ever seen him in before. There was a shiny new Mercedes in the garage. Vanda had set up the kitchen with a cook and butler from Rome; the butler wore white gloves to serve an incredibly good meal at a formally set table. The whole set-up was extremely posh, much more so than the style in which Vanda herself lived in either Rome or Florence. Yet the formality did not extend to Krinsh's attitude towards us and certainly not to our behaviour. Our ten- and eleven-year-old children were made to feel perfectly at home and he seemed to take real delight in listening to them and watching them unwind after a long day in the car.

The very first evening, after the children were in bed, we launched into our mission. We explained how much distress his criticism of the school had caused, what a controversy had been created among the students, the teachers and the feelings that had been fomented against my mother. Krinsh looked genuinely stricken.

'Kittums, I wrote that letter only to help her, it was not intended in any way to do her harm.' He grasped my knee and shook it as he frequently did when making a point.

'I shall write and straighten it all out now that I understand the problem,' he promised.

There was nothing we had told him that Rosalind had not already written him in letters and communicated to him over the phone, but we felt reassured that he did now understand, for he explained that he never intended that the Happy Valley should be identified with the name of Krishnamurti and emphasized that the Happy Valley was a separate legal body from KWInc and that he had no intention of interfering with it in any way.

The next morning, with the issue of the Happy Valley Foundation settled, Krinsh proposed we all take a drive and enjoy some of the local scenery. He guided us to Diablerets, where we rode on the ski lift across a valley, green as California could never be green. I thought of Villars long ago, when we had gone for early morning walks as the cows headed for pasture, the sound of cowbells, Krinsh rubbing his hair in the pine needles. His face then had been full of laughter, his smile radiant. I looked at his face now. It was slightly puffed with allergy. His mouth did not smile fully, even when he laughed. There was a distance in him, his eyes were not quiet. I felt he was not 'living in the moment' as he always had advocated. But suddenly a small brown furry creature scuttled between two rocks below. There was a flash of animation, a gleam of the old joy that had enriched so many moments in my childhood. 'A marmot,' he said.

We only stayed three days and each morning after breakfast we went to his room to talk. On the last morning Krinsh said with intense feeling that it was all wrong that my parents had divorced. 'That divorce should never have happened,' he said, grasping and shaking my knee again for emphasis. I could not understand why he should care so much about that one relatively small disaster in the face of the overall situation. I could not see how, at this point, it would change anything for him one way or the other. But he strongly disagreed. 'We must all remain together. It is the way it has always been and must stay like that.'

I told him I thought that was hopeless, that they had all now gone their own ways and perhaps for the best.

'Don't you see?' he insisted. 'It is all one thing. The KWInc and the Happy Valley.' I could not finally make out whether he was really talking about the two foundations, or the three individuals, or whether in his mind it really was all the same. Every time I tried to clarify what was being said he looked despairing and said I did not understand – which was all too true. He then shifted to another subject, although actually closely related.

'They say Mrs Beghe is quite mad,' he said with a sardonic smile I knew well. He had avoided using her given name or referring to her as Raja's wife.

'Who are "they?"' I asked.

'People who know her have told me that.'

'Well, it's not true. If anyone in this whole mess is mad it is certainly

A House Divided

not Annalisa.' I did not know her very well, but well enough to defend her without doubt on this point.

He moved from this to my father, and here I was on less sure ground, for I had not been a witness to many of the incidents in the past few years.

'Do you know – he has not given me any money? I had to beg from Signora Vanda to pay my doctor's bill in Rome.'

I had no answer to this and the subject was dropped. I started to describe the trip we were taking and he became more and more concerned, feeling it would be exhausting to drive all the way to Greece.

'Why don't you put the car on a ferry in Trieste instead?'

'We can't afford that; it is cheaper to drive.'

With this he jumped up from the bed on which we were both sitting, went to a drawer and came toward me with a wad of American Express cheques.

'Here, Kittums, is three thousand dollars, take it.'

'Where did you get it?' I asked.

'Rajagopal sent it.'

'Then why not use it to pay your doctor's bills?'

This did not throw him in the least and he answered without hesitation,

'I can't. It's for something else.'

I did not consider this a very satisfactory explanation, but realized there was no point in continuing the conversation. I could hardly have guessed then that nearly twenty years later I would be repeating this conversation under oath. Nor did I know then that Raja had acceded to his request for $50,000 to buy land in Saanen (a village near Gstaad) for the summer talks. A few years later a much greater sum, close to a million dollars, would be asked of Raja to build an elaborate hall. This Raja would refuse, not only because he was restricted by tax laws, a factor Krishna refused to comprehend, but because he well knew Krishna's penchant for wanting to build: halls, schools, places where he could be housed without the stigma of personal ownership, but which required unending management and upkeep. Raja was coming to feel it was time for all this to stop. He certainly wanted no more property to worry about.

On 1 September 1964, after eighteen years and in spite of Krishna's insistent advice, Rosalind resigned as Director of the Happy Valley School. She felt she had found a very competent person to take over and she was exhausted by the past years of emotional turmoil. On 29 November Louis Zalk died, leaving Rosalind on the front line of the Happy Valley Foundation. There was no one to replace Louis' and Robert's financial support of both the school and the foundation. The endowment Robert had left had not been large and had been put into the physical plant. Louis's endowment was tied into a private trust which gave only limited sums each year. Erma continued to contribute as much as she could, but the burden of making ends meet now rested with Rosalind.

In a sense it was fortunate that she had this weighty responsibility which she had already sustained for many years. Her life was her own and still very full. Because of her work she would emerge intact from the breakdown of her two closest relationships. She would in time regain some, but never all, of her radiant optimism and sense of fun.

28

A New Circle in the Shadow

Two years passed before we saw Krinsh again. In the summer of 1966, Jimmy and I exchanged our house in Santa Barbara for a friend's house in a small French village near Dreux. From there we drove to Gstaad, where once more we were invited to stay at the Chalet Tanegg.

That year we met some of what would be Krinsh's new circle, although we did not realize their importance then. He also had another new Mercedes since 1964, given to him by a rich admirer. 'Don't tell Rajagopal,' he said. Then spontaneously he asked if we would like to have it; an offer as impractical to implement as it was generous. I could see he was caught between the onerous discomfort of ownership and the joy of possession.

We were on easy enough terms with Krinsh's new friends and even teased one of them about having to use Krinsh's brand of soap and toothpaste. This was a familiar story to me, for I had seen since childhood that Krinsh wanted those close to him to use whatever product he was at the moment sold on. One day two large suitcases were brought by one of the secretaries from the London office. They contained silk monogrammed shirts and ties from Savile Row; sets for Krishna and for his new favourite. I had from that moment the intuition that this association would lead to trouble, but whose trouble I did not then guess. I did suggest to Krishna that it was going a bit far to dictate the toothpaste a person should use, but he told me very sternly to keep out of it.

While he failed to credit Raja with having provided the purchase money for the Saanen land, he made plenty of ado about his refusal to send funds for other purposes. He had not directly asked Raja to provide his new helper's salary, but used Doris Pratt's intervention. Raja, perhaps to Krishna's surprise, agreed to this salary as well as expenses; however, when the next request came for a lifetime annuity for this present 'favourite', Raja reminded Krishna of the many loyal, long-time friends who had worked steadfastly over the years: were they to be overlooked in favour of such a newcomer? Krinsh used this refusal as an example of his financial ordeal with Raja. But I was fortunately, for once, aware of the logic behind Raja's decision; a decision which would prove fortunate for Krinsh, though he never gave Raja credit for it. In due course, the newcomer would be banished from the new circle for reasons not made public, though there were those who felt he had been harshly treated. I felt compelled to warn Krinsh again, in spite of his severity toward me over the toothpaste issue, that in my opinion such an intimate appearing association could create an unfavourable impression. Instead of scolding me as I expected for such a mundane expression of respectability, so contrary to my upbringing, he did not express either a positive or negative response, but instead answered that he was aware of complications. From what he said, it seemed likely that there would be a bit of reshuffling before the new circle took its final shape.

Krinsh's young yoga teacher, Desikachar, was there too. Vanda had been put to some embarrassment over the switch in yoga teachers. Desikachar's uncle, the famous Iyengar, had been the teacher every summer and expected this to continue. Krishna had found Iyengar too rough and without notifying Vanda had arranged for Desikachar to come over from India – leaving Vanda the difficult task of explaining to Iyengar.

It was not altogether a pleasant visit for me. It had become too obvious that there was intense hostility toward my father. I was used to quarrels between him and Krinsh, but neither of them had ever discussed the other with me. Krinsh now made innuendoes which were worse than outright accusations because in arguing against innuendoes I found they took on a concrete value whether right or wrong which made them all the more difficult to dispel.

Krinsh had changed even more since our previous visit. He had always loved to tell jokes at mealtimes, mostly culled from the *Reader's Digest*. He had a very strong social commitment to be the entertaining host. But now he seemed withdrawn, his eyes veiled not only by the long straight lashes but by an inner abstraction. The rest of us carried on easily together. One day Krinsh observed us all laughing heartily and commented a trifle caustically, 'American humour, I see,' as though he were quite unable to understand it.

One day on a walk with Krinsh on the hillside above Chalet Tanegg, I suddenly asked him why he still talked after nearly forty years of saying very much the same thing.

'If everyone took you literally, listened carefully, and took in what you are saying, they needn't come back unless they want to be followers and you say you don't want followers. What would happen if your audience, by really listening to you, disappeared?'

'That is a paradox,' he answered in a moment of open candour. 'I speak to live, I do not live to speak, if there were no more talks I would die.'

No wonder then, I thought, that he needed more and more, rather than less and less of an audience. The older and frailer he became, the more he would feel that he must have a life sustained by listeners. Thousands of them. He would travel round and round the world, exerting all the strength and energy he had that it might be renewed as fast as it was spent.

We returned to California more than a month ahead of Krinsh, who would be bringing his new circle with him to Ojai. I had reported the conversations and events during our stay in Gstaad to my father as fully as possible. He was interested in our impressions but as usual offered no side comments. I think he was withholding judgment about Krishna's new associates. He could not have had the faintest idea of what, in the end, his relationship with them would be.

Krishna was now insisting on being re-instated on KWInc and would ask that his new associates be put on also. He suddenly wanted to assume full responsibility for KWInc's activities. Although Krishna had been an original member, he had soon resigned, saying he preferred to leave that end of the work completely to Raja. Thereafter Krishna had never shown the slightest interest in KWInc, any more than he had in its predecessor, the Star Publishing Trust, which had served the same purpose. Both had been established to handle organizational and publishing affairs. Raja's role in the work had always been clear to him and, until now, Krishna had given every indication that it was clear to him in the same way. As Raja saw it, he was not working for Krishna. It was because of his promise to Nitya to stand by Krishna, and Mrs Besant's request that he help in the work, that Raja had undertaken this life-long commitment: a commitment that would enable Raja to fulfil much, but not all, of his inherent potential, by employing both his financial acumen and his literary skills. Raja considered KWInc, which he had created, the funds which he had raised for it and managed, and all the publishing were his responsibility in a venture centred around, but not run by, Krishna. This arrangement was fully clear to Krishna all along, if not to the world at large. He had never expressed the slightest criticism of any aspect of Raja's performance.

Krishna had always enjoyed acquiring land and building on it. He did not like to stay around and manage this material side of his affairs, however. Over the years Raja had expertly organized and maintained all the properties for Krishna's use as well as helping with the schools in India. He could not see the justification for acquiring yet more property for which he no longer felt up to taking responsibility. He knew from experience that Krishna would not do so. Now Krishna was again in a mood to expand. He still wanted a centre in Saanen and would eventually acquire a costly estate in England, which would be used for a school. Perhaps the war years at Ojai had been too simple and too confined a way of life for him. That way of life had been appropriate to the time but was not in Krishna's natural style, as both my parents had discovered in India and as I had seen for myself in Gstaad. Raja, however, would not sympathize with these extravagant plans, nor would he co-operate. In the past, Krishna might have felt he could persuade Raja to his way of thinking, but now, because of Raja's knowledge of his long affair with Rosalind, Krishna was afraid of him. He dared not challenge him openly but he wanted Raja out of his way. Before long he would accuse him, behind his back, of usurping his responsibilities, his money, his property. Raja realized that since Krishna's affair with Rosalind had been brought into the open among them, Krishna's behaviour had changed. But he was not willing to give up his life's work and be replaced by Krishna's new friends because of Krishna's uncomfortable conscience towards him.

Raja had lost a staunch supporter when Louis died, for in spite of the distance that his marriage to Annalisa had put between them, Raja still had Louis's firm trust. Louis often told us that he would never have contributed so heavily to KWInc had it not been for his faith in my father's integrity and good sense. The death of such friends and the alienation of others due to Krishna's campaign against him would isolate Raja more and more. He seldom left his house now, even to see us in Santa Barbara. He no longer went to dinner parties, or played chess, except occasionally with his grandchildren, his days of travelling were over and nothing in the world seemed to bring him more than fleeting moments of lightheartedness.

Krinsh still maintained a privately loving manner toward Rosalind, although I noticed that he showed a new reserve when in the presence of the new circle. Being in the company of all of them at once was obviously uncomfortable for him.

When Krishna said goodbye to Rosalind that autumn, he held her

A New Circle in the Shadow

hand tightly for a brief moment and with a strange finality said, 'The first love is the best love.'

Before he left for Europe, I had one last talk with Krinsh when he came again to our house for dinner. We took a long walk on the beach. I begged him to put an end to the hostilities with my father and strangely enough he suddenly promised me that he would. The next day Raja said he had a most encouraging phone conversation with Krinsh in which they had both agreed to settle matters amicably, Krinsh promising to negotiate directly with him. However only three weeks later I heard again that Raja had received ultimatums, made almost as soon as Krishna arrived in Europe. With this reversal I felt the situation to be most depressing. So strong and instinctive had Krinsh's promise to me seemed that I had felt he really meant it. Perhaps he had at that moment.

I had my own strange farewell. Several months later, I had a dream that brought me, as no outward incident could do, a sad sense of finality.

I dreamed all my family were staying at a beautiful inn, on top of a granite mountain with gentle slopes of smooth rock, studded with small pines, surrounding us. The others were gathered in the large, monastic living-room and I had left them for the moment to see if Krinsh was all right. Someone had mentioned he might be ill. I walked through a long stone corridor to his room and he came out of the bathroom, rubbing oil in his hair and saying he did not feel at all well. He had on a mustard-coloured robe, the only colour there except for the dark green of the pine trees.

He asked me to stay and talk with him for a moment. He was deeply concerned that he would not live much longer, and before he died he must return to India and talk to his father, whom he had not seen for many years and with whom he had not had a good relationship. He wanted to ask his father to take care of Rajagopal and give him a house. It was extremely important to Krinsh that Rajagopal have this house and that Krinsh's father alone could provide it. But he thought he would have great difficulty in persuading his father to do this.

I offered to go to India with Krinsh, partly because I wanted very much to go to India, but mostly because I felt sure that even though I were a stranger to his father, I could help. Krinsh was touched and most warm and affectionate about my offer and we walked together out of his room and up a steep rocky pathway toward the crest of the narrow peak.

Just as we approached the top, Krinsh, who was in the lead, turned to face me, sat down and became a figure of stone on a stone chair, similar in pose to the statue of Lincoln in Lincoln's Memorial. But this was not a solid or smoothly sculptured statue. It was of loosely assembled stones, each piece roughly the shape of a hand or leg. I desperately began to pull apart the rocks, hoping to find Krinsh somewhere inside, but suddenly I looked up and saw the sky flaming with sunset. I walked to the top and looked over at the extraordinarily beautiful sea below and felt Krinsh in all that, the sea and the sunset, and what was really him, his essence, had gone there in freedom and left behind the dross which was the rock. My sadness at losing him so suddenly left me, knowing that he was free. But when I awoke the sadness was there again, not because I believed that he was dead, but I was struck by the contrast between my dream and reality, and I thought that if either he or Raja were to die now how terrible it would be for the one left and for all of us.

Krishna continued to persuade everyone around him, including Doris Pratt, Raja's old friend and associate in the London office, that not only was Raja arbitrarily barring him from KWInc, but that he had withheld and misspent funds intended for Krishna's use. Many of the old associates who had worked with Raja for over three decades and with whom he had enjoyed a compatible relationship now suddenly, along with Krishna's new friends, took Krishna's part, criticizing Raja for being possessive and obstinate. Raja refused to explain what underlay the real conflict between him and Krishna; he still hoped to protect both Krishna and Rosalind, as well as the thousands who he felt would be deeply hurt and disillusioned if they knew the truth. Krishna refused to recognize that before any new course of action could be taken, he must do Raja the justice of discussing their lives, with all the ramifications that had developed over the past forty years. After all it was Krishna's actions, not Raja's, that had put their personal lives on a discordant footing. Before their relationship was cleared of past misunderstandings, Raja refused to be further drawn into obvious complications with a whole new order of people and schemes.

What now looked like an open break compelled Rosalind to try again to intercede.

Ojai, California   *Jan '67*
Dear Krinsh,
    Thanks for your letter from Rome. I do hope all is well with you.

A New Circle in the Shadow

One has a strange feeling you are in orbit and not touching the earth. Please take time to work things out quietly. You once said you could never even lift a little finger against me. Surely this must apply to Raja also. I know I wouldn't or couldn't act against either of you. I also feel that you do not mind anything I may say to you. I hope I am right about this so here goes:

At the outset let me say for you and R to have and show such differences in your old age will lead to nothing but mischief and calamity. It will involve others who cannot possibly know what had been and . . . leave open the door for great trouble. *Please* give some weight & thought to all this and let's have some peace. Otherwise it is so stupid to end in a mess when one had such an opportunity to do something fine. I wonder why you do not seem to see what all this can lead to? Keep well and I hope we meet again soon.

Love,

ROSALIND

After six years of fruitless discussion, Krishna was still fulminating about Arya Vihara. Where he had once clearly stated in a letter to Raja that he wanted the house to be 'given to Rosalind outright', he now was accusing Raja of making arrangements behind his back and using this as another reason why he must be reinstated on KWInc.

Rosalind once more tried to clarify the situation in writing, after an abortive telephone call to him in London.

Ojai   *June 12, 1967*
What a strange state of affairs! It goes from bad to worse. I must tell you the sequence of events leading to 'Arya Vihara'. Mima phoned me and said they had a meeting in which it was decided to turn A.V. over to the H.V.F. for me to be able to use it in my lifetime. She said this was the only way they could see to fulfill your wishes. They all felt that the people who had put money in A.V. were anyway the people who supported H.V. There was also a letter from you saying they were both one and the same [as Krinsh had said to me in Gstaad in 1964].

I was surprised then about this offer, as once in passing when you mentioned it to me, I said that you might turn it over to the H.V.F. and I w'ld give you the money from the sale of Saro Vihara [the Logan house which Rosalind had inherited]. You did not seem to like the idea of an exchange and made me feel that you wanted to let Radha and me use it as a very kind gesture from you to us . . . You have no reason whatsoever to be concerned about this matter. Please feel free to do what you like about it in any way – sell – let others live here, anything. I will not mind in the least and I am only deeply appreciative for the many good years as well as the difficult ones that I have lived here. I thank you from the bottom of my heart for making this possible. I really do not think I could have done the work I did without the quiet and strength I got from living here all these years. Fini.

Now for the second part: I hate doing this; I would not be a person who was ever a friend, had love, or was to be trusted if I did not speak out now. I did this long ago when you arrived in Australia with Nitya. I broke his confidence to try and make peace between you before he died. Krinsh, Krinsh, what is happening to you? Such a betrayal with one who was so devoted in spite of everything. I told you that he [Raja] felt you were out to destroy him and now you are doing everything to prove it. Is it for revenge, on account of the way he has spoken to you, money, property, power – what? You discredit him to others – the talk is ugly and libelous. Send legalistic letters – highly inaccurate. How unhappy everyone is! All this has completely humiliated and insulted him beyond belief.

You came here in an odd manner. Most of the time spent on your teeth, talks, people and did you really think in this way you could solve anything decently? What can I say to a person who says he refuses to talk or listen? I have been told that I seemed to be the only person who could still talk to you. That you eliminated in one way or another all those who do not say what you want to hear and can only tolerate those who are sycophants or 'yes' men. This makes all around you suspect. What a dangerous position to be in!! Like a king who was brought up to think he could do no wrong . . . Now I feel I *cannot* talk to you. There are no words to say how sad and tragic all this has become. What is it you want? Do you know what you have done? What an ending to your lives! Louis' heart was broken when you became authoritarian. I know he wrote you this . . . No matter what has gone wrong with R and things have gone wrong . . . for you to betray him now, if you couldn't help him, but to hurt him so terribly can only make matters worse. I don't like to look at where all this must lead. He has spoken to me as badly as to you but should I harm him for this? In spite of all the above the Happy Valley

A New Circle in the Shadow

School is bursting with your ideas which is after all the *great* part of your life.

In his reply to this letter Krishna ignored her explanation and reiterated that Arya Vihara must not be given to Happy Valley. He told her that she knew nothing of what was going on and that he must be in charge of KWInc. He signed off with as much love as ever.

As Rosalind had pointed out, there was nothing for Krishna to be so anxious about. It had only been a suggestion to give Arya Vihara to the Happy Valley. There was no thought of acting without his approval. He seemed determined to find fault with Raja, even where there was none whatever. The matter of Arya Vihara was dropped; no further action would be taken.

Rosalind continued to be distressed by Krishna's refusal to see what she felt were the obvious dangers of his present course. She wrote again, this time more desperate in tone:

June 22, 1967

At least you did write to me and I am going to try to state the situation as clearly as I can. Apart from all pros and cons that you should set out to damage & defame presumably an old friend, regardless of what you think he has done – is against you not him . . . It is all so contrary to what you have said to others. Don't you see this? Before you act so hastily and rashly do please I beg you give a little more time – space – thought. There is just too much pride from both sides. It is so tragic. At the outset let me say I would not do anything to hurt either of you, about this I am clear. There is only one thing possible now as I see it – for you to come here alone and get things straight.

Even so it may be too late as there is so much damage done already. You are obviously getting very stupid advice from some who really do not know what they are doing.

Everything is in good order – every cent accounted for [and] could be explained to you very simply if you saw all the records. You never wanted to be bothered before. At one time you were asked to be a member of both boards and you refused. I can't talk to R, he blows up at me about you & me wrecking his marriage, repeats everything from the past. He had an operation which went wrong & must have another. Mima begs him not to die and leave her with this mess. I beg you to come here. I will do anything I can to make things easy. Dear Krinsh can

293

you hear me – do you remember me!! Dear God let something penetrate.

Again Krishna mistook the thrust of Rosalind's letter. Feeling she had threatened him, he warned that he would no longer answer such letters, that no good could come from them.

In spite of this, Rosalind made another attempt to meet with Krishna in person when she took Ermie, who was suffering from back pain, to the Bircher-Benner clinic in the autumn of 1967. She left Erma at the clinic and met Krishna in London, where at Wimbledon, near the scene of much happier times spent with Miss Dodge, she tried to explain that Raja had always wanted to carry out his wishes, that he had never acted against either of them and that he deserved at least an attempt at reconciliation. Krishna was absolutely impervious to her words, withdrawn and haughty. She felt totally unable to reach him. He left for Rome. In London Rosalind met an old friend who told her many disturbing rumours about Krishna and the things that were being said by him and his new associates about Raja. At first this man gave her permission to use his name with Krishna about the 'anti-Raja sentiment' and then withdrew it, feeling Krishna might resent it and that might block the possibility of a friendly conversation with him in the future. Ten days later when Rosalind saw Krishna in Rome, he had shifted aspects or, as she saw it, personalities. He was loving and appeared willing to talk. Rosalind asked him what she and Mima should do to help make things right again. She asked him also what he thought he should do. Krishna replied that he would return to Ojai, see Raja alone and try to straighten things out. Rosalind finally felt hopeful, but she had found talking to the 'two Krishnas', one in London and one in Rome, a strange and unsettling experience. She could not believe he was the same person both times. The one in Rome was the one she had always known.

Soon after, Krishna wrote his last letter to her. It was peculiarly in the style of his earlier letters, written over several days, full of concern for her well-being, with promises to set things right when he returned to California the following summer, detailed and gloomy descriptions of London and of Rome – both cities drenched in rain. He felt his age acutely and looked forward to peace and quiet. 'My love's with you always,' he ended.

Krishna did not keep his promise to Rosalind. He must have known when he made it that he could never bring himself to confront Raja alone. In the spring of 1968, when Mima was in Paris, Krishna asked her to try and settle matters for him with Raja, adding that if there was no co-operation he (Krishna) would disassociate himself from KWInc. Mima informed Krishna at the time that she would only go so far as to relay the message, not attempt to settle matters between them. When Mima returned to Ojai with this message, Raja replied that if Krishna wanted to talk about such matters he must talk to him directly, not send messengers. Krishna later accused Mima of not keeping her promise to settle things for him and of lying when she protested that she had not promised to do that.

Krishna, unable to bend Raja to his will, sent a new associate of his, a stranger to Raja, to 'investigate' the situation. The report, after investigating the way in which KWInc had been structured and functioned, all well known and approved by Krishna at the time, such as giving Raja the power of attorney over KWInc, now incited Krishna to claim that he had not known what he was signing. Even if he had never bothered to read what he was signing that was certainly not Raja's fault.

Thus continued the splitting and re-aligning of many old friendships. Those who were not by temperament devotees could more easily see Raja's side and would come more and more to stand by him as the situation became even worse.

Those who considered themselves friends of both parties tried during the next few years to bring about a reconciliation: with a few it became almost a mission that they must achieve; for others there was a great deal, psychologically, at stake. Many people who had adhered closely to Krishna over the years had done so because in various ways they felt he had literally saved them, and that they owed him a great deal for this. Others who had worked closely with Raja and were in a position to know most of the facts, which partly by nature and partly of necessity, Raja had kept private, had to face a slow, bitter disillusionment with Krishna – the same disillusionment that Raja had faced many years before and had lived with, coming to believe, much as Rosalind now believed, that Krishna was more than one person. Until a person had his own experience with the other side of Krishna, he was susceptible to believing Krishna's charges against Raja. Many old friends were deeply hurt when Krishna abruptly terminated his relationship with them because they were intrepid enough to show the slightest criticism. Among those, Carlo and Nadine Suarés, who for years had opened their homes to Krishna for lengthy stays both in Alexandria and in Paris and helped to translate his talks, most unexpectedly received this treatment.

As Krishna well knew, the Suarés had lost nearly everything in the Egyptian revolution and their circumstances were far from easy; nevertheless, when he was in Paris, they always invited him to stay with them. But on the occasion when he had asked them to include a new friend, Krishna inspected the guest room where Nadine Suarés had invited the young man to stay and said, 'A grown man cannot stay in such a hole.' Nadine told me this story a few years later, her gentle face suffused with baffled unhappiness. 'How could he say such a thing?' she asked while showing us the room, which was airy and comfortable with a bed, desk and chair. Whether Krishna's behaviour stemmed from some irritation toward the Suarés, the cause of which I am unaware, or whether he was deliberately weeding out all the old-timers who were not totally committed to him and opposed to Raja, I cannot say.

In my case, I had seen since childhood the various aspects of their triangular relationship. When I was very young, I assumed that ours was a normal household and that everyone had a Daddy, a Mummy and a Krinsh; it was a great surprise to me to find, when I started school, that this was not the case. But as there were so many other aspects of our life that were unusual, I never cast a judgmental eye over what went on under my nose. I never allowed myself to take sides in the arguments that I overheard. When they were all getting along apparently happily, I sensed that I lived in a rare and most privileged household, full of interesting events and people. There was a sense of purpose, service and worth in our daily lives, a sense re-inforced by the attitude towards us of onlookers and visitors. I was aware always of a solid front of three loving and protective adults and I was never the cause of disagreement amongst them.

It was with the greatest reluctance that finally in my early adulthood I had to separate them into three individuals and try to look at them objectively, sorting out their rights and wrongs. I found it hard to admit weaknesses and faults in any of them. On the surface both of my parents had more abrasive and generally difficult personalities than Krinsh, at least when they were upset, which happened more and more frequently. Krinsh, on the other hand was almost always lovable, fun and easy to be with. He never said a word against my mother to me, but starting in 1964 he began the grave insinuations against my father which demanded my attention.

At this point he didn't refer to him as my father but only as Rajagopal and then finally as 'he', as if the name were unspeakable. My father would frequently lament Krinsh's treatment of him, but with the grief

A New Circle in the Shadow

born of a lost friendship rather than the hatred of a discovered enemy. Krinsh's hatred ran so deep that he could hardly speak at all, as if it welled up through a frozen crust, for he was not, in his own view of himself and that of his devotees, supposedly able to feel hatred. But he did not seem to try to hide it from me. In 1966 in Gstaad, when I asked him why he had allowed my father to give his life to this work, feeling about him as he must have for so many years, Krinsh replied that he had carried him along because Raja was incapable of making any other life for himself. This was such an absurd statement that I was stunned into silence. I knew that my father had attained with high honours a further degree from Cambridge. I had been a witness all my life to his extraordinary efficiency and capability in the management of a complex organization and his deep and very human concern for the people involved in it. I realized then that there was no hope of ever returning to what I, perhaps incorrectly, remembered as the harmonious balance between them. A few years later my mother-in-law, on a visit to Gstaad, asked Krishna how, after being friends for so long, things could be so bad between him and Raja and strangely, he replied, 'He was my friend but I was never his.'

At Gstaad that summer Krishna had instigated a new attack on Raja. He called together his friends from Ojai to taped meetings in which he condemned Raja before the group and renounced all further association with him. Krishna them recommended that these tapes be played to all who wished to hear them. They even circulated as far as Australia. News of this had naturally upset Raja in the extreme.

Krishna was to stay in California for several months, mostly in Malibu, and it was here that Rosalind made one more futile attempt to bring about a reconciliation between him and Raja. Krishna said he would allow her a half-hour only of his time. He also insisted that his hostess remain in the room. Rosalind returned to Ojai to write another hopeless appeal.

3 November, 1968

After yesterday's conversation one is left with a terrible foreboding of doom . . . The stage is all set – everything you say – everything you do . . . I tried to shock – to awaken you to reality and it had no noticeable affect on you. There seems to be a total lack of feeling – without kindness – love or charity. Nethercot in his book *The Four Lives* – wrote among other things that it seems you hypnotize yourself to believe what you want to.[1] Yesterday I said you were a dual personality because you are often different people. For example the one I spoke to yesterday was like the one I spoke to in London – completely different from Rome. What is tragic is that many of your ideas were great and helpful and you are ruining it all now. Don't you see how contrary all this is to everything you have always stood for? What you have said regarding human relations and values? You have always said that any disagreement about material things was a reflection of wrong attitude in oneself. That you should descend to this kind of vicious inciting is incredible, as you have done by talking to so many and sending a tape around! These people are not directly concerned and are only harmed by being made aware of this conflict. Surely you and your advisers know that one doesn't air one's problems in public but deals directly with the principles. What you are doing is unheard of even among ordinary people. This is why so many people are deeply, silently shocked.

In the end no matter how you feel or what you do, I have a grave sense of responsibility out of the past. I would see to it that you had whatever care was necessary. This was a pledge I made Nitya the last I saw him. I will keep it.

In January 1968 Krishna went in person, accompanied by members of his new circle, to the Attorney-General's office in Los Angeles, to accuse Raja of mismanaging funds. Later he would disclaim any part, personally, in the ensuing lawsuits brought against Raja. In spite of his past statements that it would be unthinkable for him to enter into a lawsuit with Raja or to have anything to do with such matters, he was the instigator of this first step. James Vigeveno was so disturbed by these developments that a year and a half later he wrote a letter trying to cast a little light – and truth – on the situation.

Ojai   *July 1969*
TO FRIENDS OF MINE AND THOSE WHO ARE HURT:
Since 1927, now forty-two years ago, when I first met Krishnamurti, I have always been a great admirer and friend, and I have ever since been deeply interested in his teachings. During these years I have worked much for him, I have been a trustee and later Vice-President of the Krishnamurti Writings, Inc. until the end of 1966.

Rajagopal has worked for nearly fifty years for Krishnamurti's teachings and has devoted his entire life to this work . . . Most efficiently, he has made of the Krishnamurti Writings, Inc. an organization which the world will be grateful to remember one day.

But in 1960 things began to change . .. and I found myself in the middle of a growing conflict between Krishnaji and Rajagopal . . .

A New Circle in the Shadow

In private talks with me Krishnaji started to criticize Rajagopal's actions; he tried to influence me against him. Krishnaji's criticism of Rajagopal became more insistent every year when I saw him in Gstaad, and every year this matter was openly discussed at the Saanen Gatherings . . . His attitude against Rajagopal became more resentful, and he opposed him personally – not his work. Krishnaji has always admired this and has often told me: 'Nobody could do the work better than Rajagopal.'

Krishnamurti's tragic moment came in 1968, when during the Saanen Gathering an official statement was read out which announced his disassociation from the Krishnamurti Writings, Inc., and a denunciation of Rajagopal. With that you are all familiar. Much later I heard that a few friends around Krishnaji had urged him not to make this public announcement; but he had been adamant . . .

On October 31st 1968, Krishnaji called me over the telephone and said to me: 'I don't want to talk with Rajagopal alone. I want to meet with the trustees of the Krishnamurti Writings, Rajagopal and you. If this does not happen, I am out of it. If we don't meet before November 3rd, the lawyers will take charge . . . But under *no* circumstances will I see Rajagopal alone.

'I am not threatening or forcing you. I am only telling you facts. If there is no meeting as suggested, I will not see any of you again and will not answer any of your letters. This is not a personal problem; Krishnamurti Writings is a public affair. *You* are responsible.

'You are dealing with something sacred, and you are spitting on it. Rajagopal is no longer the cock of the walk, the strong man. The situation is grave, it is a sacred, holy matter . . . Don't you see the gravity of this? He refuses a man like me offering my friendship!'

After this conversation I talked with Rajagopal. Rajagopal gave up his insistence to speak with Krishnamurti alone, and agreed to send the following telegram to Krishnamurti on November 2nd, 1968.

'Answering your wish to talk with KWInc. trustees, I can arrange a meeting between you personally and the trustees at the KWInc. office, Besant Road. Please advise date and time you desire after your return from Claremont when more trustees will be available. James Vigeveno'

On November 5th I received the following answer: 'I regret very much that Rajagopal and the trustees refused my request for a meeting between all of us. I won't come to a meeting alone. The matter is now out of my hands. Krishnamurti.'

Very disillusioned I wrote the following letter to Krishnaji:

Dear Krishnaji:
The fact that Rajagopal gave up his strong demand to see you face to face, was a great step towards understanding . . . This meeting about Krishnamurti Writings matters cannot be held in the presence of persons who know nothing or very little about forty-five years of work and relationship between you and Rajagopal.

You cannot expect Rajagopal to attend a meeting with strangers and prejudiced people, but you yourself insist on that point; and because of that point alone it is you who are rejecting the friendly hand offered to you.

You say you are 'out of it'. But that is not so. Whether you personally go to court or your group of friends on your behalf, the result will be the same disaster. A lawsuit and a judgement will be directed against you personally; and the press will be eager to seize the story and dramatize it. You will be the principal figure in the spotlight. This is precisely what Rajagopal is trying to prevent, so that your life and your person will not be publicly discussed and denounced and exposed.

Dear Krishnaji, I am writing this not to criticize but to ask you to see what can happen, and look at it from the point of view of the facts.

There must be a way for two people – him who has given the teachings and him who has given his whole life to the teachings – to discuss and communicate about their problems, so that with love and goodwill an understanding can come about.'

After having refused to meet personally with Rajagopal to discuss their problem, Krishnamurti has spread the word that the money given to Krishnamurti Writings, Inc. for him has not been made available for his use. This is not true . . . all his expenses have been readily met, and specially requested amounts for himself and [his secretary] have always been sent to him by the Krishnamurti Writings, Inc. in various instalments. A few months ago, however, Krishnamurti suddenly refused the money, saying very curtly that he would no longer accept it from [KWInc] as long as Rajagopal was the head of it. In spite of this, Rajagopal had me send to Krishnaji *again* the amount, hoping that, coming from me, he would accept it . . . But again it was refused.

. . . One day, history will reveal everything; but the division in Krishnamurti himself will cast a very dark shadow on all he has said or written. Because the first thing the readers will say, is: 'If he cannot live it, who can?'

A New Circle in the Shadow

. . . I leave it to you to think and find out which of the two is nearer to the teachings and to living them. Rajagopal is not defending himself, out of love for Krishnamurti and the wish to protect him. Remember a question so often asked of Krishnaji: 'What do you do when you are attacked?' He answered: 'If you defend yourself, then the defender becomes the attacker.'

JAMES VIGEVENO

James Vigeveno's letter touched many and angered others. Beatrice Wood replied to James after receiving her copy:

Aug 1st, 1969

Dear James,

It is wonderful someone, who knew, had facts, came out so clearly to speak of the impasses between Rajagopal and Krishnaji.

I had tears as I read it. It has been obvious to me Krishnaji is not living his own teaching, that he has been making war. I am glad you not only brought that out, but also that Rajagopal with dignity has not added to the aggression, but kept silent in his own defense.

Were it wise I wish your letter could be published for many to read. From a standpoint of wisdom it might only add to the fuel. For few of us can be objective, and in the mind of devotees a world teacher can do no wrong.

Krishnaji has said he wants no followers, yet he encourages people to follow him around. Anyone who thinks independently, for himself must see the unloving attitude that Krishnaji is pursuing.

On account of my respect and affection for Rajagopal I am deeply grateful you have written so impressively and justly your thoughts.

Affectionately,

BEATRICE

Among the devotees, there were many who took grave offence at James's letter. Krishna pretended not to recognize Annie Vigeveno, when a few years later she offered him a ride up the hill to the Oak Grove. Old friends, who stood by Raja, were denounced as being part of a Judas syndrome. It is indeed hard to see that parallel. No one had acted against Krishna.

29

The Wheels of Justice

Once set in motion, the process of litigation moved slowly and inexorably towards a showdown. Raja offered terms which four years later would be accepted.

Ermie died in November 1970, leaving Rosalind in the front line alone now. There was no longer any close elder in her life to offer the solace of greater wisdom and experience. For Rosalind it was like losing a mother; Erma had cared for her since birth.

In one of her last lucid moments Ermie said to us, 'I have studied philosophy and the religions all my life and everything is still a great question.'

I will never forget the look of childlike wonder in her beautiful blue-green eyes as she said this, completely without fear, just a vital curiosity still carrying her through her last moments.

It was in January 1971, when my mother became convinced that there would be a trial and the privacy of her life would be invaded, that she sat down one day and told me all the details of her relationship with Krishna. She said she did not want me to hear it the first time in a courtroom and if he himself had not brought about the present situation she would never have told anyone. It was a relief to her when I replied that ever since I could remember I had been aware of the close relationship between her and Krinsh.

Rosalind then appealed to the attorneys on both sides, telling them how disastrous a trial would be, most of all for Krishna, only hinting at possible scandal. She was still not prepared to reveal publicly her own relationship with Krishna; it would take yet another lawsuit to wrench that from her. But her plea was disregarded.

In 1971 Krishna had returned to California, but not to Ojai, where he was refusing to talk as long as Raja was involved with KWInc. I phoned him in Malibu to plead once more that he try to end the hostilities. To open the conversation I asked him if he knew that Ermie had died. At first he acted as though he didn't know who Ermie was. When I refreshed his memory, he sounded unmoved. (Erma, while never

302

uttering a word of criticism, had, with Louis, withdrawn from personal and financial involvement with Krishna.) I heard a voice prompting him in the background.

'Can't we carry on this conversation without the help of another party?' I asked.

Krinsh denied that anyone was in the room. I was appalled by this blatant deception.

'This whole matter is something private, as you well know, between you and my father. It is something that should be settled in a closet, not a courtroom.'

I then went too far, saying, 'It seems to me it is a conflict of ego and pride and surely you of all people should be able to deal with that.'

Krinsh was outraged. His voice changed completely from a formal indifference to heated anger. It became almost shrill.

'I have no ego!' he said. 'Who do you think you are, to talk to me like this?'

I replied, 'I am nobody.' Indeed I realized he did not know me. I was a total stranger at that moment.

After this conversation which ended so badly, I did not see or talk to him again for three years. It was the first time he had ever been angry with me, although I had witnessed his anger towards others. I discovered it was a very different experience to be his direct target. Over the next few years I would meet a series of people who had suffered the same fate, often with devastating results. Strangely enough I felt I owed to him my resilience and ability to cast off his anger without injury, although I would continue to feel a great sadness for them all.

In December 1973 Jimmy and I went to India for three months. Our daughter and son, Tinka and Robbie, now in college, came with us. On an impulse I wrote to Krishna telling him we would be in Bombay in January and asking him to call our hotel there if he would like to see us. He called, and though his voice then sounded a bit remote, when we drove up to the house he was standing outside watching for us, apparently anxiously. He said he was afraid we might get lost. He was as affectionate as ever, holding my face in his hands and gazing at me for a long potent moment. There were several people at the table, although his hostess was away in New Delhi. One of the other guests had been most sweet and helpful to my mother when she had visited India in 1956, and she at least asked after Rosalind, but during lunch neither of my parents' names was mentioned once by Krinsh, nor was Ojai. A curtain had fallen on that part of the world. Krinsh showed us a model of his new school with which he was evidently very absorbed.

I left this luncheon feeling we had not really established any contact and that my farewell dream of seven years before had been indeed the true farewell.

On that trip we stayed for two weeks in the Theosophical headquarters at Adyar as guests of the late President, John Coates. We met several people who had been obliquely touched by the lawsuit between Krishna and Raja. Krishna had objected to a contract Raja had made with Quest books, a Theosophical publishing house, to publish Krishna's writings. Krishna was supposedly still taking a stand of complete aloofness from the Theosophical Society, although a very few years later he would reverse this attitude. (First he was to refer to Raja as that 'damned Theosophist', in a rancorous realization that Raja had never resigned from the society.) Mr Coates showed us the apartment that was still kept for Krishna in accordance with Mrs Besant's wishes. 'We have never locked him out as he claims,' Mr Coates told me. 'And he now claims your parents have locked him out from Arya Vihara.' 'Then Krinsh had not accepted after all,' I thought to myself, 'when my mother asked him to stay away from Ojai for those few years.' But I said nothing.

We were staying in Leadbeater Chambers, the large three-storey building that my father and Rukmini's brother Yagna, had once scampered around when it was being built. One morning during breakfast, a man appeared on our veranda and introduced himself as the person involved in arbitration of the Vasanta Vihar property across the river, now also an object of litigation. He told me how he was living in it to keep up the property until a settlement was reached. He claimed that Krishna had harried the Theosophists about both of his Indian schools and property. I was sorry later that I had not pursued a more detailed line of inquiry instead of trying to end, rather than expand, that conversation.

Rosalind had decided to build a house on Happy Valley for her use during her lifetime with funds from the sale of her Saro Vihara house. Krishna must not have known of her plans, for he sent a verbal message with a friend that Rosalind should vacate Arya Vihara as he now had a use for it. His endless statements and letters designating Arya Vihara as hers for her lifetime were not referred to and were probably forgotten by both of them.

In December 1974 an out-of-court settlement was finally reached.

The parties in the Agreement [Krishnamurti Foundation of America, Krishnamurti Foundation Trust Ltd, England, Krishnamurti and the trustees of said organizations on the one hand, and K & R Foundation, Krishnamurti Writings, Inc. of Ojai, and Rajagopal] wish to make it clear to all those who are concerned with the teachings of Krishnamurti that it is the intent of this agreement to settle all differences so that the work of Krishnamurti throughout the world may proceed effectively.

. . . the trustees of said organizations have entered into an Agreement settling and resolving all of the disputes and differences that have existed between them for a number of years. All the parties have agreed to withdraw the allegations that have been made against one another and to dismiss all legal claims based on these allegations.

Raja had sought for the previous four years to protect Krishna from the publicity that would ensue from a trial, even to the point of refusing to consider his own defence. He hoped against hope that Krishna would come to his senses and retract the absurd but terrible and imprisonable charges he had made against Raja. In the settlement, Raja offered the material properties that he had offered and that had been rejected four years ago; now they were accepted. While Rosalind's interventions may have caused some confusion for Raja, they may well also have convinced Krishna's advisers that it would be detrimental in the extreme to drag him into the courts.

Peace was to be short-lived, in spite of the judge's orders that no actions between these parties ever be resumed. Unfortunately the judge died, which was perhaps not legally relevant, but in any case alleged grounds for another action against Raja were gathered. Raja had already given up publication rights to everything after 1967, plus the KWInc land and almost all the funds, except what had been agreed in the settlement that he could keep for work on the compilation of a thirty-volume library edition of Krishna's complete works up to 1967 which Harper's had agreed to publish. This contract would extend way beyond his own lifetime for almost thirty years and after his death would pass to the Krishnamurti Foundation. Raja had sought to safeguard this project in every way he could and the publisher told me, as I drove him back to the airport after making this agreement with my father, that any publishing house would snap up the contract Raja had offered, even with the possibility of being embroiled in a lawsuit.

Raja's oldest friend, Rukmini Arundale, was among those still loyal to him. There had always been a certain rivalry with her on Krishna's part. He had been scornful of her role as the world mother (although she had not sought to be put in that position). After her husband,

George Arundale, died, Rukmini's brother Sri Ram had succeeded him as President of the Theosophical Society and, after him, John Coates. In 1980, there was another election in the society and Rukmini was one of the candidates for the presidency. She lost to her niece, Radha Burnier. Radha had for many years been a close friend of Krishna and his letters to Rosalind had mentioned her frequent walks with him on the beach whenever he was in Madras. Rukmini wrote to Beatrice Wood in August 1980 about this situation, expressing her surprise that Krishna had taken part in the campaign by saying that if Radha Burnier became President he would once more walk on Theosophical land at Adyar.

It would appear that for Krishna his life was closing full circle. He had deeply resented the snub he felt he had received from the society. His hopes as a youth to take hold of it and reform it had ended in his splitting off from it but, as his letters to Rosalind indicate, he could never walk within sight of Adyar without feeling bitter nostalgia at his self-imposed exile. One wonders how much of his thought and inner striving had been aimed at this final triumphant re-instatement.

He had also tried to stake a claim to the Happy Valley Land. The advances on his behalf had been welcomed but only if he would accept the simple few conditions which were part of the general policy of the Happy Valley Foundation towards any groups that might use the land; that there should be no cults based on a personality, and there must be a sharing of certain common facilities like the library. After receiving these terms of lease from the Happy Valley Foundation, nothing more was heard.

Once more Krishna turned his attack on Raja. Beatrice Wood expressed her feelings about the new action:

Feb 22, 1981

I am writing these notes hoping to clarify my thinking. Several weeks ago I heard . . . another lawsuit was being started over Rajagopal. This puzzled me because I understood that when the lawsuit of 1974 was terminated that it was agreed there would be no further harassment.

[K] wants all [Rajagopal's] papers, not only those which professionally have to do with activities around Krishnamurti, which are available for anyone to see, but also his private papers, which as an individual he has a right to keep. The idea being that as a 'secretary', an employee, he is keeping back papers that belong to the 'Boss'. Since Rajagopal is a man of singular integrity and accuracy, besides [being] knowledgeable about the law, I am doubtful that he would withhold papers that he should not. I have known him as being extraordinarily strict about correctness.

For forty years he has given up his life to helping, never as a secretary but as a friend, and acting without salary. This he told me himself. Dr Besant and Krishnamurti asked him to care for the business side, the publishing of books, arrangement of lectures, and he gave up a possibly brilliant career of his own to devote himself to the teachings. Until recent years Krishnamurti never wanted to have anything to do with financial nor business side of his work, and until the break came between them, he completely trusted Rajagopal's judgement and honesty, asserting he could not go on without his assistance.

Much as I admire the teachings of Krishnamurti, which have had great meaning for me over the years, it bothers me that he [is] acting in a vindictive manner, even to the extent of willingness to have Rajagopal put in jail. This is hard for me to understand, as for many years Krishnamurti lived as one family with Rajagopal and Rosalind and he lovingly helped with the bringing up of their daughter, Radha. It is sad and strange therefore that he is willing to have Rajagopal thus persecuted.

After turning from everything theosophical he now wants a school in Adyar for the training of teachers. What does this mean?

Various rumors continue to go around, and one is that Krishnamurti is supposed to have said that he is even greater than Buddha or the Christ – Christ forgave his enemies. This can be impressive to followers who do not know the whole truth, or the past. The present is the child of the past,

BEATO

When Jimmy and I returned to India in the autumn of 1981, we knew that a new lawsuit was in the offing.

We stopped on the way to spend a few days with Vanda Scaravelli in Fiesole and here for the first time she let us read a description of her experience with Krishna's 'process'. This had occurred in 1961, at a time when she admitted she was disenchanted with his behaviour, particularly toward my father. Vanda remembered Raja had asked her to take care of Krishna in Europe (not in a business sense), as he was withdrawing. Vanda had taken this as a binding commitment, though she herself would withdraw more and more from his new circle. Then she witnessed the 'process'. Her experience, though recorded with utmost sincerity and conviction on her part, struck us as another probable performance by Krishna. In this as in the others, he had attempted to attach to himself the devotion of a particular woman who was important to him at the moment. Yet Vanda still had her own objectivity about him and was one of the few who had managed to remain friends with both Krishna and my father.

'You will be in India when Krishnaji is there. Do see him. Talk to him and tell him to stop this lawsuit. He is like a child,' she said. 'He can be very naughty but he does not know what he is doing and now he wants to be grown-up and take charge but he will make a mess.'

We agreed with her in part, but felt things had gone far beyond the pranks of a naughty child. I wasn't sure at that moment that I wanted to talk to him. I told Vanda I would decide only when we got to India. Thinking it over during the long flight I felt there was nothing to lose in trying once more to reach him and that it would be much easier to see him in India than in Ojai.

On arrival in Delhi I obtained the phone number of his hostess, Pupul Jayakar, from a mutual friend. She received my call warmly and went to ask Krinsh if he would like to see us. We were invited to lunch the following afternoon.

Jimmy and I were shown into a large light room, simply and tastefully furnished with, here and there, Indian art objects of great beauty. In a moment Krinsh walked in, dressed in Indian clothes. He was more frail than in 1974, the last time I had seen him. A large bald spot on top of his head was covered by long hair swept forward in what I thought was a most peculiar styling. He had always been vain yet it surprised me that baldness should matter that much to him now. Far worse was an obvious problem with his teeth or gums, which affected his speech. The trembling of his hands was not new but was more pronounced. There were tears in his eyes as he hugged me then stood back to look and asked, 'Are you still Kittums?' to which I answered quite instinctively, 'Are you still Krinsh?' He seemed to get the point, gave a half smile and we sat down, all three together, after he had also warmly greeted Jimmy. He talked of this and that, nothing personal, until we were called to the dining-room. Here, seated on Krinsh's right at a round table, there began what I can only describe as his game of ostensible intimacy with his favourite of the moment. As a very small child I had innocently monopolized that position, but had sometimes witnessed it in his interaction with others. Now I found myself once again in that privileged place. It consisted of a sharing of morsels of food from plate to plate, being very sure I was well provided for, an occasional squeeze of knee or elbow to show that his attention was really inwardly with me. In spite of all this the conversation kept flowing smoothly from inventions to politics, thanks mostly to his efforts. Seated at the table, much to the satisfaction of a very old curiosity on my part was Nandini, whose famed beauty still lingered in spite of her white hair and gracefully ageing face. At one point, perhaps for my benefit, to show off his former Californian style of informality, or for her benefit to show that he was not neglecting her, Krinsh picked up a banana and tossed it across the table to her. This reminded me of a long ago meal at Arya Vihara, where my mother had tossed a carrot down the whole length of the table to Aldous. 'Here, Aldous, have a carrot!' Just as Krinsh now said, 'Here, Nandini, have a banana!'

As lunch was drawing to a close I said softly to Krinsh that I would very much like to have just five minutes alone with him. Now he demurred and said he must rest because he was to see Indira Gandhi that afternoon. 'Just five minutes, Krinsh,' I persisted, feeling suddenly that this was perhaps my only chance and feeling too so much of my old love for him and his for me, and that if ever one person could reach another surely it would be in such a state.

I wasted no time launching into the subject. I told him if he was planning to continue with another lawsuit, I thought it was, for his sake above all, a very bad idea – that in the end he would destroy everything he had tried to create. His schools, his teachings would all suffer and he would be remembered only for his lawsuits against a man who had given his life to helping him.

I said, even granted that he was right on all the issues, which I did not grant, but even *if* – was what he was doing still worth it? For the sake of *what*?

'Kittums . . .' Again he held my knee, closed his eyes as though searching for the right answers but none came, only questions.

'Do you not think I spend all my time thinking about this? Do you think I want it?'

'Then why?'

Still no real answers came.

'What has my father done to you? Have you any idea what the feelings are in Ojai, how people talk about him and my mother?'

At mention of her he shook me as if to stop my words.

'Don't please . . .'

'When Daddy fell over a wire walking his dog someone close to you said, "Too bad he didn't break his neck", and someone else said very much the same thing when my mother fell, and when poor Byron Casselberry had a stroke, they said it was because he had remained loyal to Raja. They are saying these things because of *you*. They think it is what *you* want. You have spawned this attitude.'

'Rajagopal has been impossible about money, if you only knew . . .'

'Please tell me.'

With this he repeated the story I had heard in Gstaad seventeen years before.

'Can't you come up with a new complaint in all these years? You told me that in Gstaad and then showed me all those travellers' cheques he had sent you.'

'Please let's not talk about this; it is pointless.'

'What else has he done, then? Do you mind him publishing the series with Harper?'

'No, no, that's all right. Let him do that. But he must return the archives where they belong so you and all of us can see them.'

'He wants to give them to the Huntington Library. Everyone could see them there. Do you object to that?'

'They must be where they belong,' he reiterated.

'Is that all? Is that what the whole thing is about?'

'Yes. I could stop this lawsuit tomorrow if I wanted to.'

'Why don't you? Why don't you meet with him alone and stop it? But you cannot expect him to meet with all those people. He has been humiliated too often. If you don't want to be alone with him, I will offer to sit and listen and not say anything, if you feel you need a witness, or just to keep peace.'

He promised he would do this. Suddenly there was a new look in his face, purposeful, and I had hope.

'Krinsh, I would love to see you in California, and you are always welcome to stay with us. But please call *me*. I cannot call *you* and go through those people around you. I don't want to be in that position.'

'I understand,' he said. 'I promise I'll call you when I get to Ojai.'

He looked washed out though, and Nandini appeared at the doorway. She had ordered a taxi for us. We were definitely being ushered out. He hugged me hard and said, 'Don't talk for a moment – just be quiet,' and then he left the room.

Pupul had disappeared and as we said goodbye to Nandini, who seemed very shy and had not spoken a word all through lunch, I remarked, 'I always heard you were perfectly beautiful and you are.' She looked astonished and followed us out to the taxi with a wide smile.

When Krinsh returned to Ojai the following spring he kept his promise and phoned to tell me that he would attend a meeting with my father, but he did not specify that it would be a private one, and consequently I had little hope that anything good would come of it. He promised to let me know the outcome. In fact he did not arrange the meeting at all, but Annie Vigeveno had suggested that there be a meeting in her house. As I would have predicted, Raja did not show up. Krishna and his trustees had walked into Annie's house, and Krishna had immediately counted the chairs before sitting down, then asked, 'Where is Rajagopal to sit?' Annie replied that he had just called to say he was not coming, with which Krishna left in a fury.

Krinsh called me two days later and this is the conversation, which I typed from memory immediately after.

K   I am calling you because I said I would call Wednesday night and tell you what happened at the meeting. We all went to Mrs Vigeveno's house Monday morning as arranged. When we entered the room I counted the chairs and asked right off where will Rajagopal sit? Mrs Vigeveno said, 'I will explain; please sit down.' I sat and she said that Rajagopal was not coming. There was no apology or explanation. I rose instantly and said there was nothing to discuss without him there and walked out. Mrs Vigeveno said that Rajagopal would like to talk with me alone and I told her that if that was the case he could telephone me directly and arrange it. He has not done so. I am telling you this, Kittums, exactly as it happened, without exaggeration. I have tried for ten years to settle this in every way I could, have sent letters . . .

R   Have you ever talked to him alone?

K   Yes. I went to his house and he taped the whole conversation. Later I caught Mrs Porter checking the tape so I know. [This took place some years earlier.] People just do not do these things. It isn't done. It's not decent behaviour. Either Rajagopal is completely mad or dishonest or he is playing games. He doesn't want this settled.

R   I know he is none of those things. It's terrible to say things like that.

K   I'm not sure. But I have done what I could, I will not go there again. Every time we have arranged a meeting he makes an excuse the last minute not to come.

R   I happen to know he really was ill this time.

K   So am I! I got out of bed to come. I don't believe him.

R   Would you be willing to see him alone if he calls you?

K   I have a definite condition otherwise I refuse.

R   What is it?

K   The archives must be returned to the place they belong, which was agreed on, and where we can all freely see them.

R   Is that the only issue, the only condition?

K   Yes.

R   Well I'm sorry it ended like this. It's very sad.

K   There is nothing more I can do; I have tried everything.

R   I don't know what to say.

K   There is nothing you can say. I am not asking you to tell Rajagopal anything.

R   No, I don't want to get in that position. When are you going to New York?

K   Next week.

R   How long will you be gone?

K   About ten days.

R   We are going to Wrightwood tomorrow.

K   There is snow there. It will be beautiful.

R   Yes, would you like to come?

K   (*laughs*) I can't go anywhere. I am in bed.

R   Well, perhaps when you get back. I'll try to call you before you go. Is there a phone number where I can reach you in the evening?

K   I am staying in Mrs —'s house and this is her private number. Nobody can have it. She has her own reasons.

R   All right, I'll call you during office hours. Thank you for telling me all this.

K   I did it because you asked me and I said I would.

Krinsh was, in fact, staying in the very same Pine Cottage where my grandmother Sophia had once stayed, where my mother had cared for Nitya and then cared for Krinsh through the first 'process'. It had been Krinsh's home for the past sixty years. From what I had heard, it had now been transformed beyond recognition into a luxurious domicile with tiled floors and modern kitchen.

There were several points in this last conversation I would ever have with Krinsh that might have been argued, but I did not feel it would be of any help. First, he had ignored the most important part of my plea and that was to see Raja alone. He had not made any effort to do so, although that had been a promise. Waiting for Raja to call him was not the same thing. Raja had been humiliated once too often by meeting

The Wheels of Justice

Krishna in the presence of his trustees. One time when they had all come to inspect the archives, as was their right under the settlement, Raja had held out his hand to Krishna and asked that they forgive and be friendly and Krishna had replied, 'You do penance first before you ask for my friendship,' and, snubbing the proffered hand, had marched out with his group behind him. This story will be unbelievable to many, but luckily Raja had witnesses of his own, and I have no difficulty after my conversations with Krishna and hearing the hatred in his voice when he spoke Raja's name in believing it.

If, as Krishna repeatedly claimed, he wanted the archives available for anyone, why had he interfered with them being given to the Huntington Library? Some had already been sent, but the charges in the latest lawsuit had quite naturally made the Huntington wary of accepting them. It was clear that Krishna really wanted the power to destroy those papers he thought would be damaging to his image.

Rosalind decided to make one final effort. She still dreaded the thought of a trial and of having her whole life laid bare, and she had known all along that a trial would mean no less.

On 8 June 1983 she wrote a complete and detailed account of her relationship with Krishna, including the abortions, the miscarriage and his behaviour over the affair in India. She sent it in a sealed envelope to Vanda, in Gstaad asking her to please have Krishna open and read it to himself, in Vanda's presence, without letting anyone see it and tear it up immediately. She hoped that if he read, precisely spelled out, what would become public knowledge in a trial he might come to his senses.

Vanda replied on 6 July from Gstaad:

Dear Rosalind,
This morning I handed your letter to K. He said 'it was too long' but read it almost all. Then he handed it to Mrs— saying that there were things concerning the foundation that she should know.
In the afternoon he tore it in front of me.

On 22 December 1983, I was standing in my husband's study when a stranger rapped on the door and thrust an envelope in my hand. It was a subpoena from Krinsh's attorneys ordering me to appear for a deposition and to bring any records or memos of phone conversations between Krishnamurti and me concerning my father. This, as nothing else had done, drove home to me how unprivate our lives had now become, how we had been thrust into an impersonal arena. It had been

313

a year and a half since my last phone conversation with Krinsh. I knew about the letter my mother had sent to him but there had been no reply to that.

If Krishna tried to deny his nearly thirty-year affair with Rosalind and his responsibility in her pregnancies, or if he tried to say that she had seduced him with Raja's condonation and it had all been over long ago, his letters to my mother over a span of twenty-five years would emphatically disprove such a claim. But it probably did not occur to Krishna that Rosalind had kept these letters. She and I were the only ones who had read them at that point.

In the autumn of 1983 the lawsuit against Raja was suddenly withdrawn, but with the right reserved to open another case in the future.

Rosalind believed that her letter ultimately had the effect of making Krishna's side drop their lawsuit. She knew that he had allowed another party to read the letter and knew that it might even have been copied to be misused at a later time. She also knew that the threat of a trial, where lies and truth about her whole life, as well as Krishna's and Raja's, would be spewed forth in a courtroom, had only temporarily been lifted. She was thus moved to allow me to use her memory and her letters in this book. She felt that since Krishna had set in motion the events that had led to the present impasse, the *whole* truth must now come out. It was a painful and terrible decision for her to make and one that involved the intrinsically self-sacrificing nature that those close to her know so well. She was fully aware of what this public knowledge could do to her final years. She had tried in her heart never to take sides between Krishna and Raja, but she could not repress her sense of justice. That doing so might hurt her as well as Krishna was not as important a consideration as the failure to clear Raja publicly of the terrible charges Krishna had made against him.

Rosalind had tried to cut herself free from her relationships with both Raja and Krishna and to go her own way. Her life with them seemed now like another life of another person. But she had been forced to come back and clarify feelings and actions of the past. She had finally freed herself from anger and from hurt. The past was almost buried and now she wanted peace; but she wanted truth more.

Raja, at last worn down by fifteen years of harassment and strongly backed by his trustees, filed a suit against Krishna and his associates, claiming slander and subjection to two previous ill-founded lawsuits, plus many other counts.

I was convinced by my last two conversations with Krishna, the one in Delhi and the one over the phone, that the basis of all Krishna's actions against Raja was his fear of what the archives contained, of what would happen to his public image if letters and statements in his own handwriting should ever come to light. He wished to acquire control over these archives by whatever means necessary. It seems not to have occurred to him that Raja's whole life had been given to protecting him, that the last thing he would ever have intended was to hurt Krishna in any way. It had taken Raja nearly twenty years of enduring outrageous charges to move to protect himself against Krishna. Up to the threshold of this last trial, he was still trying to get a settlement.

When I learned the terms of the proposed settlement, I felt my father would be accepting peace at a high price. He felt tired and old and did not want a trial which, if he had won, would have forced Krishna and his followers to retract all the charges against him and to promise never to re-open the battle, just what the judge had ordered in the first settlement of 1974. It would also have exposed all the details of Krishna's life. I wondered if my father still found it impossible to expose Krishna even if it were the only way to save himself. I realized he was not a fighter or a destroyer but in the true Hindu sense, a Vaishnavite, belonging in nature to Vishnu the preserver, for whom righteousness and *dharma* are all important. He was being pushed to go against the core of his nature and perhaps in the end would refuse.

There are those who might also see Krishna, with his multi-aspects, in Hindu terms, as a Shaivite: Shiva Nataraj, Lord of the Dance as Creator, also, Shiva the Destroyer. In tantric tradition it is realistic and even good that there be these different aspects. It is the reality of the universe. Sexuality and even lust in the gods and in yogis is a transitional part of this reality, however difficult it may be for the more puritanical among us to accept. Krishna, however, refused to associate himself with any of these traditions. He preferred to see himself as a man who successfully straddled or side-stepped the culture heritages of East and West.

In Western terms, as an alternative to the theory of the vehicle or of multiple personalities, one could still say that Krishna was a person of strongly differing aspects. The question is, to what degree was he conscious of these differences?

Was the claimed loss of memory of his early years, as well as his claim to be unconditioned, spontaneous or a deliberate effort on his part to eliminate a burdensome past? The re-writing of one's personal history is not uncommon among those who need a certain public image. Krishna was a poor, undernourished child, but not, as some have suggested, retarded. He only appeared to be. He had, in fact, an exceptional mind

315

and the sort of mental energy which is the key to productive genius. He learned early that to appear slightly moronic or helpless was a protection; first, from abusive treatment and, later, from other people's expectations which he had no wish to fulfil. Leadbeater had the acumen to perceive a spark in him and to nurture it. Krishna received intensive training that started under his own family, a training that would serve him well throughout his life. His self-discipline in adhering to a persistent regime of physical fitness, extended his probable life expectancy by about fifty years.

As for the 'process', personal interpretations and assumptions will provide a variety of conclusions. Hindu culture is steeped with the ideal of *Moksha*, generally meaning the transcendence of difference between subject and object, or as Krishna expressed it, between the thinker and the thought. And this, according to some definitions, is a more permanent state than *samadhi*.

Krishna's 'process', as Leadbeater noted, does not clearly fit this concept. But there is no doubt that it proved highly successful in gaining the devotion and love of a series of women. Even without the 'process', he knew how to gain the sympathy and the protection of the right people, from Mrs Besant to Raja and Rosalind and those who succeeded them. He could survive without deep emotional attachments (detached love is an intrinsic part of his philosophy), but he needed affection on a certain level and for this could easily substitute one person for another. There had to be someone (a woman) he could feel close to, speak to, or write to daily.

His love for Rosalind was the longest and perhaps deepest of his life. It stemmed from the early, happy years at Ojai with Nitya. For years Rosalind provided for his every emotional need. She nurtured, healed and loved him, yet refused to see him as an exalted person. This anchored and sustained the normal side of him – the side he needed to experience life as most people do, in order to talk about it. He established a true family existence with my mother and me, but he felt free to walk away when he chose. We were not his responsibility, an obligation which he was probably incapable of accepting. Neither did he feel guilt. To feel this one must first feel responsible. He often showed concern but that is not the same. Responsibility involves an ongoing and sometimes long-range commitment. Concern can be as incidental and fleeting as a moment. Therefore he enjoyed the best sides of ordinary human existence while elevating himself to a philosophical freedom from what he saw as the less desirable.

He inspired others to live spontaneously, openly, keeping alert but not judging, thus obviating the necessity of ambitious choice. But he was capable of making and enacting long-range plans. Throughout his life, he blazed his way to definite goals; he acquired houses and land for schools. He formed new circles to replace the old, without interrupting or hampering the course of his life.

Fear was central to much of his teachings, as it was central to him. It drove him to the childish solution of lying rather than confronting a difficult issue. Sometimes his lies were transparent and without guile, sometimes they were accompanied by the self-delusion that makes a lie believable. What made both Raja and Rosalind a threat was that they knew he lied. He had admitted this to them both. With a long-range view, he proceeded to discredit Raja in order to remove him from his life. For a while he thought he could control Rosalind, that she would stand by him through anything. He did not really turn against her until she came to Raja's defence in the first lawsuit. Others had been aware of his deceptions but had chosen to overlook them. Most people around Krishna were devotee types, no matter what they or he protested to the contrary. Hence they were willing, in fact compelled, to believe anything he said or did. Some would even interpret his hurtful actions as an intentional lesson for their welfare.

Krishna possessed almost all the qualities that make a person attractive (to both sexes and also children and animals). Outwardly, when he was younger, he was beautiful, charming, gentle, physically courageous and compassionate. He could focus intensely on a particular person and make that person feel he was the most important thing in Krishna's life at that moment. He could be convincing, privately and publicly, that he wanted to help, to alleviate suffering, to heal, to show individuals and mankind at large a condition of freedom. In later years he sometimes was negative, cantankerous and critical, but often the former qualities prevailed.

He had a natural gift for language, especially poetry, and had distilled with verbal brilliance the essence of wisdom, handed him by his early teachers. In his early manhood, he was a forerunner in expressing the type of iconoclasm that would bring immediate fame to cult figures fifty years later.

30

Ashes to Ashes

In the summer of 1985, the mountains of Ojai were swept by a wildfire that charred the whole north-western range. Under orders of the fire department my mother piled her dog, Beato and Beato's three dogs and a cat, into her car at midnight and drove to the Ojai Valley Inn. They had hours of delay on the road with hot ash falling around them, the temperatures in the high nineties and the dogs very upset. The inn provided for them, animals and all, along with dozens of other refugees. Knowing my mother was safe, we tried to evacuate my father, whose house was only a few blocks from the fire but he refused to leave until ordered by the police. The fire turned just then and backed over itself, diminishing its fury.

A month later we drove into the Los Padres National forest to see the last wild Californian condors.

Fog covered the hills, but under that shroud was nothing but grey and white ash where once the white sage and black sage, sumac and manzanita had flourished. Now stark charcoal stumps gave cover to an occasional rabbit.

Less than half of last year's population of condors remained in the wild. Above a valley near Mount Pinos they soared, looking for the carcasses collected off the highway by those few people who still struggled to allow the great birds their last days of freedom.

They came that day; first as black specks into the range of our binoculars, then soaring up over the rim of the nearest hill, white wing patches, head cocked at an angle watching against the odds for a morsel lying amidst the dry grass.

Species disappear from the earth every day, never to return, but the sheer size of these birds makes their disappearance more terrible. We felt this tragic finality as we drove back towards Ojai, descending now in full sunlight which revealed the horrors of the fire, no longer veiled by fog. The inevitability of change, the rightness of it, is one thing to accept rationally but days like this test the depth of one's acceptance.

Against this stark landscape there suddenly flooded memories of Ojai

Ashes to Ashes

in my childhood: playing in the orange orchards of Arya Vihara, Krinsh waiting for me to get off the school bus, hiding out of sight behind the rock wall. I thought of the care with which he taught me the small but important details of life: tying one's shoes properly, polishing them, brushing the dog. When such happy memories force themselves into the present it is hard to understand how so much could have gone so wrong.

The settlement terms were still being disputed. Finally, that winter Raja accepted that there was no hope of his own peace with Krishna. He filed for a jury trial. A court date was set for the following summer of 1986. I knew I would be a witness at this trial and would return for it in the spring, after another trip to India.

In January I drove to Ojai to say goodbye to my father, noticing now small sprigs of green prodding their way through the carpet of grey ash. There was still the threat of mudslides and floods if the rains were not moderate that winter.

I heard that Krinsh had just returned to Ojai and that he was ill, but no one I knew had any details. I had an impulse to try to see him, but realized it would not be likely that on the spur of the moment I would be allowed to do so and I abandoned the idea and left for India.

Beyond Madanapalle we followed the road still further from our course toward the Rishi Valley School. Krinsh had been there only a few weeks before. My mother had been there with him thirty years ago and had walked with him along the stream, seen the great ancient boulders and talked to his young people. I wanted to see for myself the place I had always heard was one of the loveliest spots in India.

'Krishnaji is very ill, they say he has cancer.' I could not believe these words, spoken by the headmistress who had welcomed us, without having any idea who we were. Perhaps it would have made no difference one way or the other if she had known I was Rajagopal's daughter. Her words stunned me. Cancer was the last thing I would have thought Krinsh would succumb to – even at ninety-two.

I left Rishi Valley with my thoughts a bleak veil against the gentle verdant landscape. It was getting late and we had many miles to cover before we reached the sea south of Madras, where we planned to spend the night.

The next day we returned to Adyar after a ten-year absence. Nothing much had changed. There were more graffiti; the guards at the gates, posted to keep out troublemakers and beggars, were beggars themselves asking for a small handout to buy milk for a new baby. There was a thinning of the sanctuary walls, a creeping encroachment of the real world.

We had come to see Rukmini. On the phone the day before she had said, 'Please come quickly. I have something to tell you.' I did not know whether the faintness of voice was due to weakness or a poor connection. As soon as I saw her I knew. We found her sitting in a chair in the living-room, eating her lunch. Her white hair was hanging loose and she looked very ill.

'But she is getting better,' we were told by her older sister Shivakamu. These two sisters are my father's oldest friends, I thought, since he was here at Adyar as a boy of thirteen.

Rukmini drew me close and said, 'You must give your father a message for me. I am too weak to telephone him.' Her face was drawn with illness but her eyes, still beautiful, looked at me intently.

'Of course I will,' I promised.

'A friend of Krishna's – a close friend here in India, has told him he must make his peace with Rajagopal. Krishna promised him that he would go back and do that. He is very ill you know. He will die soon. He knows that. He even came to see me after forty years of estrangement. We had a very friendly meeting. And he stood before the portrait of Leadbeater and said "pax". He has made his peace with all of us here at Adyar and even wanted to give the Rajghat school back to the Theosophists. He said it came from them and should go back to them. He asked my nephew to run it, but he knows nothing about running a school.'

She paused. This long rush of words had tired her and drawn the feeble breath from her faltering lungs. But she forced herself to finish.

'If Krishna approached your father, would Raja be receptive? Could you ask him to be receptive? I think it may be a very propitious time for a reconciliation.'

'I am sure he would be receptive, but I think it unlikely Krishna will approach him. However, I shall call him tonight from the hotel and tell him what you have said.' I hugged her and told her I loved her and how much her friendship meant to my father.

'When you get well enough to travel again, come to California, Rukmini. I will take good care of you.'

I put my arms around her again and we both cried a little. 'I'll call you tomorrow and tell you what Daddy said.' I promised.

Unexpectedly I got an excellent connection from Madras to Ojai with only a few minutes wait. I told my father every word of my conversation with Rukmini. 'Thank her for me and give her my love,' he said. 'It is a very nice thought but it will never happen. Don't have false hopes.'

'But *if* Daddy, that's all, will you see him *if* he calls you?'

'Of course, but he will never do that.'

'Nevertheless, please do something for me,' I added, 'if you have any contact with Krinsh at all, please tell him I love him and would like to be with him now. Do you know how ill he is?'

'I know nothing,' my father replied. 'There are all sorts of rumours, that's all.' I repeated his words to Rukmini the next day and we left Madras for a long drive up the east coast of India.

On 22 February I read in the *Calcutta Telegraph* that Krinsh had died five days before, 17 February (on Leadbeater's birthday.) He had said a few months earlier that he knew the exact day on which he would die but, supposedly, he had not shared this knowledge with anyone.

I had not expected his death to be such a shock. And the wave of grief that came after, was the grief for a lost parent. I had never realized how deeply I thought of him as that, though he had sometimes told me he felt I was his child. The obituary was written by Pupul Jayakar, who had been with him at Ojai a few weeks before his death. He had reiterated to her his hope that the teachings would not be distorted and that people would keep the teachings and forget the teacher.

Two days later, in New Delhi, I read that Rukmini had died. Exactly one week after Krinsh.

As my father had expected, Krishna had made no attempt to get in touch with him. Perhaps he had been too ill to try or perhaps those close to him had discouraged the idea.

Krishna's death did not bring peace to Raja nor a resolution of the strife that had been between them for twenty years. Until the eve of the court trial Raja sought a settlement and finally the trustees of the Krishnamurti Foundation signed a twenty-five page document designed to 'ensure the resolution of any and all disputes, past, present and future.'

The attorney's press release stated that:

the Krishnamurti Parties admit with respect to the prior lawsuits that the Rajagopal Parties 'have done nothing wrong, and have not committed any acts which might be the basis for civil or criminal charges or complaints'.

The Krishnamurti Parties further acknowledge that the documents they sought to recover from the Rajagopal Parties in the prior lawsuits are, in fact, Rajagopal's documents and may be kept by Rajagopal.

The K&R Foundation which Raja had formed was turned over 'AS IS' to the Krishnamurti Foundation and the latter agreed in the settlement to 'Indemnify the Rajagopal Parties . . . and hold them harmless against any claims, complaints, causes of action, lawsuits . . . or allegations of wrongdoing made by . . . any beneficiary of or successor in interest to Krishnamurti.'[1]

In other words, Raja had not only been cleared of any wrongdoing, he had been judged correct in his claim to his collection of papers. Above all, his past adversaries now had agreed that they must protect all his life's work from a potential future attack by other parties. That would have been a bitter pill for Krishna to swallow, one which he had fortuitously escaped.

Whether or not such a settlement would have been possible during Krishna's lifetime is a moot point. It is certain he would not have fared well on the witness stand. Rosalind was spared the pain of such an appearance also, although she was prepared to go through with it. Sixteen years of litigation and three separate lawsuits all dropped at the final hour, hundreds of thousands of dollars that might have been spent on schools or publications, add up to a chronicle of waste.

The settlement imposed an uneasy peace among those left to live under it but it did nothing to explain the causes of disharmony, the secret life between my mother and Krinsh, the misunderstood behaviour of my father toward Krinsh, the deceptions that had tried to the fullest his willingness to forgive.

The pepper tree where Krishna had sat one summer evening in 1922 was still alive. It had aged as he had and he wished once more to sit there. Did he think of Rosalind and Nitya watching from the veranda that night as he sat under the tree, of how she had held his head and soothed his pain. The valley was stirring with rumours of his last days. Did he really ask if any old friends from the past had inquired after him? Would he have wanted to see them if they had come? He was said to have spoken a few last words, which he wanted recorded on tape. He referred to an immense energy and intelligence that had used his body for most of his life, that would go when the body goes and it would be hundreds of years before it returned. He said nobody had lived the teachings so nobody would know that consciousness.

If he did in fact say something of the sort, was he laying the foundation for the temple which he had predicted in 1927 would be built around him after his death? He said he would never permit it in his lifetime. Or was he fading back to his earliest childhood memories – hearing

Ashes to Ashes

his mother's voice telling him he was born to be a great person? As he would have wanted, each of us must find our own answer to this and much more.

A few months later I had a letter from Shivakamu. Her nephew and Rukmini's had received one-third of Krishna's ashes in India and released them and Rukmini's together in the Ganges. The body has gone and it remains for the future to determine how much of the myth and the teachings will linger. The first steps toward immortalization have already started. Recently my mother opened her mailbox and was confronted by a four-inch profile portrait of Krinsh as well as a full-face sixty paisa postage stamp on an Indian commemorative postal letter. Would this secular tribute have pleased him?

I shall remember him in his blue denim shirt and jeans; his face full of laughter under the large straw hat, with equal enthusiasm, pitching cow pats on to the compost heap or tending his roses.

He brought to our lives love and happiness, as well as disharmony and sorrow.

To Krinsh I feel grateful for many things. From earliest childhood he taught me to be free from the desperate seeking and searching for respectability and security, for gurus and masters and ideologies. I learned from him that comparisons and labels lead to prejudice and unhappiness, that conformity leads to mediocre imitation, that there can be no freedom where there is guilt or fear. He let me be free from him and taught me not to be afraid to wander in a pathless land.

Notes and References

1 The Elders
1 Kandinsky and Mondrian and other early abstract painters found inspiration in Leadbeater's writing. Indeed, one artist evidently received a mysterious transmission of Leadbeater's 'thought forms', which he then painted. A recent retrospective at the Los Angeles County Art Museum, titled, 'The Spiritual In Art . . .' contained numerous examples of art works manifesting the influence of Leadbeater and Theosophy.
2 For this version of the story, well known among Theosophists, I am indebted to Gregory Tillett, *The Elder Brother: A Biography of Charles Webster Leadbeater* (Routledge & Kegan Paul, 1982), pp. 12–14.

2 The Vehicle
1 H. P. Blavatsky, *The Secret Doctrine*, (Theosophical Publishing House, London, 1893), p. 384.
2 *Lucifer* (July 1890) quoted by Tillett, *The Elder Brother.*
3 Annie Besant, *The Path of Discipleship*, four lectures at the 20th Anniversary of the Theosophical Society, Adyar, December 1905 (Theosophical Publishing Society, London, 1910).

3 The Vehicle Takes the Wheel
1 From the recollections of Mima Porter.

4 The New Discovery
1 C. Jinarajadasa, *Occult Investigations; Three men of C.W.L.*, published privately.
2 Ibid.

5 Back on the Path
1 From an interview with Rukmini Arundale, Ojai, 27 June 1984.

7 The Process
1 Interview with Beatrice Wood, Ojai, 1985.

2 A classical analysis of this abnormality first published in 1905 is Morton Prince, M.D., LL.D., *The Dissociation of a Personality* (Meridian Books, New York, 1957).

9   A Left Turn
1 From an interview with Rukmini Arundale, Ojai, 27 June 1984.
2 Gregory Tillett, *The Elder Brother* (Routledge & Kegan Paul, 1982), p. 220.
3 Helen Knothe Nearing's version given to Rosalind, Ojai, December 1984.
4 The Star Council Meeting, Monday, 26 July 1926, Order of the Star in the East, published in *The Herald of the Star*, vol. XV, no. 10 (1 October 1926).
5 Talk with Mima Porter, Ojai, 27 June 1984.
6 Private papers.

10   Bypassing the Masters
1 The study of dissociated or disintegrated personalities dates from the late nineteenth century and Mrs Besant was undoubtedly familiar with these theses. But she here transposed the theory to her own Theosophical framework.
2 Arthur H. Nethercot, *The Last Four Lives of Annie Besant* (University of Chicago Press, 1963), p. 390.
3 Ibid., p. 393.
4 Gregory Tillett, *The Elder Brother* (Routledge & Kegan Paul, 1982), p. 230.
5 Interview with Rukmini Arundale, Ojai, 27 June 1984.
6 *The Last Four Lives of Annie Besant*, pp. 404–5.

11   Finding the Way
1 Letter from the Star Camp, Ojai, 1928, private papers.

12   The Pathless Land
1 Arthur H. Nethercot, *The Last Four Lives of Annie Besant* (University of Chicago Press, 1963), p. 425.
2 Ibid., p. 427.
3 From a statement by Rukmini Arundale on the founding of the Rishi Valley School.
4 Gregory Tillett, *The Elder Brother*, (Routledge & Kegan Paul, 1982), p. 10.
5 Told to me by Beatrice Wood many years later.

Notes and References

13 A Cuckoo in the Other Bird's Nest
1 Interview with Rukmini Arundale, Ojai, 1984.
2 Interview with Annie Vigeveno, Santa Barbara, February 1985.

14 Childhood in the Sage Garden
1 Private papers.

16 Sages and Shadows
1 Sybille Bedford, *Aldous Huxley, A Biography*, (Alfred A. Knopf/Harper & Row, New York, 1974), p. 346.

17 A Garden of Peace in a World of War
1 Beatrice Wood, *I Shock Myself; The Autobiography of Beatrice Wood* (Dillingham Press, Ojai, 1958), p. 113.
2 Sybille Bedford, *Aldous Huxley, A Biography* (Alfred A. Knopf/Harper & Row, New York, 1974), p. 331.

20 The Shadow Deepens
1 *Time Magazine* (16 January 1950).
2 Letter from Beatrice Wood, 27 June 1987.

26 A Moratorium
1 From Rosalind's notes made at the time of the discussion.
2 Interview with Mima de Manziarly Porter, Ojai, 27 June 1984.

27 A House Divided
1 Aldous Huxley, *Island* (Harper & Bros, New York, 1962), pp. 304–5.
2 From Rosalind's notes, written shortly after Aldous died.

28 A New Circle in the Shadow
1 Rosalind was referring to the following passage in Nethercot's biography of Annie Besant, reflecting his perplexity about Krishnamurti, the man:

Here then is an extraordinary case of a man who, after a long and bizarre struggle with life, has finally got himself and his mind under almost complete control – has perhaps hypnotised himself so that he can relegate to oblivion most of the things he does not want to remember, because they recall the unhappy days when he was becoming an individual and was escaping from the domination of others whom he had cause to love and admire. One of his favorite discussion topics is that of 'exploitation', by which he means the influence on one human being by another to bring the other round to one's own point of view in order to use that individual for one's own purpose. When, however, I temerariously suggested that perhaps he might have been 'exploited' by Annie Besant in that sense, he flared up in what I would have called an angry denial in any less philosophic a person than he. I should hate to think of him as a charlatan; I prefer to think of him as a sort of schizophrenic, or at least a man of a now permanently divided personality.

Arthur H. Nethercot, *The Last Four Lives of Annie Besant* (University of Chicago Press, 1963), p. 450.

30   Ashes to Ashes
1 From the Order, approving settlement, etc. Case #79918, *D. Rajagopal, et al. v. J. Krishnamurti et al.,* Superior Court of the State of California for the County of Ventura.

Index

INDEX

INDEX

Matthias, Blanche: first meets Krishna, 129–30; and Krishna's cancelled South American trip, 135; letters from Rosalind, 141–2, 164, 188; and Udai Shankar, 163; and Rosalind's pacifism, 183–4; values life, 199; letter from Alan Watts, 225; praises Rosalind, 235; at Berkeley, 257

Mehta, Bhagvandas Chunilal, 218–19

Mehta, Nandini: Krishna's relations with, 215, 217–19, 230, 252–4, 264; Krishna's letter to, 237–9; author meets, 309–10

Meyers, Major Dev, 123, 137

Midsummer Night's Dream, A (film), 138

Narayaniah, Jiddu (Krishna's father), 21–2, 24, 32

Narayaniah, Nityananda (Nitya) *see* Nityananda, Jiddu

Negri, Pola, 13

Nethercot, Arthur H.: *The Last Four Lives of Annie Besant*, 297

Neutra, Richard, 136, 139, 210

New York Theater Guild, 87

Nityananda, Jiddu ('Nitya'; Krishna's brother): Rosalind meets, 8; childhood, 22, 25; at Adyar, 29–31; visits England, 31–2; education, 36–7; in World War I, 36–7; gambling success, 37; and Raja's arrival in England, 46; chickenpox, 47; 1921 return to India, 47–8; visits Australia, 48, 72–3; tuberculosis, 50–1, 53, 57, 70–2, 75–6; goes to California, 51–3; falls in love with Rosalind, 54–8, 66–7, 118; and Krishna's 'process', 58–60, 63, 66, 70; loyalty to Leadbeater and Theosophy, 64, 70, 72, 76, 135; 1923 trip to Europe, 65; in India, 70–1; as 'apostle', 74; death, 79; ghost, 191–2

Norway, 121

Ojai (California): described, 1, 96; Krishna first visits, 51, 53; property purchased, 64–5; Star camps, 96–7, 115–17; theatre at, 177; pacifists at, 183; 1985 fire, 318

Ojai Valley School, 176, 205

Olcott, Colonel Henry, 10–12, 16

Ommen (Holland), 69, 74–6, 78, 83, 84, 91, 98–104, 115, 120, 142–3, 156–7; as Nazi concentration camp, 192

Orcus Island, 221

Orsini, Count, 145–6

Pallandt, Baron Phillip van, 47, 69, 104

Palm, Joseph Henry Louis, Baron de, 12

Pearce (Rishi Valley school headmaster), 265

Pergine (Italy), 69

Peter Pan Lodge (Carmel Highlands), 130, 141

Pine Cottage, 312

Point Lobos (Carmel Highlands), 242

Porter, Mima (*formerly* de Manziarly): friendship with Krishna and Nitya, 38; and dying Nitya, 76; on Krishna's feelings for Rosalind, 117–18; introduces Blanche to Krishna, 129; gives dress to author, 216; in New York, 221; and Krishna's betrayal of Raja, 222; in Paris, 258, 294; and Raja's illness, 293; and Krishna-Raja conflict, 294–5; and Krishna's meeting with Raja, 311

Powell, Dick, 138

Pratt, Doris, 264, 270, 285

Quest books, 304

Quinn, Bill, 188

Rajagopal (Rajagopalacharya), Desikacharya (author's father): arranges Krishna's talks, 2; character, 7, 127; discovered by Leadbeater, 14, 36, 41; birth and background, 40–1; at Theosophical School in Benares, 42–3; education and training, 43–5; in England, 45–6; at Cambridge University, 46–7, 65, 69, 74; at Ehrwald, 65; first feelings for Rosalind, 66–8; supported by Miss Dodge, 68; cars and driving, 68, 150–1, 154–5, 173; made deacon in Liberal Catholic Church, 74–5; in Ojai, 75; and relations between Krishna and Nitya, 75–6; commitment to Krishna, 77, 110, 287, 306–7; accepts Theosophy, 77–8, 107; closeness to Rosalind, 80; runs Star, 82–3; at Eerde Castle, 85; engagement to Rosalind, 88; US citizenship, 88; and Krishna's changing views, 89, 102–3; as trustee of Happy Valley, 90; marriage, 93; separations from Rosalind, 98, 107–8; at Ommen camp, 98–101, 120–1; loyalty to Theosophists and benefactors, 102, 107, 119, 135; 1928/29 lecture tour, 103; practical organizing for Krishna, 105, 254, 263, 288; and Rosalind's pregnancy, 109; in Taormina, 109; in Athens, 110; conflicts and disputes with Krishna, 110, 134–5, 140–1, 261–2, 271, 273–4, 279, 288–9; financial skills, 111–12; gives up sexual relations with wife, 112; poor health and operations, 115, 120, 133, 229, 240, 244, 262, 264–5; cuckolded by Krishna, 117–18; 1932 visit to India, 118–19; rejects Krishna's proposals to care for Rosalind and baby, 120–1; sets up Star Publishing Trust office

333

INDEX

A NOTE ON THE AUTHOR

Radha Rajagopal Sloss was born in Hollywood. She and her husband James now live in Santa Barbara with a large and beautiful black poodle named Sindhu. The author is presently at work on a novel about the Logan family of Pennsylvania.